THE GHOST
OF FREEDOM

A History of the Caucasus

CHARLES KING

OXFORD
UNIVERSITY PRESS

2008

OXFORD
UNIVERSITY PRESS

Oxford University Press, Inc., publishes works that further
Oxford University's objective of excellence
in research, scholarship, and education.

Oxford   New York
Auckland   Cape Town   Dar es Salaam   Hong Kong   Karachi
Kuala Lumpur   Madrid   Melbourne   Mexico City   Nairobi
New Delhi   Shanghai   Taipei   Toronto

With offices in
Argentina   Austria   Brazil   Chile   Czech Republic   France   Greece
Guatemala   Hungary   Italy   Japan   Poland   Portugal   Singapore
South Korea   Switzerland   Thailand   Turkey   Ukraine   Vietnam

Published by Oxford University Press, Inc.
198 Madison Avenue, New York, NY 10016

www.oup.com

Oxford is a registered trademark of Oxford University Press

Library of Congress Cataloging-in-Publication Data
King, Charles, 1967–
The ghost of freedom: a history of the Caucasus / Charles King.
p. cm.
Includes bibliographical references and index.
ISBN 978-0-19-517775-6
1. Caucasus—History   I. Title
DK511.C3K56 2008
947.5—dc22   2007037641

5   7   9   8   6   4
Printed in the United States of America
on acid-free paper

For Maggie

Contents

Acknowledgments

IN RESEARCHING AND WRITING this book, I have amassed considerable debts, from Palo Alto to Baku. Susan Ferber, my editor at Oxford University Press, first put forward the idea of a book on the Caucasus and remained unfailingly enthusiastic as the project developed. Joellyn Ausanka shepherded the book through production. My home bases, Georgetown University's Edmund A. Walsh School of Foreign Service and its Center for Eurasian, Russian, and East European Studies along with the Department of Government, have always provided space to thrive. The Center for Russian and East European Studies at the University of Michigan offered a congenial environment during a sabbatical semester in 2004. I am grateful to the Raţiu Family Charitable Foundation for its endowment to Georgetown University, which helps support my professorship. Additional support came from the International Research and Exchanges Board (through a U.S. Department of State Title VIII Short-Term Travel Grant in 2006), Georgetown's Graduate School of Arts and Sciences, and the Körber Foundation.

The staff at the following institutions were generous with their time: Harlan Hatcher Graduate Library at the University of Michigan; Hoover Institution Archives; Firestone Library at Princeton University; interlibrary loan service of Lauinger Library at Georgetown University; Modern Papers Room and Oriental Collections at the Bodleian Library, Oxford; Library of Balliol College, Oxford; National

Archives of the United Kingdom (formerly the Public Record Office); Alpine Club Archives, London, especially Glyn Hughes; Russian State Library, Moscow, especially Galina Kislovskaia, Liudmila Zinchuk, and Liudmila Shul'ga; Russian Ethnographic Museum, St. Petersburg, especially Vladimir Dmitriev; Georgian State Archives, Tbilisi, especially Revaz Khutsishvili; Open Society Archives, Budapest; and Houghton, Lamont, and Widener Libraries at Harvard University. I am continually amazed by the resources and accessibility of one of my country's treasure houses, the Library of Congress. I wish to thank the staff of the Main Reading Room as well as the various specialized reading rooms—European, Rare Books and Manuscripts, Geography and Map, and Africa and Middle East—for their professionalism.

For helpful conversations, advice, corrections, references, comments on specific chapters and sections, and general help, I wish to thank the following: Anar Ahmadov, Sergei Arutiunov, Kazbek Balkarov and the dance troupe Khatti, Kevork Bardakjian, Thomas Barrett, Barasbi Bgazhnokov, the staff of the Center for Humanitarian Programs in Abkhazia, Rachel Clogg, Jonathan Cohen, Ararat Esoian, Ali Gara, Graham Hettlinger, Nate Hultman, Mahir Iskenderov, Fariz Ismailzade, Austin Jersild, Alexander Knysh, Gerard Libaridian, Anatol Lieven, Olga Meerson, Mark Mullen, Feliks Nakov, Ghia Nodia, Philip Remler, Alex Rondeli, Michael Reynolds, Brenda Shaffer, Victor Shnirelman, Elin Suleymanov, Willard Sunderland, Ronald Grigor Suny, Jeremy Tasch, William Todd, Erekle Urushadze, Tom de Waal, John Voll, and Taleh Ziyadov.

I owe many dinners and drinks to Daniel Byman, Georgi Derluguian, John Gledhill, John McNeill, and Cory Welt. They set aside their own projects to read the entire manuscript and more than once saved me from myself. (They, of course, bear no responsibility for shortcomings in the final product.) Two anonymous reviewers for Oxford University Press provided detailed comments that greatly improved the manuscript. My research assistants—Alejandro Ganimian, Tetyana Gaponenko, Maia Nikolaishvili, Tereza Slepickova, and Zachary Wynne—were never less than dogged in the pursuit of an elusive document or a difficult interview. Adam Goodman rescued my laptop from oblivion. Chris Robinson drew the maps. Sufian Zhemukhov is a remarkable friend who became my guide to the complexities of Circassia. With the sensibilities of a gifted writer and anthropologist, Margaret Paxson made me turn a critical eye on my own imaginings of the Caucasus and its peoples while gently teaching me to live *dobrom dobro*.

I first aired some of the ideas in chapter five and the conclusion in the following: "Potemkin Democracy: Four Myths about Post-Soviet Georgia," *National Interest*, no. 64 (summer 2001); "The Benefits of Ethnic War: Understanding Eurasia's Unrecognized States," *World Politics* 53, no. 4 (2001); "A Rose Among Thorns: Georgia Makes Good," *Foreign Affairs* (March–April 2004); and "States of Amnesia," *Times Literary Supplement*, October 21, 2005. I am grateful to the various editors for publishing my earlier work in these forums. Specific points of fact or interpretation that I owe to a primary or secondary source are explicitly acknowledged in the notes. Works that I have found especially useful in a broader sense are detailed in the "On Sources" section at the end of the book.

On Words

I N A PART of the world where ethnic, religious, and political categories are hotly contested, being sensitive to labels is particularly crucial. In speaking of the lands divided—or, rather, connected—by the Caucasus mountain range, I have used the terms "north Caucasus" and "south Caucasus." I use the term "the Caucasus" for the region as a whole. The terms "Caucasia" and "Caucasian," which one sometimes finds in older scholarly works, seem to me too redolent of racial politics to be redeemable. Since few "Caucasians" understood racially have any sense of connection to "Caucasians" understood geographically, I have avoided these terms altogether. Nor have I used the label "Transcaucasia" (Russ. *Zakavkaz'e*) for the south except in direct translations of a Russian phrase or title. Of course, the area is only "trans" if you are standing in what used to be known rather quaintly as Ciscaucasia, that is, southern Russia.

In the Russian Empire the generic term "highlander" or "mountaineer" (*gorets*) was applied to any indigenous person living anywhere except on the steppe or in lowland river valleys, people whom we might now class as Chechens, Avars, Lezgins or Georgians. The equivalent term in English was "Circassian." In its narrowest sense, however, Circassian (Russ. *cherkes*, Turk. *Çerkez*) specifically refers to speakers of Adyga languages, the major linguistic group of the northwest Caucasus. I have used Circassian in this more restricted sense, except in direct quotations or other contexts where the broader meaning was intended by a writer or speaker.

Most of the languages of the Caucasus—around forty unique to the region, plus others from surrounding areas—are dauntingly complex to native English speakers. Many have remarkable phonetic systems. Ubykh (probably extinct as a mother tongue) may hold the world record for the number of consonants (around eighty). Others have fearsome grammatical structures. The notorious Georgian verb can agree not only with the subject but also with the direct and indirect objects. Of all the major languages now spoken in the region, only a few—such as Russian, Armenian, and Ossetian—have Indo-European roots. Most of the others are marvelously idiosyncratic, so much so that their proper typology is still a matter of some debate. The Turkic family is represented by Azerbaijani in the southeast Caucasus (close to modern Turkish) and Balkar, Karachai, Kumyk, and other languages in the north. In the southwest the Kartvelian language group is composed of Georgian and the related languages of Mingrelian, Svan, and Laz (the last spoken along the Black Sea coast of Turkey). In northwestern Georgia the language of the Abkhaz is related to the Adyga family (Circassian) across the mountains to the north. The north-central Caucasus features Ossetian, while the northeast harbors the Nakh languages, including Chechen and the related Ingush, as well as the so-called Dagestani family, a mixed bag of disparate languages that includes Avar, Dargin, and Lezgin.

The north Caucasus languages use a variant of the Cyrillic scripts developed for them during the last century and a half. In the south Armenian and Georgian have their own ancient alphabets, while Azerbaijani now employs a variant of the Latin script used for Turkish. The Victorian-era explorer Douglas Freshfield once wrote that any effort to stick to the scholarly rules of transliteration for these languages produces only "words of fear," intimidating jumbles of letters unpronounceable to anyone but a specialist. I have taken the pragmatic course of using indigenous names wherever possible, Russian wherever appropriate, and English wherever they exist. Because the Caucasus remains a place where few English-language versions of ethnic and geographical names are well established, inconsistencies are inevitable.

The Gregorian calendar in use in the West was only adopted in Russia in 1918. The old Julian calendar was thirteen days behind the Gregorian in the twentieth century, twelve days behind in the nineteenth, and eleven days behind in the eighteenth. Unless otherwise indicated, old-style dates have been provided for events occurring in the Russian Empire.

The following glossary includes major terms that may be unfamiliar to many readers. Definitions reflect local usage. Alternate spellings are given in parentheses. Place names not listed here can be found by consulting the maps included in this book.

abrek	highland bandit; renegade hero
adat (*adet*)	customary law
Adyga (Adiga, Adyghe, Adyghei)	Circassian; one of the indigenous peoples of the north-western Caucasus
amanat	diplomatic hostage, usually surrendered to (or taken by) an enemy to ensure good relations
atalyk	customary rearing of young men by a nonrelative
aul	highland village
bey	gentleman; an honorific title or form of address
catholicos (*katholikos*)	supreme leader of the Georgian or Armenian church; patriarch
cherkeska	long tunic worn by men, with rows of cartridge holders on the chest
dhikr (*zikr*)	attainment of enlightenment through quiet meditation, song, or dance—particularly in Naqshbandi Sufism
fedayin	Armenian guerrillas, especially during the First World War
gazavat (*ghazawat*)	sacred struggle; holy war; jihad
gorets (pl. *gortsy*)	highlander; mountaineer
guberniia	Russian imperial province
imam	Muslim leader, often with authority over a given population
jamaat	variously a village confederation, religious order, or other broad social unit in the north Caucasus
jigit	highland warrior; daring horseman
kinjal	hiltless dagger
korenizatsiia	indigenization; early Soviet policy of creating a native administrative elite in non-Russian regions
mahalle	neighborhood
mesame dasi	the "third group," a movement among Georgian intellectuals and liberal activists in the late nineteenth and early twentieth centuries
murid	Sufi adept; general term for a follower of the nineteenth-century highland leader Shamil (hence Muridism, Murid wars)

murshid	Sufi master
naib	trusted officer in Shamil's administration
natsional'nost'	ethnicity or nationality
Naqshbandi	Sufi order prominent in the north Caucasus—especially Chechnya and Dagestan—in the first half of the nineteenth century
oblast'	Russian imperial and Soviet-era administrative district
papakha	tall, brimless hat usually made of sheepskin
Qadiri	Sufi order prominent in the north Caucasus—especially Chechnya—after the 1850s
shamkhal	title of the ruler of Tarki, on the coastal plans of eastern Dagestan
sharia	Islamic law
shashka	hiltless saber
sheikh	Sufi leader; respected elder
stanitsa	Cossack fortified village
Sufism	general term for various branches of Islamic mysticism
tariqa (*tarikat*)	a Sufi school or "path"
teip	extended clan in Chechen society
tergdaleulni	reform-oriented generation of Georgians in the late nineteenth century, literally, "those who have tasted the waters of the Terek River"

Chronology

1556	Muscovy conquers khanate of Astrakhan
1722–23	Persian campaign of Peter the Great on Caspian Sea
1762	Unification of eastern Georgian kingdoms (Kartli and Kakheti)
1763	Russia builds fort at Mozdok on Terek River
1768–74	Russo-Turkish War
1783	Kartli-Kakheti placed under Russian protection
1787–92	Russo-Turkish War
1795	Agha Muhammad Khan, Qajar ruler, sacks Tiflis
1801	Russia annexes Kartli-Kakheti
1804–13	Russo-Persian War
1806–12	Russo-Turkish War
1816–27	Gen. Alexei Ermolov serves as proconsul in Caucasus
1818	Groznaia/Grozny founded
1822	Pushkin's "Captive of the Caucasus" published
1826–28	Russo-Persian War
1828–29	Russo-Turkish War
1834	Shamil becomes imam in Dagestan
1840	Lermontov's *A Hero of Our Time* published
1844–55	Mikhail Vorontsov serves as viceroy in the Caucasus
1853–56	Crimean War
1859	Surrender of Shamil

1864	Exile of Circassians
1868	Douglas Freshfield climbs Mounts Elbrus and Kazbek
1877–78	Russo-Turkish War
1904–6	Armenian-Muslim violence in Baku
1915	Genocidal violence against Armenians and other Christians in eastern Anatolia
1918–20	Armenia and Azerbaijan are de facto independent
1918–21	Georgia is de facto independent
1931–38	Lavrenti Beria heads Georgian Communist Party
1943–44	Deportation of north Caucasus peoples, including Chechens
1953	Death of Stalin and execution of Beria
1988–	Nagorno-Karabakh conflict (ceasefire 1994)
April 1991	Georgia declares its independence from Soviet Union
August 1991	Azerbaijan declares its independence from Soviet Union
September 1991	Armenia declares its independence from Soviet Union
1991–	Georgian-Ossetian conflict (ceasefire 1992)
1992–	Georgian-Abkhaz conflict (ceasefire 1994)
1994–96	First Chechen War
1999–	Second Chechen War
2003	"Rose Revolution" removes Georgian president Eduard Shevardnadze

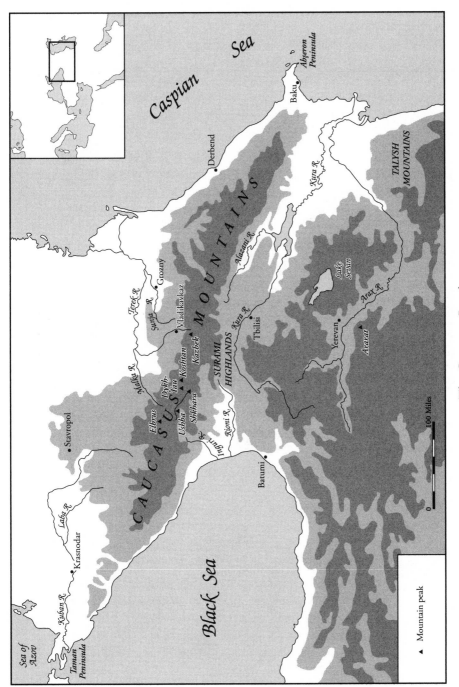

MAP 1 The Caucasus Landscape

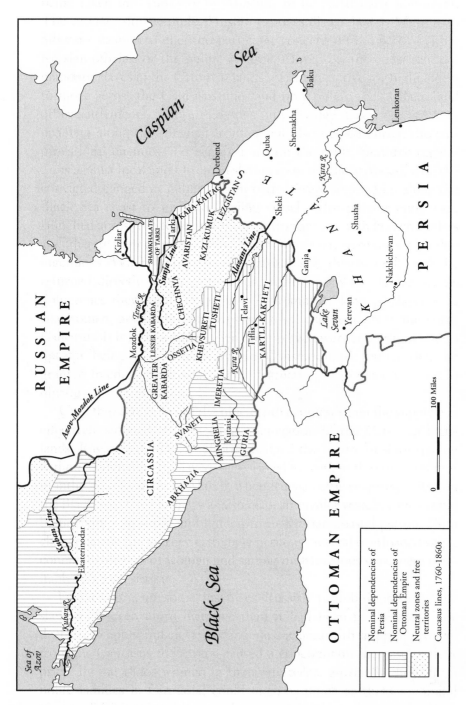

Sea of Azov

Black Sea

Caspian Sea

RUSSIAN EMPIRE

OTTOMAN EMPIRE

PERSIA

KHANATE

Kuban R.

Ekaterinodar

Kuban Line

Azov-Mozdok Line

CIRCASSIA

ABKHAZIA

SVANETI

MINGRELIA

Kutaisi

GURIA

IMERETIA

OSSETIA

GREATER KABARDA

LESSER KABARDA

Mozdok

Terek R.

Kizliar

SHAMKHALATE OF TARKI

Sunja Line

Tarki

KARA-KAITAG

AVARISTAN

KAZI-KUMUK

LEZGISTAN

Derbend

Quba

Shemakha

Baku

Lenkoran

CHECHNYA

KHEVSURETI

TUSHETI

Alazani Line

KARTLI-KAKHETI

Kura R.

Tiflis

Telavi

Sheki

Ganja

Lake Sevan

Yerevan

Shusha

Nakhichevan

Kura R.

100 Miles

0

Nominal dependencies of Persia

Nominal dependencies of Ottoman Empire

Neutral zones and free territories

Caucasus lines, 1760–1860s

MAP 2   The Caucasus circa 1780

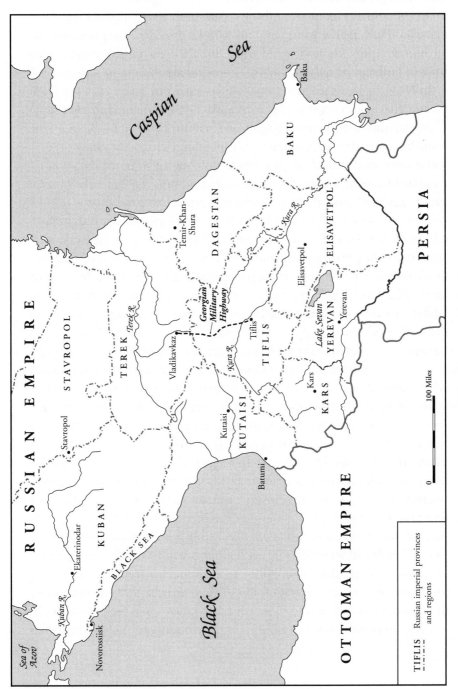

MAP 3 The Caucasus circa 1890

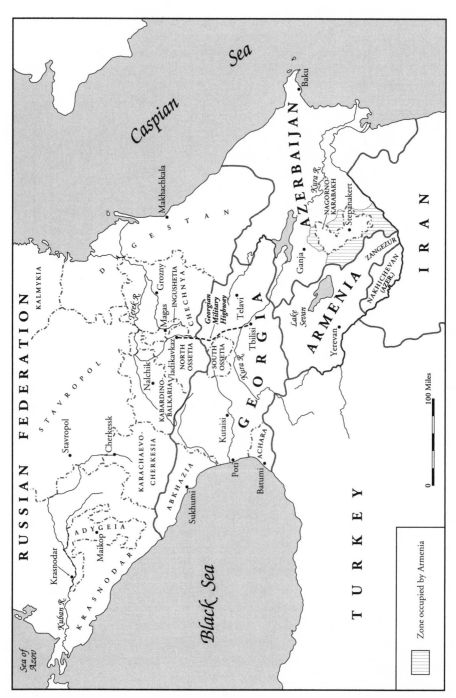

MAP 4 The Caucasus in 2008

RUSSIAN FEDERATION

KALMYKIA

STAVROPOL

Stavropol

Cherkessk

KARACHAEVO-
CHERKESIA

KABARDINO-
BALKARIA

Nalchik

ADYGEIA

Maikop

Krasnodar

KRASNODAR

Kuban R.

Sea of
Azov

Black Sea

Caspian

Sea

Makhachkala

D A G E S T A N

Grozny

INGUSHETIA

Magas

CHECHNYA

NORTH
OSSETIA

Vladikavkaz

SOUTH
OSSETIA

Georgian
Military
Highway

Telavi

Tbilisi

GEORGIA

Kura R.

ABKHAZIA

Sukhumi

Poti

ACHARA

Batumi

Kutaisi

Terek R.

Lake
Sevan

ARMENIA

Yerevan

Ganja

AZERBAIJAN

Kura R.

Baku

NAGORNO-
KARABAKH

Stepanakert

ZANGEZUR

NAKHICHEVAN
(AZER.)

IRAN

TURKEY

0   100 Miles

THE GHOST OF FREEDOM

Introduction: Nature's Bulwark

He turned his back on his native borders
And flew off to a far-away land,
Alongside the merry ghost of freedom.

Alexander Pushkin, "Captive of the Caucasus" (1822)

TWENTY-FIVE MILLION YEARS ago two great land masses col-
lided at a place we now call the intersection of Europe and
Asia. They crashed against each other with such force that,
over time, their edges soared skyward, crinkling together in a series of
long accordion folds. A string of rugged peaks and valleys, running
some seven hundred miles from northwest to southeast, rose up to
separate the great expanse of the Eurasian steppe from the arid uplands of eastern Anatolia and western Persia. From the earliest times it
has been called the Caucasus, "the longest and loftiest of all mountain
ranges," as Herodotus wrote in the fifth century B.C., a place "inhabited
by many different tribes, most of whom live off wild scrub."[1]

I first saw the mountains from south of the main chain, in a village
near Telavi, a city in eastern Georgia. The late afternoon was misty,
but the wooded hills could be seen in the distance on the far side of
the Alazani River and, beyond those, the snow-capped peaks that mark

the natural boundary between Georgia and the Russian republics of Chechnya and Dagestan.

I saw all this from inside a rattletrap Zhiguli, the ubiquitous post-Soviet automobile, as it trundled down a rough road and into what looked like an abandoned soccer field. The car pulled up to a group of men sitting at a table outside a cinderblock hut. A small aluminum camper trailer was parked near the doorway.

As I sat in the Zhiguli's passenger seat, wondering why my taxi driver had taken me here, a red-faced man with a wrestler's build walked around to my door. His breath was sour with vodka as he reached inside and tried to pull me through the window. When I resisted, he yanked open the door and hauled me out, intertwining his arms with mine as he frog-marched me around to the back of the car.

I felt a sinking feeling in my stomach. I was on the periphery of the periphery, in the far reaches of the former Soviet Union, in a village on the outskirts of a provincial city, situated in a part of the country that rarely saw foreigners. No one knew where I was, and I knew no one except for my Muslim driver, Mammed, and his mysterious Georgian friends, who were now pushing me toward the open door of the trailer. At that moment it all seemed terrifyingly clear: Mammed had sold me out. He had handed me over to a band of kidnappers who were now plotting how to make the most of their charge, an American, probably the first to have set foot in their village in recent memory.

But it was all in good fun—an instance of the oppressive hospitality for which the Caucasus has long been famous. The drunken wrestler dragged me over to a table outside the cinderblock building, where his two even drunker friends and two very large prostitutes were enjoying a late lunch. I joined them for a piece of dry cake and several toasts to Georgian women, American women, and women in general. Later, I slunk back toward the Zhiguli and made my way to Mammed's house, where his aged mother offered me a bed for the night and breakfast the next morning before driving on to Tbilisi, the Georgian capital. He had made the stop, Mammed later told me, because the Georgians owed him some money, and he thought having a stranger along—especially an American—might shame them into paying up. (It didn't.)

More than once during that trip I was convinced that I was being sold down the river, delivered into the hands of men who must surely have reckoned an American professor worth far more than they could earn by driving taxis or trading in the Telavi bazaar. After all, the Caucasus, as guidebooks point out, is a place where kidnappings are not unusual and travel off the beaten path inadvisable, even in such a relatively safe place as Georgia. However, that evening I realized that I had become a captive of the Caucasus in a much more profound sense: captive to the common vision of this mountainous land as a place of both unimaginable beauty and everyday barbarity.

I was in good company. The British painter Robert Ker Porter viewed these mountains in 1817 from the opposite slope, atop a low hill on the northern plains, near the Russian village of Severnaia. Hillocks rose from the steppe, leading on to higher, forested ridges. Beyond those stood the granite face of the main chain, the perennial snow on the summits just visible through the clouds. "I know not who could behold [the] Caucasus," he wrote, "and not feel the spirit of its sublime solitudes awing his soul."

It was not just the mountains' transcendent majesty that caused such rapture. Porter also believed that he was moving toward the frontier between two worlds. Behind him lay the Russian Empire, heir to the modernizing vision of Peter the Great, now reaching out to tame and cultivate the peoples of the Near East, from the Black Sea to the Caspian and beyond. Before him stretched the unexplored vastness, populated by primitive highlanders—some Muslim, others Christian or even pagan—whose depredations were already widely known in Europe: women sold into bondage by Tatar slavers; travelers held for ransom; bandits lying in wait in craggy defiles; rival clans waging ancient blood feuds, now prosecuted with the modern musket.

The mountains marked the troubled marches between confidence and insecurity, between civilization and barbarism—"nature's bulwark," as Porter put it, "between the nations of Europe and of Asia." Travel in these parts demanded constant vigilance, but that, in turn, had an effect on the experience itself. The inherent uncertainty of crossing through this borderland cast a shadow over the scenery, "obscuring the impressions of its grandeur, by a deeper, but less noble one, of fear."[2]

Awe and terror have often been intertwined in outsiders' conceptions of the Caucasus. For centuries travelers have seen the region as the homeland of both nobles and savages: proud highlanders who heroically resisted the onslaught of foreign empires, or backward mountaineers whose propensity for violence was matched only by their cultural chauvinism. Not long after Porter's journey, European and American newspapers would begin to carry regular stories of the struggle of Caucasus highlanders against the expanding Russian Empire. Highland chieftains toured Britain and delighted audiences with their exotic attire and stately bearing. Russians soon came to consider the

Caucasus their own wild South, imbuing it with the same ambivalent magnetism that characterized American notions of the western frontier. Russian poets and novelists, from Pushkin to Tolstoy, described the noble mien of the upland tribes or criticized their own government's increasingly brutal war against them.

There was a dark thread running through these images, one that concerned the animal brutality of the Caucasus peoples and their ferocious treatment of prisoners, their fallen state as lapsed Christians or fanatical Muslims, and their adulterated customs and identities on the frontier between Occident and Orient. In art, literature, travel writing, political reportage, and other spheres, the Caucasus was a place both attractive and repulsive to foreign visitors as well as to the Russians, who by the 1860s had established nominal sovereignty over the lowlands and highlands on either side of the mountain chain.

The end of the twentieth century resurrected and reinforced the less flattering of these views. Most of the armed conflicts that accompanied the collapse of the Soviet Union took place in the Caucasus. The independent countries of the south—Armenia, Azerbaijan, and Georgia—are beset by economic problems, social unrest, and territorial disputes. The Russian republics of the north—unfamiliar places such as Kabardino-Balkaria and tragically well known ones such as Chechnya—make headlines only after the latest hostage crisis or bombing. In fact, just counting the truly sovereign states of the Caucasus is no easy matter. The independent countries coexist with several unrecognized ones, places such as Nagorno-Karabakh and Abkhazia. Burdened by territorial conflicts, radical religious movements, terrorism, corruption, kidnappings, human trafficking, and ethnic nationalism, the Caucasus, as used to be said about Ireland, must surely be a place of very long memories and very short tempers.

Yet the history of this place is more than an interminable tale of social ills and political disorder. It is about the successes and failures of building modern states as well as the late conversion of ancient social practices into the accoutrements of nationhood. It is about the ways in which political and social modernization—whether in the Russian Empire or the Soviet Union—often produced unexpected results. It is about the place of a mountainous land at the confluence of Asia and Europe in the imaginary geography of both East and West, and how such tenaciously ambiguous labels as "empire" and "nation" have been transformed over the last two centuries.

This book tries to make sense of a part of the world that has seemed, during the past twenty years, the epitome of senselessness, where governments have had no qualms about bombing their own citizens, where terrorists have held hospitals and schools under siege, and where acts of selfless hospitality and unspeakable cruelty seem to be two sides of the same cultural coin. This is a history of the modern Caucasus as a place from the beginnings of Russian engagement down to the present day. But it is also a history of the Caucasus as an array of contrasting ideas—of liberty and lawlessness, of things both awe-inspiring and awful.

The main chain of the Caucasus mountains extends from the Taman Peninsula on the Black Sea to the Abşeron Peninsula on the Caspian Sea. The mountains form a series of high parallel ridges. In the west the mountains rise as low, wooded hills. In the center of the range they become imposing granite edifices, girded by snow and ice. In the east they split into two different chains and flatten out, continuing as a mass of high tablelands cut by deep gorges. The entire range thus forms a vast arrow, its flèche fanning out toward Asia and its tip pointing toward Europe.

The height and number of peaks in the Caucasus eclipse those in the Alps, although they do not approach the scale of the Himalayas. Near the largely uninterrupted main chain rise some of Eurasia's most impressive mountains—Elbrus (18,510 ft.), Shkhara (17,064 ft.), Dykhtau (17,054 ft.), Kazbek (16,558 ft.), to name just a few—which have been favorite challenges for climbers for more than a century. There are formidable peaks even beyond the main chain, lying on spurs and parallel walls that break off from the central cluster. Altogether the mountains form a complex jumble of highlands and plateaus packed into a rather small corner of the world. The distance between Elbrus in the Russian high Caucasus, usually labeled the tallest mountain in Europe, and Ararat (16,804 ft.) in eastern Turkey, one of the tallest in the Middle East, is only about three hundred miles.

Until relatively recently, there were only a few ways of getting from one side of the main range to the other. One was to travel along either of the two seacoasts, bypassing the highlands entirely by sailing around them or by going overland along the narrow passage between mountains and water. The route along the sandy shore of the Caspian, the so-called Derbend gap, was known in antiquity. It was a frequent point of encounter between the peoples of the Eurasian steppe and those of the Near East. The land route along the Black Sea was only completed in the 1890s, when tsarist administrators built an artificial coastal road and, later, a rail link that flanked the ridges of the western Caucasus.

Another option was to go straight through the middle of the range. Beginning north of the mountains, one could go upstream along the banks of the Terek River into the mountains, trek through narrow ravines and over highland passes, and then descend through the valley of the Aragvi River in the south, reaching out from the headwaters of one major river to link up with those of another. This road would eventually become the overland route through the heights, the course now followed by the famous "military highway" that leads from Vladikavkaz in Russia to Tbilisi in Georgia. Other routes were available, but they were usually no more than shepherd's trails and single-track paths until the last century, when Soviet planners devised ways to bridge over and blast through this grand continental divide.

The main chain marks off two broadly distinct regions. The northern slopes lead down to the Eurasian steppe. The southern slopes slip into lush river lowlands, the Mughan plains along the Caspian, and the rough uplands of Turkey and northern Iran. Although the icy mountains attract most of the attention, the entire Caucasus region is a land of considerable geographical diversity. Rich agricultural zones flank the wide lowland rivers. Expansive prairies run into green hill country. High plateaus provide summer grazing lands for cattle, sheep, and goats. The experience of taking the Georgian Military Highway south, squeezing through the treacherous Darial Gorge, and then coming upon the Aragvi River and the hills of Georgia below was an experience that enthralled travelers. Jacques-François Gamba, the French consul in Tiflis (later called Tbilisi), recorded his impressions on first passing through the mountains in 1820: "Italy, the Tyrol, Switzerland: none offers anything more admirable and romantic than the valley of the Aragvi.... After the steep crags which continually threatened to crush travelers under their debris, after the mountains covered in snow and ice...now came hills and prairies of the most beautiful verdure.... Before us, the landscape was alive with a throng of villages set amid well-tended agricultural lands."[3] The Caucasus has never been one place but many, including arid plains, semitropical foothills, craggy gorges, and alpine peaks. Moving through these varied landscapes—crossing rivers or coming down out of the hills—literally meant exiting one world and entering another.

The variety of topography and climate helps account for the multiplicity of political, cultural, and economic influences that have long defined the region. Roman writers claimed that scores of translators were required when traders sought to do business there, while Arab geographers sometimes labeled the region the *djabal al-alsun*, the mountain of languages. According to the tenth-century Arab scholar al-Masudi, the peoples who lived there could only be numbered by Him who made them.[4] In the 1870s the American traveler George Kennan expressed a similar view: "The Caucasian mountaineers as a whole are made up of fragments of almost every race and people in Europe and Western Asia, from the flat-faced Mongol to the regular-featured Greek.... How such a heterogeneous collection of the tatters, ends, and odd bits of humanity ever blended into one coherent and consistent whole I don't know; but there they are, offering problems to ethnologists and comparative philologists which will be found very hard to resolve."[5] The same sentiment would continue to be repeated—at times in equally racist terms—down to the present: the Caucasus as an impenetrably complex ethnic space, where the bonds of kith and kin have been reinforced by geographical isolation. The ecological diversity of this narrow causeway, lying between two major Eurasian seas, has meant that the range of disparate cultures has been even more extreme than in most places. One cannot help but be struck by the many languages, religious practices, and social structures concentrated in a territory smaller than Texas.

In the northwest forested mountains and hills slope down to the plains that run toward the Sea of Azov and the Black Sea, cut by the course of the Kuban River. Here traditional farming and herding were practiced by those who spoke a range of similar languages often collectively labeled Adyga (or Circassian), along with several Turkic peoples. Islam touched the region from its earliest moves north of the mountain chain, but periods of re-Islamicization—via the Ottoman Empire, the Crimean Tatars, or indigenous proselytizers—washed over the area through the nineteenth century. The region is today divided into three Russian republics—Adygeia, Karachaevo-Cherkesia, and Kabardino-Balkaria—as well as the much larger Stavropol and Krasnodar provinces to the north and west. Only in Kabardino-Balkaria do ethnic Circassians constitute the majority of the population.

In the middle of the Caucasus lies the republic of North Ossetia, separated from South Ossetia by the border between Russia and Georgia and populated by a largely Christian population cultivated by the Russian Empire as a buffer between Muslims in the eastern and western highlands. Farther to the east, along the course of the Terek River, are the lands of Nakh-language speakers, which were divided by later ethnographers into the categories of Chechen and Ingush. Islam was present here, too, but the influence of various syncretic systems of belief and practice—combined under the blanket label of Sufism—often blocked attempts to corral religion into purer forms.

The Chechens are now considered exemplary of the mountaineers' historic resistance to Russian rule, but that reputation is only partly deserved. People who lived much higher in the mountains—the Svans and Khevsurs of northern Georgia, for example—were generally the most antipathetic to outsiders; their religious practices, infused with animist beliefs, set them farthest apart from their Christian and Muslim neighbors. The real engine of the highlander uprisings of the nineteenth century lay farther to the east, in Dagestan. The very name of the region—literally "the mountainous land"—is evidence of its central geographical feature: mountains and plateaus cut by fast-flowing rivers. A congeries of distinct languages and customs has long been characteristic of the area, with social ties formed along lines of clans, extended families, and village groupings. The major ethnic groups—the Avars, Dargins, Kumyks, and Lezgins, among others, with none accounting for more than 30 percent of the population—today represent the dominant factions in Dagestan's precarious balance of regional, ethnic, and clan interests.

Across the mountains, to the south of Dagestan, lies modern Azerbaijan. Until the 1820s an array of Turkic-speaking Muslim khans held sway in this transitional zone from mountains to hills and plains. The khanates were nominally controlled by Persia, but they usually took advantage of their position on the international trade route between Central Asia and the West to exercise control over their own affairs. Eventually they all succumbed to the power of the Russian Empire, but the long history of contact with Persia left indelible marks in terms of cuisine, musical styles, and other areas. Conversely, the Qajar dynasty of Persia, which ruled from the 1790s to the 1920s, might just as well be called Azerbaijani as Persian. The Qajars were originally Turkoman nomads who managed to gather the Persian lands after the turmoil that followed the end of the Safavid dynasty. Although they speak a language closely related to Turkish, most modern Azerbaijanis share an additional cultural trait with Persia—Shi'a Islam—which sets them apart from the Sunni variant dominant in Turkey.

To the west of Azerbaijan are the lands inhabited by speakers of Kartvelian languages, which include Georgian and the cognate languages of Mingrelian, Svan, and Laz, a family unrelated to anything around it. The Georgian states of the Middle Ages—Kakheti in the east,

Kartli in the center, Imereti in the west, plus other lesser principalities—were in sustained contact with Russia from the sixteenth century onward. It was not until 1801, however, that Kartli and Kakheti formally became part of the Russian Empire, with their largely Orthodox Christian population extended the protection of the Christian tsar. It would be several decades before the rest of Georgia's many kings and princes would recognize Russian authority. Prior to that, political elites were usually able to play off neighboring empires against one another and enjoy a degree of autonomy. International trade; the produce of the agricultural lands along the Alazani, Kura, and Rioni rivers; and strategic necessity combined to make Tbilisi, the former seat of the Kartlian kings, the jewel in the crown of the Russian imperial Caucasus.

To the south of Georgia lies Armenia, today the smallest of the Soviet successor states but geographically a vast area stretching into modern Turkey. Here rough hill country descends to the valley of the Arax River from the mountains of the so-called Lesser Caucasus. Armenians speak one of the few indigenous Indo-European languages in the Caucasus, but the real seat of early Armenian civilizations lay farther to the south and west, in the lands on the frontier of eastern Anatolia and western Persia. Hellenistic kingdoms, Persian satrapies, and vaguely independent Muslim khanates successively controlled the territory that would become the modern Armenian republic. As with other Christian peoples, the Armenian Apostolic, or Gregorian, Church remained an important vehicle for a sense of cultural identity among Armenian farmers and traders even under Muslim rule. However, the church's ancient see at Echmiadzin, not far from the modern capital of Yerevan, has long competed with other poles of attraction, both cultural and political. The problem of who speaks for the Armenians—the people who have clung resolutely to this tiny bit of territory or the much larger diaspora now scattered across the globe—is still acute.

"Except that the risk of being eaten or pierced by poisoned arrows is gone," wrote one Caucasus traveler in the 1870s, "the mountains are much in the same state as they were in the time of Herodotus or Strabo."[6] He could not have been more wrong. Intense interaction among Caucasus peoples and Cossack communities, Russian colonists, and religious dissenters; the sedentarization of nomadic populations; the forced deportation of targeted ethnic groups; and the piecemeal assimilation to Russian culture and language—all have continually reshaped the ethnic and political contours of the Caucasus. The geographical and cultural diversity of the region went hand in hand with a long history of mutual influence and exchange. The Caucasus mountains created an arena where shepherds met farmers, ox drovers interacted with camel breeders, and kings and clan chiefs vied for power with steppe khans and highland emirs. Given the region's linguistic diversity, skill in multiple languages was historically the normal state of affairs. Based on set patterns of seasonal livestock grazing, local commerce, and long-distance trade, people higher in the mountains found it useful to learn the language of the people in the valleys and plains in addition to a lingua franca: Turkish, Arabic and, later, Russian.

Mountains have never been impenetrable barriers to the sharing of culture, from languages and legends to music and foodways. The Caucasus mountains, like the Andes and the Alps, have been both dividers and conduits, isolating distinctive communities while also providing channels of communication and interaction. Arabs, Mongols, Ottomans, and Russians were all able to command varying forms of loyalty on both sides of the Caucasus chain. Nor are mountains the only explanation for cultural fragmentation. The cultural landscape of flatlands can be just as complicated as that of highlands. One normally thinks of mountains as brimming with difference and plains as soporifically uniform, but neither is an accurate representation of the lives and social practices of the people who live there.

Mountains are not just one thing. There are high mountains and plateaus, where settlement is seasonal, with people moving from lowland to highland or from one upland valley to the next. There are middle, forested mountains, where highlanders are in sustained contact with people residing in valleys and along river courses. Lowlanders move along rivers or take to the mountains in times of distress. Valley farmers supplement their income with herding and raiding. Moreover, none of these categories is fixed, especially in circumstances in which states and empires have forcibly rearranged populations through relocation, mass exile, and genocide. Over the course of a single generation, lowlanders can be moved into the hills or mountaineers refashioned into prairie farmers. These processes are invariably traumatic, and they produce profound social changes in any landscape.

If there is a lasting geographical division in the Caucasus, it is not the one between north and south but rather between east and west. In the middle of the main chain two sets of uplands jut out toward the north and south at oblique angles. In the north the Stavropol hills glide down toward the plains. In the south the Surami mountains lead on to the Armenian plateau and the heights of the Lesser Caucasus. These ridges mark the watersheds of the Caspian and Black Sea basins. In the east the Terek, Kura, and Arax rivers empty into the Caspian. In the west the Kuban and Rioni rivers flow toward the Black Sea.

Cultural and political influences have been mapped onto this basic east-west division. Before the Russian conquest, elites in the western Caucasus were most likely to communicate in a variety of Turkish. For those in the east it was often Arabic or Persian. Western Georgia and the northwest Caucasus were under strong Ottoman influence for centuries. Eastern Georgia and the lands of modern Armenia and Azerbaijan were tied to Persia. Bridging the north-south divide was rather easier than overcoming the east-west one. Russia had major footholds in the eastern Caucasus, on both sides of the mountains, before it could fully control the west. The northwestern highlands were only subdued in 1864; the southwestern highlands succumbed at about the same time. The major connector across the Caucasus range, the Georgian Military Highway, was scouted by the Russian army in the 1760s and upgraded into a passable route for large-scale transport in the 1790s. Good roads connecting east and west were far later in coming. Not until the completion of the Transcaucasus railroad in the 1880s were the Black and Caspian seas finally joined by a modern, direct land route. (It is "trans" in the sense that it lies on the other side of the mountains from Russia, connecting east and west, not north and south.) Indeed, since antiquity the main way of getting from one sea to the other was not to traipse across the south Caucasus but rather to paddle up and down rivers in the north: to go upstream on the Don River from the Sea of Azov, portage across the steppe, and then set down again on the Volga and float to Astrakhan on the Caspian. A modern east-west connection on the northern side of the mountains, the North Caucasus railroad, was completed in 1917. Today the east-west divide still marks off important boundaries that from time to time eclipse the political distinctions between north and south.

The tenor of writing about the Caucasus alternates between the triumphalist and the tragic. The narrative is about either the ancient roots of a particular people and their survival, despite all odds, into the modern era, or about the age-old oppression of one group by a nefarious other. The concepts of empire and nation form the warp and weft of the historical narrative—a story of Russia's push to the south, the ensuing conflicts with Persia and the Ottomans, and the enduring resistance of small nationalities caught up in the clash of Eurasia's empires.

However, there are other, more complicated stories as well. Borders, allegiances, and identities have often been on the move. Looking across the entire region, one can see modern nationalisms that barely existed a century ago, long-standing cultural identities that are now nearly extinct, and peoples, languages, and cultures that have appeared, disappeared, and reappeared in a different form—often within a very short span of time. Consider a few examples.

The Armenians were perhaps the most privileged non-Muslim group in the Ottoman Empire. Their recognition as a distinct, protected community went back to the very beginnings of the Ottoman imperial system. Yet by the 1890s they had become the target of horrific state-organized violence and of genocide during the First World War. The modern Armenian republic is a direct result of these events. In the late Middle Ages a place called Georgia disappeared from the map, replaced by an array of combative feudal kingdoms and principalities. It would take many decades, from 1801, for the Russian Empire to gather them together again. Yet today there is a sense of common political identity among Georgians that is all the more remarkable for its long absence. The name "Azerbaijani" had no clear ethnic sense at all until the twentieth century. Today it is the basis of a strong national sentiment, not to mention a state. During the Caucasus wars of the nineteenth century it was the Adyga peoples (Circassians) who produced the longest-lived resistance movement against Russian rule. Now the Adyga are among the most politically loyal of all the constituent peoples of the Russian north Caucasus, while a bloody guerrilla struggle has raged among the Chechens since the mid-1990s.

Interstate relations have also moved in unpredictable directions. Georgia was the real partner of Russia in the conquest of the Caucasus in the nineteenth century. It later produced some of the central figures in the history of the Soviet Union, such as Lavrenti Beria and, of course, Joseph Stalin. Yet since 1991 relations between Russia and Georgia have been tense at best. Azerbaijan is now a solid ally of Turkey despite deep religious differences. By contrast, Armenia—the world's oldest Christian country, with links between religion and the state that run back to the fourth century—now enjoys cordial relations with the Islamic Republic of Iran.

Two hundred years ago the map of the Caucasus looked very different from the one that exists today. Unified places called Georgia and Armenia had long ago disappeared, the former in the fifteenth century and the latter in antiquity. Both were geographical rather than political expressions. A place called Azerbaijan, when the term was used at all, was more likely to refer to what one would now call northwestern Iran. It was not until the first decades of the twentieth century that these three names would be applied to modern states with clearly delineated borders, drawn along boundaries that had few historical antecedents. That point applies equally to the republics of the Russian north Caucasus—Adygeia, Karachaevo-Cherkesia, Kabardino-Balkaria, North Ossetia, Ingushetia, Chechnya, and Dagestan—places that would only appear on political maps much later, some not until well into the twentieth century. And the game is not yet finished. The conflict in Chechnya, the spread of violence to Russia's other north Caucasus territories, and a series of unresolved border disputes in the south Caucasus may eventually lead to even more changes.

Identities have been equally slippery. Only a century ago a traveler would have encountered someone we would now call a Georgian who spoke Turkish or an Armenian speaker who was a Muslim. There were Russian-speaking Buddhists, Orthodox Christians who spoke Chechen, and Armenians who considered Turkish their native language. Little is known of the daily lives of the inhabitants of the Caucasus until modern times. But one thing that is certain is the fact that their identities were always relational. One might be a Christian in contradistinction to a Muslim, a Gregorian Christian as opposed to an Orthodox one, a highlander rather than a lowlander, a farmer rather than a nomad, or—often most critically—a person from one clan or village rather than another. Categories such as "Georgian" and "Armenian," among others, have existed for centuries and perhaps even millennia. However, that is not the same as claiming that these categories have always meant identical things to the people who used them, nor is it to say that the social groups to whom these labels applied have existed in an unbroken line from the foggy past into the present. In the days before border guards, passports, and censuses, the boundaries between states and the bonds among the people who inhabit them were far more fluid than they are today. The decisions of empires and governments, the outcome of treaties, the forced and voluntary movement of populations, the interplay between social practice and official cultural policy, the fortunes of war, and the ruthless determination of individual political leaders have all played a role in making the modern Caucasus and the identities of the people who live there.

For centuries the political environment in the Caucasus was shaped by the struggle for influence among three Eurasian empires—the Russian,

Ottoman, and Persian. Muscovites reached the Caspian Sea with the conquest of the khanate of Astrakhan in 1556, yet it was not until the time of Peter the Great that Russia began to take advantage of its position as a Eurasian maritime power. Peter captured Derbend and Baku in 1722 and extended his reach almost to the Black Sea, but his successors soon surrendered these territories in the face of a revived Persia and a still powerful Ottoman Empire. During the next century Russia performed what the historian W. E. D. Allen called a great flanking maneuver: swinging around the eastern edge of the Caucasus, reaching up the river valleys of the southeast, and moving westward to touch the Black Sea, before bringing things full circle by subduing the highlands in the northeast and finally, by the 1860s, the northwest.[7]

Russia ended up as the historical winner. The Persians relinquished most of their claims to the region in the 1820s, and Ottoman authority was whittled down during the rest of the century. Except for the brief period of turmoil during the Bolshevik Revolution and the ensuing civil war, the entire Caucasus would remain within the Russian sphere until the collapse of the Soviet Union. Today the north lies within the Russian Federation. In the independent south, Russia continues to play a significant role in the economy, energy politics, and security policy of the region.

This outcome, however, was not predestined. In the very early nineteenth century much of the eastern Caucasus—which was tied to Persia by bonds of religion, culture, and commerce—might naturally have remained part of the Iranian realm. Russia secured territorial concessions from Persia in 1829, but in the same year the entire Russian diplomatic representation to the shah was brutally murdered in Tehran. Tsar Nicholas I's only response was to demand an official apology, which was delivered to St. Petersburg in solemn fashion by the shah's grandson. To do otherwise, the tsar feared, would have provoked an untimely war with the Persians, on whom Russia depended for trade and as a balance against the Ottomans. In the western Caucasus the Ottoman Empire retained some residual authority among Muslim populations in the highlands as well as in the western lowlands of Georgia. Wiping away the last vestiges of Ottoman influence there required not only Russian strategic acumen and military firepower, but also twin policies of what one would today call genocide and state terrorism—the systematic burning of villages, wholesale killing of native peoples, and forced deportation.

Conquering this imperial frontier took more than a century and a half, from Peter the Great's initial forays along the Caspian coast to the brutal subjugation of the northwestern highlanders and Black Sea coastal peoples in the 1860s. Even then, Russian control was never completely certain. Several independent republics emerged in the chaos of the First World War, all of which were snuffed out by the Bolshevik army in 1920 and 1921. During the Second World War, Stalin forcibly exiled hundreds of thousands of Chechens, Ingush, Karachai, Balkars, and other ethnic groups. Since the end of the Soviet Union, the Russian Federation has fought two brutal wars in Chechnya and has worked in more subtle ways to extend its economic and military power over Armenia, Azerbaijan, and Georgia. The modern history of the Caucasus is thus neither one of straightforward imperial conquest nor of the inexorable logic of Russia's manifest destiny in the south.

What happened in the Caucasus was, at various times, a major issue in the foreign policies of European powers, in the activities of religious and charitable organizations, and even in the popular culture of both Europeans and Americans. The Caucasus played a role in the Near Eastern strategies of Britain, France, and Germany. Writers from Alexandre Dumas to John Steinbeck visited and recorded their impressions. Oilmen drilled the wells of Baku. Engineers tapped the rich veins of copper and manganese that lay beneath Georgia. Sportsmen hiked the peaks and meadows of the highlands. Even people who had never been to the Caucasus could come face to face with it at Buffalo Bill's Wild West Show, which featured skilled horsemen from the Georgian lowlands. A mainstay of American dime museums was the "Circassian beauty," a voluptuous woman in fanciful costume, who would regale visitors with tales of her alleged abduction from the Caucasus and the erotic depravities of the Turkish harem.

By the time the Russian Empire finally conquered the last of the highlanders, another process of appropriation was already underway: the conceptualization of the Caucasus as a distinct place by generations of Russian and foreign writers, artists, and travelers. The mountains became metaphors for both love of liberty and unspeakable barbarism. Tribal allegiances were evidence of both inchoate national feeling and the inherent primitivism of local societies. The Caucasus was cast as either the fount of civilization (and of its highest representative, the "Caucasian race") or the antithesis of civilization itself. Today these visions still play a powerful role in politics, foreign relations, and communal interactions. National self-conceptions are wrapped up in them. Rights to territory are justified by reference to them. Notions of native and alien, friend and enemy, flow logically from them.

The greatest literary evocation of these themes is Alexander Pushkin's narrative poem "Captive of the Caucasus," first published in 1822. In the poem a young Russian aristocrat, seeking adventure beyond the confines of high society, is captured by mountaineers and taken to their village. In time he comes to appreciate the rugged beauty of the Caucasus and its people. A native woman falls in love with this strange outsider and helps him escape, but when he rejects her affection, she drowns herself in a mountain stream.

The poem contains all the elements of European romanticism: the quest for excitement by a bored European man; a Christian hero both captive to and captivated by exotic Asiatics; the sublime effects of an untamed landscape. However, there is a more subtle theme running through the text, one that concerns the very meaning of freedom and the ambiguous results that can come from seeking it. The Russian sets off to find adventure and the primordial freedom associated with the mountains, but he ends up chasing ghosts. The quest for liberty leads to bondage. The search for the unfamiliar breeds a longing for the comforts of home. The promise of love ends in death.

The peoples of the Caucasus, including Russians, have understood these ironies only too well. Russia's expansion in the nineteenth century, cloaked in the civilizing mission of a European empire, was prosecuted with incredible savagery. In the early twentieth century the promise of national self-determination produced an array of sovereign Caucasus republics, but their short-lived independence collapsed in the face of internal disorder and the aggression of the Bolsheviks. The rhetoric of liberation for the toiling masses underlay the grand experiment to create the Soviet Caucasus, but that, too, produced political and intellectual legacies that have been difficult to escape. In the late 1980s and early 1990s the promise of emancipation was the impetus for the popular movements that gave birth to the region's newly independent countries. Freedom for whom and from whom—including where borders should lie, how democracy and political order are to be balanced, which nations deserve self-determination and which do not—are still open questions.

The search for the elusive ghost of freedom—by the peoples of the Caucasus and by the many outsiders who have gone there looking for it themselves—is the central theme of this book. It is organized, in the main, chronologically. The first chapter covers the period from the late eighteenth century through the 1820s, from the beginning of Russia's energetic movement into the region until the end of the first phase of the wars of conquest. The second chapter continues through the

1860s, when the highlands came under full Russian control and the entire Caucasus was integrated into a modernizing empire. The third chapter highlights a few key episodes from several periods to illustrate the ways in which the Caucasus was imagined as a distinct place by generations of Russians and foreigners. The fourth chapter spans the early 1900s through the 1970s, from the emergence of cosmopolitan cities and briefly independent states through the fitful process of so-vietization. The fifth chapter brings the story up to the early twenty-first century, from the transformation of the region in the late Soviet period through the even more monumental changes wrought by the failure of the Soviet Union. The conclusion considers the region's possible future, as well as its connections with Europe.

"In writing these Travels," commented Julius von Klaproth, a nineteenth-century Caucasus explorer, "I have almost always adopted the plan of describing the country lying on both sides of the road."[8] This book, metaphorically speaking, tries to do the same, namely, to serve as a guide to the controversial terrain of Caucasus history by discussing multiple interpretations of contentious issues and taking seriously the inconstancy of names, identities, and popular memory. Although its geographical scope includes the Caucasus narrowly defined—the hills and plains on either side of the main mountain chain—it ranges beyond as well, from the chambers of government in major European capitals to the circus sideshows of late-nineteenth-century America. Each chapter addresses issues that are critical in terms of understanding the recent past and the uncertain present of this region: the power and impotence of boundaries, both territorial and social; the sources of resistance to, and accommodation with, imperial outsiders; the emergence of the Caucasus as an imaginary geographical and cultural space in literature, ethnography, travel writing, and other fields; the protean meanings of nationalism and the burdens of historical memory; the Soviet revolutionary experiment and its legacies; and the vicissitudes of state- and nation-building in Eurasia.

The story begins two centuries ago, when the political environment was about to undergo a fundamental transformation. Imperial powers were seeking new clients. Old allegiances were being reworked. Religion and nationalism were being mobilized by rival claimants to legitimacy and by outside forces vying for influence. Soon Russians and Europeans would begin to see the Caucasus as a major arena in the strategic jockeying, underground intrigues, and business gambles that accompanied the quest for empire on the borderlands of Europe and Asia.

ONE

Empires and Boundaries

*But the Persian Geographers cease not . . . to stretch their Empire out, in their most
modern Descriptions, as far as those Boundaries, which it had of old, alleging,
that they are still in Right and Fact, the Bounds of their Country.*

Jean Chardin, French traveler (1670s)

*The mountains are full of free and ungoverned people, where renegades can always find
refuge under the cover of laws which are contrary to our interests.*

Gen. Alexei Petrovich Ermolov (1820)

IMPERIALISTS ARE CONGENITAL optimists. They consistently over-
estimate their own power and underestimate the resolve of those
they aim to conquer. They eventually come to believe the bombas-
tic titles they bestow on themselves and their subordinates. In the sixteenth century Muscovite grand princes claimed for themselves the
title of lords of Georgia and Kabarda and of the Circassians and other
mountaineers even though no Russian ruler until the nineteenth century would really control all these lands and peoples. By the time of the
Bolshevik Revolution, the tsar's full title extended to several para-
graphs, cementing his claim to kingdoms and principalities that had
not existed in any meaningful sense for centuries. The Ottoman sultan

and the Persian shah were little different. This pattern extended even to imperial subalterns. In the eighteenth century the king of eastern Georgia was still calling himself "The Most High King, by the will of our Lord, King of Kings of the Abkhaz, Kartvelians, Kakhetians, and Armenians, and Master of All the East and the West" despite the fact that he and his predecessors had been under Persian or Ottoman overlordship off and on for several hundred years.

Before the period of Russian conquest, such optimistic assessments about the extent of one's own power were understandable. The problem in the Caucasus was not a lack of clear boundaries but rather a surfeit of them. A local strongman could charge his own customs duties, which might or might not be surrendered up to a higher sovereign. Nominally independent powers could declare themselves vassals of a larger one. Client states could switch sides. Figuring out who really controlled which piece of real estate was a challenge. In the early 1820s the French diplomat Jacques-François Gamba traversed the lands of the Circassians and the Abaza, in the northwest Caucasus, yet he was uncertain about when he had crossed a real boundary line between one political realm and another: "I could never quite determine if these limits were established by politics or by invasions, or if they naturally separated two peoples who have nothing in common in terms of language, traits and character."[1] The limits—of an empire, a cultural group, or even a continent—were usually in the eyes of those who believed they had stepped over them. "We have just crossed the Terek [River]," wrote the wife of a Russian official in 1811, "and are now out of Europe."[2]

Until the late nineteenth century the borders separating the many different political entities in the Caucasus were often opportunities for extraction—collecting tolls for safe passage, for example—not solid walls delineating one sovereign's realm from another's. Modern maps that show great swaths of colored territory as clearly belonging to one or another khanate, kingdom, principality, or empire are fundamentally misleading about the real nature of sovereignty on the ground. The goal of any political power was to control the locus of extraction, such as a key bridge, port, mountain pass, or fortress.

When borders did serve something like a modern purpose, they were usually meant not to keep people out but to keep them in. As a labor force, a symbol of power, and a resource to be drawn on for raising armies, people were a commodity not easily replaced. Peace treaties between Russia and its neighbors in the eighteenth century often included clauses about the mandatory return of people displaced by war, a practice that today would be called the forced repatriation of refugees. Even in peacetime the wanderlust of an emperor's subjects could be a problem. In 1771 one major group of nomads on the Eurasian steppe, the Kalmyks, decided to pick up their tents along the Volga River and head east to better grazing lands in China. Catherine the Great responded by sending an army to return them to her domains. In the end the Kalmyks—perhaps numbering three hundred thousand—outran Catherine's Cossack cavalry and ended up as vassals of the Qing emperor despite the empress's protestations that the Chinese return them to their rightful sovereign.[3]

It was not until much later that the concept of borders began to change. Improved surveying techniques and cartographic conventions allowed boundaries to be determined more precisely. Concern over the spread of infectious diseases, such as the plague and cholera, also inclined autocrats to rethink the concept of what a border was good for. Gradually the focus became controlling foreigners' entry into a territory rather than preventing locals from exiting. Having a quarantine facility and not just a garrison or a customs office became the essential feature of border posts. Before then the array of overlapping political forms was so great that the modern notion of sovereignty—recognized control over a defined territory—was difficult to apply.

Imperial Dreams

Despite the problems of delineating boundaries, there was a clear sense, going back to antiquity, that the Caucasus represented a kind of borderland, a frontier where different peoples, empires, and social systems came into contact. In Greek mythology, it was the far edge of the world where Prometheus the fire-stealer was exiled by the gods. The Qur'an speaks of the Caucasus as a mountainous land beyond which lie the marauding peoples of Gog and Magog, held in check by a huge metallic wall. In the sixteenth century, well before the arrival of the Russians as a major player, the Caucasus was a battleground between the two great powers of the Islamic world: the Ottomans and the Safavid dynasty of Persia. From the 1530s to the 1550s one campaign after another devastated the lowlands of the south Caucasus and pitted local powerbrokers against their rivals on the other side of the imperial divide. Finally, in 1555, under the terms of the Peace of Amasya, the Ottomans and Persians agreed to a formal division of spheres of influence. The Ottomans assumed nominal control over the areas west of the Surami highlands, which encompassed the Georgian kingdom of Imereti, ruled by a Christian king and his subordinate princes, and the coastal lands of the Black Sea. The Persians were to control the east, which included the Georgian kingdoms of Kartli and Kakheti, the Muslim khanates of Yerevan and Nakhichevan, and the various Muslim potentates in the lands stretching from the mountains down to the Caspian Sea. A similar division extended north of the mountains, with the Ottomans claiming the Black Sea coast of Circassia and inland Kabarda and the Persians claiming Dagestan in the east.

The exact nature of political influence varied by region and by period. The several Christian kings and princes of Georgia, scions of the ancient Georgian ruling house of the Bagrationi, learned how to survive within the interstices between two powerful Islamic empires. Over the centuries they became practiced in the art of playing off one regional authority against another, often with the goal of using that relationship to gain some advantage over their own distant relatives. As a general rule, the Ottomans retained greater influence in the lowlands of the west, including the river valleys leading to the Black Sea, than in the east, along the course of the Kura and Alazani rivers flowing toward the Caspian Sea. In the mid-eighteenth century the kingdoms of Kartli and Kakheti, united under King Erekle II, managed to carve out something close to independence from their Persian suzerains, creating a powerful but short-lived state that ruled the Muslim khans, steppe nomads, and Armenian nobles of the south and east. Even then, western Georgia remained outside Erekle's domains.

The Ottomans enjoyed nominal sway over the Muslims of Circassia and Kabarda in the northwest Caucasus. However, power was exercised only indirectly through the intercession of the khans of the Crimean Tatars, who were themselves unruly vassals of the sultan, frequently raiding local villages and threatening to draw the Ottomans into a war with Russia. Farther to the northeast, in Dagestan, the Ottomans had certain advantages over the Persians. They were Sunnis like the Dagestanis, and the several attempts by the Persians to subdue Dagestani tribal leaders were usually rebuffed as an onslaught by Muslim schismatics. "If any Persian king is a fool," went a Persian proverb, "let him march against the Lezgins," one of the major tribes of Dagestan.[4] In fact, if there was a single pole of attraction to the political and religious leaders of Dagestan, it was not Turkey or Persia but Yemen, the great center of a major school of Sunni Islam. Still, with the exception of brief periods when the Ottomans managed to march troops into the Persian Caucasus and assert their control temporarily, the basic east-west division remained in place for the next two centuries after the Amasya accord of 1555.

The imperial balance of power in the Caucasus teetered in the middle of the eighteenth century. The immediate cause of the realignment of political influence was the rapid decline of the Safavid dynasty in Persia. The Safavids had reached their apogee during the reign of Shah Abbas (1587–1629), when Persian rule extended over all the Georgian kingdoms and the Muslim khanates of the south and east. In the late seventeenth and early eighteenth centuries those achievements were reversed. Tribal raiders from Dagestan made incursions from the north and threatened Persian vassals in the south Caucasus. In the 1720s Afghans invaded Persia proper and took the Safavid capital of Isfahan. The Safavid shah, Tahmasp II, launched an ill-considered war to recover territory that had been taken in the interim by the Ottomans, but his defeat on the battlefield led to his overthrow at home. Nadir Shah, a distinguished military commander, stepped in and managed to restore order, but his assassination in 1747 ushered in a period of civil war.

The empire broke apart. The kingdoms of eastern Georgia—Kartli and Kakheti—emerged from beneath Persian overlordship and began to develop stronger ties with Russia, which increasingly portrayed itself as protector of fellow Orthodox Christians across the Near East. Farther south and east a series of functionally independent khanates emerged, controlled by local Muslim elites professing loyalty to either Persians or Ottomans and surviving by monopolizing trade and the natural wealth of their domains. Dagestan, which was never really commanded by the Safavids at all, was dominated by an array of local elites who sometimes raided lowland settlements and survived with little concern for the machinations of empires farther afield.

In earlier centuries it was the Ottomans who were most prepared to take advantage of Persian weakness. Now it was the rising power to the north, Russia. Since the sixteenth century Russia's influence had been growing. Ivan IV's capture of the Tatar khanate of Astrakhan in 1556 extended Muscovy's reach to the Caspian Sea and laid open the coasts of Persia and Central Asia. Relations developed apace with lowland Muslim rulers, such as those of Kabarda. Cossacks, too, were present along the river courses of the north Caucasus, and in time they would provide a channel of influence into the hills and a border force to secure the expanding southern frontier against highland raiding parties. Throughout the late sixteenth and early seventeenth centuries Muscovy also sent a series of embassies to the leaders of Georgia in order to establish relations with these ancient Christian kingdoms, reconnoiter the Caucasus borderlands, and provide much-needed geographical information to Russian military planners.[5]

Ivan IV's immediate successors were more involved in dealing with Russia's internal unrest than capitalizing on these relations. However, by the time of Peter the Great, Russia's strategic gaze once again turned to the south. Under Peter, Russia developed a maritime presence not only in the Baltic Sea—to protect the newly created capital of St. Petersburg—but also on the Sea of Azov, the antechamber to the Black Sea. Peter captured the strategic fortress of Azov, located near the mouth of the Don River, from the Ottomans in 1696. He was forced to give it up soon thereafter, but just as the Don had been the highway to the Black Sea, so the Volga became the route to the Caspian. In the early 1720s Peter used his new naval might to launch an expedition along the Caspian coast. The justification was an attack by Dagestani highlanders against Russian subjects trading in Persian lands. However, in quick succession Peter's forces took the strategic fortresses at Derbend and Baku. The Persians were forced to relinquish these and other territories in the eastern Caucasus and the Caspian littoral.

In the end, none of Peter's grand designs in the south could be realized. The formal cession of Persian territory did nothing to bring these lands fully under Russian control. They would eventually be surrendered by Peter's successors or lost during the sweeping campaigns of Nadir Shah, who managed to unite some of the old Safavid domains in the 1730s and 1740s. The Russians contented themselves with shoring up their holdings in the north. For the next several decades Russian leaders assiduously ignored pleas for assistance from local rulers, both Christian and Muslim. The Ottomans were still too powerful on land and sea, and their strong relations with many of the Caucasus uplanders dampened Russia's ability to forge further friendly relations inland. Peter's exploits had lasting importance, though. They set the stage for the growth of Russia's own sense of entitlement to the Caucasus, the idea that not only Russia's security but its very identity— now as a proper empire, with feet in both Europe and Asia—depended on ending Ottoman and Persian control.

Those twin visions were partially realized later in the eighteenth century. Catherine the Great initiated a wide-ranging plan for extending Russian influence in the Caucasus, both north and south, as part of her broader aim of eventually unseating the Ottomans and placing a Russian prince on the throne of a restored Byzantium. Defensive lines were strengthened, first between existing Cossack settlements, or *stanitsas*, and later between newly built forts. New communities of

Cossacks were moved into the region as border guards. The Ottomans, who were looking out for their own fortunes in the region after the weakening of Safavid power, were not prepared to accept Russian moves. In 1768 war erupted between the two empires. Highland tribesmen sacked Russian forts. Ottoman and Crimean Tatar armies pushed into the northern steppe. Russians moved south through the mountains and attacked Georgian and Ottoman holdings alike. During the war Russian forces under Gen. Gottlieb Heinrich von Todtleben crested the main ridge of the Caucasus in 1769, following the courses of the Terek and Aragvi rivers and laying the foundation for what would eventually become the key overland route to the south, the Georgian Military Highway.

After several seasons of fighting, the war was ended in 1774 by the Treaty of Küçük Kaynarca. The treaty marked a monumental change in Russia's relations with its neighbors to the south and, by extension, the Ottomans' relations with theirs to the north. Russia was given effective control of Crimea and other areas on the Black Sea littoral. The sea, previously closed to foreign ships, was opened to Russian-flagged commercial vessels. In the north Caucasus, Russia stepped up pressure on the lowland chiefs of Kabarda by strengthening the line of fortified settlements. Some local chieftains resisted, appealing to the Ottomans for assistance, but Russia continued its policy of building forts and encouraging the settlement of Cossacks, Armenians, and other groups considered loyal to the empress.

South of the mountains, the relationship already forged with eastern Georgia, specifically the united kingdom of Kartli-Kakheti, was further enhanced. After the end of the Russo-Turkish conflict, Catherine promised Russian protection against future attacks by the kingdom's external enemies. This protective guarantee, sealed by the Treaty of Georgievsk (1783), would later provide the basis for absorbing eastern Georgia fully into the Russian Empire. From the Georgian perspective, however, the new arrangement was little different from the relationship that had existed with the Persians in centuries past. The Georgian family line would be confirmed in its position as hereditary kings, while simultaneously assuming the title of governor-general of Georgia in the service of Russia.

These developments were of considerable concern to the Ottomans. In systematically violating the terms of the Treaty of Küçük Kaynarca—such as annexing the Crimean peninsula and its large Muslim population—Russia seemed committed to expansion. In 1787 a second war erupted between the two empires. At its close in 1792 Russia was granted control of the entire northern littoral of the Black Sea, all the way to the Kuban River. Parts of the Caucasus coast and the highlands were assumed to be functionally independent, but Russia had already begun to strengthen its position north of the mountains and to the south as well, through its special relationship with eastern Georgia.

At this time another power began to rise on the ruins of the Safavids and to reassert rights to the eastern Caucasus. The Qajars, a Turkoman family with traditional grazing lands in Persian Azerbaijan, gradually took advantage of the weakening of the many dynastic potentates who had staked their claims to power following the end of Safavid rule. In the 1780s the eunuch Agha Muhammad Khan, leader of the Qajars, began to extend his reach over the old Persian lands, including the eastern Caucasus. It was expressly to protect eastern Georgia from Qajar incursions that Erekle II, the king of Kartli-Kakheti, had signed the protective treaty of 1783 with Catherine—even though he had earlier been a supporter of Nadir Shah, who had permitted a degree of Georgian autonomy that the Qajars would not countenance.

Catherine's commitment to Kartli-Kakheti was less than complete, however. Faced with continuing tensions with the Ottomans, Catherine withdrew the Russian garrison from the Kartlian capital of Tiflis in 1784. There followed a decade of wrangling between Erekle II and Agha Muhammad. However, in 1795 the Persians tired of Georgian intransigence and marched on Tiflis, sacking the city despite the Russians' explicit promise to defend it. The city was left in ruins. Much of the population, both in the towns and the countryside, was killed, expelled, or enslaved, with the total number of households in Kartli-Kakheti reduced by perhaps as much as half.[6] The following year Agha Muhammad had himself crowned shah of a renewed Persian Empire and relocated the capital from the old Safavid center of Isfahan to Tehran, a city better suited to guarding Qajar interests in the Caspian and eastern Caucasus.

Despite the Persians' war on eastern Georgia, the eastern Caucasus was not completely brought under Qajar rule. The king of Kartli-Kakheti remained on his throne; an array of sovereign khanates, only nominally subject to the Qajars, existed throughout modern-day Armenia and Azerbaijan; and the various hereditary rulers of Dagestan looked after their own affairs with little regard for the dictates of Tehran. Kartli-Kakheti was in a particularly vulnerable position, however. The Qajars had already proven their strength by marching on Tiflis. There was nothing to stand in the way of cavalry galloping out of northern Persia, and with a series of friendly Muslim khans along the way, the army could easily provision itself.

This difficult situation eventually forced the Georgians into establishing an even deeper relationship with Russia. The 1783 agreement with Kartli-Kakheti provided a Russian foothold in the south Caucasus, but Georgian royals had long argued that the Russians had never really lived up to their end of the original bargain. Georgievsk had placed eastern Georgia under Russian protection, yet it required that the Russians actually defend the kingdom against attack from other Georgian kings, from the Qajars, and from the persistent raids of Lezgins and other Dagestani highlanders. By the late 1790s, however, all Russian troops had been withdrawn from the kingdom, leaving little in the way of defense. In September 1799 Erekle's successor as king of Kartli-Kakheti, Giorgi XII, sent a personal petition to St. Petersburg requesting that his kingdom be made a part of the Russian Empire "on the same footing as the other provinces of Russia." In return, the Russians were to ensure that Giorgi's family—the Bagrationi—remained on the Georgian throne, that he and his heirs received hereditary titles and property within the bounds of the empire, and that, as had happened with other territories, the Georgian nobility be absorbed into the elaborate Russian system of ranks.[7]

Before any of this could be accomplished both Giorgi and Paul, the Russian emperor, died. The new tsar, Alexander I, proved far more decisive than his predecessor. Faced with the growing assertiveness of Napoleon and persistent worries about the power of the Persians, Alexander decided to use Giorgi's offer as a pretext for outright annexation. In September 1801 he issued a proclamation that made Kartli-Kakheti a part of the Russian Empire while also deposing the ancient royal house. Placing eastern Georgia under the emperor's control was not intended to "increase my powers, secure profit, nor enlarge the boundaries of an already vast empire," the tsar wrote in justifying the annexation, but was meant to "establish in Georgia a government that can maintain justice, ensure the security of persons and of property, and give to everyone the protection of law."[8] The following year he appointed Prince Pavel Tsitsianov—of Georgian descent—imperial governor and commander of Caucasus military forces. When he arrived in Tiflis in early 1803, Tsitsianov's first task was to remove any malcontented royals who might become a source of opposition to tsarist rule.

This proved more difficult than he had imagined. In April Tsitsianov received word that Mariam, the widow of Giorgi XII, together with the queen's mother and other members of the family, were preparing to flee to Khevsureti, a mountainous region of northern Georgia. Russian authorities feared that they would use their support among the populace to launch a revolt against the tsar. The Khevsurs were known as fierce warriors, and the deposed royals could perhaps link up with Lezgins and other peoples north of the main chain, igniting a full-scale war along Russia's southern border (a possibility that nearly came to pass a few years later).

Before the family could depart, Tsitsianov dispatched Maj. Gen. Ivan Lazarev, the commander of Russian troops in Tiflis, to the queen's residence. Lazarev arrived on a Sunday morning in full mufti, along with his interpreter, a military band, and two companies of infantry. The formality of the occasion, however, was not matched by the general's demeanor. He stepped into the royal chambers to find the queen seated and waiting for him, her seven children still sleeping on the oriental carpets that draped her divan. He informed her curtly that she was to accompany him as a guest—that is, a prisoner—of the imperial representative. When the general approached her, the queen drew her husband's dagger from beneath a cushion and plunged it into his left side, killing him. Lazarev's soldiers rushed to his defense, felling the queen beneath a barrage of rifle butts. They then trundled her out of the house, along with the rest of the family, and threw them into carriages that were waiting in the street below.

Word of the indignity quickly spread throughout the city and the countryside. As the carriages left Tiflis and rumbled up the Georgian Military Highway, throngs of Georgians lined the route, crying and bidding the family farewell. When the convoy arrived in Russia, the queen was dispatched to a convent in Voronezh, where she spent the next seven years surrounded by other nuns, removed from the grand surroundings of her royal residence and her native land. She died several decades later, still an exile, in Moscow.[9]

Over the next few years, Tsitsianov's administration worked to secure the full incorporation of eastern Georgia. New internal administrative boundaries were created, new regulations issued on everything from local government to noble ranks and educational institutions, and provisions made for shoring up the security of the vulnerable Georgian lands against highland raiders. Soon Russian forces began pressuring the surrounding khanates, headed by hereditary rulers who looked to Persia for support. In early 1804 the Russian army subdued the khanate of Ganja in modern Azerbaijan, a city that was renamed Elisavetpol, after the wife of Alexander I. Later in the year a similar move was made in the south, against the khanate of Yerevan, but with little success. Two years later Tsitsianov's forces again opened a front in the east, marching on the khanate of Shirvan, which was easily taken, and then Baku.

Although the khan of Baku was formally allied with the shah, he readily capitulated, offering to ride out from behind the city walls and personally surrender to the representative of the tsar. But when Tsitsianov moved forward to meet him, the khan's men opened fire, leaving the general fatally wounded. The Russian army beat a hasty retreat. The khan then ordered the commander's head and hands to be hacked off and sent as trophies to Tehran. Later in 1806, even without Tsitsianov's leadership, a new military campaign was launched, which ended in the complete capitulation of both Baku and Derbend, the strategic choke point along the Caspian coast.

These moves inevitably provoked a war with the Qajars, the khanates' main protector, as well as with the other interested party in the region, the Ottomans. From 1804 through 1813 Russia was formally at war with the Persians, and from 1806 through 1812 with the Ottomans as well—in addition to the even more serious problem of Napoleon in the west. Each season brought renewed fighting throughout the north and south Caucasus as local leaders, both Christian and Muslim, sought to take advantage of Russia's engagement and the preoccupation of its imperial rivals to reinforce their own spheres of authority.

Russian forces were able to seize strategic outposts, but these were often subsequently overrun by Persians and Ottomans or were simply handed back by the Russians to one or another local power broker in exchange for nominal loyalty. At the same time, the Russians faced opposition in Georgia, supposedly the *place d'armes* of imperial interests south of the mountains. The king of Imereti, another scion of the Bagrationi household, stubbornly refused to submit to Russian control. Revolts were also launched in Kartli-Kakheti by members of the former royal dynasty. Although these uprisings were eventually quelled, they remained a major distraction for Russian forces during the Persian war and after. In fact, the full subjugation of all the Georgian lands would occupy the entire first half of the nineteenth century.

The Ottoman and Persian conflicts were ended by the treaties of Bucharest and Gulistan, in 1812 and 1813, respectively. These peace treaties changed the strategic balance in the Caucasus and along the coast of the Black Sea. Under the former, Russia gave back to the Ottomans virtually all of the conquests that had been made during the war, including the vital Black Sea ports of Poti and Anapa, as well as the inland border fortress at Akhalkalaki. Under the latter treaty,

Russian control was confirmed over both eastern and western Georgia—the old kingdoms of Kartli-Kakheti and Imereti—as well as over the Muslim khanates of Karabakh, Ganja, Shaki, Shirvan, Derbend, Baku, and Quba to the south and east. However, Persian influence remained in two important areas in the south, the khanates of Yerevan and Nakhichevan. Although Russia was at last formally recognized as a Caucasus power, the victory was an ambiguous one. The Ottomans could still influence the Muslim highlanders of the western Caucasus, especially through their military presence in Anapa. The Persians, too, retained a solid foothold north of the Arax River and on the plains stretching to the Caspian Sea.

The political situation by the 1810s and early 1820s was more settled than it had been a few decades earlier, before the emergence of the Qajars and Romanovs as rivals. However, the political map was still complex. In the north Russian forces held a defensive line that stretched between the Black and Caspian seas. They also controlled the corridor through the central Caucasus, the Georgian Military Highway. The fort at Vladikavkaz on the Terek River, founded under Catherine but repeatedly abandoned in the face of highlander raids, was once again firmly under Russian control and served as the jumping off point for the overland journey to the southern slopes. Eastern Georgia was formally a part of the Russian Empire, albeit with a disgruntled royal house that felt the tsar had reneged on his promise to protect their hereditary privileges. Western Georgia—the kingdom of Imereti and its associated principalities—was racked by civil discord and still vulnerable to the blandishments of the neighboring Ottomans. To the southwest Georgian-speaking Muslim frontier lords professed loyalty to the sultan and looked out for his interests on the new borderland with Russia. To the southeast an assortment of Muslim khans, highland chieftains, Armenian and Jewish merchants, and Kurdish, Turkoman, and other nomads jockeyed for influence and control of local economies, sometimes cooperating with the Qajars and at other times waging war against them.

Yet surveying the fault lines of imperial conflict reveals little about the factors that would ultimately determine the political fate of the region—the way in which the interests, ambitions, and visions of local rulers and their subjects intersected with the new strategic designs of outsiders. Beneath the rarefied strategic gambits of Persians, Ottomans, and Russians lay the everyday experiences of generations of men and women: lowland farmers along the Kuban and Terek rivers; Cossack communities that had emerged from a mix of Slavic peasants, renegade serfs, and natives; the noble families of the south Caucasus, the Christian kings and Muslim khans who had spent many centuries making their peace with more powerful neighbors; foreign merchants, travelers, and adventurers; and the expansive category that Russians would come to call the *gortsy*—"highlanders" or "mountaineers"—who have continued to play a complex game of accommodation with and resistance to Russian rule right up to the present. Not simply recipients of the grand plans of Eurasian imperialists, local societies across the Caucasus had long ago established their own forms of political power and social organization, which were now coming under pressure from both the north and the south.

Kings and Khans

An important literary form of the Enlightenment was the *description géographique*, a comprehensive catalogue of the flora and fauna, people and social mores, economy and political life of a distinct region. These works fulfilled educated Europeans' desire for descriptions of such faraway places as eastern Europe, overseas colonies, and even the villages that lay beyond the gates of one's own city. Some of the most interesting of these treatises were written by educated young men on the periphery eager to provide some account of their native realms to the wider world.

In the Caucasus one of the most important of these works, dating from the 1740s, was written by a certain Prince Vakhusht. Few details are known about him other than the fact that he was a member of the ancient house of the Bagrationi, the royal dynasty whose many branches ruled the Georgian lands until the union with Russia. He was probably born around 1696 and spent most of his adult life in Russia, one of the many Georgian nobles who, across the centuries, were absorbed into the Russian nobility through marriage or assimilation.[10] He may have undertaken the work as a way of securing Russian and European interest in the plight of the old royal family, which was then dispersed among a number of rival kings and princes, all threatened by both Persians and Ottomans.

Throughout his book the prince attempted to illustrate the commonalities that united the peoples who lived in historical Georgia, but what is most striking about his account is the incredible diversity of the political and cultural landscape. The Georgians, says Vakhusht, "love arms and are bellicose, proud, and intrepid. They seek glory to such a degree that, in order to acquire it, they will spare neither country nor sovereign.... They know nothing beyond reading and writing, singing and dancing, and making war, and they think of this as a great science." However, Vakhusht had in mind only one particular group—the people of his own realm, the kingdom of Kartli. He was less complimentary about others: "Those who live in the mountains have something of the character of wild animals, but they are intelligent." Although he admitted that the people of Samtskhe, the marches along the border with the Ottoman Empire, resembled the Kartlians, "at feasts and meetings, the important people speak Turkish and use Georgian only among themselves and with their friends." The Kakhetians, neighbors of the Kartlians in the fertile eastern hills, resembled the Kartlians "in their manners and their clothes," but they were "proud, presumptuous, boastful, verbose, querulous, intrepid, above all peasants, and faithful." The Svanetians, who resided in the mountains of the north, were "known to plunder, show no mercy, and are coarse and without manners.... They have their own language, but know also Georgian."[11]

Vakhusht had no doubt that all these people were actually Georgians. Many knew the language and were even subject to the same religious authority, the Orthodox Christian *catholicos* of Kartli—for Vakhusht the most important criterion in deciding who was Georgian and who was not. Nevertheless, the political and cultural diversity of the Georgian lands is the great theme of his work. There were people he called Georgian but who spoke a different language. There were groups loyal to the Orthodox church but who were animists in practice. There were others who had converted to Islam, spoke Turkish, or felt themselves subject to Ottoman or Persian suzerainty.

This mélange of cultural, political, and religious groups characterized the Georgian lands when Vakhusht was writing, in the mid-eighteenth century on the eve of intense Russian involvement. Mutually antagonistic kings, princes, and local strongmen ruled the lands that Vakhusht saw as part of a unified Georgian cultural realm. The medieval Georgian kingdom had disappeared by the middle of the fifteenth century, rent asunder by the conflicting interests of ever more powerful regional elites. The old Bagrationi kings claimed a common descent, going all the way back to the biblical David and Bathsheba, but that did little to produce political unity. A period of warfare and court intrigues raged until the mid-eighteenth century, when the thrones of the eastern kingdoms of Kartli and Kakheti were once again united under a single crown worn by Erekle II. However, surrounding this renewed Georgian state were neighbors who resisted incorporation: Turkish-speaking frontier lords along the Ottoman border, upland chieftains in the Caucasus foothills, and kings and princes of the lowland areas along the Black Sea coast. Not until the nineteenth century would nearly all the lands claimed by medieval Georgian monarchs be united within a single state—this time the Russian Empire.

The contentious kings and princes of Georgia existed at the intersection of complex imperial interests, and local rulers sought to balance one set of empire builders with another, often by marrying strategically. "There is scarce a Gentleman in Persia, whose Mother is not a Georgian, or a Circassian Woman," wrote the French traveler Jean Chardin in the 1670s, "to begin with the King, who commonly is a Georgian, or a Circassian by his Mother's side."[12] Even within the same family imperial bargains could be struck in different ways. Consider the example of the sons of Vakhtang V, king of Kartli, who ruled a few decades before Vakhusht composed his *description géographique*.

The eldest son, Archil, was placed by his father on the throne of the western Georgian kingdom of Imereti, but in 1679 he was deposed by an invading Ottoman force. Archil turned to the Russians for support and was given refuge in Moscow. While in Russia, he gathered sufficient money and political support to launch a successful bid to retake the Imeretian throne. His reign, however, was marred by the disloyalty of local nobles, who plotted to oust him. Fed up with the infighting in his kingdom, Archil returned to Russia, where he was absorbed into the Russian nobility. His son accompanied Peter the Great on his famous mission across Europe and fought valiantly at the Battle of Narva against the Swedes. Archil himself ended his days in Moscow.

Archil's younger brother, Giorgi, had a rather different experience. On the death of their father, Giorgi ascended to the family's hereditary seat, the throne of Kartli, then a dependency of the Persian Empire. Not long thereafter he was replaced by a rival claimant and transferred to a governor-generalship on the Afghan frontier. His tenure in the east was stellar. He served the shah loyally and achieved some success in quelling rebellions by Afghan tribesmen. He was soon elevated to the position of commander in chief of the entire Persian army and was dispatched to Kandahar, then under siege by the Afghans, with a detachment of four thousand Georgian horsemen. He died there in 1709, defending the interests of the shah at precisely the time his brother and nephew, now "Russians," were serving the tsar.[13]

The same mixture of self-interest and commonsense calculation that lay behind the decisions of Archil and Giorgi also characterized politics and family life in other parts of the Caucasus. South of Kartli and Kakheti lay the highlands of the Lesser Caucasus and, beyond, the Armenian plateau stretching into Anatolia. Political power sometimes shifted from season to season, since the area had long been the battleground between the Ottomans and the Safavid Persians. Local rulers under various titles—khan, emir, sheikh—controlled trade and provided military support for one or another side, normally managing their own affairs with little regard for the broader political aims of their imperial protectors and tormentors.

A similar situation existed farther to the east, in the highlands of Karabakh, on the Mughan steppe, and along the river courses leading down from the Caucasus toward the Caspian Sea. Over the centuries Muslim khans had carved out political control in this borderland, benefiting from commerce and providing a host of goods for both Ottomans and Persians, including horses, rugs, agricultural products, and slaves. In the Safavid lands were a series of khanates, most of which were dominated by hereditary Muslim rulers who governed populations both nomadic and settled, Muslim and (mainly Armenian) Christian.

The borders of the khanates were often indistinct and the precise power of the rulers changeable. Each differed in economic and military importance. The khanate of Yerevan, centered in the modern city of the same name, boasted one of the finest citadels in the Persian Empire. Its location on the border of the Ottoman lands, commanding the heights above the fertile Arax plain, meant that it was the Persians' first line of defense—but also one of the first points of attack from the north and west. To the south the khanate of Nakhichevan was poor by comparison, having far fewer villages, a large population of Turkoman herders, and little tillable land. Farther to the north and east the khanates of Ganja and Karabakh could take advantage of abundant plains, timberland, and silk production. In the latter hereditary Armenian princes, or *meliks*, shared power with Muslim khans or were recognized as supreme by the shah. Even farther east khanates such as Shirvan, Quba, and Baku were well placed to profit from trade in silk, livestock, fish, and salt. In Baku there was also oil, extracted from hand-dug pits and used, even before the industrial age, for lighting, waterproofing, and encouraging silkworms to weave their valuable cocoons. The kingdoms and khanates of the south Caucasus were classic border powers, with wealth derived from their position as transit points along major international trading routes from Central Asia to the Persian Gulf, Constantinople, and the Mediterranean. But they were also centers of learning and artistic creativity in their own right. The khans' courts both hosted and produced poets, musicians, and clerics known throughout the Muslim world.

The political situation in the north Caucasus was more complicated still. On the one hand, all north Caucasus societies had a great deal in common in terms of lifestyle, dress, spiritual beliefs, and folk customs. Several groups shared a remarkably complex oral literary tradition, encapsulated in the magnificent sagas about a race of giants—the Narts—who were said to have inhabited the Caucasus before the arrival of humans. Many had well-established folk ethics that governed personal behavior, interpersonal relations, and gender roles, which are still invoked to this day.

On the other hand, the tribal societies of the uplands were distinct in important ways. Some groups, such as the peoples of mountainous Dagestan, had been in contact with Islam for centuries. Others, such as the peoples of Chechnya or Abkhazia, conserved elements of traditional animist religions even as Christianity and Islam began to make inroads. Languages were wholly separate. The Adyga languages of the northwest (Circassian) bore no relation to the Nakh languages (such as Chechen) of the northeast. These, in turn, were distinct from the mix of indigenous languages spoken in Dagestan. At various times and in various contexts, Arabic and a variety of Turkish served as languages of sacred and secular communication in a region where speakers of mutually unintelligible languages might be separated by only a mountain or river.

The social structures of tribal societies also differed. In some areas, such as Kabarda, society was organized according to an intricate feudal hierarchy, with a princely caste governing nobles, free peasants, and slaves. Farther to the east political and economic power resided with several regional Muslim elites, known by such titles as the *shamkhal* of Tarki on the coastal plans of eastern Dagestan, the khan of Avaristan in the mountainous west, and the sultan of Ilisu in the northern part of what is today Azerbaijan. These hereditary rulers represented something closer to the recognizable political authority of the Georgian kings and princes. Official visitors to their domains were often impressed by the hospitality and grandeur with which they were received. Jacques-François Gamba, the French consul in Tiflis, gave an account of an evening spent with the *shamkhal* of Tarki in the early 1820s: "They carried before us four immense chargers laden with white breads and cakes of diverse sorts, and a rice pilaf of extraordinary dimensions. Sorbets and beautiful fruits completely covered the chargers, which were placed on the ground. That same night, they killed several sheep and two steers. They supplied to our caravan, free of charge and in plentiful portions, all the victuals and necessary provisions."[14] Leaders such as the *shamkhal* also competed with numerous village alliances and confederacies—more than sixty in Dagestan in the early nineteenth century—whose affairs were regulated by a complex system of customary law.[15] The rulers of Dagestan were in large measure sovereign only by the grace and favor of those they claimed as their subjects. Their real power extended only over the settlements immediately surrounding their capitals. In time of war they were reliant on village leaders to provide the troops and other resources to launch a campaign or rebuff an external attack. "The Avars...have a Khan whom nobody obeys," noted a Russian officer in 1830, "especially if they cannot see their own advantages."[16] In other areas, such as western Circassia or Chechnya, social power tended to be even more widely dispersed. Individual upland villages, or *auls*, oversaw their own affairs under the leadership of a village elder or council.

In broad terms, the nature of the Russian conquest in the nineteenth century differed depending on what kinds of societies the Russians encountered. In areas with essentially vertical social ties—that is, an established feudal hierarchy or a large princely class—absorption into the empire was relatively straightforward. Unlike in many other modern empires, the nobility at the core of the Russian imperial system was remarkable for its ability to embrace the aristocracy of neighboring peoples. Social status or estate, rather than ethnicity or race, was the critical factor in determining the social distance between Russians and others, at least in the earliest period of empire building. By contrast, in areas with horizontal social ties—where social systems were based on clans or village alliances rather than allegiance to a powerful lord—the Russians faced a much more difficult time. Most of the south Caucasus, Kabarda, and parts of lowland Dagestan belonged to the former category; Chechnya, western Circassia, and mountainous Dagestan fell into the latter.

Historians have come to label these different social systems "aristocratic" and "democratic" based on the romantic visions of Russian ethnographers and European travelers. Such labels can be misleading, however. The real issue was not how many "nobles" or "democrats" might have existed within any Caucasus society but rather the degree to which political and economic power was concentrated or dispersed.

In areas in which a small group of seigneurs controlled productive resources—for example, owning grazing lands and forests, or profiting from the slave trade—the Russian Empire had to deal with only a limited set of power brokers, which meant that the Russians could by and large count on native elites to control their own populations. In regions where the political economy was based on cooperative arrangements among discrete households or loose networks of extended families, there were few credible elites on whom the Russians could rely. In these areas military force rather than economic or other forms of persuasion would eventually be the preferred method of extending Russian influence.

This broad view of events requires some qualification, though. The central problem that faced Muscovite and, later, Russian rulers was the absence of centralized political authority in the highlands. In none of the areas of the north Caucasus were there political elites who could claim to speak on behalf of large numbers of people or, more to the point, force their will upon them. From the earliest Russian encounters with the Caucasus until the end of the wars of conquest in the 1860s, the primary Russian strategy was thus to designate particular individuals as putatively legitimate leaders. The Russians became practiced in the art of manufacturing their own allies, investing them with titles, and recognizing them as the sole legal and political authority in their domains, in return for which they pledged allegiance to the tsar. Like empire builders before and since, however, they sometimes picked the wrong ones. The protracted wars of Russian conquest in the nineteenth century thus had this fundamental problem at their root: how to strengthen traditional hierarchies in the highlands as a first step toward bringing these elites into the administrative structure of the empire. It was not so much a question of how to divide and rule as how to unite and absorb.[17]

In practice, therefore, Russia's expansion into the Caucasus was always a matter of altitude rather than latitude. The lowlands on either side of the main chain, with their established kings and khans, were integrated into the imperial system more than a half century before the tsar could command the allegiance of the last of the highland peoples. The "conquest of the Caucasus" is thus a fundamentally misleading phrase. Some parts of the Caucasus, such as lowland Kabarda or eastern Georgia, did not need to be conquered at all and were rather easily joined to the empire through the fiat of the tsar and the acquiescence of local notables. Other parts, such as the khanates of modern Azerbaijan and Armenia, were taken from neighboring empires as a by-product of peace treaties. Still others, such as stretches of the Black Sea coastline, were joined to the tsar's domains simply because other empires no longer insisted on denying the Russian claim to them. But the theme of conquest does apply to the areas that plagued imperial strategists from the very beginning: the districts of the upland Caucasus inhabited by people the Russians knew as the *gortsy*.

Life on the Line

Until the first decades of the nineteenth century Russian policy toward its southern flank was primarily defensive. Territories acquired from other empires or from acquiescent local elites were settled with Cossacks and state peasants, joining indigenous farmers and nomads who had been there all along. These settlers and subjects presented the Russian government with an immediate security problem: the need to protect the new territories and their inhabitants from raids launched by groups left outside the sphere of imperial control, particularly Muslim highlanders who had yet to recognize the power of the tsar. To this end Russian state policy involved the establishment of forts and defensive outposts, first as pinpoints of imperial power and later as fortified lines—with watchtowers, Cossack villages, and smaller forts, all connected by newly constructed roads—designed to prevent large-scale incursions out of the mountains.

The lines were meant to create an effective barrier between unpacified and inconstant natives on the far side and Russian forces, loyal locals, newly arrived colonists, and others living on the near side. The line between the forts at Kizliar and Mozdok on the Terek River was completed in the late 1760s. By the 1830s additional lines had been erected that spanned almost the entire breadth of the Caucasus, from the Caspian to the Black Sea. The architecture of war redefined the landscape. By the middle of the nineteenth century some thirty-five major forts and dozens of smaller fortifications dotted the countryside.[18]

In the century from the 1760s to the 1860s Russia's overall strategy was to attempt to increase the distance between the empire's subjects and the armed groups that threatened them in the uplands.[19] Although the lines were central in achieving that end, the fortified frontier was not only a barrier; the line system had clear social, economic, and even ecological consequences on both sides of the divide.[20] After all, an entire century elapsed between the completion of the first fortified line and the final conquest of the north Caucasus, and during this period a great deal changed. The nature of the lines themselves, how people made their lives on them, and how the lines facilitated connections as much as—or perhaps more than—they prevented them are themes usually left out of the story of Russia's southward expansion. But as any modern border guard knows, erecting physical barriers usually fuels the creativity of those seeking ways to get through and around them.

The Russian settlement of the north Caucasus plains and foothills was never a matter of Slavic colonists arriving to put down roots on virgin soil. Nomads, local livestock breeders, and indigenous farmers were already present, and even when new groups arrived, they were often from outside the Russian Empire—such as Scottish missionaries and German farmers, who were given the right to live on the imperial frontier. Moreover, there had long been a Slavic presence in the region in the form of Cossacks. Until the early eighteenth century that overly broad term referred to a whole range of escaped peasants, military deserters, and no doubt a good many highlanders as well, who had carved out independent communities along the river courses of Eurasia. They lived at the intersection of competing political and economic interests—the Ottomans and their nominal clients, the Crimean Tatars; various subordinate Muslim khans; and Muscovy—and exploited their position as intermediaries. Although they would later be cast as hordes of knout-wielding cavalrymen, Cossacks were also farmers, fishermen, traders, and in some periods even skilled mariners on both the Black and Caspian seas.

Already by the time of Peter the Great the tsar had come to recognize the power of Cossacks as a border force, a hardy militarized society with a proven ability to adapt to local customs and acquire the local knowledge needed to protect the new frontier being created in the south. Cossacks were encouraged to build fortified settlements along the major rivers of the north Caucasus, particularly the Terek in the east and the Kuban in the west. In time these *stanitsas* became key components of the line system, literally the dots through which the lines were drawn. By the end of the eighteenth century Cossacks were no longer freelance border guards but had been absorbed into the Russian imperial system. Catherine the Great closed down the headquarters of the Zaporozhian Cossacks on the Dnepr River, in modern Ukraine, and relocated many of them to the north bank of the Kuban

River. Henceforth they would be known as the Black Sea Cossacks, the empire's first line of defense in the northwest Caucasus. Similar Cossack groups, each with its own communal traditions and (later) even regimental identity, evolved across the region.

Many of the Cossack communities had for centuries been in direct contact with highlanders; indeed, it was often difficult to tell them apart. The Cossacks were normally Christians, although their faith was often more declared than observed. The highlanders were largely Muslim, yet their beliefs and practices were likewise rarely conventional. The dress of the two communities was similar, with men arrayed in the *papakha* and *cherkeska*—the tall fur hat and long, tight-fitting tunic outfitted with cartridge slots on the chest—that would eventually become the stereotypical image of the "Cossack." Their weapons were largely the same, and it was the highlanders who usually supplied them, especially the high-quality swords (*shashkas*), hiltless daggers (*kinjals*), and finely crafted muskets.

If anything, the line system probably deepened this contact rather than diminished it. The rise of Cossack *stanitsas* and, later, settler towns provided established points of exchange. In the early 1840s the German naturalist Moritz Wagner visited Ekaterinodar, the headquarters of the Black Sea Cossacks, and was astonished to find so many Circassians strolling about the town: "It is a strange thing to see these men, who had invaded the country a few days before, perhaps, plundering and killing, now moving about peaceably among groups of Cossacks. The Russian system consists in offering a friendly reception to the neighbouring tribes on the other side of the Kouban, in not forbidding access to their towns and stanitzas to their known enemies, and in giving a free passage to all Circassians who do not crowd together in too large bodies."[21] This, however, was often the normal state of affairs in the *stanitsas* and frontier settlements, that is, daily interaction between men and women who, a few nights before or after, might have found themselves on opposite sides of a military clash.

There was considerable interdependence across the lines. Highlanders traded with villages in the plains or even directly with Cossack towns and Russian colonies. Mountaineers provided livestock, animal products, leather goods, wood from upland forests, and weaponry (even though the last of these could, in turn, be used against them). Lowland villagers and Russian settlers provided salt (a crucial commodity in the highlands), metals (often returned to the settlers in the form of handicrafts), and manufactured goods imported from Europe or other parts of Russia.[22] Intermarriage between Cossacks and native women was common. The offspring of those unions might become either Cossacks or natives, depending on individual circumstances. Cossacks, lowland villagers, and Russian soldiers engaged in the same kind of bride kidnapping that was customary in the highlands. In turn, it was not unusual for mountaineers to descend on towns and villages and carry off women for the purpose of marriage or sale to a Tatar or Ottoman slave dealer. In an environment in which cultural exchange was the norm, the exigencies of love, lust, and economics made the lines between imperialist and native necessarily indistinct.[23]

Yet despite all the evidence of mutual contact, the lines were still military devices. The experience of soldiers and average citizens was fundamentally one of boundary maintenance even if boundary transgression was a fact of life. The lines themselves were often drawn along a natural barrier, such as a river: the Kuban in the northwest, the Terek in the northeast, and the Alazani in the southeast. Near their mouths rivers could serve as effective dividers, with a few strategically placed Cossack watchtowers sufficient to catch bands of guerrillas or raiders paddling across the wide and deep waters at night. Farther upstream the lines were more heavily fortified since the narrower, shallower river bed meant that the natural frontier was easier to breach.

In addition to physical barriers there were also man-made ones. Watchtowers, or *vyshki*, were the most visible of these. The towers were usually little more than wooden platforms, some as high as thirty or forty feet, that commanded a view across a river.[24] They were occasionally covered with a makeshift roof, but more often the Cossack watchman was left to face the elements with only his thick sheepskin cape, or *burka*, for protection. The tower was accessed by a ladder, and watchmen were sent up the towers on shifts, with the most important being at night, when raiding parties were most likely to attack the towns and *stanitsas*. When the sentry spied movement in the shallows and determined that it was a raiding party, he would set fire to a stack of dry reeds or a barrel of pitch and then untie his horse and race to the nearest village or fort. If the garrison managed to see his smoke signal before he arrived, they would fire a cannon shot, which would alert the soldiers on duty and call them to arms.[25]

Behind the towers were further elements of defense. The poorest Cossack *stanitsas*, although usually described as "fortified villages," were little more than dusty congeries of shelters protected by meager barricades. Moritz Wagner, who toured the settlements of the Kuban line, found collections of wattle and daub huts, covered with thatched roofs, with perhaps a stone church or other public building in the center. They were occasionally surrounded by a shallow ditch, but usually a simple bramble hedge or piled brush served as a shield. The brush could be set alight in the event of an incursion across the river, but that was only a temporary defense and, in any case, had an obvious downside: The presence of so much combustible material meant that setting a fire to dissuade a raiding party could end up destroying the entire settlement. If a group of raiders managed to slip into a village or town and quickly light the brush or the houses themselves, they could literally smoke out the villagers before anyone had time to muster a counterattack. As one Caucasus commander complained: "Strong parties of highlanders carry out raids with great impertinence, knowing that we cannot quickly assemble a sizeable cavalry detachment and that the infantry cannot catch them. They openly come over the Line, rush toward their selected point for attack, and with their spoils, return via a different route, thereby escaping the forces sent after them."[26]

The tactical logic of the line system meant that the response to an attack was almost never to try to defend villages with superior force but rather to catch the perpetrators on the retreat. When a Cossack sentry sounded—or, more accurately, lit—the alarm, other watchtowers along the line would send up their own signals. In short order cavalry would assemble and rush to the point on the river where the first signal had been sent up. Rather than attempting to fight a pitched battle inside a village, which would have created even more of a threat to life and property, the tactic was to prevent the raiders' withdrawal to the other side of the line.[27]

Besides the Cossacks and settlers, members of the regular Russian imperial army were stationed in forts along the lines or integrated, often uneasily, into local Cossack communities. Conditions in these outposts were dire. Disease was a major concern, especially in the forts along the Kuban River and the Black Sea. Each year some portion of the soldiery was lost to malaria and summer heat; in plague years as much as a sixth of any garrison could die. Easily accessible forts, such as those located directly on the seacoast, were probably better supplied, but even then soldiers would often have to make do with limited stores, perhaps only salted meat, during the winter, when shipping was difficult. Scurvy and other diet-related ailments were common. All this meant that the temptation to trade with—or, frequently, loot—native villages was irresistible, which in turn did little to endear the Russian soldiers to the highlanders. "Our soldiers are forced to steal a little," a Russian commander told Wagner sheepishly.[28]

As in other regions of Russia, corporal punishment remained an option for officers who needed to discipline insubordinate soldiers. On the Caucasus lines, however, there was a twist. Many of the soldiers were married, often to native women from nearby villages or to Russian women specially imported for that purpose, and corporal punishment could be applied to the wives as much as to the husbands. There was yet another variant, too. With so many women present in a military environment, soldiers could offer up their wives as sexual partners to officers as a way of avoiding punishment. For all these reasons, the desertion rate on the lines remained high. The distance between being a uniformed captive in Russian service and a hostage of the highlanders must not have seemed particularly great.[29]

The Caucasus lines were most effective not because they created distance between the empire and the mountaineers but because they did precisely the opposite. They created spaces of interaction in which, from the mid-eighteenth century to the mid-nineteenth, the clear distinctions between "Russian" and "highlander" gradually became blurred. Forms of speech and dress, food and customs, were exchanged along the very lines that were intended to define difference. "No people upon earth detest each other more cordially," wrote one visitor upon seeing the interaction between Black Sea Cossacks and Circassians along the Kuban River.[30] Anyone who looked across a river from a Cossack watchtower would have known fear. A movement in the reed beds or the dust kicked up by horsemen far in the distance could be the prelude to a deadly attack. But this was not only, not even mainly, a fear of "the other." It was often the more intimate terror that "the other" might look disturbingly familiar.

In the early decades of the nineteenth century the Russians, like other contemporary empires, were only beginning to understand how to deal with the determined guerrilla resistance represented by highland raiders, moving beyond the cavalry-and-square combinations of European land campaigns and toward more dynamic forms of offense and defense. The French in Algeria, the British in Afghanistan, and the Americans on the Great Plains would all eventually discover how genuinely useless fortified lines could be against a determined, mobile, and culturally adaptable foe. As time progressed, Russian strategists would come to advocate a radically new way of warfare: taking the fight directly to the *gortsy* rather than waiting for them to bring it to you. In the end, it was a single-minded general who helped to transform the lines of the Caucasus into something other than defensive barriers and zones of exchange.

"Ermolov Comes!"

Portraits of Alexei Ermolov show him to be nothing if not determined: the knitted brow cantilevered over a slight scowl, the deep-set eyes and flared nostrils, all framed by ample sideburns and a shock of unruly hair. Even in his dotage he practically leaps from the canvas. Juan van Halen, a Spanish major in Russian service, recalled meeting Ermolov in his field camp in 1819. "Ermolov is of an almost colossal height and very well formed, with a vigorous constitution and a martial attitude: these traits are very strongly pronounced, without being harsh; his expression is full of energy and vivacity; and his penetrating look reveals him to be a superior man."[31] He was said to travel in a rudimentary carriage and to sleep on a simple carpet. Anyone who met him gave a similar assessment, one captured in typically poetic form by Pushkin as "the head of a tiger on the torso of a Hercules."[32]

Ermolov was the quintessential frontier conqueror. He was the first to employ a comprehensive strategy for the subjugation of the Caucasus highlands, and his ruthless methods would be used, in one form or another, by tsarists, Bolsheviks, and Russian generals into the twenty-first century. He was one of the pioneers of Russia's permanent war on its southern periphery, the longest-running conflict in the history of the empire and one that has continued to plague Russian strategists, in rather different forms, up to the present day. His tenure marked the start of a long series of wars of conquest in the upland Caucasus, which would come to a close only in 1864.

Ermolov was the most celebrated and, at the same time, the most hated of Russian commanders in the Caucasus theater. To St. Petersburg society he was the gallant, Latin-quoting senior officer. For generations of indigenous mountaineers he was the dreaded "Yarmul" who razed villages and slaughtered families. Although he gained the supreme confidence of one tsar, Alexander I, he was treated with suspicion by another, Nicholas I. He was responsible for implementing a series of policies that were at the time hailed as vehicles for civilizing the benighted Caucasus frontier but that today might well be called state-sponsored terrorism.

During Ermolov's decade in the field, Russia became an empire based not on the complex policies of bribery, cajoling, and trickery associated with the Muscovites' earliest advances into the north Caucasus but rather on the war-fighting techniques then being developed by other empires around the world: wanton destruction of property, mass deportation, and indiscriminate killing—all committed in the name of bringing true freedom and enlightenment to backward tribal peoples. The political landscape of the Caucasus also began to change. By the time Ermolov was dismissed from his post in 1827, the Caucasus was no longer an imperial borderland that embraced various forms of autonomy and accommodation. It was quickly becoming a place defined by the full incorporation of outlying regions into a centralized state. Through Ermolov's efforts, Russia's possessions in the Caucasus moved from being part of a premodern imperial order toward becoming, for better or worse, part of a fitfully modern one.

Alexei Petrovich Ermolov was born in 1777. From early on he was distinguished by his military prowess. At the age of sixteen he fought in the Polish campaign under Field Marshal Alexander Suvorov. He continued his service in Italy and the southeastern Caucasus, seeing action during the storming of Derbend and Ganja. During the Napoleonic Wars he participated in the Battle of Austerlitz and was a field commander during the assault on Paris. He was not yet forty when he became one of the most highly decorated officers in the empire, a central figure in the transition from the Catherinian wars to the campaigns of Tsar Alexander I.

Fresh from his glories in the west, in 1816 Ermolov was elevated by the tsar to the position of chief administrator of Georgia, a post that effectively gave him control over all military affairs in the north and south Caucasus, as well as ambassador to the court of the shah. After a diplomatic visit to Persia designed to conciliate the Qajar shah Feth Ali and secure Russian possessions gained under the Treaty of Gulistan, Ermolov returned to Tiflis with the centerpiece of his strategic vision already in mind: the reinvigoration of the north Caucasus lines.

Ermolov saw himself as an imperial commander, one serving on the very edge of civilization, in which the toughness and resolve of the finest Roman generals had to be combined with an unbending will to use barbaric tactics against the barbarians themselves. "I desire that the terror of my name," he once declared, "should guard our frontiers more potently than chains or fortresses."[33] Even more important, Ermolov was an artilleryman, not a cavalry officer like other commanders in the Caucasus theater. That professional orientation, combined with his self-image as a bearer of enlightenment, contributed to the nature of Russian military planning under his leadership.

Ermolov appreciated the power of modern weaponry. He had seen it up close during the Napoleonic Wars: the devastating effects of cannon on wood, stone, and flesh; and the ability of mobile field guns to decimate infantry and frustrate a cavalry charge. Ermolov's plan involved the construction of a series of new, larger forts that would serve as anchors for military operations in the central Caucasus. From these secure centers, men and weapons could be assembled and dispatched against highland raiding parties and, eventually, against the raiders' homes and families. In the summer of 1818 he ordered the construction of a new outpost on the Sunja River which he called Groznaia ("terrible" or "menacing"), later to become the modern city of Grozny in Chechnya. The fort soon earned its name. Chechens came down to the river each evening to fire on the construction works. To counter them Ermolov ordered that a field gun be left outside the walls in plain view of the raiders. When the party returned to steal the gun, the fort's artillery opened fire, leaving more than two hundred dead and wounded around the abandoned weapon.[34] Following the raising of Groznaia, Ermolov continued the newly fortified line to the east. In 1819 Fort Vnezapnaia ("surprise") was built near the eastern border of Chechnya. Two years later Fort Burnaia ("stormy") rose in Dagestan and completed the link between the Caspian Sea and the older facility at Vladikavkaz ("ruler of the Caucasus"), at the head of the overland route to Georgia.

However, building new forts was, in and of itself, no solution to the problem of highlander incursions, and Ermolov understood the military inadequacies of the line system. There were never sufficient forces at every point along the line to repel a concerted attack, and the fact that soldiers and civilians lived so close to the enemy—sometimes just across a river—meant that there was inevitably unwanted fraternization. The number of soldiers stationed in the forts was never particularly high; those along the Black Sea coast rarely had more than five hundred men.[35] Fortifications also presented irresistible targets of attack. Potshots from snipers were a daily occurrence, and outposts could and did fall to sustained sieges by highland forces, even though the highlanders would usually sack rather than occupy the facility. Nor were they of great use as staging posts for concentrating military might. Any military campaign required the assistance of Russian forces in Tiflis, a far more secure and desirable place to live, especially for the officer corps.

Ermolov's solution to these problems—probably designed by his chief of staff, Alexei Vel'iaminov—was to treat the line as no more than a rear-guard position, patrolled by loyal Cossacks, and to advance beyond it with the goal of meeting the uplanders on their own ground.[36] One of his first acts as commander was to allow Russian cavalry to pursue raiders back across the Kuban River, which earlier had been forbidden for fear that soldiers might contract the diseases known to rage there.[37] Ermolov believed that only the energetic punishment of raiding parties and the full integration of the highland tribes into the political structures of the Russian state would create a completely secure environment. This, in turn, demanded a clear understanding of highlander tactics, good intelligence, a forward military presence, and above all the stomach to carry the war to the highlanders themselves, including putting aside any scruples about destroying villages, forests, and any other place where raiding parties might seek refuge.

Targeted assassinations, kidnappings, the killing of entire families, and the use of disproportionate force in response to small-scale raids were to become central to Russian operations in the opening decades of the nineteenth century. In a famous passage from a later essay on mountain warfare, Vel'iaminov summed up the stratagem that his commander sought to pursue: "The Caucasus may be likened to a mighty fortress, marvelously strong by nature, artificially protected by military works, and defended by a numerous garrison. Only thoughtless men would attempt to escalade such a stronghold. A wise commander would see the necessity of having recourse to military art; would lay his parallels; advance by sap and mine, and so master the place."[38] Vel'iaminov was not alone in believing that unbending commitment was essential to victory over the highlanders. Pushkin conveyed the same view, if more poetically. "Caucasus! Bow down your snowy head. / Submit! Ermolov comes!"

By 1822 the string of new forts and Ermolov's recent tactical changes had yielded remarkable results. The interior khanates of Dagestan—including the Avar, the Tabasaran, and the Kumyk—had successively fallen to Ermolov or his subordinates. The khanates to the south and southeast—in the eastern hill country and the Lesser Caucasus and along the Caspian coast—were likewise absorbed into the empire through a combination of diplomatic guile and threats of force. There were still those in the most remote parts of the mountains who remained untouched by Russian control. For example, the peoples of Chechnya would continue to oppose Russian encroachments. But the buttressing of the Caucasus lines, the extension of military power beyond them, and the consolidation of Russian influence over established rulers meant that Ermolov could reasonably claim that his policy was a success.

The price, however, was constant vigilance since punitive expeditions had to be mounted in response to any perceived threat, no matter how small. There were also attempts by mountaineers to launch large-scale attacks on the new Russian forts. In 1824 and 1825 a major uprising spread from Dagestan all the way to Kabarda. Although the revolt collapsed as a result of internal dissent, it foreshadowed the sort of full-scale war that would engulf the entire region beginning in the late 1820s. Nevertheless, throughout the early part of the decade Ermolov could remain relatively confident in his gains. Each victory added to the general's fame in St. Petersburg and swelled the ranks of the imperial soldiery as newly defeated native rulers pledged their services to the tsar. His tactics were occasionally criticized by imperial observers, but when even the tsar became squeamish at reports of atrocities, Ermolov had a ready answer: Gentleness would be viewed as a sign of weakness, and every act of cruelty on the part of Russian forces would only increase their respect in the eyes of the Muslims of the mountains.

Two developments outside the region shattered this relative stability. One was the death of Tsar Alexander I in 1825 and the officers' revolt that soon followed it, the Decembrist uprising. Ermolov had few overt connections to the leaders of the rebellion in St. Petersburg, but the new tsar, Nicholas I, remained nervous about virtually any powerful senior officer, even those who had loyally served his predecessor.

At the same time, tensions with Persia began to rise. Under the old Treaty of Gulistan, Persia had ceded significant territory along the border with Russia: the cities of Baku and Derbend on the Caspian Sea, the latter of which effectively gave Russia control of the land route to the east of the mountains, as well as the districts of Karabakh and Shirvan. The shah and the Qajar military resented having been made to surrender so much; the Russians felt that Persia had not surrendered enough. In 1825 Ermolov occupied a border district northeast of Yerevan, putting pressure on the Persian garrison there and threatening to take under the tsar's authority one of the last major fortifications in the south Caucasus still under Persian control. Emboldened by success in the highlands, and convinced of the inefficacy of diplomacy when engaged with an Eastern enemy, the general confronted the Persians in the same way he had dealt with the mountaineers over the previous decade. It proved to be an ill-considered move.

For the Persians the timing for a strong military reaction was propitious. Not only had the Russians violated an international agreement by engaging in hostilities, but the domestic political crisis in St. Petersburg also seemed a heaven-sent distraction. From Tehran's perspective, the Decembrist uprising would surely preoccupy the new tsar, and the punishment he was now doling out to his own officer corps would have repercussions on the Caucasus front as well. Ermolov was suspected by Nicholas of having been sympathetic to the Decembrist cause. Although it is doubtful that the Persians had an inkling of this particular fact, it nevertheless made a military reaction even more well timed than the shah might have imagined.

Things were crumbling. There were fewer than thirty-five thousand men under Ermolov's command in the south Caucasus, and calls for reinforcements went virtually unheeded.[39] Each of the khanates that had seemed loyal to the tsar now moved toward revolt as news reached them of an impending assault by Persian forces. Facing a disaster—potentially even another invasion of Tiflis by both Muslim *gortsy* and Persians—the tsar dismissed Ermolov in the spring of 1827 and replaced him with Ivan Paskevich, another senior officer in the southern theater. On the eve of a new war, Ermolov retired in disgrace to his estate south of Moscow, the once powerful commander now reduced to inaction against the combined threat of a Persian attack, the khans' mutiny, and risings among unpacified highlanders.

Political turmoil, a demoralized officer corps, and a new commander—these would have been serious inducements to any military leader seeking to strike a blow against Russia, and at the time of Ermolov's removal from office they were all in place. The Persian army, commanded by Crown Prince Abbas Mirza, seized the opportunity to oust the Russians from the borderland that Ermolov had ill-advisedly occupied, as well as from some of the territories ceded under the Treaty of Gulistan. But the Russians, now under the command of Paskevich, overwhelmed the Persians, pushing them south and overrunning one fortress after another. Russian troops occupied Echmiadzin, the ancient see of the Armenian church, followed by the khanate of Nakhichevan. Yerevan was placed under siege.

At this stage Paskevich could have pressed his advantage and continued on to Tabriz, but the heat of summer, the lack of supplies, and the general's own congenital indecisiveness caused him to halt. That provided the breathing space Abbas Mirza needed, and in late summer 1827 the Persians returned to march on Echmiadzin. When they appeared before the holy city the Armenian *catholicos* held aloft one of the monastery's chief treasures, the spear said to have pierced the side of Christ. The sight of the relic was credited with giving the Russians hope during the darkest hours of battle.[40] Abbas Mirza's army withdrew and Echmiadzin was saved. With no Persian relief, it was only a matter of time before the khanate of Yerevan capitulated. In recognition of this achievement, Paskevich was honored by the tsar with the epithet "Erivanskii," which he added to his surname.

With the Russians threatening to march on to Tabriz or even Tehran, the British—who enjoyed special influence in Persia—finally put pressure on the shah to make peace. To drive home their point, the British withheld the generous subsidy that had previously been paid to the Qajars, arguing that the shah had launched a needless war to end a dispute that could have easily been settled through negotiations.[41] With the Persians wavering, in the autumn of 1827 Russian troops occupied Tabriz, Persia's second city and a key trading center, after little resistance. Paskevich himself, fresh from receiving the honors of conquest in Yerevan, entered the city in mid-October.

The shah was now in no position to negotiate. With British mediation, in February 1828 Russian and Persian negotiators met in the small village of Turkmanchai on the road between Tabriz and Tehran. The shah was persuaded to pay an indemnity and give up the districts of Yerevan and Nakhichevan. The new border between the two empires was now to follow the Arax River, then dip south toward the Caspian Sea, leaving the port of Lenkoran and the Mughan steppe inside Russia. The Treaty of Turkmanchai marked the end of Russia's territorial expansion in the southeastern Caucasus and established the northern border of Persia, which has remained in place, with slight alterations, until the present day.

The great success of Russian (and British) diplomacy during the course of the war was to keep the Ottomans out of it. That situation lasted only for a while, however. Even before the ink had dried on the treaty, war broke out on the Ottoman front. This was potentially far more damaging to the Russians than the opportunistic moves of Abbas Mirza. War with the Ottomans would not be limited solely to the Caucasus but would have to be waged in multiple theaters in eastern Anatolia, the Balkans, and the Black Sea against armies that were larger than those of the defeated Persians.

In the end, insufficient Ottoman provisioning and Russian experience in the recent Persian war worked to the tsar's advantage. The key fortress at Kars fell in midsummer 1828. The fort at Anapa and the port at Poti on the Black Sea, the sultan's vital channels of military influence in the western Caucasus, succumbed to a combined land-sea assault. Russian forces overwhelmed the frontier garrisons at Akhaltsikhe and Ardahan, the Ottomans' chief levers against the Georgians. During the next campaign season in the summer of 1829, Paskevich finally entered Erzurum, the central strategic objective in eastern

Anatolia, which opened the way to the headwaters of the Euphrates. With his forces exhausted, the tsar opted for peace.

The Treaty of Adrianople ended the Russo-Turkish War in September 1829, but only some of the most daring military advantages gained by Paskevich were sealed in the deal. The strategic redoubts in the south Caucasus were retained by Russia, but the important Anatolian fortresses of Kars and Ardahan were returned to Ottoman control. Adrianople was something of a compromise designed to secure what was really far more important to Russian interests—control over the ports of Anapa and Poti on the Black Sea, through which the Ottomans had previously supported the highlanders of the western Caucasus.

The great mystery of the 1820s is that the highland peoples remained relatively peaceful during a period when the Russian Empire was at its most vulnerable, with a much-hated commander in chief in office, followed by an imperial succession crisis, and then two wars with other Eurasian empires. Any indigenous military commander worth his salt would have launched a full-scale, organized war at the time, descending on the Caucasus lines, attacking undermanned frontier posts, and destroying the forts from which Ermolov had earlier directed his campaigns in the interior. Yet unity was always elusive. Chieftains fought against one another. Traditional intertribal raiding could escalate to the equivalent of range wars. Religious dissension and struggles for power among khans and sheikhs drained energy that might have been spent fighting the Russians. The lesson for Russian strategists was to concentrate on preventing sufficient numbers of disgruntled local elites from banding together to form a solid front against imperial encroachments. As long as powerful elites could be bought off or cajoled into Russian service, the possibility of a united front emerging in the Caucasus was relatively slim. With the victories of 1828 and 1829, which eliminated the Persians and Ottomans as major sources of support for highland Muslims, Russia's hold on the Caucasus appeared more secure than ever.

"Living a life close to that of primordial savagery," wrote a Russian officer a few years after Ermolov's dismissal, "they are not accustomed to rational thought, but act according to ancient traditions as if by instinct."[42] Ensuring that these "ancient traditions" were oriented toward Russia was the entire point of Ermolov's system. By harshly punishing opportunistic raiders or other guerrillas, the Russians were protecting their new forts and Cossack settlements while simultaneously helping to convince indigenous elites that supporting the

Russian side was in their best interests. However, while Ermolov and his successors were transgressing the fortified frontiers and pushing the empire into the highlands, literally tens of thousands of men and women, both Christian and Muslim, were moving in the opposite direction—being carried as captives across the physical lines between Russia and the highlands, the geopolitical ones between empires, and the metaphorical ones between religious and cultural communities. If there was a single cultural lens through which Russia would come to understand its own Caucasus possessions and the peoples who lived there, it was the trope of being made a prisoner.

Captives

Early Muscovite relations with the peoples of the Eurasian steppe often involved the threat of capture. Raiding parties would descend on Slavic settlements and carry off both men and women, who might eventually find themselves sold into slavery as far afield as Constantinople. According to one calculation, as many as 150,000 to 200,000 people, mainly ethnic Slavs, may have been abducted in the first half of the seventeenth century alone.[43] Efforts to free these captives became a part of Russian state policy. Church coffers and specially established state funds were marshaled to pay ransoms. The release of captives became a subject of diplomatic relations between the court of the Muscovite grand prince and steppe nomads.

When Russia approached the Caucasus, there had thus already been a long history of interaction with indigenous peoples over the issue of captive-taking. For the highlanders, the slave trade and punitive raiding were weapons that could be used to resist the Russian advance or, more often, to secure a better deal with the new imperial presence. Unlike in the past, however, the victims were now not simply Russian villagers but often prominent individuals whose cases attracted the general interest of the Russian public. In 1774 the famous botanist Samuel Gmelin, sent to the Caucasus by Catherine the Great to engage in scientific reconnaissance, was abducted by the ruler of Kaitag, in Dagestan, and died while awaiting the payment of a ransom. Even less well known individuals could find themselves the object of considerable public attention. In March 1816 Pavel Shvetsov, a major in a Georgian grenadiers regiment, was captured while en route from Georgia to the fort of Kizliar by Chechen hillmen, who demanded a considerable sum for his release. A huge public campaign in favor of the imperial officer ensued. Articles and appeals flooded Russian newspapers, and a public fund was established to accept contributions from average citizens. Ermolov, then commander of the lines, decided to take his own hostages by ordering the arrest of the local notables through whose lands Shvetsov and his captors had passed. The ploy seemed to work, for the ransom was eventually reduced to ten thousand rubles—still an enormous figure at the time—and Shvetsov was released.[44]

The Shvetsov incident illustrates one of the central points about Caucasus captivity: It was never a one-sided affair. Since the Muscovite period the mutual surrender of hostages (*amanat*) had been a mainstay of diplomacy between Russians and peoples of the Eurasian hinterland. The sons or other relatives of political authorities would be handed over to the other side to seal a political alliance or provide insurance against war. Inevitably many of these captives—especially if they were young and their detention of long duration—would become more comfortable in the culture of their captors than that of their birth. Captivity could thus become a form of acculturation as much as one of punishment.

It is difficult to generalize about the experience of captivity given the many forms it could take. Being a prisoner of war was different from being taken in a raid. Being a female captive was certainly different from being a male one. There is also the problem of evidence. Most of the captivity narratives that have survived—even the ones whose veracity is not suspect—are those of people who wanted to get away from their captors and were successful in doing so. But there are entire classes of captives whose voices are rarely heard: highlanders taken by Russians, highlanders captured by other highlanders, and Russians and others in imperial service who were carried off to the highlands and eventually found themselves wanting to stay there.

Desertion from the army of the Caucasus was a problem throughout the period of the highland wars. The move from being a Russian soldier to being a willing prisoner of war simply required one step—often a rather small one—in an entire chain of captivity. An ordinary soldier might begin life as a serf, the effective property of one or another Russian landowner. He might be drummed into the army or navy, under terms and for a period of service over which he had no control. He might then be taken prisoner in battle or defect, with the assurance that, were he to return to the Russian side, he would be incarcerated for treason. He might eventually marry a local woman and find himself making a new life for himself as a highlander, prevented from returning to Russia by the bonds of love—or the vigilance of watchful in-laws.[45] For average Russian infantrymen or seamen the leap from soldier to prisoner and back could be a move from one form of captivity to another.

This was certainly the case with one particular kind of deserter—the runaway Pole. After the crushing of the Polish uprising of 1830–31, Russian imperial policy was to send Polish soldiers, especially the sons of nobles whose loyalty to the empire was now suspect, to serve in the Caucasus. It is uncertain how many Polish young men ended up on the frontier in this capacity. In fact, some ordinary Russian deserters were known to call themselves "Poles" in the hope that they would be better treated by their highland captors.[46] But many European travelers were astonished to find, while visiting some highland valley or town bazaar, young men who could converse in German or French and who might admit, secretly, to being Catholic.

The story of Jan Saremba is not untypical. The son of a Warsaw glazier, Saremba fought in the Polish uprising against the tsar, but with the fall of Warsaw to Russian forces, he was assigned to a Russian military unit preparing for deployment to the Caucasus. Based in a regiment outside Tiflis, Saremba found himself in the company of sixteen other Poles, almost half of whom had been sent south as punishment for their participation in the revolt.

The harshness of army life pushed the Poles toward planning their escape. They spent months acquiring the necessary skills and information that would allow them to leave, make their way to the Ottoman lands, and perhaps return home from there—or, if not, then at least fight against the Russians in the next Russo-Turkish war. One evening they quietly loaded up their knapsacks and set out through the forest and toward the Russian-Ottoman frontier. (One Pole, who had married a Cossack widow, elected to stay behind.)

They eventually made contact with a group of local Muslims, who agreed to assist them in crossing the border in exchange for a promise that they would convert to Islam once they reached Ottoman territory. The Poles duly pledged to change religions, all the while quietly asking the Virgin to intercede on their behalf for their denial of the true faith. With the Muslims' assistance the Poles managed to cross the border undetected by Russian sentries. Soon, however, they found themselves captives once again. The Ottoman bey in charge of the frontier zone initially promised to help them navigate the region's rough terrain, but the escorts he appointed turned out to be slave dealers.

Saremba ended up as the property of a Muslim merchant. During a trip to the city of Trebizond, on the Black Sea, he managed to escape to the house of the French consul, who took him under his protection. Free at last, Saremba married a Greek woman, fathered two children, and earned a decent living from the old family profession of making windows. He supplemented his income by serving as factotum to European travelers, which is how his story is known: He accompanied the German naturalist Moritz Wagner on his tours of the Caucasus and Persia in the 1840s.[47]

The problem for Russia was not simply that the desertion of men like Saremba depleted the ranks of the Caucasus army. Rather, trained soldiers—including those with valuable skills, such as artillerymen and sappers—might well end up fighting on the wrong side of the battle lines. As the commander of the Black Sea coast reported with alarm in 1838, "In skirmishes infantrymen have charged our lines shouting in the Polish language."[48] Highland leaders eventually came to understand the usefulness of such men. Concerted efforts were made to reach out through them to other non-Russian nobles in order to create a common front among the empire's dissatisfied minorities, from Central Europe all the way to Central Asia.[49] Poles were sometimes organized into special regiments and even accompanied Ottoman forces in the invasion of western Georgia during the Crimean War.

Beyond the problem of desertion, there was an additional concern for the friends and families of those who had crossed the Russian lines—either voluntarily or against their will—and found their way to the highlands. It was the worry that someone who left might become a renegade and eventually "turn Turk." A renegade is literally someone who has reneged on an implicit contract, renouncing his true identity and withdrawing from the obligation of loyalty to his God, his family, and his people. Stories of tsarist soldiers who fled to the mountains and eventually adopted Islam are legion. The individual reasons for this shift in religious allegiance are varied. Some may have converted out of genuine belief, others as a result of force, and still others for love—the desire to wed a highlander's daughter, for example. Moreover, the lines between being obviously Christian or obviously Muslim could be indistinct. In the Caucasus people in both religious categories enjoyed alcohol, were far removed from clerical authority, and practiced a form of folk religion that bore only scant resemblance to the orthodox varieties found elsewhere.

For all the fluidity of religious belief and practice, there were still those who refused to budge, usually to their own detriment. In the early 1820s the French businessman Edouard Taitbout de Marigny met a Caucasus prisoner—a Russian named Ivan—in a coffeehouse in the Black Sea port of Anapa.[50] Fifteen years earlier Ivan had been on his way to Tiflis with a company of Russian merchants. As the group prepared to cross the Kuban River, a party of Circassians suddenly emerged from the reed beds and took him captive. He was subsequently sold to a wealthy Abaza prince who took him high into the mountains. From that time forward he became known to everyone as Osman. On several occasions Ivan/Osman tried to escape, once even reaching as far as the Kuban, but he was always recaptured and severely beaten.

Tired of constantly having to drag him back from the frontier, his master decided to wed him to a Circassian woman. He would thus be bound by the chains of love and familial obligation rather than by the threat of beatings and other corporal punishments. Ivan/Osman was at first less than enthusiastic about the idea, but the prince locked him in a room with his intended bride, Khani, and two days later he agreed to marry her. The beatings continued, however, especially when the prince was drunk. One night, after a particularly heavy binge, Ivan/Osman loaded up his wife and their meager possessions and set fire to the prince's house. The old master was trapped inside and perished. Ivan/Osman then offered himself and his wife as slaves to one of the prince's enemies, who warmly received them.

For many years Ivan/Osman lived happily with his wife, but after her death he expressed a wish to return to Russia. His new master declined to grant his freedom unless he converted to Islam, which Ivan/Osman refused to do. For his piety he was repeatedly traded or sold. He often managed to escape to a new master—eighteen different ones, according to his count—and at last ended up as the slave of a wealthy Ottoman merchant. That is how he came to be sipping coffee in Anapa, where Taitbout recorded his tale.

Such stories became one of several stock captivity narratives, not only in the Caucasus but in other imperial settings as well: the long-suffering prisoner who refuses to renounce his faith despite the cruelties of the fanatical Mohammedan. But things were much more complicated than this. Although Ivan/Osman declined to change his religious affiliation, in most other ways he was fully acculturated to Circassian society. He married a local woman, carved out a tolerable if not ideal existence by jumping from one master to a better one, and by his own account lived happily with his wife until her death robbed him of his most important tie to the highlands. It is difficult to know which kind of story—the pious Christian, the impious renegade, or the ambiguously in-between—is most representative of the experience of

Caucasus captivity. The evidence, in any case, is skewed. The voices of the pious have been carefully preserved, whereas many of the stories of those who crossed the line between Christian and Muslim have been lost. The former served the growing imperial narrative of steadfast Christians battling backward mountain Muslims. The latter, by showing that the lines between religions and social categories were not nearly so clearly demarcated, fundamentally undermined it.

The reasons for taking captives were multiple. Captives could be held as a form of insurance of an ally's good faith or against an enemy's ill will. They could be used as labor, especially if they possessed an artisanal skill.[51] They could be ransomed for cash if the captives were known to have wealthy relatives. In some instances, they could be used as sources of intelligence, such as the disposition of Russian or indigenous military forces. One of the most famous instances— the abduction in 1854 of two prominent Georgian princesses, Anna Chavchavadze and Varvara Orbeliani, by the highland leader Shamil— incorporated many of these elements and held the Russian public enthralled as a distraught family worked over the course of several months to secure the women's freedom. In addition to a substantial ransom, Shamil demanded the release of one of his sons, who had earlier been taken hostage by the Russian army.[52]

Captivity could also give rise to its own secondary economy. There were individuals ready to provide advance payment of a ransom in exchange for a certain percentage in interest. There were couriers who could be paid to deliver messages or packages. In the mountains there were even people who would provide loans directly to the captives, allowing them to purchase food and clothing locally in exchange for IOUs to be honored when they were eventually released. There was sometimes an otherworldly calculus of costs and benefits as well. Christian missionaries in the north Caucasus were known to purchase children from highland families and rear them as Christians, with each new child counting as a soul rescued from the depravities of Islam and paganism.[53]

In general, the number of those who experienced Caucasus captivity as hostages, deserters, or renegades was probably relatively small. According to one estimate, from the beginning of the nineteenth century until 1864, perhaps six thousand Russian soldiers and fewer than one hundred officers were taken captive.[54] These numbers, while significant, pale when compared to the quantity of people trafficked out of the Caucasus as human chattel, sold into bondage and sent off to serve in the palaces and harems of the Ottoman Empire.

Total figures are difficult to come by, but at the slave trade's peak in the nineteenth century perhaps as many as two thousand slaves per year were removed from the Caucasus, adding to the already enormous numbers taken from the mountains and the Eurasian steppe during previous centuries.[55] These people, mostly young women, were taken from highland and lowland villages and loaded onto ships anchored off Black Sea ports. They might first reach Trebizond, the major entrepôt on the southeast coast, and from there continue on to Constantinople, where they were sold in open-air markets, one located near the Tophane docks on the Bosphorus, another situated in the very center of the old city.

Charles White, who lived in Constantinople in the early 1840s and became an astute observer of Ottoman society, visited the slave market on several occasions. The market, he reported, was located just outside the central bazaar, south of the silk house and the jewelers' shops. People entered the space through a large wooden gate, which was open from eight in the morning until midday except for Fridays. A watchman stood guard to inspect those entering and to prevent the escape of slaves who had managed to get out of their locked quarters.

The market was a large rectangular space surrounded by a wooden colonnade. In the center was a two-story building that housed the dealers as well as newly imported slaves. A series of platforms was set up between the columns, where slaves could be offered for sale. Private quarters for the most desirable slaves—women, especially those from the Caucasus—ringed the market. During a normal business day men would meander through the colonnade, inspecting women on the platforms and haggling over prices. Women would be led around by their owners, but only in rare cases would they be physically restrained, a punishment also infrequently applied to male slaves. In good weather slaves would be arrayed in the central portion of the bazaar, where they would stand or sit on mats, unveiled but not unclothed.

The price of a female slave, White said, depended on several qualities. Slaves from Africa usually fetched less than those from the Caucasus or other parts of Eurasia. A slave who had previously been trained in the domestic arts could command a higher price. Age, physical condition, and norms of beauty also mattered. Black female slaves could go for as a low as 1,500 piastres but never more than 2,500. White women with no "defects" could fetch up to 15,000. (By comparison, the cost of hiring a boat for a month was only 600 piastres.) The average number of slaves housed in the market at any one time was no more than three hundred, and it was rare to find new women from the Caucasus being traded there. They would be taken directly from ships to a market nearer the Bosphorus and sold on the spot to middlemen, who might then resell them in private transactions with families of some social standing.

In the spring of 1842 White had the opportunity to visit the house of a wealthy Ottoman, where young Circassian women were being trained as domestic servants. He was accompanied by a Turkish acquaintance who feigned an interest in purchasing a girl from the head of the household. When the guests arrived, they were escorted into the receiving room by their host and offered coffee and a pipe. In due course a string of eleven girls was paraded before the men:

> Daughters of Circassian serfs, reared in servitude and taught from their cradles to consider themselves as marketable articles, there was nothing to them novel or degrading in slavery or the preparatory exhibition. So far from it, they appeared to watch the countenance of the pretended purchaser with anxiety, and their faces flushed with hope rather than shame when prices were mentioned. . . . They are aware that many of their countrywomen have become mothers, and *pro forma* wives of sultans; that many also have been and are married legitimately to influential and wealthy men; and, if similar good fortune be their lot, that they will be happier than could possibly be the case in their mountain fastnesses.

"Divest it of the name," White concluded, "and slavery, as it exists in Turkish families, loses almost all its severity."[56]

In the nineteenth century, one's position on the slavery question usually depended a great deal on one's opinion of the Ottoman Empire in general. Those who saw in Ottoman society a debauched, un-Christian immorality, overlaid with a harsh oriental despotism, condemned slaveholding as an affront to the dignity of women—especially white women. Those who saw the Ottomans as allies of Europe against an aggressive, autocratic Russia were quick to downplay the differences between slavery in the Ottoman lands and the position of women in many other societies, including European ones. It was their own ambition for wealth and social advancement, not compulsion, that brought women to the slave market, claimed James Longworth, a London *Times* correspondent, during his sojourn in the north Caucasus. "Their views in this respect are much the same as those of our young ladies who are shipped from England to India."[57] Longworth's assessment was echoed by many observers, who were frequently surprised when they encountered women who seemed to find life in the harem a liberating experience compared to the fate that awaited them in the mountains—poverty, hunger, abduction by an enemy clan or Russian soldiers, perhaps even de facto slavery in the house of a local notable.

It is impossible to know whether these women genuinely desired to spend their lives in Ottoman or other households far removed from their native lands, especially when most of the evidence comes from European men gazing on societies in which the power of women was limited. However, the institution of slavery in the Caucasus and in Muslim lands in general was different from the sense that the term connotes in the history of western Europe and North America.

For one thing, slaves were never "bred" in Muslim societies. Their manumission after a period of servitude was normal, and slave status rarely passed from parent to child. Moreover, Ottoman slave trading intersected with established practice in the Caucasus itself. The institution of *atalyk*—the farming out of male child-rearing to a non-blood relative—was a longstanding tradition in Circassia. The extension of that tradition to the "sale" of sons to a Muslim from Trebizond or Constantinople—or, indeed, to Christian missionaries seeking to "save" children from their highland parents—may not have been that difficult. The cultural bases of slave-holding and slave trading were even more pronounced in the case of women. Bride kidnapping—the real or feigned abduction of a woman by a suitor as a prelude to marriage—was a common custom among many Caucasus highland peoples and had been practiced at times by Russians, Cossacks, Georgians, and others. In native societies in which a woman's lot in an upland village was severely circumscribed, and in which her sisters, aunts, and neighbors told stories of the wonders of the Ottoman capital, the attractions of life in the home of a wealthy Ottoman official may have been considerable. However, the majority probably found the reality of life abroad a pale imitation of the promise.

Throughout the nineteenth century the Russian government attempted to stop the outflow of women from the northwest Caucasus to the slave markets of Constantinople. Tsar Alexander I had already banned the slave trade in Russian lands as early as 1805, making Russia the second European country (after Denmark) to pass such legislation. Yet the issue for tsarist officials was not slavery as an institution. Indeed, when Alexander's ban was first put into effect, it was still possible for Russian landowners to buy and sell serfs. Rather, Russian attitudes were determined by cultural considerations as well as strategic ones.

Like other European empires, Russians found the idea of Christians being taken into captivity by Muslims to be particularly abhorrent. The reverse—for example, Muslim captives dispatched as laborers to Siberia—seemed to elicit no particular concern on the part of either Russian officials or the public at large. Moreover, the consistent demand for slaves in the Ottoman lands was an incentive for highlanders to move across the Caucasus lines and prey on Cossack villages and other settlements. Those raids not only created a constant security problem along the fortified frontier but also helped enrich the empire's local enemies. To clamp down on the trade, punitive regulations against local and Ottoman slavers were regularly passed, with the convicted hanged in public. Naval patrols were stepped up along the Black Sea coast to interdict slaving vessels. Hot-pursuit raids were launched across the Russian-Ottoman frontier to catch known traders and liberate their charges. These efforts, however, were somewhat disingenuous. When women were seized at sea, they would rarely be returned directly to the port or the region from which they came. Sometimes they were simply placed in another kind of slavery—as charwomen, prostitutes, or wives in Cossack settlements in the north Caucasus. It is little wonder, then, that women were sometimes said to opt for being sold into slavery in Constantinople rather than be granted freedom in Russia.[58] The distinction in practice was not as obvious as it might seem.

Until the second half of the nineteenth century, when the supply was effectively stopped after the final subjugation of the Caucasus highlands, Russian interdiction efforts changed the nature of slave trading without eliminating it. Slavers were forced to work in the stormy winter months from October to March, when Russian cruisers rarely sailed on the Black Sea. The journey was also made in smaller vessels, which could be pulled up on shore and hidden from Russian coastal patrols. Both changes made the journey extremely perilous. Several overloaded ships, containing dozens of women and sailing on hazardous seas, were inevitably lost each season.

Furthermore, in some instances Russian prohibitions made the slave trade even more lucrative than it had been in the past. The decreased supply and elevated danger associated with shipping women from the Caucasus to Turkey caused a concomitant increase in their price. By the 1840s women in their late teens, especially those from noble families in Circassia, could fetch as much as thirty thousand piastres.[59] This price rise proved a powerful inducement even to Russian officials. Successive Russian consuls in Trebizond, for example, seem to have been key players in the game. Not only would they turn a blind eye to the trade, but they would issue Ottoman sea captains with charters certifying that they were traveling from an Ottoman port to the Russian port at Kerch to take on a cargo of wheat. Such charters were apparently given with full knowledge that the ships would be turning east instead of anchoring in the north, that is, heading toward the Caucasus coast in order to pick up their cargo of girls. With a legitimate document in hand, the Ottoman captain could easily put off any nosy Russian naval officer who might intercept the ship at sea.[60]

For nearly the entire nineteenth century an imperial army and navy, largely composed of forced conscripts who had been born into servitude as Russian peasants, claimed to be liberating men and women who may well have had some complicity in their own bondage. Once liberated, these former slaves might end up as forced laborers or concubines of the very men who had liberated them. In such a context, the boundaries between slavery and freedom, compulsion and complicity, were very difficult to fix. Nevertheless, in time this particular form of captivity—white women sold into bondage and lapsed Christians (as highlanders were sometimes described) made to serve the infidel Ottoman—became a call to action in the Caucasus. The Russian Empire—like the British and the French—thus came to see its imperial mission as both strategic and fundamentally humanitarian.

Generations of men and women moved freely across the lines of the Caucasus, but as the nineteenth century progressed, the region's many boundaries—separating one empire from another, highlands from lowlands, Christians from Muslims—began to harden. One of the great achievements of the early stages of Russian conquest was to make borders matter. Soldiers stabilized frontiers. Cartographers mapped the coasts and hinterlands. Administrators built new political and social institutions across territories secured for the empire by war and treaty. In a way, however, these processes also marked one of the empire's great failures. They excluded certain styles of life that for centuries had ensured the survival of individuals and the flourishing of cultures at the intersection of different imperial domains. In time those old customs became specters of a lost way of life, habits that were all but impossible to maintain within a modern, consolidated empire.

TWO

Rule and Resistance

The Circassians hate us. We have forced them out of their free and spacious
pasturelands; their auls are in ruins, whole tribes have been annihilated. As time
goes on, they move deeper into the mountains, and direct their raids
from there. . . . What can one do with such people?

Alexander Pushkin, Journey to Erzurum *(1829)*

Russia, in order to deceive the world, conceals the very object of her continual warfare against
us and ours. She diffuses the report amongst the civilised world that she is fighting the
Circassians simply because they are a savage, uneducated, and unruly people.

Circassian leaders Hadji Hayder Hassan and Kustan Ogli Ismael
petitioning Queen Victoria (1862)

IT IS EASY TO THINK of the north Caucasus as an Islamic wall
blocking the expansion of Russia toward Christian populations in
the south such as the Georgians and Armenians, as well as toward
the warm waters of the Mediterranean and the Persian Gulf, "the
north Caucasus barrier," as it has been called.[1] It is equally tempting,
especially given the nature of political violence in the north Caucasus
since the early 1990s, to see the highlands as the homeland of devout
Muslims who have spent the last two centuries chafing under the
Russian yoke. However, these views oversimplify the place of religion

in the social life of the region, as well as the role of Islam in promoting political mobilization.

Islam in the Caucasus—or anywhere, for that matter—has never been just one thing. There are important divisions, both theological and social, between Shi'a and Sunni, the two major traditions of the Islamic faith. Muslims long influenced by the spiritual and cultural traditions of Persia, such as the Turkic-speakers of the southeast Caucasus, were traditionally Shi'a. Much of the northern and western Caucasus, where spiritual life was shaped by contact with Crimean Tatars and Ottomans, belonged to the Sunni branch. Even among the Sunni, however, there are distinct schools of religious law and textual interpretation. The north Caucasus, like the other fringes of the Islamic world, became an important outpost of Sufism, the catchall term for several different paths, or *tariqas*, of Islamic mysticism. In Dagestan the Naqshbandi-Khalidi *tariqa* held sway after the late eighteenth century and formed the basic spiritual inspiration for—and perhaps the underlying social network of—the highland guerrilla movements of the nineteenth century. In Chechnya, by contrast, the Qadiri school arose after the Russian defeat of Naqshbandi leaders in 1859.

Each of these traditions had distinct and often conflicting positions regarding right conduct, the interpretation of scripture, and the relationship between sacred and secular authority. Even more complicated was the way in which orthodox religious law, or *sharia*, interacted with the complex system of customary law, or *adat*, which varied not only from region to region but even from village to village. Overlaying all of these differences was the Russian imperial system, which sometimes opposed traditional religious practices, hierarchies, and legal codes and at other times attempted to embrace or reshape them as tools of imperial management. All Muslims were not opposed to Russian imperialism, nor were those who resisted it always Muslim. There were Muslims throughout the Caucasus who were relatively easily absorbed into the empire (for example, the Kabardians of the northern lowlands or Muslim herders of the southwest) while some Christians fought long and hard against it (for example, certain Abkhaz princely families or the Imeretians of western Georgia). Just as there has never been one Islam in the Caucasus, so there has never been a unified "Islamic resistance" to Russian power.

The advent of Islam in the region dates from the earliest days of the religion itself. In the mid-eighth century Umayyad armies conquered Derbend and brought it into the realm of the Arab caliphate. That early influence probably remained in place only in Dagestan, where some local rulers traced their lineage to Arab governors and where Arabic remained the language of learning well into the modern period. In other areas traditional religious practices—the veneration of local saints, sacred trees, and springs—were combined with Islamic doctrine to create a unique form of folk Islam. In still other parts of the Caucasus, Islam encountered well-established religions—Orthodox Christianity in the Georgian lands, Zoroastrianism in Azerbaijan, and Judaism among some upland tribal groups—that were able to resist Islam or modify Islamic practices to suit local conditions.

Subsequent waves of Islamic influence continued to arrive. Trade ties with the centers of Islamic scholarship in Central Asia and the Persian Gulf provided channels of exchange. Periods of imperial conquest by Ottomans and Persians or, more frequently, dynastic marriages stimulated conversion. A network of religious academies (*madrasas*) in Dagestan, with links to the scholarly traditions of Syria and Yemen, produced successive generations of proselytizers. Personal desire, self-interest, family pressure, and duress to adopt one or another identity combined to ensure that, over the centuries, Islam in its many different forms took root in some parts of the Caucasus but not in others.

At times, however, Islam did play an important political role if for no other reason than the fact that it provided a rallying point around which talented indigenous leaders could mobilize their own populations. The first large-scale, organized resistance to Russian expansion in the Caucasus highlands was a rebellion led by Sheikh Mansur, also called Ushurma. Little is known about Mansur, his followers, or his major political aims. Whether he was even an "Islamist" leader in any meaningful sense is still a subject of debate. Periodic rebellions along Russia's southern frontier were a fixture of the seventeenth and eighteenth centuries, and Mansur may well have been a regional leader in the same mold, someone able to take advantage of the strategic intersection of different empires and lead a genuinely multiethnic frontier coalition against a distant sovereign.

Mansur first appeared in 1785 as a local military leader in Chechnya, perhaps as an adept of the Naqshbandi *tariqa*. He issued a call for a holy war—a jihad or, as it is generally known in the Caucasus, a *gazavat*—against the Russians. A range of groups in the northeast—including the Avars and the Nogais—answered the call. Mansur's forces attacked Russian outposts and staged guerrilla operations against Russian troops on the move. Despite some substantial military successes, internecine rivalry among Mansur's forces weakened his support. In the late 1780s he and his remaining followers fled into Ottoman territory, where he continued to execute small-scale forays in support of the sultan, who was then at war with Catherine the Great. By this time, however, enthusiasm for the *gazavat* had waned. The chieftains of Kabarda—who were essential to the success of any pan-Caucasus movement—remained loyal to the Russian side. Mansur himself was captured in the Ottoman fort of Anapa and sent to the Schlüsselburg fortress near St. Petersburg, where he died in 1794.

Although the Mansur movement achieved little at the time, it did illustrate that traditions of clan raiding, glorification of social bandits (*abreks*), and esteem for youthful warriors (*jigits*) could be combined with broader economic and political goals. Given the right circumstances, a martial ethos and feuding culture could be transformed into a movement of organized rebellion and, on occasion, infused with Islamic significance. By the late 1820s religious issues came to the fore when for the first time the empire faced a sustained and large-scale movement that claimed to be the bearer of Islamic purity. This also placed the Russian Empire in a new and even more difficult position. Rather than seeking to quell resistance aimed primarily at the power of the tsar, as had been the case with earlier frontier rebels, the empire was now being pulled into what amounted to a civil war among north Caucasus communities themselves.

The Murid Way

From the perspective of both Russian strategists and highland leaders the Caucasus was never a single arena of conflict. Historians often present the Caucasus wars as a decades-long struggle to subdue the region and bring it into the Russian sphere. However, the military subjugation of the highlands involved two quite different theaters, each with its own players, tactics, and challenges.

The simplest way to understand the situation is to think of it in the terms that a Russian commander looking southward from St. Petersburg would have used. The Caucasus consisted of two distinct flanks. Broadly speaking, on the right, or western, flank was the territory bounded by the Black Sea to the west and the Kuban and Inguri rivers to the north and south. This region encompassed the coastal Abkhaz tribes as well as the many varieties of Circassians living in the mountains, on the coast, and in the hills sloping down toward the Kuban River. On the left, or eastern, flank was the territory bounded by the

Caspian Sea to the east and the basins of the Terek, Kura, and Alazani rivers to the north and south. This region included the peoples of Chechnya and the upland communities of Dagestan. Between these two flanks ran the Georgian Military Highway, the umbilical cord linking Georgia to the rest of the empire. The middle ground between the right and left flanks was also home to a variety of peoples, some of whom were loyal to the tsar, while others lived in out-of-the-way areas and consequently posed no immediate threat to imperial power. Among the latter groups were the Turkic-speaking Karachai and Balkars,; the Ossetians, whose villages helped insulate the road against highlander attacks; and the peoples of mountainous Georgia, the Svans, Khevsurs, Pshavs, and Tush. The great dream of some highland leaders was to unite the two flanks, which were separated by no more than 150 miles, into a single front. The great success of Russian policy was that it prevented them from ever doing so.

The struggle on the right flank was of longest duration, lasting from the earliest encounters between Muscovites and Kabardian princes in the 1500s until the conquest of the last of the Circassian tribes and the Abkhaz in the 1860s. There was little in the way of comprehensive strategy here, however, since the Russians rarely faced a united enemy. Highland fighting mainly involved raids across the Kuban line or periodic investments of Russian forts along the Black Sea. On the Russian side, fighting primarily consisted of uncoordinated, punitive expeditions of short duration, whose main aim was to suppress a local strongman or to secure formal acknowledgment of tsarist suzerainty, such as the payment of tribute or taxes.

At the beginning of the nineteenth century, the situation on the left flank looked to be even simpler than that on the right. In some areas the lack of cohesive native elites allowed the Russians to play one group off against another. Over time, concessions were secured that enabled the building of forts deeper into the mountains and the advance of the Caucasus lines toward the south. Although elites in Dagestan were far stronger than in other areas, they generally accommodated themselves to Russian encroachments, looking to the new imperial suzerain as a way of securing their own positions against local challengers.

Things changed radically in the late 1820s. The northeastern Caucasus quickly became a region where old allegiances no longer mattered and where a new military-political movement opposed both the Russians and traditional elites. A new generation of indigenous activists gradually built up a sense of unity through a combination of mobilized Islam, clan loyalty, and personal charisma, a movement that would come to be known to Russian observers as "Muridism." The term is derived from the Arabic word for a disciple, or *murid*, of a particular Sufi leader, or *murshid*. In essence, the bond between *murid* and *murshid* is a spiritual one, the tie between an adept seeking the path to enlightenment and an experienced teacher who can shepherd the student along the true path. It is not substantially different from the disciple-teacher relationship found in the mystical strains of other faiths.

There had long been a custom of venerating particular Muslim teachers in the north Caucasus, especially in the largest of the Sufi traditions in the region, the Khalidi branch of the Naqshbandi order. The Naqshbandis traced their religious heritage to the fourteenth-century Bukharan mystic Baha al-Din Naqshband, who advocated a form of silent prayer and meditation, or *dhikr*, which the faithful used in emulating the qualities of the Prophet Muhammad. Only through strict observance of the teachings of a venerated master could adepts hope to attain the perfect "recollection of God" made possible by the *dhikr*. In the late eighteenth century the ideas of Naqshband spread to the Caucasus, with an added emphasis on restructuring society around the strict adherence to *sharia*. Changing society and not simply the heart of the believer became a major goal.

However, Naqshbandi Sufism was not only—nor even mainly—political. There was a great debate among Sufi scholars about whether the faithful were required to join in holy wars declared by respected sheikhs or imams, and whether the purity of the Naqshbandi way was, in fact, soiled when it was implicated in politics. From the Russian perspective, though, Sufi sheikhs were always—at least potentially—military commanders-in-waiting. The sheikh was a religious leader who could transform his spiritual adepts into guerrilla fighters, ordering them to attack Russian settlements and forts and conceivably mobilizing entire swaths of the highlands against the Russian presence. Beginning early in the nineteenth century, Naqshbandi Sufis were periodically repressed or exiled. Imperial administrators watched the movement closely for signs that leaders were overstepping the boundary between religious contemplation and political action.

When Naqshbandi Sufism assumed a military cast, it was usually in response to the policies of the empire itself. By 1824 almost the entirety of Dagestan had come under Russian rule, first through the extension of direct control over khanates and free communities by outright conquest, then through Persia's renunciation of interest in the affairs of Dagestan in the Treaty of Gulistan. With the subsequent absorption of the khanates south of the mountains, Dagestan was isolated from direct Persian influence. There were now plenty of reasons for the appeal of a movement promising radical religious return and social change. Traditional sources of livelihood, from farming to slave trading, had been disrupted by Russian operations. New settlers had encroached on grazing lands. The expeditions of Ermolov had decimated upland villages and pushed people higher into the mountains or into lowland settlements, where they competed with indigenous farmers and herders as well as Cossacks and Russian settlers. The Naqshbandi-Khalidi *tariqa* in and of itself may not have been the impetus for resistance, but it certainly provided a social network through which dissatisfaction could be expressed and armed opposition organized.

The origins of "Muridism" as a political movement date from the rise of Ghazi Muhammad al-Daghestani, known to the Russians as Kazi Mullah, the first of three eminent spiritual and military leaders in the north Caucasus. Born in the early 1790s, Ghazi Muhammad grew up in the unique religious environment of upland Dagestan. He studied under a succession of prominent clerics before being initiated into the Naqshbandi-Khalidi order and developing a reputation as a respected scholar of *sharia*. In 1829 a gathering of Naqshbandi leaders proclaimed him imam of all Dagestan. He quickly issued a decree to indigenous rulers that *sharia* was now to be implemented across the region.

Ghazi Muhammad's authority was hardly universal, however. Few political leaders recognized the authority of this upstart. His zealous attempts to enforce obedience both to religious law and to his own dictates threatened to ignite a full-scale civil war among the tribal chieftains and free communities of Dagestan. Indeed, despite the degree to which both highlanders and Russians would later see Ghazi Muhammad as an archetype of Muslim resistance, the struggle in Dagestan was as much internecine as anti-Russian. Muhammad Tahir al-Qarakhi, the chronicler of the career of the later highland leader Shamil, offered this account of Ghazi Muhammand's encounter with the powerful *shamkhal* of Tarki: "An enraged Ghazi Muhammad once came to the *shamkhal* by himself. In a harsh voice, he gave him an order: 'Establish the *sharia* in your territory!' The *shamkhal*'s face lost its color: When he went limp and responded, 'I will do this! I will do this!' Ghazi Muhammad left. The *shamkhal* told his servant, 'By God, I almost wet my robe from fear of him.' He made as if he were going to fulfill this promise but did nothing."[2] As al-Qarakhi's story made clear, the imposition of Islamic law presented a challenge to traditional religious and political leaders. In order to secure their positions, they might go along with the Naqshbandi, only to turn against them once more attractive offers were extended by the Russians. These disputes established a pattern that would be followed throughout the highland wars: the effort by a military-religious leader to enforce his will across a region, followed by a period of intra-Muslim war, then a series of harsh pacification campaigns by the imperial army, which in turn temporarily united highland elites against the common Russian enemy.

The initial Russian response to the rise of Ghazi Muhammad was spotty and disorganized. Ivan Paskevich stepped down as commander in May 1831 and was soon transferred to Poland to deal with the ongoing rebellion there. The new commander, Grigorii Rozen, found it difficult to draw up a comprehensive strategy, in part because the actions of his enemy were hardly strategic themselves. Ghazi Muhammad's raids were often opportunistic, with no clear aim of establishing lasting territorial control over specific villages. However, in the summer of 1832 Rozen launched a full-scale expedition aimed at subduing Ghazi Muhammad. The idea was to move out from the central Caucasus and spread across Chechnya in force, with perhaps twenty thousand men, systematically destroying villages that had provided fighters to Ghazi Muhammad's army.[3] The push into Chechnya caused Ghazi Muhammad to retreat to upland Dagestan and to explore the possibility of peace. At this stage the Russians pressed their advantage. Word was sent to the imam that only complete surrender would be considered. The imam found himself increasingly isolated as other highland leaders made their own accommodations with the Russians and hastened to steel themselves against a new campaign, which was to be coordinated by the able field commander Franz Klüge-von-Klugenau. In the autumn Klugenau's forces surrounded the imam's redoubt at Gimri and stormed it with little resistance. Ghazi Muhammad had already been abandoned by all but a few dozen followers, most of whom, including the imam himself, were killed by Klugenau's troops.

What the Russians did not know at the time was that a new imam was already being groomed to take Ghazi Muhammad's place. Soon after the battle at Gimri, a gathering of Naqshbandi leaders proclaimed Hamzat Bek the new leader. Hamzat could not claim the devout pedigree of his predecessor. A member of the Avar nobility of

Dagestan, he passed his youth at the court of Pakhu Bike, the widow of the khan of Avaristan. Tradition has it that he spent much of his time drinking. He later fell under the religious influence of Ghazi Muhammad. Hamzat Bek seems to have been involved in guerrilla activities before Ghazi Muhammad and may have helped transform the first imam from Islamic scholar into military leader.[4] By the early 1830s Hamzat Bek had emerged as one of his most trusted lieutenants.

When Hamzat Bek assumed the mantle of imam, few political elites in the north Caucasus recognized the succession. Ghazi Muhammad had himself never secured the loyalty of all the major figures in Dagestan and Chechnya, and over the course of his campaigns many of those initially loyal to him had fallen away. During the year that followed his elevation, Hamzat Bek launched a series of attacks both against those leaders who refused to pledge their allegiance and against villages that failed to acknowledge the sovereignty of *sharia*.

Rozen was well aware of Hamzat Bek's actions, which had produced a renewed civil war in Dagestan. He moved to take advantage of fissures within the Dagestani side. Pakhu Bike, the imam's former benefactor, had grown suspicious that Hamzat Bek was plotting to undermine the khanate. Her suspicion proved prescient, for in the summer of 1834 Hamzat Bek led an attack on the khan's residence. He encircled the Avar capital and demanded that Pakhu Bike surrender. When she refused, he stormed the citadel, overwhelmed the defenders, and had the woman's head lopped off.[5] All the members of the Avar ruling house were summarily executed. Sources differ as to whether the murders were planned or were simply the result of wartime chaos. Either way, they illustrated the essentially fratricidal nature of highland warfare, with Muslim leaders killing one another with as much zeal as they killed Russians.

Pakhu Bike's death was a turning point. Those not yet loyal to Hamzat Bek now saw him as little more than a murderer; those who had already pledged their allegiance came to feel they had been duped. Hamzat's social reforms, especially the prohibition against tobacco use, further undermined his popularity. In the same year, conspirators within his own camp—some of whom sought blood revenge for the assassination of the Avar dynasts—killed him while he prayed in a mosque.[6] The elimination of Hamzat Bek at the hands of highland Muslims themselves signaled the waning of the power of the most radical Naqshbandi leaders and reinforced the prerogatives of the established elites on whom the Russian Empire had long depended. However, the nature of warfare in the Caucasus would soon undergo changes that not even Ermolov, the hardnosed imperial innovator, could have predicted.

Raiding and Retribution

Fighting the Caucasus wars was unlike anything the Russians had experienced in their encounters with the French, Persians, or Ottomans. In combat with other imperial forces, Russia's battlefield operations involved a set of skills broadly similar to those that had been required for the previous two centuries: infantry drill and fighting in lines and squares against similarly arrayed ranks; the cavalry charge and flanking maneuvers; the deployment and placement of field artillery; and the siege of fortified cities.

In the north Caucasus these techniques had to be adapted to both a new environment and a new enemy. In the "Murid" forces of both Ghazi Muhammad and Hamzat Bek in the northeast, as well as in those of the Circassians in the northwest, the Russians faced an entire army of what might be called irregular dragoons: a stellar example of multipurpose light cavalry, with the added advantages of being highly knowledgeable of local terrain and armed with lethal long guns. (It was precisely this deadly combination of abilities—possessed by Kabyles in Algeria, Pashtuns in Afghanistan, and Lakota Sioux in the American West—that frustrated other modern armies as well.) The legendary horsemanship and daring of Caucasus fighters were acknowledged even by their enemies. Russian painters depicted engagements between Cossacks-of-the-line and their Circassian and Dagestani counterparts, with riders galloping at full tilt toward one another, meeting with the clash of saber and lance.

However, such engagements were probably the exception rather than the rule. The Caucasus wars were always partly guerrilla campaigns—what would today be called seasonal counterinsurgency operations. They rarely involved anything approximating pitched battles, at least of the type that Russian officers and men knew from their wars with other empires. There were certainly occasional large-scale clashes, with casualties running into the hundreds on either side, but most involved relatively small operations, with mobile groups stealing across imperial boundaries to secure needed supplies or pick off soldiers on the march. In this form of warfare, the support of local populations was crucial for both the Russians and their enemies. Loyalties were often divided and inconstant, however. Native farmers and herders might side with or against highland guerrillas, depending on the season or the scope of the military operation. Mountaineers might cooperate with Russian forces against a local rival or, more rarely, unite in great pan-clan and even pan-religious confederations to counter a major Russian expedition. Where families, villages, and larger communities positioned themselves in the struggle depended on individual circumstances rather than clear-cut lines of religion or political allegiance.

Three general approaches to mountain warfare would animate Russian commanders up to the end of the Caucasus wars. First, punitive responses were to be made for every act of violence. Any attacks on fortified positions were to be met with a lightning and merciless counterattack, thus raising the stakes for guerrillas, whose natural inclination would be to seek the prizes to be found behind the fortified walls. Second, the lifelines of guerrilla combatants had to be cut. Villages that had—or could have—harbored them were destroyed. Crops were burned or ordered ploughed under. Herds of cattle and flocks of sheep and goats were slaughtered or stolen. Such expeditions had the added advantage of securing the spoils of war for Russian soldiers, including livestock, weapons, wood, and even people. The signal disadvantage, of course, was often to drive local populations into the arms of the Murids or other highland fighters.

From the highlanders' perspective these two techniques represented a stepped-up version of the warfare they had known for centuries: tit-for-tat raids and long-running blood feuds involving rival clans or tribal alliances. However, the third Russian technique— altering the physical environment of battle—was genuinely novel. The hills, forests, and upland villages where highland horsemen were most at home were cleared, rearranged, or destroyed in a concerted effort to shift the advantage to the regular army of the empire. If the mountaineers depended on knowledge of local geographical features, then the advantage conveyed by that knowledge could be reduced by modifying the geography itself. Edmund Spencer, who witnessed a series of coordinated Circassian attacks on Black Sea coastal forts in the 1830s, noted the ease with which mountain fighters used their familiarity with the terrain: "An enemy can never calculate upon their movements, for, appearing as if endowed with ubiquity, they are found now in one place, and then in another, and even creep, like a snake in the grass, and surprise the sentinel on duty at the gates of the fortress: in short, every tree, crag, and shrub, serves a Circassian as an ambuscade."[7] To counter these tactics, new, durable roads were laid to permit the rapid movement of troops and equipment over long distances. Along these avenues, lines of fire were secured, which usually entailed the felling of trees in broad swaths alongside the roadway, up to the distance of a musket shot. Into these spaces Russian settlers could be moved or "pacified" highlanders resettled, creating nominally loyal farming communities to provide food and personnel for the Russian forts. During the final stage of the Caucasus wars, in the 1850s and 1860s, clear-cutting of forests was pursued with particular vigor, creating a vast and lasting denuded landscape in parts of the north Caucasus.

Leo Tolstoy, who served as a cadet on the Terek line, incorporated descriptions of the results of these clear-cutting policies in his short story "The Wood-Felling." He described the stretch of stumps opened up by a detachment of ax-wielding infantry. The milky-white smoke of burning brush piles created a haze across the landscape. In the distance a small group of mounted highlanders would occasionally come into view, and now and then a bullet would chuck itself into the muddy forest floor or ricochet off downed trees. The Russian artillery could do little more than respond after the fact, aiming their cannons at the spot where the puff of smoke from a mountaineer's musket still hung in the air. Encounters such as these, Tolstoy noted with sarcasm, were always portrayed in the best possible light: "The affair in general was successful. The Cossacks, as we heard, had made a fine charge and brought back three dead Tartars [Muslims]; the infantry had provided itself with firewood and had only half-a-dozen men wounded; the artillery had lost only [one man] and two horses. For that, two miles of forest had been cut down and the place so cleared as to be unrecognizable. Instead of the thick outskirts of the forest you saw before you a large plain covered with smoking fires and cavalry and infantry marching back to camp."[8]

These operational innovations, from targeting civilians to destroying forests, produced a particularly horrific form of warfare. Here is how a Russian officer recalled an expedition in Chechnya in 1852: "At this moment, General Krukovskii, with saber drawn, sent the Cossacks forward to the enemies' houses. Many, but not all, managed to save themselves by running away; the Cossacks and the militia seized those who remained and the slaughter began, with the highlanders, like anyone with no hope of survival, fought to their last drop of blood. Making quick work of the butchery, the ataman [Cossack commander] gave out a cry and galloped on to the gorge, toward the remaining villages where the majority of the population was concentrated."[9]

Many participants in the Caucasus wars frequently mentioned the viciousness of fighting, but it is difficult to argue that one side had a particular penchant for cruelty. The taking of trophies—right hands were prized—was practiced by all sides.[10] The wholesale destruction of villages became a standard feature of the tactics of the Russian regular army and Cossack units, as well as a form of retributive justice practiced by highland commanders against disloyal communities. Even when punitive expeditions were not ordered, soldiers had to feed themselves in the field by foraging, an activity that must have seemed to highlanders little different from retributive raiding. "How can one blame them now," noted a Russian lieutenant in his diary in 1837, "for the fact that, having become accustomed to freedom, they do not want to make peace with us and instead protect their lovely homes?"[11]

When the Russian column was on the move, force protection was the foremost goal. Light field artillery was deployed in the front and rear. Cavalry, heavy artillery, and supplies were placed in the middle of the column, with a line of infantry stretching down the sides. All around the column snipers were deployed at musket range to ward off attack and keep the column from being rushed from the flank. From time to time the snipers might find themselves isolated from the main column, with little to accompany them but the unfriendly forest and the crunch of the enemy's footfalls in the distance. Men in the column could hear the occasional skirmish in the trees, the pop of muskets, and the cries of their comrades felled by unseen assailants. Artillerymen, forced to stay back and cover a retreat, might be left behind by the main column, surrounded by well-spaced highland sharpshooters against whom the artillery pieces would be useless. At their most successful, the highlanders could keep soldiers pinned down on rocky roads, trap them in defiles, or sow confusion when they passed through unfamiliar terrain. In "The Wood-Felling" an old Cossack, having lived on the line for decades, laughs at the close-order drill practiced by the regular army. "I used to watch your soldiers in amazement," he says. "What fools! There they'd be, marching away all huddled together with their red collars! How could they not be shot down?"[12]

From the annexation of eastern Georgia in 1801 until the end of the Circassian campaigns in 1864, as many as twenty-four thousand Russian soldiers and eight hundred officers were killed in the Caucasus wars, plus perhaps three times that number wounded and captured.[13] (The losses on the native side, while probably far higher, are impossible to calculate.) The wars seared themselves into the Russian imagination not because of the death toll—which was small in comparison to losses against the French, Ottoman or other imperial armies—but because the nature of the fighting and the alien environments in which soldiers found themselves created indelible memories of both romance and horror.

The experience of war differed depending on who one was and where one joined the fighting. Young officers, scions of the leading families of St. Petersburg and Moscow, could bring along servants and baggage handlers on their annual expeditions into the mountains. Junior and senior officers were prized as prisoners by the highlanders, and the fact that they were often surrounded by nonfighting personnel made their capture particularly easy. Then there were conscripts, men sent from villages throughout Russia to fight in surroundings that were wholly foreign, both culturally and geographically. In addition to members of the regular army, there were also Cossacks drawn from fortified villages and settlements, as well as local auxiliary forces, both Christian and Muslim, provided by indigenous rulers who—at least for the coming campaign season—had professed their allegiance to the tsar.

In the flatlands along the major north Caucasus rivers, the prevention of raiding was the chief concern. Soldiers stationed in outposts or seated on watchtowers kept an eye on a river crossing or villages just across the frontier. In upland areas soldiers were engaged in annual campaigns, with long columns traipsing into the mountains to sack a particular settlement or relieve a vital military outpost under siege. Beyond the dangers of warfare itself, auxiliary killers also took their toll. Infectious diseases, diet-related illnesses, hunger, and cold killed far more soldiers than highlanders' musket balls. Nevertheless, it was the nature of violence in the northeast, in the upland *auls* of Dagestan and the forests of Chechnya, that average Russians would come to see as the quintessential form of warfare in the Caucasus. Likewise, it was the famous and long-serving successor to Hamzat Bek—Shamil— whom Russians would view as the embodiment of the indefatigable *gorets*: part brigand, part cultural hero, part worthy adversary in an empire's fight to subdue the Caucasus highlands.

The Imam and the Viceroy

Born in 1796 or 1797, Shamil was the child of a free noble of Avaristan and was related via his mother to the ruling house of Kazi-Kumuk, a once powerful khanate in Dagestan. Like many young men from this social background, Shamil was given to a respected *murshid*, Sheikh

Jamal al-Din, and exposed to the tenets and practices of the Naqsh-bandi *tariqa*. It is through the *murid-murshid* relationship that Shamil was also introduced to the circle of the first imam, Ghazi Muhammad, for whom he became a trusted fighter. Shamil was present at the siege of Gimri in 1832 and miraculously emerged as one of only two survivors, a feat that would later be pointed to as evidence of the divine favor that surrounded him.

Following the murder of the Hamzat Bek, Shamil became a leading candidate to succeed him. In the early autumn of 1834 an assembly of religious leaders, many of them drawn from Shamil's own home village, proclaimed him as the third—and, as it turned out, last—imam capable of garnering widespread support in Dagestan and Chechnya. As with the two previous military-religious commanders, there was serious opposition to Shamil's claim to supreme leadership, not only among other Sufi adepts but also among the traditional clan and princely rulers whose positions had been recognized by the Russians. The first two years after his elevation to imam were spent consolidating his authority among the remnants of Hamzat Bek's forces and defeating local rivals.

Shamil might well have suffered the fate of his predecessor—assassination by former allies—had it not been for the general Russian disengagement in the northeastern Caucasus in the early 1830s. Preoccupied by problems in the west—such as risings in Circassia and the maintenance of a coastal blockade on the Black Sea—military planners paid scant attention to a relatively young and unknown Dagestani leader who had so far presented no obvious threat. By the time that Rozen, the supreme commander in the Caucasus, again turned his attention to the northeast, the situation had changed markedly. Raiding parties were already hitting Chechnya, and Shamil's followers were putting pressure on otherwise peaceful leaders in Dagestan to turn away from the Russians and implement *sharia*.

The Russians responded by attacking Shamil's strongholds, including his mother's native village, but with little result. In the autumn of 1837 Gen. Franz Klüge-von-Klugenau made diplomatic overtures to Shamil, seeking to win his agreement to visit Tiflis or at least to send envoys to the Russian side. The timing was particularly sensitive from the Russian standpoint. Tsar Nicholas I was due to tour the Caucasus that autumn, and having a full-blown, armed resistance in the northeast would hardly have matched the image of the region as a docile segment of the imperial domain. A meeting between Klugenau and Shamil produced a disappointing result. Shamil professed his willingness to seek peace but blamed his intransigent lieutenants for continuing the struggle.

Rozen duly arranged grand receptions and dinners at which uniformed officers and bureaucrats, loyal mountain chiefs, and an assortment of Persians, Englishmen, and other foreign envoys, all in mufti, lined up to greet the tsar during his visit to the region.[14] Soon after the sovereign's visit, however, Rozen was replaced by Evgenii Golovin, who soon embarked on a new campaign to subjugate Dagestan and Chechnya. In response to news of an impending Russian expedition, Shamil fortified the stronghold of Akhulgo, in northern Dagestan, and prepared to make this the center of his resistance. He ordered food stockpiled and access routes cleared. Stone fortifications that had been destroyed a few years earlier by a Russian assault were rebuilt.

Shamil also sought to enlist the help of outsiders, a strategy that had long been pursued by indigenous leaders in the western Caucasus but one that Shamil himself had thus far eschewed. He appealed both to the Ottoman sultan and to the pasha of Egypt, Muhammad Ali, underscoring the religious nature of his struggle and the obligation of other Muslims to come to his aid.[15] Shamil's war had previously been an attempt by a religious zealot and military commander to consolidate his power among an assortment of fellow Muslim leaders, some loyal to Russia and others equally resistant to Russian rule and to Shamil's hegemony. It was now a movement with a self-consciously religious claim to the allegiance and support of all fellow Muslims, both inside and outside Dagestan.

Far more than his predecessors, Golovin concentrated his efforts on the left flank. In the summer of 1839 troops under Lt. Gen. Pavel Grabbe reached Akhulgo after a difficult journey across lands denuded of supplies by the scorched-earth policy of Shamil's fighters. The location of the citadel—protected by a river on three sides and perched atop steep hills—meant that conducting the siege was to be extremely difficult, from the placement of field guns to the prevention of the enemy's communication with the outside. As the siege wore on, both sides agreed to negotiations, but Grabbe demanded that Shamil first surrender his son—in a sign of good faith—as a hostage. After initially refusing, Shamil dispatched his eldest son, Jamaladin, to the Russian side, paving the way for the exploration of terms of surrender. Grabbe proposed that Shamil command his troops to lay down their arms and, after surrendering to the Russians, accept exile from his homeland. Those terms were refused, and Grabbe then launched the full force of his troops against Akhulgo. After two days of bloody fighting, he secured it for the Russian side. Grabbe next ordered a series of expeditions to find, capture, or kill any remaining highlanders. Shamil, however, had escaped from the village on the first night of the final attack, leaving most of his men behind to be slaughtered and his son in Russian hands.

Akhulgo proved a decisive battle. Shamil's resistance had been broken. The former leader could find no quarter in either Dagestan or Chechnya. Russia's traditional allies in the north Caucasus were now reaffirming their loyalty. New tribal chieftains were daily coming forward to submit themselves to the tsar. Yet Russian commanders drew precisely the wrong lessons from these developments. Rather than consolidating their victory by attempting to buy off the allegiances of other leaders in Chechnya and Dagestan, Golovin launched additional operations throughout the entire northeast Caucasus. The harshness of these expeditions—which also involved the ill-considered attempt to disarm all Chechen hillmen by force—triggered an inevitable reaction. By early 1840 Chechens and Dagestanis were preparing for yet another round of fighting.

In the meantime Shamil had taken refuge in Chechnya—a journey that his followers would later compare to the Prophet Muhammad's flight from Mecca to Medina. From there he extended his power over the clans and rulers of Chechnya, much as he had done in his native Dagestan. Rather than fall into the earlier trap of defending a fortified village against a Russian attack en masse, Shamil now concentrated on developing mobile guerrilla forces that could take advantage of their superior knowledge of the terrain and lure Russian troops into forests and gorges, where soldiers could be picked off one by one. From this point forward Shamil pursued neither the small-scale raiding of traditional Caucasus warfare nor the concentrated counter-siege tactics of the first years of his revolt. His well-organized operations were now designed to fatigue Russian detachments and then to crush them.

The results were almost immediately apparent. By the end of 1843 Shamil had overrun more than a dozen Russian forts, captured field artillery and other weaponry, and seized hundreds of horses to swell the ranks of his cavalry. These new operations were coordinated by a complex administrative and military system, with a clearly delineated structure, uniforms that distinguished rank and function, and even a military band. At the top stood the imam himself: the central political decision maker, commander in chief, religious authority, and judicial arbiter. Throughout the 1840s and 1850s Shamil fashioned something resembling a state in the lands he controlled, a political entity that attracted more and more people—both highlanders and Christian deserters—and significantly reduced the number of those who were willing to make peace with the Russians.[16]

Shamil was known by many epithets, both in the highlands and among his Russian opponents, but one frequent label was the Arabic *amir al-mu'minin*, or "commander of the faithful." This is perhaps the one that reveals the most about the motivations of those engaged in the drawn-out war in the northeast.

Shamil's fighting corps was built on top of the social connections of Naqshbandi Sufism. The Sufi brotherhoods provided an overarching ideology and could be called upon when needed. They represented a template for relations between leader and follower that could be sanctified by reference to religious tradition and the adept-master structure of Sufi Islam. However, it is a considerable leap from admitting the social power of Naqshbandi Sufism to the idea that Islam as a faith was the driving force behind the prolonged resistance to Russian imperialism. Some Muslims, such as the Shi'a of Azerbaijan, remained consistently hostile to Shamil. Others, such as the noble houses of Dagestan, were only intermittently loyal. Still others, such as the Circassians of the northwest Caucasus, carried on their own fight against the tsar with little regard for the imam. Moreover, the most important Muslim powers in the region—the Ottomans and the Persian Qajars—continually kept Shamil at arm's length despite his repeated calls for assistance.

Still, in the self-understanding of northeast highland leaders, the central thread linking the three imams with each other and with earlier political-spiritual leaders, such as Sheikh Mansur, was not the fact that they were all committed anti-Russians but that they were committed Muslims. Their central goal was to return Muslim communities to a strict interpretation of the Qur'an and away from the soiled traditions of customary law and folk religion. The zeal for spiritual and dogmatic purity could also be directed against Muslim and secular authorities. For example, Shamil's representative, or *naib*, in Circassia was said to have substituted Shamil's own name for that of the caliph—the Ottoman sultan—in the benedictory passages of Friday prayers.[17]

In the writings of Shamil's associates and even of the imam himself—one of the few instances in which an indigenous military commander left a remarkable literary record—there is no clear sense in which all Muslims were obliged to join him in the *gazavat* against the Russians. The message is that Muslims are called upon to be good Muslims first and foremost and to turn away from their spiritually corrupt leaders. The fight against the Russians appears as a by-product of the struggle to purify Islam. One of the major extant chronicles of Shamil's exploits is *The Shining of Dagestani Swords in Certain Campaigns of Shamil*, which was written in Arabic by Muhammad Tahir al-Qarakhi, his scribe and advisor.[18] It portrays Shamil not as a protonational leader against Russia but as a pious man seeking to root out wicked laws and replace them with *sharia*. The chronicler has Shamil argue for the unity of Islam, denying the traditional divisions of authority in the highlands and even dismissing the differences between distinct schools of Islamic thought. Almost the entire narrative concerns Shamil's exploits against other Dagestani and Chechen communities, not against the Russians. It is his apostate and worldly fellow highlanders, not the Christian imperialists, who come in for the harshest criticism.

A similar theme runs through Shamil's letters to his subordinates and his public pronouncements. Written in formulaic Arabic, with invocations wishing God's blessings on his correspondents, they range from minor decrees transferring *naibs* from one post to another, to complaints about the amount of tax revenue collected in particular districts, to explicit orders to assassinate a traitor. Throughout his letters, however, Shamil consistently admonishes his followers to practice *sharia*, resist evil, and continue the struggle against the enemies of God. "Our wish, first of all, is that you remain under the protection of God, the Highest," he wrote to the people of Dagestan in June 1850.[19] Shamil rarely uses the term "Russians" to describe his enemies. Rather, he classes them into two categories—the "unbelievers" (*kafirs*) and the "hypocrites" (*munafiqs*)—the former consisting of those non-Muslims who resisted the hegemony of Islamic law, the latter those who cooperated with the enemies of Islam. As Shamil wrote in his final testament, a summation of his life addressed to his descendants and followers, "We waged war on oppression and enslavement.... [W]e did not fight against the Russians or the Christians: we fought for our freedom."[20]

What the Russians were encountering in the person of Shamil, as in his two immediate predecessors as imam, was a renewal movement within the highland Muslim community. It had implications for Russian imperial control not because it was Islamic but rather because it challenged the religious hierarchy, social mores, and administrative order with which the tsarist government had long interacted. From Sheikh Mansur all the way down to Shamil, religious leaders who combined the struggle for piety with the struggle against imperialism were never wholly embraced by the communities they claimed to represent. Russian commanders eventually learned to use these divisions to their advantage. Overtures were made to leading Muslim clerics, urging them to denounce Shamil as an apostate and to compile lists of deviations from *sharia* and misinterpretations that Shamil himself had supposedly advocated.

If the clash of religions is not a particularly helpful way to understand Shamil, neither is ethnicity. Although newspaper accounts of the modern wars in Chechnya frequently portray the Chechen nation as eternally resistant to Russian rule, such assertions apply an ethnic template to what was, until the twentieth century, a fuzzy cultural map. Some of the people whom we might now call Chechens joined Shamil's resistance, while others accommodated themselves to the new reality of Russian power and profited from the proximity of Russian forts and Cossack settlements. Some groups in Dagestan—especially those associated with old ruling families and hereditary nobles—consistently resisted Shamil, seeing the Russian presence as essential buttresses to their power.

Moreover, if one were to look for a nationalist precursor of the Chechen warlords of the 1990s, one would have to look past Shamil. The imam was, if anything, an Avar insofar as he was born in the region of Dagestan controlled by the Avaristani khan. As in much of Dagestan, his language of official communication was Arabic, and it is likely that he used a variety of Turkish, the broad lingua franca of the highlands, in everyday speech. He may have spoken Avar, but there is no evidence that he thought of himself as an Avar in a modern ethnonational sense. He also spent a good deal of his career fighting the hereditary rulers of his native region. While Shamil did make his political and military comeback in Chechnya after 1839, that was a matter of necessity rather than nationalism. His previous ruthlessness and the defeat at Akhulgo had so alienated his fellow Dagestanis that he was left with little choice but to regroup beyond his old homeland.

Russian and Soviet writers tended to see Shamil's statelike creation as a form of "oriental despotism." By contrast, in the popular memory of Dagestanis, Chechens, and others, his imamate is today often regarded as symbolic of the desire for national independence across the north Caucasus. Both views are idealized versions of the realities of Shamil's system of governance and warfighting since territory was seized and surrendered from season to season. Yet if Shamil was unable to create all the trappings of statehood in the highland Caucasus, it was often equally difficult for the Russians to do so. "The system of our activity, being based exclusively on the use of force of arms, has left political means completely untried," wrote Prince Alexander Chernyshev, the Russian minister of war, in 1842.[21] It would fall to one of the foremost Russian military and civilian leaders in southern Russia, the worldly and accomplished Mikhail Vorontsov, to put in place the rudiments of a civil administration in a part of the empire that had known mainly conflict.

Before the late 1820s, the "conquest of the Caucasus" mainly involved incorporating previously well established political entities into a larger imperial order, that is, absorbing or unseating old elites and transferring the productive resources of defined territories from traditional khans, kings, and princes to the tsar. From the late 1820s until the early 1860s conquest meant something entirely different, namely, counterinsurgency, not the older imperial techniques of persuading, cajoling, and redrawing borders, which had worked in Georgia or the khanates of the southeast.

Yet running parallel to the long military campaign was the creation of an imperial administration throughout the areas that had been "pacified" or otherwise brought safely into the empire. The Caucasus lines remained central to that task, a way of ensuring that the instability in the uplands did not spread to the hills and lowlands on either side of the main chain. There were also more mundane but no less important projects. Cities had to be modernized. Streets had to be laid and roads built. Quarantine and other public health facilities had to be erected. Taxes had to be collected and state funds distributed to relevant agencies.

The central figure in the fulfillment of these goals was Mikhail Vorontsov, one of the most accomplished Russian administrators on the southern frontier. As the first imperial viceroy in the Caucasus, Vorontsov built an administration concerned with improving the basic civilian infrastructure of areas that were quickly being transformed from a faraway borderland into an inseparable part of Russia proper. Vorontsov was born in 1782 in Britain, where his father served as Russian ambassador to the Court of St. James. He was reared in an English environment, attending Cambridge and moving to Russia only when he reached the age of sixteen. Like many aristocratic young men of his day, he was offered a military commission and saw action in the Caucasus during the generalship of Pavel Tsitsianov. During the Napoleonic Wars, he was wounded at the Battle of Borodino and commanded Russian occupation forces in France.

At the age of forty-one he was handed the governor-general's post in New Russia, the stretch of territory along the northern rim of the Black Sea, which he fashioned into the showcase of the Russian south during his two decades of service there. The city of Odessa was transformed from a dusty Tatar village into a modern seaport with a population of some seventy-eight thousand and a famous cascade of steps that connected the upper city to the docks below. Farther east he laid the foundations for Sevastopol, the naval base of the Russian Black Sea fleet and an arsenal that would soon become the envy of the Ottoman Empire and its protectors in western Europe. In recognition of his achievements, in November 1844 Tsar Nicholas I bestowed on him the grand title of *Glavnokomanduiushchii voisk na Kavkaze i Namestnik vo vsekh oblastiakh s neogranichennym polnomochiem*—commander in chief of Caucasus forces and viceroy of all domains with full and unlimited powers.

It was the first time that the tsar had specifically delegated his full authority to a subordinate. Previous individuals had held the lesser title of *glavnoupravliaiushchii*, or chief administrator, and often shared power with a host of ministerial legates and commanders dispatched from St. Petersburg. Even Ermolov, who had the personal confidence of Alexander I and was informally known as the "proconsul" of the Caucasus, had never been granted the explicit powers Nicholas awarded to Vorontsov. There had long been friction between local administrators, who called for greater sensitivity to Caucasus customary law and cultural norms, and central authorities who were prone to ignore the special considerations that governing the Caucasus required.[22] These problems resulted in both administrative chaos and military stagnation. By giving a grander title and full authority to an already proven reformer, Nicholas hoped to bring about the same transformation in the Caucasus that had recently been effected in New Russia. From this point forward the military dimensions of Caucasus policy were to go hand in hand with the creation of a stable and workable civil administration.

Once Vorontsov arrived in Tiflis, he quickly set about surveying and revamping the political structure of the region. One of his initial tasks was to reform the basic territorial administration of the areas south of the main mountain range. These lands—the old kingdoms of

Kartli and Kakheti and the several khanates of present-day Azerbaijan and Armenia—were then still being referred to by their ancient names even though power had been concentrated in the hands of the Russian chief administrator and commander in chief. Applying the same techniques he had pioneered in New Russia, Vorontsov reconsidered the question of boundary lines and overlaid the older labels with new ones—in this case derived from the names of towns and cities that were to serve as provincial centers. New administrative units, such as the provinces of Tiflis and Yerevan, were put in place.

Within these new entities Vorontsov delegated power to assemblies of nobles and incorporated prominent local elites into the structures of governance, in some cases even fusing customary law with Russian state law. The Russian state had considerable experience with co-opting indigenous elites, but few administrators before Vorontsov had attempted this systematically. Especially in Georgia—where barely a decade before his arrival a conspiracy of nobles had been foiled by tsarist authorities—ensuring the loyalty of local elites was critical to cementing Russian power. As in New Russia, he focused on educational and cultural initiatives, even funding many himself. Specialized secondary schools were established in Tiflis and Kutaisi, and other institutions were opened as part of a thoroughgoing reform of state-supported education. In the early 1850s the new Caucasus school system was fully incorporated into the Russian imperial network, with graduates of Caucasus schools regularly going on to Russian universities. Libraries, museums, and scholarly societies were also set up.

Vorontsov was convinced that the Caucasus needed a genuine political, cultural, and economic center—much as Odessa had become the effective capital of New Russia—and Tiflis was to be it. Parts of the city had remained in ruins since the Persian onslaught of 1795. Vorontsov laid down plans for its rebuilding, creating wide thoroughfares and designing new residential districts on both banks of the Kura River. The first drama theaters were established in 1850 and 1851 (one for Georgian plays, another for Russian), and the famous Tiflis opera house was soon inaugurated, complete with an Italian company regularly performing well-known pieces. While not exactly up to European standards, the booming cultural life in Vorontsov's Tiflis was a sign of the city's gradual rise from garrison town to urban imperial outpost.

Vorontstov applied a similar level of energy to reforming the nature of highland warfare. Prior to his tenure, the Russian army had won most of the battles but had made little progress in winning the war.

Expeditions would penetrate deep into the mountains, young men would be killed or captured and villages torched, following which the expedition would retreat, satisfied that its aims had been met, to the nearest major fort. Within weeks, however, Shamil's lieutenants would be active in the recently pacified area, with new adherents now flocking to join the movement as a result of the outrages committed during the last Russian incursion. Not only were such expeditions largely fruitless, but they were also extremely costly to Russian soldiers. In the brushland of Chechnya snipers could decimate columns on the march. In the higher-elevation villages of Dagestan soldiers could be mowed down as they struggled to clamber up rocky edifices toward an enemy bastion.

Vorontsov's initial plan was to advance the Caucasus lines deep into the forests and mountains, taking the fight directly to the power centers of Shamil's movement—a redoubled version of Ermolov's old operational imperative. His first forays, however, were not as successful as he had hoped. In the summer of 1845 a campaign against Shamil's new capital of Dargo—the most famous single campaign in the history of the Caucasus wars—ended in the destruction of the stronghold. But the disastrous retreat through the forests of Chechnya came at a huge cost. Faced with repeated attacks from hidden musketeers and occasionally from homemade or captured artillery, the Russian column was able to advance only a few miles a day. During the retreat, two Russian generals and nearly two hundred officers were killed, along with over three thousand men killed or wounded.[23] By the time the remaining soldiers reached a secure outpost, the detachment was said to resemble a mare set upon by wolves.[24]

Following the Dargo campaign, Vorontsov developed a strategy that would come to characterize his period as commander in chief, namely, the systematic attack on Shamil's redoubts and the elimination of the highlanders' ability to move, communicate, and extract resources from the local population. This plan was different from the ad hoc punitive expeditions of the early nineteenth century or even Ermolov's scorched-earth tactics. Vorontsov combined military ruthlessness with what would now be called a hearts-and-minds campaign. He worked to discredit Shamil, portraying him as a despot and a bad Muslim. He established cordial relations with highland leaders who had long-standing personal rifts with the imam.

To achieve his aims Vorontsov ordered the beefing up of fortifications on all the Caucasus lines. Regiments were reorganized and moved around. New lines were put in place to protect strategic communication routes. Forests were cut back to reduce the cover for harassing fire, both musket and cannon, from guerrilla positions. Crops and livestock were destroyed and villagers were urged to move to areas out of reach of Shamil's forces. The Russians even cultivated potential rivals within Shamil's own camp as a way of weakening the imam's hand. In 1851 Vorontsov sought to capitalize on the disaffection of Hadji Murat, one of Shamil's trusted lieutenants, who defected to the Russian side. The early successes of Vorontsov's new system were limited, however. Sieges often ended in failure since Shamil's associates had developed better defensive techniques, just as the Russians were developing better offensive ones. An inconstant guest of Vorontsov's field commanders, Hadji Murat attempted to escape back to Shamil's side and was killed by a Russian patrol in 1852.

Although this shift in strategy would only begin to show results after Vorontsov had left office, his one undeniable military success was in preventing Shamil's forces from gaining their own vital strategic objective: the expansion of the war from the northeastern Caucasus to the northwest. Despite a concerted effort beginning in the late 1840s, Shamil never managed to extend his power westward into Kabarda and Circassia from his bases of support in Dagestan and Chechnya. Had he managed to do so, he would have created a vast front between the Caspian and Black seas and presented the Russians with a single wall of resistance, fueled by the martial traditions of the highlands and infused with the language of Muslim revival. It was to remain the imam's unfulfilled dream and the viceroy's unrealized nightmare.

Vorontsov retired from office in the spring of 1854. The immediate reason for his departure was that he had received permission to travel abroad for medical treatment. At this point the viceroy, then in his early seventies, was exhausted from his decade-long conflict with Shamil, but he must also have reckoned that he now had little chance of defeating the imam, given the preoccupation of the imperial court with larger affairs of state. The previous autumn the empire had embarked on what would become a costly and unsuccessful conflict with the Ottomans and their European backers.

Faced with a brewing conflict over the holy places in Jerusalem, Tsar Nicholas I ordered an attack against the Ottoman fleet, which was lying in its winter quarters in Sinop, on the southern coast of the Black Sea. The strike decimated the fleet and brought the two empires into full-scale conflict, the beginning of what would come to be known as the Crimean War. By the spring of 1854 Britain, France, and Sardinia had joined the Ottomans and launched their own assaults on the tsar's forces on both the Baltic and the Black seas, an effort to prop up the faltering Ottomans against what the Allied powers saw as an overly ambitious Russia. The Russian regular army and reserve forces were now being mobilized along the southern frontier, in the Caucasus and in Crimea, for an anticipated attack by land and sea. For Vorontsov the coming war was not only a major distraction from what he believed to be the empire's chief task in the south—taming the Caucasus highlands. It was also an uncomfortably intimate affair: Sidney Herbert, the British secretary of war at the time, was Vorontsov's nephew.

The Crimean War might have been expected to contribute significantly to Shamil's cause. Already in the summer of 1853, before the outbreak of hostilities, Shamil had dispatched a representative to Constantinople to engage in talks with the Ottoman authorities on coordinating action in the event of a war. The idea was to mount an attack on Russian positions in the Caucasus at the same time that the Allies were preparing to challenge the tsar in the Baltic and on the Crimean peninsula. In the late summer Shamil ordered raids along the borders with Kakheti and on the upper Alazani River. By the time war was declared that autumn, both the highlanders and the Ottomans were in remarkably good positions. Ottoman troops were concentrated in the border districts of Ardahan, Kars, and Batumi, and they far outnumbered Russian forces south of the Caucasus: seventy thousand versus roughly twenty thousand Russian regulars and Georgian militia.[25] Shortly after the declaration of war, the Ottomans launched a double land offensive along the eastern Black Sea coast and toward the old border stronghold of Akhaltsikhe. Yet these early moves failed to yield the lightning victory that Ottoman planners had expected. With each successive season of war, Ottoman troops suffered increasingly from disease, lack of supplies, and general exhaustion. Efforts to invade western Georgia were frustrated, as were attempts to coordinate action with Shamil's forces in Dagestan. By the summer of 1854, Shamil had effectively decided that cooperation with the Ottomans was fruitless.

Before his retirement, Vorontsov had been able to push the imam into a defensive position, seeking to hold his own in the highlands of western Dagestan. Shamil was now tiring. There were few large-scale expeditions, and periodic raiding against lowland settlements in Chechnya and Dagestan diminished his reputation among locals. Moreover, dissension in his officer corps had descended to grumbling among the rank and file. His efforts to win over the Circassians by encouraging an uprising of commoners against the Circassian aristocracy bred only disunity. The young, daring military commander of the 1830s and 1840s was now guarded and rightly wary of his associates.

The Allied powers attempted to secure highland assistance in the fight against Russia. British and French spies were dispatched to make contact with tribal leaders across the north Caucasus and ascertain the degree to which they might be encouraged in their war with Russia.[26] There was surely no more propitious time for the Circassian, Chechen, and Dagestani leaders to unite, given that British ships were now patrolling the Black Sea and the entire Russian southern fleet was hemmed in at Sevastopol. However, little came of these efforts. Highland leaders were by and large reluctant to join together against Russia, in part because of the old lack of unity among political actors, in part because of rational calculations of self-interest.

Furthermore, they had been disappointed by the Allies' overtures before. Since the 1830s British agents along the Black Sea coast had been promising aid, encouraging the view that London would look kindly on a Circassian uprising against Russia but providing little in terms of practical support. Shamil's Dagestani and Chechen fighters were also less than eager to look to the Allies. Britain and France were engaged in their own imperial battles against Muslim warriors in Afghanistan and Algeria, a fact that was known and resented in the Caucasus uplands. The feeling of distaste was often mutual. After Shamil's abduction of the Chavchavadze and Orbeliani princesses in 1854—a story that had filtered into western Europe, often in sensationalized form—even once sympathetic observers were disinclined to offer their wholehearted support.

Russian forces were crushed in the Crimean War. Russian fortifications along the Black Sea coast were dismantled and the size and gunnery of ships restricted. However, the Allied victory paradoxically did little to alter the strategic landscape. Britain, now facing the 1857 Mutiny in India, had concerns well beyond the Caucasus, and earlier advocates of the highland cause in London and Paris came to seem little more than cranks. After all, the highlanders had failed to strike hard against the Russians at the most opportune moment since the 1820s. With one war just ended, the Allied powers were loath to support a frontier conflict on the far edge of the Black Sea. Moreover, there were more Russian forces in the Caucasus theater than ever before—perhaps two hundred thousand men, dispatched to the south to meet the threat of a full-scale Ottoman invasion.[27] Now there was nothing to prevent a concerted Russian drive against Shamil in the northeast and against the Circassians in the northwest.

The task of launching a new campaign was entrusted to Prince Alexander Bariatinskii, who had become commander in chief and viceroy in early 1856. He immediately undertook a series of reforms that would prove decisive. The structure of the Caucasus army was altered, with power devolved to separate commands under talented field officers. New equipment was supplied to soldiers, especially rifled weapons, whose effectiveness had recently been proven in Crimea. Roads and bridges were improved and lines strengthened. The clear-cutting of forests was renewed with vigor.

Over the course of 1858 and early 1859 Bariatinskii's successes were rapid. The Chechen lands were brought under control with relative ease, and even Shamil's new capital in Dagestan was encircled and taken with little bloodshed. The reason was due in part to the coordinated, multipronged attack that the Russians were now launching. Three separate armies, each under an operationally independent general, pushed deep into western Dagestan from different directions. Meanwhile, Shamil managed to escape with a small band of followers to the Dagestani village of Gunib, perched on a high plateau.

The collapse of Shamil's forces had been rapid. His flight to Gunib was as much a retreat from disgruntled highlanders, who now saw that the tide was turning, as from the advancing Russians. Bariatinskii's detachments encircled the redoubt and made the final assault in late summer 1859. The Russian army, now augmented by local fighters, met with fierce resistance, but in the end Shamil feared for the safety of his family, which had accompanied him in the retreat, and sent word to the Russian commander that he was prepared to capitulate. He rode out to meet Bariatinskii on his own horse, surrounded by a few dozen fighters. The general reportedly accepted his surrender while seated on a stone, which was later inscribed with his name and the date: August 25, 1859.

Whereas previous enemies of the empire had been imprisoned, killed, or exiled, Shamil became a national celebrity. After his surrender, he settled into a comfortable retirement in Kaluga, southeast of Moscow. "By the will of the Almighty, the Absolute Governor, I have fallen into the hands of the unbelievers," Shamil wrote to one of his sons in November 1859. "The great emperor...has settled me...in a tall, spacious house with carpets and all the necessities."[28] Over the dozen years of his captivity, he became something of a sideshow oddity, the once valiant Lion of Dagestan now surviving on a generous pension awarded by the tsar. He was introduced to the wonders of Russian civilization, traveling by railway to St. Petersburg, parading through the imperial capitals, and touring everything from paper mills to sugar factories. He was attended by two of his wives, three of his sons, four daughters, and their families. Shamil spent most of the remainder of his life in Kaluga before being allowed to make a final trip to the Muslim holy places. He died in 1871 while on pilgrimage and was buried in Medina.

Various fates awaited other members of his family. His son Jamaladin, who had been educated in the style of a young Russian nobleman while being held hostage by the tsar, had already been returned to Shamil's care in 1855 in exchange for the release of the two princesses whom he had abducted in a raid on eastern Georgia the previous year. Jamaladin died in the mountains soon after his return, unable to resign himself to his alienation from the Russian world he had known as a child. Another son, Magomet-Shefi, became a bureaucrat in the Russian imperial administration. A third son, Gazi-Mehmet, turned to the sultan and served as an Ottoman officer in the Russo-Turkish War of 1877–78. Of all his immediate descendants, only Said Shamil, one of the imam's grandsons, continued the struggle in the mountains, fighting for Dagestani independence during the Russian civil war.

Shortly after the beginning of his gilded captivity, Shamil was asked about the prospects for renewing the Caucasus struggle. He dismissed the idea. "The Caucasus," he said, "is now in Kaluga."[29] But that was only partially true. As Shamil was beginning his retirement as Kaluga's most celebrated resident, upland fighting was still raging. For the last five years of the Caucasus wars, the center of conflict was not mountainous Dagestan and Chechnya, where Shamil had been active for some three decades, but rather the hills, valleys, and beaches of Circassia.

"The Tribes That Remain"

The first reference to Circassians in English dates from 1555. Thereafter the term became the equivalent of the Russian *gortsy*, a blanket label for virtually any exotic Eurasian highlander, whether dark or fair, caftaned or trousered, noble or commoner. But the real Circassians— the native Adyga peoples of the northwestern Caucasus—proved to be a persistent problem for Russian officialdom. They attacked Russian forts along the Black Sea coast and raided settlements north of the

Kuban River. They repeatedly affirmed that their region had long been independent, not a part of the Ottoman Empire, and that the sultan therefore had no right to cede their territory to the tsar as he had done in 1829 under the terms of the Treaty of Adrianople.

The Circassians were both the first and last of the indigenous peoples of the Caucasus to be incorporated into the Russian Empire. The earliest formal contacts between Russia and Circassian communities date to the sixteenth century. The Circassian-speaking Kabardians of the northwest Caucasus lowlands were important allies of the Muscovites in their efforts to counter the depredations of the Crimean Tatars. Yet there were also those who consistently resisted Russian rule, continuing the fight even after the capitulation of Shamil.

Throughout the nineteenth century the Circassians were of considerable interest to strategists in western Europe. In the early part of the century the French worked to obtain preferential trading rights with them. Later the Circassian cause came to play a particular role in the overall strategy of Britain, Russia's main rival in the Near East. Just as the Afghans were meant to provide a brake on Russian expansion toward British possessions in India, so the Circassians represented a similar bulwark against a Russian push to the south, toward British interests in Persia. It was through the Circassians' place in the grand gambits of the "Great Game" that their reputation as noble freedom fighters first became cemented in the Western imagination. It is no exaggeration to say that for several decades in the middle of the nineteenth century "Circassia" became a household word in many parts of Europe and North America. Correspondents from major newspapers found their way to Circassia or gleaned information from foreign consuls and merchants in Trebizond and Constantinople. The "Circassian question," the political status of the northwestern highlands of the Caucasus, was debated in parliaments and gentlemen's clubs. For a time in the 1830s British spies crisscrossed the region, seeking to mold the disparate Circassian tribes into a unified military force. In fact, even the Circassian national flag—which bears a stars-and-arrows design that today can be found flying across the northwest Caucasus and among the ethnic Circassian diaspora—was the handiwork of David Urquhart, a querulous Scottish publicist who became the highlanders' chief intercessor in the West and took on their cause as his own.

These efforts came to little, however. The Circassians remained skeptical of the often lukewarm British assistance, and over time the plight of faraway highlanders gave way to more immediate foreign-policy concerns among European powers. Moreover, when the

Dagestanis and Circassians failed to band together and assist the Allies during the Crimean War, enthusiasm for their cause in Western capitals dissipated altogether. In a plaintive letter to Queen Victoria two Circassian leaders tried to explain the difficulties of coordinated action: "During the Crimean war, we were accused by the Allied Powers of want of sincerity, not having participated with them against our common foe," they wrote a few years after the war's end. "This is true, but it was not the fault of our nation, as it proceeded from want of union and energy between our leaders."[30] The conclusion of the war in Dagestan and Chechnya, followed by the end of the Crimean conflict, allowed Russian planners to turn their full attention to the continuing struggle against the Circassians. The new military offensive that ensued would mark the final chapter in the Caucasus wars of the nineteenth century and the beginning of a long history of Circassian exile.

From the earliest days of Russian movement into the Caucasus, the rearrangement of populations was an essential part of the empire's political and military strategy. The burning of crops and destruction of villages, on their own, were imperfect methods of ensuring obedience. Crops could be replanted and houses rebuilt. After any particular campaign season, Russian troops might return to a previously pacified area to find villagers once again providing assistance to the native resistance. In time Russian commanders came to understand that the complete dislocation of populations could ensure that communities conquered during one season did not become rebels during the next. The result was the frequent and substantial alteration of the demographic landscape of both the north and south Caucasus over the course of the nineteenth century.

In a policy memorandum of 1857 Dmitrii Miliutin, chief of staff to Bariatinskii, summarized the new thinking on dealing with the northwestern highlanders. The idea, Miliutin claimed, was not to clear the highlands and coastal areas of Circassians so that these regions could be settled by productive farmers, as had happened in other parts of the empire's periphery. Rather, eliminating the Circassians was to be an end in itself—to cleanse the land of hostile elements. Tsar Alexander II formally approved the resettlement plan, with the goal of moving Circassians out of the Caucasus and into the lowlands along the Kuban River. Miliutin, who would eventually become minister of war, was to see his plans realized by the early 1860s.[31]

In a series of sweeping military campaigns lasting from 1860 to 1864—overseen by Miliutin in St. Petersburg, Bariatinskii in Tiflis, and Nikolai Evdokimov, commander of the right flank, in the highlands—the northwest Caucasus and the Black Sea coast were virtually emptied of Muslim villagers. Columns of the displaced were marched either to the Kuban plains or toward the coast for transport to the Ottoman Empire, which had earlier made provisions for resettling Muslim co-religionists. (Tens of thousands of Tatars had been removed from Crimea to the Ottoman Balkans and Anatolia following the Crimean War.) One after another, entire Circassian tribal groups were dispersed, resettled, or killed en masse.[32]

As Russian forces moved farther and farther into the northwest Caucasus uplands, lists of groups targeted for expulsion were drawn up and orders given to move them out of their villages and down to the coast. Russian detachments would march up through river valleys on the north slope, cresting the peaks and then pushing people toward the Black Sea on the other side. Russian diplomats repeatedly assured their European colleagues that the expulsions were not meant to be bloody, and that removing the highlanders was the only way to extinguish banditry and organized rebellion.[33] "The war in the Caucasus will not be completely terminated until our soldiers have crossed all the mountain ranges and have expelled the last inhabitants," a correspondent for the *Journal de St. Pétersbourg* wrote, "but it is to be hoped, at least, that we will no longer encounter stubborn resistance anywhere and that, because of their numerical weakness, the tribes that remain in the highland gorges will no longer offer us the least bit of danger."[34]

The scale of the emigration and the suffering experienced by refugees on the coast seem to have taken the Russians by surprise. Circassians arrived not only with their families and their possessions but also with slaves, livestock, and other people and goods. Few provisions had been made for housing them or for safely transporting them either to the Kuban River or, if they desired, to Ottoman ports. It was not until 1862 that a special state commission was established and funding appropriated to organize transport across the sea.[35] While the Russians had long been acquainted with many of the largest and most powerful tribal groupings in the western Caucasus, the final campaign revealed the existence of additional communities about whom the Russians knew little. In one instance, a secretary in the Russian foreign ministry informed Lord Napier, the British ambassador, that a previously unknown tribe had been discovered in the mountains. They, too, were scheduled for expulsion.[36]

The mass exodus of the early 1860s was preceded by a smaller emigration of war refugees throughout the late 1850s and followed by a series of further expulsions as late as 1867, when the Muslims of

Abkhazia were at last compelled to leave. Additional refugees flooded out of the empire during the Russo-Turkish War of 1877–78. The total number of people who left the highlands is thus difficult to determine. Contemporary Russian figures claimed that, out of an estimated 505,000 mountaineers in the northwest Caucasus, between 400,000 and 480,000 left in the early 1860s. Other estimates put the aggregate figure at between 300,000 and 500,000, most of them in the period from 1862 to 1866. Besides those who immigrated to Turkey, there were also countless numbers who were resettled in the lowlands, so that the real number of those displaced by the last phase of the Caucasus conquest is probably unknowable. Overall, however, the number of those who left the Caucasus, both highlander and lowlander, from the time of the capture of Shamil until the end of the Russo-Turkish War of 1877–78 may be on the order of two million people, many of whom perished at some point along their journey northward to the plains or across the Black Sea to the Ottoman Empire.[37]

The picture is clearer at a higher resolution: in terms of the numbers of individuals and families scrutinized by Russian, Ottoman, and British officials resident in the ports of embarkation or arrival. In December 1863 there were already 7,000 immigrants in Trebizond, with 3,000 more arriving in only three days in February 1864. By May there were 25,000 camped around Trebizond and another 40,000 at Samsun. As many as 150 were dying each day from disease and starvation. In September 4,000 people arrived in Smyrna, with 2,346 arriving in Cyprus in November, all in similarly deplorable conditions. A sense of the scale of death and disease can be gained from the number of people who passed through the Bosphorus—and could therefore be counted by health inspectors—on their way to resettlement in western Anatolia and the Balkans. In the first nine months of 1864 alone there were just over 74,000.[38] To that number, of course, must be added the many who were shipped directly to western Black Sea ports, such as Varna, or were dispersed overland from Trebizond.

Conditions during the passage were inhuman. Refugees—as many as 1,800 per ship—were squeezed onto sailing vessels provided by the Ottomans or by the Russian government.[39] Livestock and household goods crowded the decks. Those who could not secure a place on a larger ship took to the sea in small boats, which often foundered during the Black Sea's frequent storms. Even on the more stable vessels, overcrowding led to dehydration and produced outbreaks of disease. The bodies of the dead were thrown overboard and washed up on the beaches along the entire eastern stretch of the Black Sea. These "floating graveyards," as contemporary observers called them, would sail into Ottoman ports with only a remnant of their original human cargo alive. Once the refugees arrived in the Ottoman lands, there were frequently too few provisions for them. Food, clothing, fuel, and medicine were scarce. Public health was threatened as dead bodies were carelessly buried or abandoned, sometimes even finding their way into freshwater reservoirs in the port cities. "Circassia is gone," concluded a foreign diplomat in a report from May 1864. "What yet remains to save is the Circassians."[40]

By the middle of the 1860s, the traditional lands of the Abazakh, Shapsug, Ubykh, and other Circassian tribal groups had been abandoned. As a local saying had it, even a woman could now travel easily between the harbor cities of Sujuk Kale and Anapa since she could be assured of never meeting a single person on the way.[41] A decade prior to the expulsions, there were perhaps 145,000 people living in the Abkhaz lands and another 315,000 Circassians belonging to various tribes, plus tens of thousands of other coastal and highland peoples.[42] Yet at the time of the first general imperial census in 1897, there were only about 60,000 people living on the coasts of Circassia, and of those only 15,000 had been born there.[43] Among these were the last remnants of the populations now exiled across the sea, as well as the offspring of the first generation of Russian settlers who had been sent to take their place. "In the mountains of the Kuban district one can now find bears and wolves," wrote one observer, "but no highlanders."[44]

The forced movement of Circassians had a profound effect on the nature of intercommunal relations in the Ottoman Empire. Part of the Ottoman resettlement strategy was to place the Circassians in areas where either Muslim or Turkic populations were low—the mirror image, in fact, of the policy pursued by the Russians. Circassian families were sent to Syria, the Balkans, and eastern Anatolia and resettled amid restive communities of Arabs, Slavs, Kurds, and Armenians. These new arrivals were looked upon by locals as an invading force, foreigners favored by the imperial government who were now demanding their share of land, food, and other scarce resources.

Circassian migrants were sometimes farmed out to local families, with the Ottoman government requiring every four households to provide food and lodging for one batch of Circassians.[45] Resentment on both sides—local Muslims and Christians for having extra mouths to feed, Circassians for being foisted on disgruntled locals—was inevitable. Social problems also began to emerge as new migrants competed with locals for grazing lands. Traditional raiding practices, which had been an accepted component of inter-clan feuding in the high-lands, were now carried out in a new environment where raiding was considered little more than thievery. Slavery was another sensitive issue. The Ottoman government, like the Russian, had previously attempted to squelch the slave trade with the Caucasus, but the influx of Circassian migrants—among whom slave ownership was a long-established social norm—seems to have spurred the trade once again.[46]

These tensions led to conflict. Within a few years of the mass migration, the very word "Circassian" had become a byword for "highwayman" in much of Anatolia and the Balkans. There were undoubtedly successful examples of assimilation and intermarriage between Circassians and local Muslims, but by and large the Circassians remained a foreign presence for more than a generation. The problems created by the forced migration only added to the disorder in southeastern Europe and eastern Anatolia in the 1890s and during the First World War, when the combination of intercommunal ill-feeling, foreign invasions, and state-organized genocide decimated the regions' local populations, both Muslim and Christian. As had happened repeatedly in Caucasus history, the victims in one era became the perpetrators in another.

The Circassians were eventually subsumed within the general category of "Muslim" in the late Ottoman Empire, thereafter becoming simply "Turks" with the establishment of the modern Turkish Republic. Some sense of identity has remained alive. In parts of the Arab world Circassians are still recognized as a distinct social group, and there are plenty of Turks today who claim Abaza, Shapsug, or another tribal designation as part of their heritage—identities left over from the days when shiploads of refugees docked at Trebizond and Samsun and offloaded their desperate human cargo. Real cultural affinities have weakened, however. Tevfik Esenç, the only known native speaker of Ubykh, was celebrated by the small coterie of Caucasus linguists and activist Circassian intellectuals. When he died in Istanbul in 1992, with him went one of the last living links to the exiled peoples of the northwest Caucasus and the Black Sea coast. But the idea of Circassia—if not its reality—would live on, not only among the diaspora now scattered across the Middle East but also in the romantic visions of generations of writers, travelers, sideshow conmen, and anyone else seeking to profit from the exotic Orient. Even after the surrender of Shamil and the depopulation of the northwestern Caucasus, the Circassians would remain an integral part of the imaginary borderlands of the Russian south.

THREE

The Imaginary Caucasus

*The Alps we already knew, and the Pyrenees, but this was finer than anything we had
ever seen or even imagined in our wildest dreams! This was the Caucasus. . . . How I
wished I had brought with me my copy of Aeschylus!*

Alexandre Dumas père *(1858)*

*I have cultivated in myself a sixth sense, an "Ararat" sense: the sense
of attraction to a mountain.*

Osip Mandelstam (1930)

B Y 1864 THE CAUCASUS WARS had come to an end. There were
still periodic uprisings among one or another mountain people,
and as the century wore on, even the Georgians would begin to
question the cost that their language and national culture had borne in
joining the empire. But in the second half of the nineteenth century the
Caucasus was—as it had never really been previously—a Russian space.
Cities such as Tiflis were becoming nodes in an expanding imperial
administration. Even once sleepy ports such as Baku and Batumi were
reinvigorated by the discovery of oil and the advent of modern modes
of transportation, from steamships to railroads.

The Caucasus had been absorbed not only into the administrative structures of the multinational and multiconfessional Russian state, but also into the imperial mind-set of average Russians. "Kavkaz!" exclaimed Vasilii Potto in the opening lines of his influential popular history of the Caucasus wars, published in the 1880s. "What Russian heart does not thrill to that name, bound by bloody bonds to the historical and intellectual life of our fatherland?"[1] In art, music, literature, cuisine, and popular culture Russians were gradually coming to see themselves as tied, both culturally and emotionally, to the Caucasus. They read adventure stories about the Murids and attended public spectacles reenacting the capture of Shamil. They spent their holidays in the spa resorts of the north and enjoyed the salubrious air of the Black Sea coast. They conversed over glasses of fine Georgian wine and cheered at the sight of uniformed highland regiments during official parades. Imagining the Caucasus as a place both far away yet intimately familiar would soon extend beyond the boundaries of the empire to the drawing rooms, museums, and circus midways of western Europe and America. This trend began with the process of categorizing the many treasures, both human and material, that the Caucasus was believed to hold.

Inventing the Highlander

Classifying people—whether based on race, language, culture, or any other criterion—is always more complicated than it might seem. Words signify different things in different contexts. The English term "Caucasian," for example, today denotes a racial category developed by an eighteenth-century German anatomist to identify the allegedly primordial form of humankind, with light skin and round eyes. Yet the equivalent term in Russian (*kavkazets*) refers to a person having family ties to the Caucasus, with perhaps dark hair and olive skin. Virtually any other identification that might have currency today—Georgian, Chechen, Muslim, Sufi—was imbued with different meanings in the past. The collective categories that would eventually come to be used for ethnic groups, nationalities, and religions in the Caucasus were not present, fully formed, when the Russians arrived. They were products of the imperial system itself—negotiated, reworked, and in some cases wholly invented as part of the process of imperial absorption and administration. In the twentieth century Soviet demographers, ethnographers, census takers, and party officials devised further ways of delineating and categorizing people, literally calling them into being or obliterating them with the stroke of a pen.

From their earliest encounters with the Caucasus, Russian military planners and administrators began to devise their own ad hoc ways of classifying the people they met. What usually mattered most were collective labels that circumscribed political and economic power. Russian generals were concerned with who could exert effective control over people and places and who could be called upon to counter the plundering expeditions of the Crimean Tatars or, in extremis, repel a concerted Ottoman invasion during the next Russo-Turkish war. For those groups not under the clear purview of one or another of the lowland or mid-altitude princes, khans, or sultans, the term was usually simply *gortsy*. Beyond that, Russian military and administrative elites knew little more.

This situation began to change under Catherine the Great, who commissioned several expeditions to help her and her court better understand the range of new acquisitions on the southern frontier. When Catherine ascended the throne in 1762, Russia's dominions stretched nearly to the northern shores of the Black Sea and touched the wall of the north Caucasus. Beyond lay a mosaic of kingdoms, khanates, and upland free communities, sometimes paying nominal obeisance to the Ottomans or Persians. In 1768 Catherine ordered the outfitting of five expeditions under the aegis of the St. Petersburg Academy of Sciences. The expeditions coincided with the first Russo-Turkish War (1768–74) of her reign. With even more former Ottoman territory under her control at the war's conclusion, the leaders of the various scientific parties could report back that they had explored the vast reaches of the newly acquired lands and found them to be unbelievably rich in minerals, wildlife, and people. The effort was coordinated by Peter Simon Pallas, the greatest of naturalist-travelers in Catherine's Russia, who also served as general editor of the scientific works published as a result of the expeditions' research. In the Caucasus the task of exploration fell mainly to Johann Anton Güldenstädt, a Baltic German with a medical background, who found himself at ease in the company of the many other German academics, some Russian-born, others imported, then in Catherine's service. It is to Güldenstädt that Russians' most deeply held beliefs about the Caucasus—indeed, many of the things that the peoples of the Caucasus believe about themselves—owe their origins.

Güldenstädt was only twenty-three when he left St. Petersburg in the summer of 1768, arriving via the Volga River in Astrakhan, on the Caspian Sea, the following winter. The work of exploring this part of the imperial borderlands was divided between Güldenstädt and Samuel Gmelin, another German academic, who was assigned the Caspian coast. Güldenstädt was given regions farther to the west, specifically Georgia and the northwest Caucasus. After passing several months preparing for the trek into the mountains, Güldenstädt left Astrakhan and headed for Kizliar, the Russian fort on the delta of the Terek River, which became his base of operations.

Güldenstädt moved slowly, recording his impressions, noting down the most propitious travel routes, the size and type of settlements, and the natural endowments of the lands he traversed. His traveling companions—a group of students and assistants, plus an artist to make sketches—collected numerous specimens and artifacts for shipment back to the academy. Güldenstädt also made contact with important political figures (another part of his brief), including the leaders of the Georgian states, Erekle II of Kartli-Kakheti and Solomon I of Imereti. He traveled widely in the north Caucasus, although he never managed to penetrate Dagestan in the northeast, which had been assigned to Gmelin. He returned to St. Petersburg in the spring of 1775 after having passed the better part of seven years on the road.

Güldenstädt spent the next several years collating his notes and trying to bring some order to the treasure trove of information that he and his associates had dragged back to the imperial capital, including drawings, inscriptions, plants, animal carcasses, ancient coins, and virtually anything else that could shed light on the history and culture of the Caucasus. However, he died prematurely in 1781, the victim of an infectious fever then raging in the city. The task of publishing his material was taken up by his boss, Peter Simon Pallas, who devoted additional years to sifting through Güldenstädt's notebooks.

The product of all this effort was a two-volume work entitled *Travels in Russia and the Caucasus Mountains*, which was published in German in 1787 and 1791.[2] It had taken just over two decades, from the beginning of the Güldenstädt-Gmelin expedition until the publication of the first volume. By the time the second volume appeared, Catherine was still on the throne, but Russian power now extended across the entire northern coast of the Black Sea. The empire could make a reasonable claim to significant portions of the eastern coast as well, and eastern Georgia was now a Russian protectorate. Much of the territory that Güldenstädt had explored was closer than ever to becoming a real component of the empire.

The unassuming title of Güldenstädt's book belied its contents. Thanks to this posthumously published account, the author became the leading authority for every significant academic, writer, and traveler in the Caucasus from the late eighteenth century onward. His catalogue of the peoples of the Caucasus served as the basic inventory for generations to come. He provided a linguistic classification of the major ethnic groups and compiled lists of words in languages ranging from Georgian to Chechen to Lezgin. It is to Güldenstädt that we owe the very names of most of the territories in the north Caucasus, including Kabarda, Ossetia, Ingushetia, Chechnya, and Dagestan. Although he was not the first to use some of these terms, no one before had attempted to fix the boundaries of these lands and to insist that geographical labels be used with greater precision. Well into the nineteenth century Russians frequently republished excerpts from Güldenstädt's work to be used as primers for administrative personnel newly assigned to the Caucasus service.[3]

The *Travels* was a product of its period, displaying the same Enlightenment urge to taxonomize that motivated other scholars of the day. Güldenstädt makes a fetish of scientific objectivity, categorizing with no explanation of why his categories accord with reality. He goes into minute detail in some areas yet seems satisfied with cursory generalizations in others. Despite his insistence on accuracy of language, he is maddeningly inconsistent with respect to terminology and spelling. On balance, Güldentstädt was more interested in collecting zoological and botanical specimens, and in breaking down the region into its component geographical parts, than in describing the mores of the native peoples by whom he was surrounded.

Anyone associated with the production of Güldentstädt's book must surely have known all this—and probably been a little embarrassed by it. The editor, Pallas, was a careful scholar who in the 1790s produced his own studies of Russia's southwestern frontier, Crimea, and the Black Sea littoral. But times were hard. Gmelin, the other academician sent to the Caucasus, had been abducted and killed by Dagestanis in the summer of 1774. With Güldenstädt now gone as well, one can imagine Pallas and his associates poring over the expedition's archive in the grand chambers of the Academy of Sciences, desperately trying to make sense of a dead man's notes, drafts, and drawings, before finally throwing up their hands and sending the mess off to the printer.

Within only a few years of the publication of the second volume, the academy decided to try to do a better job of things. The administrative board ordered the outfitting of a new expedition, to be headed by yet another German named Julius von Klaproth. Klaproth was born in Berlin in 1783, the son of a noted chemist and university professor. Early in his career he became widely known for his innovative studies in Asian linguistics and ethnology, and this fame earned him an invitation to decamp to St. Petersburg and take up a post in the imperial academy. When the institution finally got around to commissioning a supplement to Güldenstädt's volumes, Klaproth was the natural choice: young, energetic, and already a distinguished student of Asian cultures rather than a doctor-cum-traveler like Güldenstädt. There had been other scientific expeditions to the Caucasus since the 1790s, but the academy felt that their conclusions did little to fill the gaps left by Güldenstädt.

The instructions delivered to Klaproth in 1807 were clear concerning the purpose of the new expedition. "What is particularly expected of Mr. de Klaproth is this, to make us acquainted with the country."[4] He was to describe each region in detail, being sure to note down anything that might be useful for the future development of the territory. He was to give an assessment of which peoples were capable of being well governed by the Russian emperor and which, for reasons of their unpolished cultures or their martial sensibilities, were best left outside the purview of St. Petersburg. Klaproth was to make the acquaintance of the principal person in each district—the local headman, khan or chieftain—which would not only facilitate his travels but also provide essential intelligence to the emperor. "It is certain that many calamities have happened in Russia in consequence of the want of information respecting distant provinces," wrote the academy, "so that he who furnishes correct notions concerning them renders an essential service to the state."[5]

The academy was highly specific about the kinds of things on which Klaproth was expected to report. Are there traditions respecting the existence of Amazons? Who are the likely descendants of the Scythians, the ancient steppe dwellers described by Herodotus? Where are the passes in the mountains? What is to be found in the districts south of the highlands, especially along the Black Sea? What is the word for "tribe" in the Lezgin dialects? Are the women of the Caucasus as beautiful as is often claimed? As one reads through the academy's instructions to Klaproth, it is shocking to realize how little Russian academicians—the most learned men of their day—knew about a territory where their empire would shortly embark on a series of long and costly wars of conquest.

After receiving his charge, Klaproth left Moscow in the autumn of 1807. By November he had reached the steppe land beyond the Don River and the Russian fort at Mozdok. From there he took the well-established route through Kabarda to Vladikavkaz and picked up the Georgian Military Highway for the overland trek to Tiflis. He returned to St. Petersburg early in 1809 and set about preparing the results of his research for publication.

Like the work of Güldenstädt, Klaproth's *Travels in the Caucasus and Georgia*, which was published in German between 1812 and 1814, became an essential text.[6] Unlike his predecessor's writings, however, Klaproth's book was soon translated into English and French, which further enhanced its reputation as the basic guide for travelers. The author's findings cemented many of the ideas that would inform popular opinion about the Caucasus for the balance of the nineteenth century. He saw the Circassians as inherently thievish, erroneously attributing even their name to a Turkic word meaning "highwayman." He felt that the Muslims of the Caucasus were such in name only and that some could profitably be converted—or reconverted, since he saw Islam as a foreign import—to Christianity. He extolled the beauty of the women, particularly the Circassians and the Lezgins. He reinforced the view that Caucasus peoples were wildly extravagant in their hospitality but cruel to those who did not fall within the category of protected guest. The Ingush, for example, represented the typical Caucasus mixture of refined and retrograde: "In the observance of the rights of hospitality, in the possession of their property in common, in the equitable division of what fortune or accident throws in their way, they lose the appearance of savage life, and seem actuated by more humane sentiments than we rapacious Europeans who style ourselves polished and civilized. . . . Freedom, wildness, and gravity, are expressed in their looks."[7] This picture would become standard fare in Russian and European writing down to the present day, an image born of ethnographic conjecture, gross generalization, and a certain romance about the serenity and savagery of mountain dwellers. To his great disappointment, however, Klaproth confessed that he had been unable to verify the existence of Amazons.

Klaproth believed that the mountains had taught him something. If he left St. Petersburg as a scholar, he returned as a strategist, interested less in obscure questions of ethnic origin and more in how best to deal with restive highlanders jealous of Russian encroachments. Klaproth was one of the first publicly to propose a comprehensive plan for dealing with the problem of raids across the lines: build more forts; remain on good terms with native elites; prevent unregulated trade between Cossacks and highlanders (which tended to break down the boundaries between servants of the emperor and those inimical to him); launch punitive strikes when necessary; and enforce a system of dependence on the empire by controlling the trade in salt to the mountaineers. In various forms, these were precisely the policies that would define Russian engagement with the peoples of the Caucasus for decades to come.

—◆—◆—

Güldenstädt and Klaproth had a great deal in common. Both were part of the same group of talented Germans who contributed to Russian cultural achievements in the eighteenth and early nineteenth centuries. Both were working on imperial commissions. Both aimed to produce an objective, comprehensive account of Russia's southern frontier, a land of growing strategic concern to Catherine and her successors.

Both were also academics. Their goal was to communicate with their learned colleagues, not necessarily to disseminate information to a wider reading public, which in any case did not really come into existence in Russia until much later in the nineteenth century. Today the names of Güldenstädt and Klaproth remain obscure outside scholarly circles, even if their ideas about the Caucasus form the bedrock of popular understandings of the region. Yet they had little to do with their own success. Güldenstädt's complete text was not translated into Russian until 2002.[8] Klaproth's book has never been fully translated. Their lasting influence is due to the work of yet another author, an obsessive enthusiast named Semyon Mikhailovich Bronevskii.

Bronevskii was the author of a book with the straightforward title *The Latest Geographical and Historical Information on the Caucasus*, published in Moscow in 1823.[9] He listed himself not as the author of the work but as its "compiler and elaborator," which is precisely what he was. His great contribution was not to offer something genuinely original but rather to take the material contained in the works of Güldenstädt, Klaproth, and other authors, check it against the reports and studies that had accumulated over the previous three decades, and then write his own overview. What emerged was a book that represented the most comprehensive assessment of the geography, flora, fauna, and cultures of the Caucasus that Russia had thus far produced.

Bronevskii prefaced his book with an explanation of its rationale. The aim was to provide people who wished to travel to the Caucasus with an accessible guide to what was to be found there, especially since "the interior . . . has remained almost as little known as the interior of Africa." Learned books had been published in foreign languages, and scholars had been kept busy cataloging the plants, animals, and people of the mountains and plains—often in exhaustive detail. Little of this had filtered down beyond the rarefied heights of the Russian academy, however. "It is at last time," Bronevskii wrote somewhat defensively, "to bring science out of the hothouse and into the open air, and to transplant it in Russian soil."[10]

Bronevskii was in effect saying that the time had come for the study of the Caucasus, like the region itself, to be made fully a part of Russian consciousness, directly rather than through the medium of learned but non-Russian academics. Bronevskii then proceeded to provide, in readable Russian, a remarkable array of facts, figures, and opinions on every conceivable aspect of the Caucasus, all in two volumes totaling more than eight hundred pages. His themes included geography, history, religion, language, morals and habits, traditional governance and folk justice, trade, demography, natural history, the vexed question of slavery and the sale of captives (to which he devoted a substantial section), as well as detailed descriptions of all the major regions and peoples, from Abkhazia and Circassia in the west to the khanates of the east.

Nothing quite like this had ever been produced, even by those scholars who enjoyed the imprimatur of the imperial academy. Bronevskii's achievement is even more remarkable when one considers the fact that he was no more than a dedicated amateur, working quietly on his own over the course of several decades. He was born in 1763 into the provincial Russian nobility and held a succession of rather minor administrative posts before finally securing a position on the military staff in Tiflis. This allowed him to experience at first hand a region that had long fascinated him and to spend several years traveling and collecting materials. From there he ascended to the directorship of the Asiatic Department of the Russian Ministry of Foreign Affairs, which provided still further access to information and intelligence. He finished out his government career in Crimea, as mayor of the coastal city of Feodosiia, where he died in 1830. All this was a far cry from the backgrounds and careers of the illustrious German professors who preceded him as interpreters of the Caucasus.

We know that Güldenstädt and Klaproth had a major influence on later conceptions of the Caucasus simply because their views continued to pop up in Russian and foreign travel accounts, ethnographies, and other works throughout the nineteenth century. They are still routinely quoted by Russian scholars. However, their ideas would never have had such staying power had it not been for the person who translated them—literally and figuratively—for a wider audience. If one looks carefully through the most important Russian and western European writing on the Caucasus, including works of literature, Bronevskii is there lurking between the lines. Some authors suggest him as a source for readers who wish to explore the region on their own, while others mention him in their correspondence and occasional writings as having influenced their thinking.

There is yet another piece of evidence attesting to Bronevskii's influence, and it is contained in *The Latest Information* itself. At the back of his text Bronevskii provided a list of all the people who paid for its publication by taking out subscriptions to cover the cost of printing. The list includes over two hundred individuals and institutions, including the most respected families in St. Petersburg, Moscow, Kiev, and other cities and towns—the Volkonskiis, the Dolgorukovs, the Golitsyns—as well as schools and learned societies. That was the meaning of Bronevskii's point about bringing the sciences out of the "hothouse" and transplanting them in Russian soil. What had largely remained hidden in the work of academicians was at last accessible to a broader public. "Semyon Bronevskii's *Latest Information on the Caucasus*," wrote the poet and novelist Alexander Bestuzhev-Marlinsky in a review, "merits both the attention of Europeans as well as the special gratitude of the Russians."[11]

Tellingly, almost all of the subscribers to Bronevskii's book lived outside the Caucasus. This was a book by a Russian, in Russian, for Russians—for the new generation of readers who still thought of the Caucasus as exotic and far removed, but as a land that was now appealing, within reach, and, most important, almost theirs. The author's timing could not have been better. The exploits of Ermolov were already well known among the party-going class in St. Petersburg and Moscow. A new cohort of young, well-bred men, frustrated by the authoritarian backwardness of their own society and looking longingly toward the primordial freedom of the mountains, was coming of age. By the early 1820s the basic building blocks of Russia's romantic vision of the Caucasus were in place: the exploits of a brave general against wild frontiersmen; a readable and carefully researched compendium of the riches to be found there; and even a popular poem—Pushkin's "Captive of the Caucasus," published a year before Bronevskii's work—that painted a vivid picture of the unruly south. Russia was finally prepared to step into the mountains.

Prisoners, Superfluous Men, and Mopingers

If Bronevskii was the unsung popularizer of the real Caucasus, Pushkin was its most celebrated literary creator. Earlier writers had treated the region in works of fiction and travel, albeit obliquely. But it was through Pushkin that the storybook image of the Russian Caucasus was forever sealed: a land of pristine beauty and noble savagery, where valiant heroes could test their mettle against obstacles both natural and man-made. Pushkin was to the Caucasus what Byron was to the Near East and James Fenimore Cooper to the American frontier—the literary pioneer to whom every later writer of poetry and prose owed some artistic debt.

Born in 1799, Pushkin was a descendant on his mother's side of Avram Ganibal, an African of perhaps Abyssinian or Chadian origin, who was raised from childhood in the court of Peter the Great. On his father's side Pushkin was descended from the minor Russian nobility. That background allowed him to gain admission to the imperial lycée, which had been established to train a cadre of civil servants based on European standards. After graduating Pushkin took up his expected post as a secretary in the Ministry of Foreign Affairs. While still in school he had begun to distinguish himself as a poet, and as a fashionably eccentric young man in cosmopolitan St. Petersburg, he burnished his reputation with the publication of *Ruslan and Liudmila* (1820), an epic romance set in the days of Kievan Rus'. Pushkin's other works—odes to liberty and satirical barbs aimed at members of St. Petersburg society, including those who had the ear of powerful ministers and of Tsar Alexander I—attracted the attention of imperial authorities. The tsar came close to ordering the poet exiled to Siberia but was eventually persuaded that a transfer to the staff of a provincial official in New Russia would allow him to have all the liberty he could stomach on the treeless steppe.

This was to be the first of only two direct experiences with the Caucasus: two months spent in the spa town of Piatigorsk in the summer of 1820, and an extended trip lasting several weeks down the Georgian Military Highway and on to eastern Anatolia in 1829. The object of Pushkin's first journey south was to report to his new assignment in the state institution in charge of supervising the colonization of the New Russian prairie, based in Ekaterinoslav (modern Dnepropetrovsk, Ukraine). Not long after his arrival in the town, Pushkin met up with an old friend from his days at the lycée, whose father was the formidable general Nikolai Nikolaevich Raevskii, one of the heroes of the Napoleonic Wars. The Raevskii family was planning to take the waters in the springs of Piatigorsk, located in a hilly region rising from the north Caucasus plains. Pushkin, who had contracted a chill after bathing in the Dnepr River, was invited to join them. His supervising officer gave him leave to do so, and the entire entourage set off for the Caucasus.

The warm, sulfurous springs around Piatigorsk had been known since antiquity, but it was only in the late eighteenth century that they began to be developed as a destination, with their curative powers extolled by Russian and foreign visitors. Piatigorsk itself was merely a collection of tents and huts on a tributary of the Kuma River, in what is now the Stavropol region of Russia. To call it part of the Caucasus is also stretching things a bit. Several small mountains loom overhead, extinct volcanoes that jut up from the undulating prairie—hence the Russian name Piatigorsk and its Tatar equivalent Beshtau (lit. "five peaks"). The main chain of the Caucasus is quite distant. Piatigorsk was always well north of the lines and was in an area populated by Cossacks and friendly villagers, none of whom presented any danger to travelers.

Still, it was close enough to make an impression on the young poet. "I traveled in sight of the hostile lands of the free mountain peoples," Pushkin wrote to his younger brother, Lev, the autumn after his visit. "Around us rode sixty Cossacks, behind us was drawn a loaded cannon, its match lit. Although the Circassians nowadays are relatively peaceful, one cannot rely on them; in the hope of a large ransom they are ready to fall upon a well-known Russian general.... You will understand how pleasing this shadow of danger is to the fanciful imagination."[12] Pushkin's vision, refracted through his own fanciful imagination, was the product of his gazing at the faraway mountains, hearing the stories of Cossacks and former prisoners in the taverns of Piatigorsk, and mixing it all with a fair amount of Byron, whose works he had read in English during his rustication in the southern provinces. Bronevskii may also have had an indirect influence: Pushkin spent two days at Bronevskii's Crimean dacha that same summer and later reportedly kept a copy of *The Latest Information* in his library.[13]

All this, however, is immaterial. The real importance of Pushkin is not whether his views of the Caucasus accorded with reality, but the simple fact that generations of Russian readers were convinced that they did. In his writings Pushkin sought to persuade his audience that his fiction was grounded in truth. His essential aesthetic was the literary equivalent of *cinéma vérité*, an unabashedly romantic subject rendered with gritty realism. The most important example is his poem "Captive of the Caucasus," which he wrote in the months following his excursion to Piatigorsk. It was first published in 1822.

The story line concerns a Russian man of good breeding who has become burdened by life in the more cultured parts of the empire. He determines to set out for the Caucasus frontier and seek adventure in the mountains. He is soon captured and taken to a remote upland village. At first frightened by the strange customs of the unwashed natives, he eventually comes to appreciate their unique appeal. He is charmed by the beauty of a young Circassian maiden, and in time she helps him to escape. However, when he confesses that he cannot return her love, she throws herself into a river. The poem ends with the maiden's tragic death, the ripples expanding as she sinks deeper and deeper beneath the moonlit waters. The Russian escapes to the Cossack line, the glint of the sentries' bayonets signaling his return to civilization and his true liberation.

"Captive of the Caucasus" was intended as more than a simple romance. Pushkin's earlier paeans to freedom now found an especially suitable vehicle in the boundless expanse of the mountains, the untamed wilderness, and the unbowed highlander. Pushkin was also concerned to provide as much *vérité* as possible. The poem has been described as "a Baedeker in verse," and that is no overstatement.[14] The work is filled with information on folk customs, foreign terms, and ethnography—all of which give it an almost scholarly timbre that seems out of keeping with the dark romance of the main narrative.

With no journalists covering the Caucasus wars for the Russian public, heavy censorship of information about what was happening on the Caucasus lines, and little in the way of firsthand battle memoirs yet available, Pushkin's fictional account played a role that was both entertaining and educational. The extended section of the poem in which Pushkin describes the culture of the Circassians was printed separately at least six times during the poet's lifetime—a putative primer on regional ethnography drawn from a work of poetic fiction.[15] The Caucasus was no longer a fanciful frontier but an exciting, dangerous, and real place, one that could be explored, penetrated, and understood by a Russian public only then discovering its own newly opened south. All of this, however, was something of a closed circle. Ideas that originated with Güldenstädt and Klaproth were interpreted and popularized by Bronevskii, who may have contributed something to Pushkin's vision, who in turn provided the most enduring literary image of the

Caucasus, the veracity of which any reader could confirm by consulting a copy of Bronevskii, which could then be buttressed by a quick perusal of a German edition of Güldenstädt or Klaproth.

———◆—◆———

There is much that any reader in the first quarter of the nineteenth century would have found of interest in Pushkin's captivity tale: the exoticism of the frontier; boredom as an impetus for adventure; the mysterious ways of the *gortsy;* the inherent tragedy of romantic love. Decades later soldiers sent to the Caucasus theater would have the poem in mind as they sat around a campfire in Circassia or bivouacked in the dark forests of Chechnya.[16] But the overarching theme of the poem must also have resonated at the time. Russia itself was a captive—to a war that showed no signs of ending and to a political and social system that increasingly seemed out of step with the dominant trends in other parts of Europe. Fleeing to the Caucasus was not merely a form of escape for Pushkin's hero. It was also a way of achieving freedom from the conventions of a hidebound imperial society and the despotism of an all-powerful emperor. Many would follow Pushkin's hero south, but unlike the poet himself they went all the way—into mountain villages, trussed up in gray woolen uniforms and dressaged in military columns, across snow-covered highland passes, and through dark defiles to carry out some retribution for a Circassian or Dagestani attack.

Pushkin never experienced the horrors of conflict. One of the few times he fired a gun was when he was also killed by one, during a duel in 1837. Even though he issued a clarion call to defend the empire on the brittle frontiers of Asia, the men who responded returned with a more nuanced view of what the wars of conquest had wrought. From the 1820s to the 1860s countless sons of aristocratic families, along with hordes of Russian peasants drafted into the army, participated in the campaigns to subdue the Murids in Dagestan and Chechnya in the east and the Circassians and Abkhaz in the west. Some published memoirs of their experiences. These contained a mix of bravado and patriotism but were tinged with a more realistic assessment of the difficulties of fighting formidable enemies in an extreme environment. Others turned to literature, using poetry and fiction as ways of conveying the meaning of war. The most influential member of this new generation of soldier-authors was Mikhail Lermontov.

Born into a military family in 1814, Lermontov spent his childhood on the family's country estate southeast of Moscow. He studied at a school for the children of the nobility and then briefly at university, before embarking on military training and taking up a billet as a junior officer in a regiment of hussars based near St. Petersburg. During this period Lermontov began to exercise his talents as a poet. His themes were essentially those of his generation of disaffected young men: the stultifying nature of tsarist rule; the pretentiousness of high society; the disappointment of quashed freedom. The seminal event for these aristocratic youths was the crushing of the Decembrist uprising of 1825. Scores of officers and thousands of average soldiers were banished to the Caucasus, the "southern Siberia," which became a holding pen for military men who had fallen afoul of the tsar and his camarilla.

But it was Pushkin who indirectly helped launch Lermontov's career. Lermontov's passionate poem "The Death of a Poet" blamed the "greedy, hungry pack, corrupters of the palace" for Pushkin's death at the hands of a fellow duelist, the "murderers of Freedom, Genius, Fame" who now wielded undue influence at court.[17] The poem earned Lermontov a form of internal exile to a dragoon regiment in Georgia. He was in the south for less than a year—in fact, he failed to report to his unit—but that brief experience marked his future work, since he interacted with older officers who had been banished to the Caucasus as sympathizers of the Decembrists. Lermontov was reassigned to St. Petersburg in 1838, where he launched his publishing career to considerable acclaim. However, when he fought an ill-advised duel with the son of the French ambassador in the winter of 1840, he was court-martialed and sent back to the Caucasus. This time his exile was less leisurely, for he now saw active fighting in Chechnya. This, too, was to be of short duration because Lermontov, like Pushkin, fell victim to a duelist's pistol in 1841. He died in Piatigorsk, at the foot of Mount Mashuk, the very place where Pushkin had begun his engagement with the Caucasus a little over two decades earlier.

Although Lermontov was only fifteen years Pushkin's junior, the generational difference was immense. Lermontov's cohort had no real memory of the glories of the defeat of Napoleon or the early triumphs of Ermolov in the south. Where Pushkin saw the mountains from a distance and gleaned what he could around the smoking hearths of Piatigorsk, Lermontov saw things in much grittier detail: gory battles; villages burned; women and children murdered or displaced; military units welcomed back to their forts in triumph, only to find, days later, highland warriors preparing to exact their revenge. "I love my native land but love it strangely," Lermontov wrote, "The glory bought by blood and treason, . . . The sacred chronicles of the heroic nation— / None ever strikes a spark in my imagination."[18]

For Lermontov the mountains bore ancient witness to the vainglorious search for conquest and control. In "The Debate," written in 1841, he imagined Mounts Elbrus and Kazbek in conversation about the grand conflict between East and West. Kazbek is at first indifferent to humans' impact on the landscape: the sleepy Georgians, the hookah-smokers of Tehran, the slow-moving Nile—nothing in the East has changed, he says, for a thousand years. But Elbrus advises him to turn his eyes to the north, where a country is on the move, sweeping down to overwhelm the leaden, dawdling Orient. Battalions on the march, drummers flailing, cannons creaking forward, their wicks already lit: "Onward crawls the mighty army, / Like a cloud released; / Dark, enveloping, alarming, / Heading for the East." Whereas Pushkin would have seen the thundering ranks of Russians as the magnanimous bearer of civilization southward, Lermontov was more skeptical. "And the great Caucasian mountain, / Gloomy and morose, / Tried but could not finish counting / The advancing rows."[19]

Lermontov gave a darker hue to Pushkin's sanitized image of the Russian conquest, but he could also invert it. His subjects are more often deserters than valiant officers, soldiers locked in the confusion of battle rather than stepping out on parade. He challenges prevailing conceptions of Caucasus natives and frames Russian strategy as imperial occupation and enslavement.[20] In his narrative poems "Mtsyri" and "Izmail Bey" Lermontov provides another version of the Caucasus prisoner, one from the other side of the battle lines. In "Mtsyri" he tells the story of a young highland boy, left in a Georgian monastery by a Russian officer and raised to speak "the alien tongue" while still casting "long glances toward the East." As he grows older, the mountains reveal to him his own true identity. "And through the mist I saw at times / How unassailable, in snows, / The Caucasus in glory rose . . . / And from my half-forgotten past / A misty veil was dropped at last."[21] He recalls his earliest memories of his father's house, his beautiful sisters, and dignified old men relating tales of war. He runs away from the monastery, across the fearful mountains, through tangled forests and down treacherous ravines, in an attempt to reach his homeland. His quest is ultimately unfulfilled, however. Delirious, he finds himself once again on the outskirts of the monastery, prepared to die in exile. The eponymous subject of "Izmail Bey" is likewise reared in a Russian environment but heeds the call of the mountains to return to his native comrades. The poem contains a harsh rebuke of Russian atrocities in its highland wars. Where Pushkin's young hero went to the Caucasus seeking freedom, Lermontov's highlanders yearn to recover theirs in a land taken hostage by the northern invader.

Many of these themes found their way into what became Lermontov's most famous work, his novel *A Hero of Our Time*, which appeared in 1840. Beyond its setting in the Caucasus, the novel is episodic rather than linear, with multiple narrators and plots. Its playful approach to chronology, sweeping forward and ebbing back, is distinctly anti—even post—modern, as is the book's central conceit, namely, that much of the text is derived from the journals of the main character, the young officer Pechorin, and is only now being published posthumously by yet another narrator. The action is set in the 1830s, with Pechorin serving in the Murid wars. He spends time in Piatigorsk, where he woos a woman and emerges victorious from a duel, for which he is relegated to service in Chechnya. After further adventures among the Cossacks and in Georgia, Pechorin dies while returning from Persia. Throughout the novel Lermontov weaves details of Caucasus life into the broken story line, with appearances by cartloads of Armenians, lethargic Ossetians, and plucky Circassian brigands on swift horses.

The setting of the novel is, in a sense, incidental since the focus is on Pechorin himself, an archetype of what in Russian literature later came to be called the "superfluous man" (*lishnii chelovek*)—intelligent and idealistic yet powerless to correct the injustices that surround him. "I'm never satisfied," he confesses early in the novel. "I grow used to sorrow as easily as I do to pleasure, and my life gets emptier every day. The only thing left for me is to travel."[22] Pechorin is a man of deep introspection who yearns for freedom yet finds himself bound by the shallow conventions of society and his bleakly reactionary government. The Caucasus is uniquely suited to such a character, a figure who turns out to be heroic in a complicated, ambiguous, and melancholy sense. Where else, Lermontov seems to ask, could a man like Pechorin demonstrate his superfluity than in a part of the empire where meaningless action—an unending frontier war, a spiral of violence and retribution—had become the order of the day?

Writers of all ranks, from belletrists to the titans of the Russian literary canon, returned again and again to the Caucasus as a subject and a setting. Lermontov was Pushkin's successor as a narrative and lyrical poet, but his accounts of the nature of warfare and conquest set

Russian literature on a rather different track, one involving a more realistic assessment of the costs—to both Russia and the Caucasus itself—of the long history of upland fighting.

In the second half of the century Leo Tolstoy followed that intellectual path to the south. Like Lermontov, Tolstoy experienced the Caucasus during a period of intense warfare in the early 1850s, when his brother was a lieutenant in one of the regiments stationed on the Terek line. Tolstoy served as a cadet in the northeastern theater and later saw even more extensive action as an officer during the Crimean War, where he witnessed the siege of Sevastopol. Like Lermontov, his literary vision of the Caucasus was born of real experience. Even more than his predecessors, however, he understood the insanity of war and the grinding boredom of life in a part of the empire that, some thirty years after the exploits of Ermolov, was still scarred by conflict.

In his short story "The Wood-Felling," set in a Russian military unit during a campaign in Chechnya, Tolstoy mocked the gullibility with which outsiders approached the Caucasus. Decades after the beginning of the wars of conquest, average Russians still knew relatively little about the region. In the story Tolstoy has a Russian soldier, Chikin, recount how people back in his home village quizzed him about life in the Caucasus campaigns. Chikin decided to have a bit of fun with his peasant neighbors, inventing peoples and customs that stretch the imagination:

> "Well, so they asked, 'What's that Cherkes fellow or Turk as you've got down in your Cawcusses,' they say, 'as fights?' and so I says, 'Them's not all of one sort; there's different Cherkeses, old fellow. There's the Wagabones, them as lives in the stony mountains and eat stones instead of bread. . . .
>
> " 'Then,' says I, 'there's also the Mopingers,' " continued Chikin, making his cap slip onto his forehead with a movement of his head: " 'These others are little twins, so big . . . all in pairs,' says I, 'they run about hand in hand at such a rate,' says I, 'that you couldn't catch 'em on a horse!'—'Then how's it, lad,' they say, 'how's them Mopingers, be they born hand in hand?' " He said this in a hoarse bass, pretending to imitate a peasant. " 'Yes,' says I, 'he's naturally like that. Tear them hands apart and they'll bleed.' "[23]

Chikin's story continues in this fanciful vein. The only thing the peasants have a hard time believing is the one thing that turns out to be true: that the snow remains year-round on the summits of the Caucasus peaks. How can that be so, they ask, when the hillocks on the steppe lose their snow early in the thawing season? Peaks nearer the sun must surely be hotter.

At another point in "The Wood-Felling" Tolstoy underscores the fact that it is not simply ignorant villagers who have been charmed by the imaginary Caucasus. "All of us who came to the Caucasus in obedience to tradition made a terrible mistake in our calculations," says Bolkhov, the unit commander. "Why in Russia they imagine the Caucasus to be something majestic: eternal virgin ice, rushing torrents, daggers, mantles, fair Circassians, and an atmosphere of terror and romance; but in reality there is nothing amusing in it. . . . All that I, in obedience to tradition, came to the Caucasus to be cured of has followed me here, only with the difference that there it was all on a big scale and now it is on a little dirty one where at each step I find millions of petty anxieties, shabbiness, and insults."[24] For Tolstoy the tradition to which Bolkhov has sworn obedience is the one pioneered by Pushkin, of the Caucasus as a place of escape, even refuge, from the outside world. For soldiers who found themselves there, it turned out to be anything but that: virgin ice and rushing torrents, yes, but also the terror of unexpected violence, a bloody anti-insurgency campaign, and the crushing tedium of camp life. Riding around Piatigorsk, Pushkin found the specter of danger an agreeable fillip for the imagination. Tolstoy knew that the substance of danger was a different thing.

In *The Cossacks*, a novella published in 1863, Tolstoy described life on the Terek line in the 1850s, a time when Chechen raids across the river were still frequent. The central character, a cadet named Olenin, has left Moscow for the same reasons as Pushkin's young man—to find freedom on the frontier, escape unpayable debts, and have some fun. As he travels south, the trappings of civilization recede and the memories of his past life fade. In the Caucasus, Olenin muses, "the people are not really people—I mean, none of them knows me or will ever move in my circles in Moscow or hear anything about my past. Nor is it likely that anyone in Moscow will ever find out anything I do here."[25] What happens in the Caucasus, in other words, stays in the Caucasus. These illusions, however, are soon shattered. Violence and boredom, not adventure, are Olenin's dominant experiences. "Your men slaughter ours," says a Chechen to a Cossack, "ours butcher yours."[26] His love for a Cossack woman remains unrequited—Pushkin's trope of unreciprocated romance now flipped on its head. The novella ends with

Olenin riding away from the Cossack *stanitsa* where he has been stationed. The woman does not even deign to watch him go.

These themes are bound together in Tolstoy's most famous work on the Caucasus, the novella *Hadji Murat*, written at the beginning of the twentieth century. The novella is Tolstoy's version of the life of the title character, who found himself in a blood feud with Shamil after the imam took his wife and children hostage in an attempt to induce him to join the resistance against the Russians. Hadji Murat appeals to the Russians for assistance, encouraging them to trade their own prisoners for the lives of his family. Frustrated by their broken promises, he decides to leave the Russian side and attempts to liberate his family single-handedly. He is soon mistaken for an escapee, hunted by imperial soldiers, and beheaded. Like Lermontov's "Mtsyri," *Hadji Murat* is in essence an inversion. Tolstoy concentrates not on the life of Shamil, the central figure in the Murid wars, but rather on a turncoat. It is a story of multiple betrayals—of Shamil by his former lieutenant (and vice versa), of Hadji Murat by the Russian generals whom he had previously assisted, and of the Caucasus by an empire that arrogated to itself the right to conquer.

Tolstoy opens *Hadji Murat* with a metaphor. He describes strolling through a field to pick wildflowers for a nosegay. During his walk, he comes upon a beautiful crimson thistle that he wishes to add to his bouquet. Yet when he struggles to remove it from the soil, he ends up destroying it—"a flower that looked beautiful in its proper place" but that he had ruined in attempting to uproot.[27] Hadji Murat, Tolstoy's literary stand-in for highlanders in general, was precisely that: a deracinated native, a leader whose alternating loyalties mirrored the shifting fortunes of the Caucasus peoples and their variable relationship to Russian power. Their commitment to liberty in all its forms and meanings ended in tragedy.

The tenacity and ambiguity of highland resistance was something only a soldier who had served on the lines could fully appreciate. Shamil, the old adversary, ended up a celebrated but cloistered guest in Russia. Hadji Murat, who had at times cooperated in the conquest, ended up the great antihero of the Caucasus campaigns, the highland equivalent of a superfluous man. Many Muslims—"Tatars" in Tolstoy's language—ended up in exile, uprooted from the highlands like unwanted plants from a garden. The mountains were increasingly denuded of the very peoples who were supposed to have welcomed the civilizing influence of the northern, Orthodox Christian empire. In the period between Pushkin's day and Tolstoy's, many of the crimson thistles had been pulled.

Convoy to Tiflis

During the sojourns of Lermontov and Tolstoy in the Caucasus, the normal route was to approach the mountains from the north. The Black Sea coast was also an option but only for the most adventurous. As long as the major port, Batumi, remained under the control of the Ottoman Empire, and with no secure means of further overland conveyance to Tiflis, travel by sea was difficult. After 1830 the tsar placed the coast under a naval blockade in order to prevent guns, salt, and other provisions from reaching highland fighters in Circassia.

Most visitors reached the mountains after spending days on the Volga or Don rivers and then "posting" across the southern Russian steppe. Posting involved riding in rough wooden carts of various sorts—especially the bone-rattling, four-wheeled *telega*, which was pulled by three horses—or perhaps a sturdy carriage purchased or hired in St. Petersburg or Moscow. The deeply rutted roads were either rough as washboards in the dry, hot summer and icy winter or vast, mucky sloughs in the spring. Tossed and bounced about, a traveler might even be thrown out of the cart and land, dazed, by the side of the road. At different points along the route state-regulated post houses offered some refreshment and provided new horses for the next stage of the journey. The traveler was required to procure a signed order (*podorozhnaia*) for horses from a local official. That document, issued for a small fee, permitted travelers to hopscotch from post house to post house, picking up a new team of horses and driver at each one, until they reached the final destination marked on the travel document.

Post houses rarely offered more than minimal comforts: some straw for bedding; some tea or a simple meal if the hour were not too late. The experience was not for the traveler expecting sumptuous oriental surroundings. "That the progress of civilization in the country is sluggish is evinced by the noxious condition of inns and post-houses," wrote a British naval officer, "which swarm with all manner of insects."[28] For other travelers the discomforts of the post house were nothing compared with the thought of loading up one's bags each morning for a full day in a bumpy cart. "Whilst we gradually accustomed ourselves to endure such hardships as hunger, dirt, and vermin," wrote the German diplomat Max von Thielmann, "each successive morning we regarded the *telega* with increased horror."[29]

Although some form of posting could be found in the south Caucasus, the even shoddier state of the roads there made traveling by horseback more advisable. In any case, no traveler could cross the mountains alone. In the early nineteenth century the likelihood of disasters—from avalanches to bandit attacks—meant that the only option across the highlands was to join one of the periodic postal convoys leaving from the Caucasus lines. For most of the first half of the century the fort at Mozdok on the Terek River was the starting point for the journey south to Tiflis. The fort was founded in the 1760s, when a Kabardian prince ceded his territory to the Russian Empire. Mozdok became a key point of attraction for natives from Kabarda and Dagestan as well as from south of the mountains. (Mozdok would later be succeeded by Vladikavkaz as the Georgian Military Highway's northern terminus.)

The main purpose of the convoy was to transport mail and provisions across the mountains to and from Georgia, but since it was the only protected conveyance through sometimes hostile territory, travelers were allowed to trail along in their own vehicles under the aegis of the Russian military. The group that set off from Mozdok on May 15, 1820, gives some idea of the nature of the convoy. From front to back, it consisted of:

> two pieces of artillery, each pulled by four horses
> ten Cossack cavalrymen
> the postal *brichka*, or covered wagon, pulled by eight horses
> a large assortment of carts, wagons, and sturdy carriages with scores of
>   passengers, both Russian and foreign
> fifty Kabardian horsemen
> one hundred oxcarts filled with wheat
> fifty infantrymen
> a few more Cossack horsemen bringing up the rear[30]

Starting out from Vladikavkaz nearly a decade later, Pushkin gave a similar description. He recalled that some five hundred people gathered at the meeting place at nine o'clock in the morning. A drum roll signaled the departure, and the entire assembly began moving, with cannons leading the way. Four-wheeled carriages came next, followed by the creaking oxcarts driven by Muslim teamsters. Great herds of horses and oxen flanked the convoy, while Nogai nomads, clad in thick felt *burkas*, swung their lassos to keep the animals in check. Thin wisps of smoke rose from the cannon wicks, which were kept lit in case of attack. Soldiers would occasionally run up to light their pipes from the smoldering guns.[31]

As more and more travelers began to make the journey—Georgian ladies coming back from St. Petersburg; Armenian traders on their way to Tabriz; European travelers seeking adventure in Tiflis—the convoys correspondingly became more cumbersome, stretching up to two miles in length. They moved at a snail's pace since they could only travel as fast as the slowest components, the infantry and the oxen. (Pushkin reported that his group covered only fifteen *versts*—about nine miles—during the first day on the road.) That made them a potentially attractive target. If the outriders spotted a raiding party, a signal was given and the infantry formed up into a fighting square, with the artillery placed in front. If a fort were nearby, the entire column might make a mad dash for the protected walls, hoping to outrun the raiders but in the process leaving the slow-moving carts and buggies behind.[32]

Given the government's increasing control of the highlands and the general success in keeping the eastern and western theaters of war separate, travelers rarely had reason to fear. Even early in the century some visitors felt that the journey should have been more exciting than it was, especially when they failed to see any real Circassians swooping down from the hills. Russian policy was to resettle relatively peaceful Ossetian villagers along the route of the Georgian Military Highway, thereby creating a demographic buffer between the road itself and less friendly peoples in Circassia or upland Georgia. These population changes meant that hostile Circassian horsemen—at least along the highway—existed mainly as fantasies. If one avoided traveling at night and took an escort, one was unlikely to be molested.[33] "The pass over the Caucasus is like many a terror that requires only to be approached to disappear," wrote a traveler in the late 1820s. "There are no dangers or difficulties that can frighten the most timid female," except for the fact that the bad roads rendered light carriage traffic impractical.[34] The situation in the eastern Caucasus was different, even in the latter half of the century. There were some areas in Chechnya and Dagestan that were best left unvisited due to the prevalence of banditry. Still, "travelling as one necessarily does under Russian protection, and being further supposed to be well armed," wrote another visitor in the 1880s, "one need be under no apprehension as to one's personal safety."[35]

There were various reasons to make the journey. Adventure travel was one, but as war and periodic raiding subsided, there were other, less violent attractions. Decent hotels were to be found in Tiflis, such as the Hôtel de Londres and the Hôtel du Caucase. The hot springs along the Kura River and the picturesque bazaar winding down from the imposing Narikala fortress were not to be missed. In the north Caucasus the most important destination was the array of spa resorts that grew up around the region's numerous sulfurous and iron-laden springs. The springs were credited with relieving a host of ailments, from digestive disorders and menstrual irregularities to nervousness and incontinence. The landscape itself was even thought to have salutary effects. "You have before you the steam from the hot water, and in the distance the mountains eternally covered in snow," noted an early guidebook to the springs. "What a striking contrast! What a rich field for the artist's brush or the poet's pen!"[36]

Pushkin as a young man and Lermontov as a child had experienced the curative power of the springs in Piatigorsk, and locals were quick to take advantage of the growing demand. The 1820s and 1830s witnessed a building boom, as pavilions, bathhouses, and restaurants sprang up to welcome visitors. Even old Cossack *stanitsas*, such as the modern city of Kislovodsk, were retooled as resorts if the waters were found to have therapeutic value. When Pushkin returned to Piatigorsk in 1829, he marveled at how much the town had changed since his last visit nearly a decade earlier. During his earlier stopover, the baths were no more than shacks; the healing waters flowed out of the mountains in all directions, with white and red mineral deposits staining the rocks. Now there were proper bathhouses, a boulevard lined with linden trees, painted park benches, neat flowerbeds, and little bridges. The police had even tacked up lists of proper behavior to be followed in the baths. "I confess: the Caucasus spas offer more conveniences nowadays," Pushkin wrote, "but I missed their former wild state."[37]

At the very beginning of the nineteenth century, Russian writers had already begun to record their experiences during the journey south. Tales of dangerous gorges, feral tribesmen, and snow-covered passes dominated—so much so that, as one writer complained in 1823, the Russian reader would little understand the wealth and beauty awaiting the traveler at the end of the journey in peaceful Georgia, "the Russian Italy."[38] Soon newspapers and journals were littered with letters, travel notes, and excerpts from diaries describing trips down the Georgian Military Highway or around the south Caucasus provinces. At least 78 such accounts were published in Russian-language sources in the 1830s, 71 in the 1840s, and 103 in the 1850s.[39]

Many of these were simple itineraries—notes on road conditions, post houses, and distances—but they began to appear at a time when the Russian public was becoming more familiar with the peoples and places of the Caucasus thanks to the work of writers such as Pushkin and Lermontov and popularizers such as Bronevskii. Even so, it would take time before large numbers of Russian travelers made the journey across the mountains. It would take even longer (because of tsarist censors) for Russian readers to discover the details of their own government's war against the highlanders. Far more people were content to stop at the spas around Piatigorsk, where a whiff of danger could be had within the comfortable confines of an ornate bathing house.

But as travel became safer, exploration of Russia's southern provinces was a challenge that more and more people were willing to take on. The Russian Steam Navigation Company began operations in 1857 with a commission from Tsar Alexander II, running routes across the Black Sea to the major Caucasus ports. In 1885 the Transcaucasus railway was opened, joining Baku on the Caspian with Batumi on the Black Sea. Travel no longer required bouncing along in a horse-driven convoy, swatting flies and peeking at the mountains through a phalanx of Cossack or Kabardian outriders. It was now a matter of purchasing a ticket on a train, steamer, or regular coach and then sitting back to enjoy the ride.

Soon, a new reason to go to the Caucasus also appeared on the agenda of European and Russian visitors. The mountains themselves, previously the bailiwick of unknown highlanders, were emerging as a destination for hikers, climbers, and sportsmen—people who had become bored with the Alps and for whom an easy sojourn at a Tiflis hotel provided little excitement. The mountains could be reached from London or Paris in a little more than a week via several different routes: by train from St. Petersburg and Moscow or by steamship to Rostov, Novorossiisk, or Batumi; then overland to the main chain from the north or the south. A new generation of visitors, looking down from the high summits and finding the entire Caucasus spread out before them, would craft their own visions of the primordial freedom to be found at the edge of Europe.

"There Is Something to Be Gained on the Heights"

From a mountain climber's perspective, most of the Caucasus range is of little real interest. In the west the mountains of Circassia and Abkhazia are impressive from the coast, where ranks of green hills march up shale pathways toward the granite peaks, but these present few real challenges. In the east Dagestan consists of a series of high massifs gouged by deep ravines but with little in the way of alpine environments. Few summits on either end of the chain are higher than about fourteen thousand feet—the height of the famously accessible Pikes Peak in Colorado.

It is the jumble of snowy peaks just to the west of the midpoint between the Black and Caspian seas—the so-called central group—that has attracted the most attention. In this area, bounded by the Klukhor Pass to the west and the Georgian Military Highway to the east, are clustered the region's most formidable mountains: the famous Elbrus, an old volcano with its crater still strikingly visible; the fearsome Shkhara, part of a prickly fin of rock and ice rising up along the range's spine; the sprawling Koshtan, with ridges radiating out in all directions; the awesome double-horned Ushba; and the stately Kazbek, hemmed in by glaciers.

Exploration, description, and charting of the area above the tree line were activities pursued in earnest by a dedicated, at times fanatical, band of European climbers who began to filter into the Caucasus in the late 1860s. Local villagers knew the lower passes and meadows intimately, but they had little reason to venture to the heights, where there was no food for livestock, no hidden lakes for water, and no springs yielding salt. Nor was there a tradition of Russian exploration and mapping at altitude. Expeditions had been undertaken by the army's general staff as early as the 1840s. The empire's first mountaineering organization, the Society of Nature Lovers / Caucasus Alpine Club, was founded in Tiflis in 1878. However, organized Russian travel and exploration did not begin to flourish until the very last years of the nineteenth century.[40] The first Russian alpine guidebook for a popular audience—Merkulov's *Guide to the Mountains of the Caucasus*—was not produced until 1904.[41]

In western Europe several things sparked an interest in Caucasus climbing after midcentury. Because of the Crimean War, Europeans were far more familiar with the Black Sea and Caucasus than they had been previously. Families often had personal connections to the region via a brother or uncle who had served with the Allies. War correspondents and photographers had also accompanied the British and French forces, providing firsthand images of the Russian south to the European public. These changes all occurred at a time of growing demand for new climbs. Most of the major summits in the Alps had been taken, with the Matterhorn, the last unclaimed prize, being conquered in 1865.

Alpinists had also begun to organize themselves into groups of what might be called professional amateurs: men, often with private incomes, who had the time and money to spend the climbing season scaling unknown peaks and seeking out ever more spectacular routes. The British Alpine Club was founded in 1857, and over the next four decades the club produced a generation of men who would make the first recorded ascents of almost every significant mountain in Europe and Eurasia. "To those who have the health, strength, experience and energy," said Clinton Dent, president of the club, in a stirring public address, "I can but say—THERE, in that strange country, those giant peaks wait for you—silent, majestic, unvisited.... Go there!"[42] Soon so many people were visiting the central group of the Caucasus that it could rightly be called "the new playground which had at last proved to be accessible to Long Vacation travellers."[43]

The climber who wrote those lines was Douglas Freshfield, undoubtedly the most important foreign traveler to the high-altitude Caucasus in the nineteenth century. As a child Freshfield had spent most summers in the Alps. By the time he finished his final exams at Eton, he had already reached the top of Mont Blanc. His summer holidays at Oxford University were likewise spent on climbing expeditions. Shortly after he took his degree, he convinced three companions to seek out new adventures in the unexplored Caucasus, "the first step," he later recalled, "towards converting the Prison of Prometheus into a new Playground for his descendants."[44] What writers from Aeschylus to Pushkin had thought of as an archetypical jailhouse was now becoming a recreation area for well-to-do Europeans.

In 1868 Freshfield was part of the team that made the first documented ascents of the two most famous peaks in the Caucasus: Elbrus, the highest mountain in Europe, and the more diminutive Kazbek, the unmistakable guardian of the northern reaches of the Georgian Military Highway. That expedition, undertaken soon after he passed through the gates of University College, Oxford, was only the beginning of what would become, during the next thirty years, an unequaled career as explorer, climber, and writer. Freshfield himself claimed to have been one of the original "discoverers of the Caucasus," and in a sense that claim was justified.[45]

Before the 1868 expedition, none of the major peaks had been scaled in a recorded climb, none of the passes described, and none of the place names fixed or features mapped. Although the Russian military survey had been under way since the 1840s, it had thus far produced charts that provided only cursory descriptions of the highlands of the central group and even omitted many of the major peaks. By the late 1890s—when he at last sat down to collect his personal notes, public speeches, and previously published travelogues into a single work—Freshfield had traversed the main chain of the Caucasus no fewer than eleven times by eight different routes.

Freshfield's book *The Exploration of the Caucasus*, published in two volumes in 1896, remains the single most influential work on Caucasus mountaineering ever written. It includes accounts of his ascents throughout the western and central Caucasus, detailed summaries of the most interesting and challenging climbs, and vivid descriptions of peaks, valleys, and glaciers. Fortunately, Freshfield had the good sense not only to compose lucid prose but also to engage the talents of Vittorio Sella, one of the greatest mountain photographers of his era. His striking panoramic images are scattered throughout Freshfield's text, and the crispness of their detail is awe-inspiring even more than a hundred years after the photographs were taken.

Freshfield had no illusions about the difficulty of some of his climbs. Many of them, such as getting to the top of Elbrus, were relatively easy. But to think in those terms, Freshfield believed, was to miss the entire point of the endeavor. Writing some thirty years after his first ascent, Freshfield recalled the panorama that spread out before him as he stood atop the summit of Elbrus: "The scene brought under his eyes, at first overwhelming in its vastness, suggests, as he gazes on it, some harmonious plan, a sense of ordered masses, of infinite detail. And to this majestic landscape, of a scale and splendour so strange as to seem hardly real, the sky supplies ever-shifting effects. New subtleties of tint and definition, of luminous colour in the depths and clear outline on the heights, are brought out by every passing alternation of light and shadow, by the progress of the sun across a vault that has not the blue of lowland skies but a depth and darkness as of 'sheer space begun.' "[46] Freshfield was not just waxing lyrical. He was building up to what is, in fact, the central message of *The Exploration of the Caucasus*: that mountains can be something other than playthings for bored sportsmen.

Freshfield was writing at the close of the golden age of European climbing, an era when climbers were not merely technically proficient in their craft but also amateur botanists, ethnographers, geologists, and passable writers as well—Klaproths at altitude, as it were. The great peaks had been scaled by multiple routes. More and more people were coming to the Caucasus seeking adventure rather than revelation.

Freshfield believed that the surge in popular interest was not without its costs. That was why he decided to include Sella's panoramas in his book. "And here let me make a confession," he admitted with feigned embarrassment, "which may surprise many and shock some modern climbers. I love summit-views, and I sincerely pity those who can find in them no charm or beauty.... It is time to insist that there is something to be gained on the heights, that the great peaks have revelations to bestow on their faithful worshippers."[47] *The Exploration of the Caucasus* ends on this melancholy note. The book is a paean to the spiritually rehabilitative effects of altitude, an ode to the corrective influence of Nature on the gloom of Progress, and a hymn to the power and majesty of mountains. All these themes would have been familiar to Pushkin, Lermontov, and any other visitor who found in mountain vistas an indispensable balm for a soul suffering from modernity. But they were slipping out of fashion in Freshfield's day, when technical challenge, not the thirst for knowledge, was becoming the chief motivation for setting off for the heights.

There was one particular view that stood out in Freshfield's mind, however. It was a scene from a point not far below the summit of Koshtan, the fourth highest peak in the central group. In a talk delivered to the Royal Geographical Society, Freshfield recalled it vividly: "The day was cloudless, the air crystalline, space was for a moment annihilated.... The many passes and heights of the central ridge of the Caucasus lay literally at our feet.... Every detail was distinct as on a mapman's model, yet the whole was vast and vague, wonderful and strange, creating an impression of immeasurable shining space, of the Earth as it might first appear to a visitant from some other planet."[48] The scene was painfully out of keeping with the task that Freshfield and his climbing companions had set themselves. They were building a small monument, no more than a pile of stones, to four of their comrades who had been missing for nearly twelve months.

As Freshfield well knew, such views came at a price. Men could become not only prisoners of the technical skill of climbing but also prisoners of the mountains themselves. They could fall victim to the capriciousness of the very peaks that they set out to conquer, lured to their deaths by a false foothold or a hidden crevasse, or perhaps even abducted or killed by unfriendly locals. Freshfield had journeyed to the mountains on this occasion, on a saffron-colored day in the summer of 1889, not to scale an unexplored summit or map an uncharted route. He was there to solve one of the greatest mysteries in the history of

Caucasus mountaineering: Which of these fates had befallen the lost party?

— ❦ —

By the late 1880s almost all of the mountains in the central group had been scaled by foreign mountaineers. Freshfield and his team took Kazbek in 1868. The same group also ascended the eastern peak of Elbrus, although the real credit may well belong to a Circassian climber who reportedly scaled the mountain in 1829.[49] Elbrus's western peak was reached by another British expedition in 1874, and from 1884 to 1887 many of the major mountains—all well above fifteen thousand feet—fell in rapid succession: Gestola, Tetnuli, Dykh-Tau, Shkhara.

The grand exception was Koshtan, located in what is today the Russian republic of Kabardino-Balkaria.[50] At just under seventeen thousand feet, it was known to be particularly challenging. Its summit was shaped like the hump of a charging ox and steep on all sides; roaring winds made clinging to the icy walls and snowfields exceptionally dangerous. It was only a matter of time before European alpinists attempted to add Koshtan to the list of conquered peaks. The assault occurred in the summer of 1888. Three British explorers assembled in Nalchik, on the plains skirting the northern edge of the highlands. The team consisted of Clinton Dent and W. F. Donkin, both experienced climbers and president and secretary, respectively, of the Alpine Club, along with the younger Harry Fox, who was also well known in climbing circles. Even before base camp had been set up, Dent returned to Britain owing to ill health, leaving Donkin and Fox to make the climb themselves, accompanied by two Swiss guides.[51]

The four-man group set out during the final days of August. Donkin and Fox planned to attack the mountain by a roundabout route, to ascend the glacier that falls from the northern slopes of Koshtan and then to work their way around to the western side and attempt an ascent from that direction. However, the party encountered a large rock wall barring their way on the western slope. The new strategy was to backtrack around to the northern face and trek around the summit to the east in order to attempt an ascent from there. They sent word to their outfitter to prepare the heavy baggage that they had left behind and to meet the climbing party and their guides in Karaul, a pasturage on the southeast side of Koshtan.

In late September word reached London that things had not gone as planned. The outfitter in Nalchik dispatched a telegram to Dent informing him that he had not heard from the climbers in three weeks. They did not make the scheduled rendezvous in Karaul, and locals had reported no sign of the four men. A search was organized by Russian authorities, but due to the lateness of the season, the search could only be conducted below the snow line, where the climbers were unlikely to have met with an accident. No traces were found. A further search was undertaken on the personal order of Tsar Alexander III, but friends and associates feared the worst—that the climbers had been killed in an accident. "We feel sure," Dent wrote to the brother of one of the Swiss guides, "that our brave companions are lost."[52]

The international climbing community mourned the loss of two senior explorers, victims of a sporting culture that had already been widely criticized for treating the safety of its practitioners too cavalierly. However, in the following months rumors began to circulate claiming that Donkin and Fox had met with a different sort of tragedy. Highly placed sources in the Russian government were convinced that the climbers and their guides had inadvertently crossed into Svaneti, a region of northern Georgia known for its inaccessibility and hostile inhabitants. The climbers, it was increasingly felt, had not been swept away by an avalanche or slipped into a crevasse. They had been murdered by ferocious highlanders.

That version of events soon became standard fare in Russian newspapers, both in the imperial capitals and in Tiflis. The Svans on the southern slope of the Caucasus were known to be antipathetic toward outsiders. The recent quashing of a revolt in the area had left local populations more discontent than ever. Perhaps the climbers had wandered across the main range and fallen into the hands of the Svans or other natives. Details seemed to point toward foul play. A man in one of the local villages turned up with an unexplained injury, which could well have been made by an ice ax. Although the man had an alibi for the period when the climbers had most likely disappeared, his unusual wound fueled suspicion. Villagers also reported that they had seen footprints leading off the Koshtan glaciers and toward Svaneti or Balkaria, areas less visited than the environs of the major peaks. The Russian government dispatched Cossacks to several communities to flush out a possible perpetrator.

Dent, the president of the Alpine Club, had his own reasons for believing in the murder scenario. His earlier experiences in the region had taught him to distrust the natives, whom he found at best lazy and at worse venal and treacherous.[53] Freshfield, too, had had run-ins with unfriendly villagers. Several times during the 1868 expedition he found himself with ice ax or pistol in hand, ready to fend off an attack by a highlander eager to seize his equipment or demand payment beyond the amount agreed upon for some service.[54] Nevertheless, Freshfield remained skeptical. The basic geography of the region would have made an accidental incursion into Svaneti unlikely, and he remained unconvinced that the generally affable highlanders could suddenly have turned into murderers. Would Donkin and Fox be credited with making the first confirmed ascent of Koshtan, or would they go down in history as mere victims of the landscape and peoples of the Eurasian frontier? Freshfield set about organizing a new party whose chief purpose would be to determine, once and for all, the fate of the climbers and their guides.

The new team represented perhaps the finest array of foreigners ever assembled for a high-altitude expedition in the Caucasus: Freshfield, with his two decades of experience in the region; Dent, the public face of British mountaineering; Charles Herbert Powell, a captain from the Indian Army who knew Russian and served as interpreter; and Hermann Woolley, a noted photographer. The group was joined by four guides with experience in both the Alps and the Himalayas, including the brother of one of the lost guides. The team set out from Vladikavkaz in midsummer 1889. The plan was not to follow the route taken by Donkin and Fox but rather to begin the search from the point where the missing climbers were to have rendezvoused with their outfitter. From there they could make their way up the slopes of Koshtan and hopefully find some evidence of what had happened to their comrades, now missing for nearly a year.

It is impossible to overstate the difficulty of the task that the members of the search party had set for themselves. They were covering a vast stretch of mountainous territory, where rockslides, avalanches, floods, and storms were constant dangers. They had no reliable maps. Many of the passes, glaciers, and safe routes were unexplored or unnamed. Worse, a prominent physical feature, such as an escarpment or valley, might be called one thing by local villagers or Russian informants and another by experienced British climbers.

As it turned out, Dent and Freshfield were not searching in the dark. There was a critical piece of evidence that the earlier Russian rescue parties had recovered from the base camp—Fox's diary—which gave a sense of what had happened in the final hours before the ascent. The last entry, dated Tuesday, August 28, also contained several ominous asides that seemed to point toward exactly the fate alleged by Russian authorities and newspapermen.[55] Fox recorded that one of the highland villagers had accompanied the climbers to base camp and had proceeded to quiz them about their precise route. A native intimately familiar with hidden passages across the glaciers could well have set a trap for the foreigners. There was also a reference to Donkin having spent time in camp firing his revolver at "imaginary enemies." Was Donkin merely killing time or had some earlier incident given him reason to believe that he needed to hone his skills as a marksman? From Karaul the search party began the ascent toward the pass separating the northern glacier from its southern counterpart. On July 28 one of the guides stopped suddenly. "Der Schlafplatz!," he cried out, the sleeping place! In the snow a small tin box, used for holding snow glasses, sparkled in the sun.

With nothing to go on but their own suppositions about the likely route that Donkin and Fox had taken, the Dent and Freshfield party had come upon exactly the spot where the men had made their final bivouac, a high pass between two glaciers, at an altitude of about fourteen thousand feet. It was a small outcropping next to a sheer precipice, guarded by a makeshift wall of piled-up stones. The search party hacked away at the rock and ice that nearly covered the encampment and managed to dislodge what remained of the lost climbers' personal effects: a stew pan, rucksacks, sleeping bags—even Donkin's revolver. No trace of the men was found, but the key to their mysterious disappearance lay in what was not there. Three things were conspicuously absent: the team's supply of climbing rope, their ice axes, and Donkin's camera.

That was enough to convince Dent and Freshfield of what had happened eleven months earlier. The climbers had probably left their camp to make the final assault on the summit, which lay about three thousand feet above them. They had taken only light gear, including ropes for the ascent and a camera to record the event, expecting to return to the bivouac in due course. From the ledge the only route to the summit was along a narrow ridge, which dropped sharply away on either side, and even the first part of the ridge was separated from the sleeping place by the flat face of Koshtan. An accident along this route would have sent the men plunging thousands of feet to the rock, ice, and snow that lay below.

"As we looked along the stupendous cliffs of this great peak," Dent wrote to the London *Times* upon his return, "we felt that any accident whatever in such a place meant almost instantaneous death."[56] The expedition surveyed the cliffs and the valley floor for signs of the party but to no avail. Anything left of the climbers and their guides would have been covered by the snow of the previous winter. "We were well satisfied to leave the mountaineers in their high tomb," Freshfield concluded in his report, "warded by the frosty walls and watched only by the stars, with the brightest peak of the Caucasus for their perpetual monument."[57] Today, somewhere deep inside the glacial ice and crevasses of Koshtan, the remains of Donkin and Fox await their accidental discovery by some future visitor.

The Dent and Freshfield expedition was intended not only to settle the question of the fate of the climbers and their guides but also to get at a deeper question: Were the peoples of the Caucasus still so backward that they could be suspected of murdering foreign travelers in cold blood? Was it still safe, as it had been for decades, to travel into the mountain vastness with little thought of being waylaid, robbed or even killed by rebellious mountaineers?

On this score there was one final bit of evidence that seemed, if not conclusive, then at least convincing: Donkin's ice-encrusted revolver, recovered from the final sleeping site, was still fully loaded. Even if a group of natives lacking professional equipment had managed to climb up to fourteen thousand feet—across glaciers, rockfalls, and sheer cliffs—solely in order to rob two foreign climbers and guides, it seems highly unlikely that they would have done so without encountering at least some resistance.

The local Turkic-speaking villagers—today's ethnic Balkars—were greatly relieved that the expedition had finally placed the blame squarely with the mountains themselves. "You have come from far to remove the suspicion and its consequences from us, and we thank you from the bottom of our hearts," one elder reportedly told Freshfield.[58] As the search party passed through villages on their way back to Vladikavkaz, there were numerous gatherings at which the story of the lost climbers was recounted in detail, through translators, to the assembled highlanders. As Clinton Dent later recalled, the search party made sure to round out its account with a declaration that the locals had been fully cleared of any wrongdoing. The memory of the search team's exoneration of the highlanders remained fresh well into the twentieth century. When British climbers first returned to the mountains in 1958, they were greeted enthusiastically by a bearded old man. He explained that his father had assisted the Dent and Freshfield expedition and that it was only Dent's account to Russian authorities that had prevented the men of the village from being rounded up by Cossack cavalry and punished as murderers. The ghosts of Donkin and Fox, captives of the landscape but not of its inhabitants, helped to prevent the mountaineers from becoming victims of their own government's reprisals.[59]

There was something to be gained on the heights, Freshfield concluded, but also much to be lost. The Caucasus produced the sublime and also consumed it. That, however, was part of the region's undeniable appeal: a place where danger lurked beyond each rockfall and where the promise of emotional fulfillment was counterbalanced by the prospect of tragedy. It does not take a great deal of imagination to uncover these sentiments in the work of Güldenstädt, Bronevskii, Lermontov, or virtually any other writer since the late eighteenth century. To be in the Caucasus was to exist on the edge, at the extreme limits of civilization, propriety, and human emotion, where the rules of polite society no longer applied and savagery was within reach.

The Caucasus was a place whose gentle contours and fissures could be probed not only for scientific and artistic reasons but also for the opportunity to interact with the transcendent beauty of the mountains. Journeying there could even become, in a way, an erotic experience. These elements would eventually come together in one particularly enduring vision of the imaginary Caucasus—that the people who lived there were not simply valiant denizens of the unmastered heights, as Pushkin believed, nor merely welcoming inhabitants of an unforgiving landscape, as Freshfield thought. They were also extremely sexy.

Eros and the Circassian

In David Lean's masterful film *Lawrence of Arabia* there is a scene in which Lawrence is taken captive by an Ottoman bey, played with oleaginous verve by José Ferrer. The sadistic overtones of the scene are clear. Lawrence is stripped to the waist, held down over a bench, and whipped while the bey looks on voyeuristically from behind his office door, his tubercular cough occasionally interrupting the whack of the cane. At the beginning of the scene the bey approaches the demure Lawrence. "You have blue eyes," he says. "Yes, effendi," replies Lawrence. "Are you Circassian?" the bey asks. "Yes, effendi" is again the reply. Then the beating begins.

The bey's question is reasonable enough. In the Levant during the First World War, it would not have been unusual to find a light-skinned man in Bedouin garb, a descendant of the Circassians who had been expelled to the Ottoman lands in the 1860s. (Their descendants are still there today, a privileged military elite serving as personal bodyguards to the Jordanian king.) However, in the context of the film there is something significant in that word "Circassian." It points unmistakably toward the homoerotic, the subtle setup for what Lean, in his editing notes, called "the buggering"—Lawrence's rape while in Ottoman custody. The bey's question concerning his captive's ethnic origins follows a well-worn cultural groove—the equation of Circassians, and often Caucasus peoples in general, with sex.

In the art, literature, and popular culture of Russia, Europe, and America, there is a long tradition of eroticizing this otherwise straightforward ethnic label, which can either refer to a specific ethnic group—the Adyga of the northwestern Caucasus—or serve as a catchall term for Caucasus highlanders generally. From the eighteenth century onward, plays and novels featured Circassians as slaves in Eastern seraglios. Orientalist paintings showed Circassians as odalisques whiling away the hours in a harem. How all this came about reveals a great deal about the place of the Caucasus in the imagination not only of the Russian public but also of writers, readers, and consumers who had little direct connection with this distant land.

Throughout the nineteenth century, as more and more Europeans became familiar with the Caucasus they were fascinated by the physical appearance of Circassians. The men were said to be tall, dark, and lithe. Their long mustaches, silver-studded weaponry, and close-fitting clothing—especially the *cherkeska*—enhanced their noble, war-like mien. "In the first appearance of a Circassian," wrote Edmund Spencer, a major Caucasus travel writer of the mid-nineteenth century, "there is something extremely martial and commanding: his majestic look, elevated brow, dark moustachio and flowing beard, his erect position, and free unconstrained action, are all calculated to interest the stranger in his favour. No half-civilised people in the world display so pleasing an exterior."[60] The reactions of male Europeans upon first encountering real, live Circassian men often verged on the homoerotic. In 1862 two Circassian chiefs, Hadji Hayder Hassan and Kustan Ogli Ismael, came to Britain on a tour to promote the anti-Russian resistance in the mountains. The *Dundee Advertiser* giddily reported that "the Chiefs are two remarkable-looking men. Their imposing bearing, their romantic dress . . . and their natural dignity of mien, stamp them as very superior men. . . . Raven-haired, black-bearded, broad-browed, with wide springing eyebrows of sooty black . . . these bronzed and armed children of the mountains tend to put us out of love with our own specimens of men, and suggest thoughts not complimentary to the types of manhood by which, in this country, they are surrounded."[61]

For all the breathless descriptions of the men—and there are plenty like this in nineteenth-century sources—it was the women who remained most intriguing. Spencer, who met a Circassian princess near the Black Sea coast in 1836, called her "one of the handsomest women I think I ever beheld." She was about eighteen, he said, with regular features "of the Grecian cast; eyes, large and dark." Her complexion was clear and tanned, her hands and feet delicate. Her dress and demeanor, he noted, were "studied with no small degree of coquetry" since she allowed her dark hair to fall in tresses around her shoulders.[62]

Such views were not limited to romantic Victorians. Russian writers could also wax poetical, even while Russian soldiers were killing and being killed by Circassians. Semyon Bronevskii, for example, claimed that the beauty of the Circassian woman was renowned since the earliest times, and that such praise was fully deserved. Her dark eyes and dark-brown hair, elongated but not aquiline nose, and small mouth combined to give her "the lineaments of the face of the Ancient Greek, mixed with the light shade of the Roman." If added to this were "a full, high bosom, a graceful figure, and slender legs, then you will have a general picture of the dimensions of the face and physique of the Circassian beauty."[63] The women were frequently cast as modern instantiations of a genuinely timeless beauty, the perfect form of the ancient Greek ideal, perhaps implanted into the Circassian population in the days when the Hellenes' beak-prowed ships sailed along the Black Sea coastline in search of gold, grain, and slaves.

The image of the sensuous Circassian woman was so frequently repeated in travelers' accounts that later in the century something of a backlash set in. Some visitors complained that the alleged comeliness of mountain maidens was grossly exaggerated. "The women are a little disappointing," wrote one visitor in the 1890s, a result of "too exalted anticipation."[64] Others turned the very notion of Circassian beauty back on its creators, seeing it not as a reflection of reality but as a romantic projection of overeager and undersexed young men. In *The Cossacks* Tolstoy has Olenin rhapsodize a fantastic encounter with a highland girl while on his way to serve on the line: "She stood there in the mountains, a Circassian slave girl, slender, with a long braid and deep, docile eyes.... He imagined her kisses, her shoulders, her sweet voice, her docility. She was beautiful but uneducated, wild, and rough. During the long winter nights he would begin to educate her.... She would also have a knack for languages, read French novels, and even understand them—she would surely love *Notre-Dame de Paris*. And she would be able to speak French."[65] Tolstoy here captured the essential attributes of the imaginary Circassian female: simple, wild, rough, unformed but welcoming, a sexual *idiot savant*.

It was not long before astute businessmen seized upon this complex cultural image. In western Europe in the 1860s, a popular skin treatment was marketed under the label "Circassian cream," a product whose purpose was to soften the skin while also blanching it by using ingredients said to come from the Caucasus.[66] Soaps, hair oils, and many other beauty products peddled by both legitimate salesmen and charlatans bore the "Circassian" moniker. Being pure, white, and hailing from the imagined Caucasus turned out to be an irresistible combination for marketers, especially given the widespread use of the term "Caucasian" in Western languages to denote an allegedly superior racial group.

The ultimate expression of Circassian eroticism, however, was to appear in a rather unexpected place—in the circus midways and dime museums of Victorian-era America. A century ago many Americans would have easily recognized a Circassian. They had probably even met one. Ushered into a darkened room and directed toward rough wooden benches, a crowd would gather as a pump organ ground out a slow dance. Men in scratchy woolen suits, women with paper fans, and rowdy boys who had managed to sneak past the ticket taker looked on expectantly as a burlap curtain opened on a makeshift stage. There, a pale-skinned woman lay on a velvet chaise while her desultory servant waved a fan fashioned of peacock feathers. She might even recount—in English, no less—a Tatar raid on her village, the sea journey to Constantinople, the prods and examinations in the slave bazaar, and a new life in the confining luxury of the sultan's palace. She might sigh as she stroked the wild thicket of dark hair that shot up from her head.

In the late nineteenth century no circus sideshow or museum of "freaks" was complete without such "Circassian beauties," as they were called. Like the dwarfs, albinos, and bearded ladies who populated these public exhibitions of the odd and the grotesque, they were just the kind of rarity that anyone would pay to see: a voluptuous woman, perhaps descended from the Amazons, who was once fierce and untamed, then sold into sexual bondage and now, following her rescue and journey to America, an emblem of vicarious adventure and erotic possibility.

The great showman Phineas T. Barnum was probably responsible for introducing the Circassians into American popular culture—or at least took credit for doing so. In 1841 he purchased a collection of human oddities in New York City from a less able businessman. Barnum immediately saw the entertainment value of the collection, which he renamed simply the "American Museum." Soon his museum of "freaks"—including exceedingly tall and short men, hirsute girls, and eczema sufferers—was charging twenty-five cents (rather than the standard ten cents) for admission.

Exactly how the Circassians joined this cast of characters is uncertain. Later in the century it was not uncommon to find entertainers from the Caucasus touring around America. Buffalo Bill Cody's Wild West Show featured skilled horsemen from Guria, in western Georgia, who were intentionally mislabeled "Cossacks" for publicity purposes.[67] Barnum, however, seems to have pioneered the connection between the Caucasus and showmanship. According to his own version of events, he dispatched one of his agents, John Greenwood, to the Mediterranean in 1864 in order to collect interesting human specimens for the museum. While on Cyprus, Greenwood heard stories about the ethereal beauty of Circassian women, who might be purchased in the slave markets of Turkey. With the Circassian name already having some resonance among the American public, and with the additional titillating whiff of sexual bondage that came with them, Barnum instructed Greenwood to see what could be done to secure "one or more Circassian women for exhibition in my Museum."[68]

Once in Constantinople, Greenwood adopted a technique known to many male travelers intent on experiencing the wonders of the Orient. He disguised himself as a "Turk" and managed to gain admission to a slave market. (Given the considerable number of men who reported such activities in the nineteenth century, there must have been a thriving business providing "disguise tours" to gullible Westerners.) Greenwood reported that he "saw a large number of Circassian girls and women, some of them the most beautiful beings he had ever seen"—which would have been difficult, given the fact that the largest slave markets were no longer in operation. In any case, a month later he was on a steamer bound for Marseille and then Baltimore, having picked up "many treasures" for his employer.[69]

Barnum and Greenwood's correspondence concerning the procurement of Circassian women indicates that Barnum was prepared to pay as much as five thousand dollars in gold for a woman with "a striking kind of beauty," perhaps more if she were accompanied by a eunuch.[70] Not long afterward the American Museum began exhibiting women who, given their supposed origins in the Caucasus highlands, were said to be exceptionally pure examples of the "Caucasian race."

Any museum proprietor or midway hawker who advertised a Circassian beauty for inspection by the paying public had to clothe and present her in the style established by America's master showman. First was the hair. The iconic Circassian beauty had hair like a briar patch: Dark and unkempt, it fanned out in all directions from her head. Her skin, by contrast, was light and smooth, like fine porcelain. She was dressed in Eastern garb, in flowing garments of rich fabrics, and often revealed a hint of shoulder, forearm, and décolletage to convince the public that her alabaster skin was not the result of talc.

We know what these women looked like because the most famous became minor celebrities and appeared in photographic portraits that could be traded like baseball cards. Many of these photographs, some taken by the famous Bowery photographer Charles Eisenmann, have survived. The women are shown in a variety of poses. Some lounge against an urn or other atmospheric prop, their faces exhibiting the gratified desire and congenital boredom of the harem. Others stand defiantly against a painted backdrop of the white Caucasus mountains, their ancestral homeland. Their stage names—uniformly suggestive of the women's otherworldliness—were often penciled onto the backs of the photographs, such as the famous Zalumma Agra, the "Star of the East," or Zoe Meleke and Zoberdie Luti.

As the fame of the Circassian beauties spread, the public demanded even more information about them, and Barnum was prepared to oblige. He began to publish short biographies of the women, which were later expanded into pamphlets that provided details about the women themselves and their native region. In one such pamphlet, published in 1868, the women of Circassia were held to be "as beautiful as houris" and were therefore especially prized by the sultan in Constantinople. The region was one of high mountains and pristine glens, a place of untold natural beauty and wealth, "another California" whose riches would soon be revealed to the world through "the onward march of civilization." The particular subject of this sketch, Zalumma Agra, was said to hail from a port city on the Black Sea, where she had been "a daughter of one of the petty princes of the country and a niece of the Prophet Schemyl [Shamil]." According to the pamphlet, she ended up in Barnum's care after having been expelled from her homeland by the Russians. The intrepid Greenwood had seen her in Constantinople, secured her guardianship, and then proceeded to transform her into what she had now become, "a refined, intellectual, and Christian woman."[71] Any visitor to Barnum's museum—as well as to scores of imitators, from Baltimore to

The Georgian Military Highway, photographed in the early twentieth century. Time and Life Pictures/Getty Images.

Portrait of Alexei Ermolov, by George Dawe. © The State Hermitage Museum, St. Petersburg.

Shamil (center) with two of his sons, Gazi-Mehmet (left) and Magomet-Shefi (right), Kiev, 1869, from a nineteenth-century postcard. Author's collection.

Idealized image of Circassians, from a nineteenth-century engraving. Author's collection.

Dagestani man and woman, circa 1910. Library of Congress, Prints and Photographs Division, Prokudin-Gorskii Collection.

Zobeide Luti, an American "Circassian beauty," circa 1860. Author's collection.

A street in Tiflis/Tbilisi, with the Narikala fortress above, 1931. American Geographical Society Library, University of Wisconsin–Milwaukee Libraries.

A village in upland Dagestan, 1933. American Geographical Society Library, University of Wisconsin–Milwaukee Libraries.

Armenian orphans in a school outside Yerevan, 1919. Library of Congress, Prints and Photographs Division.

Muslim/Turkish orphans in eastern Anatolia, 1919. Library of Congress, Prints and Photographs Division.

Lavrenti Beria (center) with Nestor Lakoba (left), Aghasi Khanjian (right), and Ghazanfar Musabekov (far right), Moscow, 1935. Hoover Institution Archives, Nestor A. Lakoba Collection.

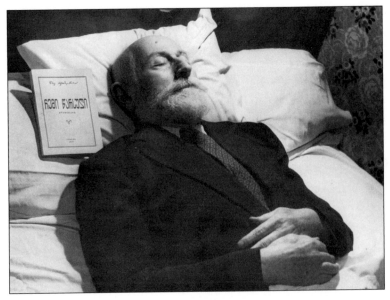

Noe Jordania lying in repose, Paris, 1953. Hoover Institution Archives, Boris I. Nicolaevsky Collection.

An informal memorial to victims of the Beslan hostage crisis, in the gymnasium of School No. 1, Beslan, North Ossetia, 2006. Photograph by the author.

The funeral procession of Azerbaijani president Heydar
Aliyev, 2003. Getty Images.

Georgian president Mikheil Saakashvili addressing the European Parliament, 2006. AFP/Getty Images.

Chicago—would thus have been treated not only to an erotically charged conversation with a woman of the mountains but also to a quick geography lesson—part fantasy, part reality—on the Caucasus itself.

The truth is that these women had no connection to the Caucasus at all. Most were probably local talent—Irish girls from lower Manhattan—who were hired by Barnum and outfitted in bizarre costumes. That is why, as hedges against prying questioners, the pamphlet on Zalumma Agra helpfully explained that she had lost all knowledge of her native language and had only dim recollections of her homeland. The wild coiffures were achieved by having the women shampoo their hair in beer and then tease it out vigorously with a comb. The hair may have been an effort to suggest blackness rather than whiteness, a nod to popular conceptions of African female sexuality, or there may have been a degree of gender bending going on: The tall, fuzzy hat (*papakha*) often worn by Caucasus men may have morphed into female hairstyles. Whiteness, slavery, the Caucasus, and a physical appearance that suggested both racial purity and the mythical earthiness of the black female—the multiple cultural symbols embodied in the Circassian beauties provide ample testimony to Barnum's particular marketing savvy.[72]

This prototype of the Circassian woman reached its zenith in the 1880s, but in time popular interest waned. Barnum's American Museum burned down already in 1868, and he soon turned his attention to other pursuits. With the arrival of the First World War, Circassian beauties had all but disappeared, although some shed their vaguely foreign names and simply billed themselves as women with bizarre hairdos. The Circassians went from being notable as epitomes of female beauty to being grotesque perversions of it. Bad hair, not the exoticism of the East, had become a more profitable selling point.

The Caucasus was viewed through different cultural lenses at different times but always in ways that revealed more about the viewer than about the mountains, plains, and peoples of the region itself. On his way to Erzurum in 1829, Pushkin stopped in Orel, south of Moscow, to visit Ermolov. It was early morning, but the general was already out and about. When he returned, he received Pushkin cordially with a warm but forced smile. The inactivity of retirement was obviously weighing on him, although he still had traces of the old lion in his gray eyes and bristly hair. His dress and surroundings provided unmistakable echoes of his earlier career on the troubled southern frontier. He was dressed in a green *cherkeska*, and Circassian swords and daggers lined the walls of his study.[73] The Caucasus was now in Orel.

There is no better symbol of the reciprocal effects of the conquest of the Caucasus than the fact that Ermolov could be found in his retirement dressed in native attire and encircled by mementos of the mountains. That, however, is the way of all empires. They and their makers are irremediably changed by the experience of conquest, finding in the peoples and cultures of the frontier something indescribably appealing. Empires, as much as imperialists, can go native.

Such was the case with Russia. Already in 1828 Tsar Nicholas I had added Caucasus mountaineers, decked out in colorful *cherkeskas*, to his imperial retinue. Later, special detachments of Georgians, Armenians, and Muslim highlanders were added to the corps, dressed in costumes that were as traditional as those of Victorian Scottish regiments, that is to say, largely modern inventions rather than borrowings from a tribal past. State-sponsored spectacles replayed the capture of Shamil, while cheap works of fiction told of indefatigable warriors and lovely highland princesses. Even modern forms of entertainment could be mobilized to rework old themes. One of the first Russian feature films to be shot on location in the Caucasus, in 1911, recounted the familiar story of captivity at the hands of charming natives. Two films on Shamil were produced in 1913.[74]

Things can also proceed in the opposite direction, that is, natives can go imperial. Empires depend on a panoply of subalterns: local notables whose authority is cemented by the sovereign; paid functionaries recruited from among the native population; and new generations of peripheral elites trained in the academies and institutions of the imperial center. Although these privileged peripherals are crucial components of imperial rule, they are also its most dangerous element. It is within their ranks that anti-imperial ideologies of nationalism, liberty, and self-determination usually arise.

The writings of Güldenstädt, Klaproth, and Bronevskii worked out exactly who these "natives" were. Pushkin, Lermontov, and others created the image of the romantic highlander. Following the Crimean War and the fall of Circassia, Russian ethnographers and naturalists descended on the Caucasus with renewed vigor. If the early nineteenth century was about mapping the region and its complexities, the latter half was about making it simpler: dividing it up into a manageable and understandable array of clearly delineated peoples; creating a historical narrative for each one; cataloging the cultural traits that defined them; and, finally, packaging these things in ways that could be communicated to the public through museum exhibitions and other public displays. A history of fitful incorporation, tactical compromise, and brutal warfare was now recast as the story of Russia's inevitable triumph in the south. Soon, however, a new generation of Caucasus elites would read the same history as a narrative of oppression, Russification, and the struggle for social reform and national freedom. The meaning of the Caucasus and its past could be as malleable on the ground as it was in the overactive imaginations of European climbers or American showmen.

Ideas of social justice, enveloped in new visions of national identity, were emerging at precisely the time that the Caucasus was becoming increasingly important to Western governments. The Ottoman Empire was weakening. Russia would soon find itself in the throes of a popular revolution, followed by harsh reaction and even more monumental upheavals. The Caucasus, located at the intersection of these fragile imperial orders, had become a prize that no strategist could ignore. By the end of the First World War, much of the Caucasus would be transformed from a place of diminutive kingdoms and satrapies of one or another empire into a congeries of small, fragile, and notionally independent republics. Freedom, no longer merely an obsession of poets and travelers, was becoming a matter of practical politics.

FOUR

Nations and Revolutions

*In the end, who will establish himself in the Caucasus? Who will use the oil
and the most important roads leading into the depths of Asia, the Revolution
or the Entente? That is the whole question.*

Joseph Stalin (1920)

The difference between poetry and truth is not yet recognized in the mountains.

Essad Bey (Lev Nussimbaum), Baku-born writer (1931)

IN THE 1820s, Semyon Bronevskii gave what seems from a modern perspective like a confused inventory of peoples and territories in the north Caucasus. From west to east, his list included the following:

the Circassians who live beyond the Kuban River
Greater and Lesser Kabarda
the land with no name
the area controlled by the Bragun chieftain
the Kists
the Ingush
the Karabulaks
the peaceful Chechens

the mountain Chechens
the Kumyks, of three types
the Nogai nomads, scattered about in all parts[1]

Bronevskii's list represented an amalgam of geographical, linguistic, and political labels. Some are still in use today, while others have disappeared. However, this was the lens through which Russian empire builders saw the region in Bronevskii's day: a mix of poorly understood groups, some free and others under Russian suzerainty, with still others connected to one or another powerful local ruler; some living in the mountains, others on the plains; some settled, others nomadic.

It was only later, after the final conquest of the uplands, that something approaching modern conceptions of cultural identity became the natural way of thinking about who lived there. In the late nineteenth century the Russian mental map of the Caucasus became populated by distinct ethnic groups, each with its own language, dress, territory, and way of life.[2] In 1851 the Russian Geographical Society established a branch in Tiflis and inaugurated a series of specialized journals and monographs on the history, archaeology, folklore, and ethnography of every corner of the Caucasus. A statistical committee and archaeological commission were formed in the 1860s to provide numerical data on economic and social development and to uncover the roots of modern cultures in the buried past. In the 1870s a special state commission began publishing detailed ethnographic descriptions of the highland populations on both sides of the mountains. Linguists, ethnographers, statisticians, and historians—both professionals and amateurs, Russian and indigenous—found common cause in the new drive to understand the Caucasus.[3]

As early as 1867 some of the artifacts assembled by these scholars were housed in a new Caucasus Museum in Tiflis. Its director, the energetic Gustav Radde, created a local industry in the collection and dissemination of information about the natural and cultural peculiarities of the region. Situated on Golovinskii Prospekt, the city's main thoroughfare, the museum was attracting some six thousand visitors per year by the 1890s.[4] Some of the exhibition halls were dedicated to the flora and fauna of the region, with dioramas of leaping ibexes and scampering pheasants. Others were filled with mannequins dressed in ethnic costumes and placed against painted scenes of appropriate habitats: shield-bearing Khevsur and Tush warriors in one mountainous tableau, caftaned Turkmen in another, Jews and Armenians engaged in some transaction in still another. Anyone who walked through the museum's doors would have had an immediate visual representation of the relationship between the imperial center and the Caucasus periphery. A vast mural on the staircase entitled *The Arrival of the Argonauts in Colchis* depicted a mythical encounter between Greeks and Colchians, the bearers of Western civilization reaching out to the ancient inhabitants of Georgia. All of the Greek faces, however, were portraits of prominent Russian imperial leaders.[5]

In 1897 the social inventory of the Caucasus was fully revealed in the first comprehensive imperial census.[6] The census categories were built around the three most important criteria for defining groups in the Russian imperial imagination: social category or "estate," religion, and language. At the turn of the twentieth century the category of ethnicity or nationality (*natsional'nost'*) did not yet have the all-powerful sense that it would acquire under the Soviets. Nevertheless, one can get a clear sense of how administrators and scientific professionals viewed the human landscape, as well as how much the view had changed since the early days of imperial expansion. Bronevskii's vision had given way to one in which the Caucasus was seen to be peopled by clearly delineated religious and linguistic groups. The universal category of "highlander" had disappeared, replaced by an array of terms that closely mapped modern ethnic categories, such as Circassians, Abkhaz, Ossetians, Chechens, Ingush, and Avars.

Administratively, in 1897 the Caucasus was divided into provinces (*guberniias*) and districts (*oblasts* and *okrugs*). In the north the Kuban district and Stavropol province stretched from the steppe land along the Kuban River and Sea of Azov and into the foothills of the main mountain range. The Terek and Dagestan districts comprised the area that had seen much of the fighting during the Caucasus wars: the forests of Chechnya, the ravines of Avaristan, plus other regions where Shamil's influence had been most pronounced. South of the main range lay the Chernomorskaia, or Black Sea, province, the strip of coastal Circassia that had been emptied of natives more than three decades earlier. Historic Georgia consisted of the Kutaisi and Tiflis provinces, named for two of the major Georgian cities. Farther to the east lay the Elisavetpol and Baku provinces, with their large Muslim populations. The border with the Ottoman Empire was bounded by the districts of Batumi and Kars and the province of Yerevan, areas that had repeatedly been trampled during the successive wars between tsar and sultan.

The population of the Caucasus numbered around nine million. The region was a vast patchwork of linguistic and religious groups, although the influx of Russian colonists in some areas, the forced migration from the highlands, and concerted campaigns of proselytizing by the Orthodox Church had made it a more Russian and Orthodox environment than it had ever been before. Just under half the total population was Orthodox Christian, both Russian and Georgian. Around 12 percent were Gregorian Armenian or Armenian Catholic (Armenians in communion with Rome). About 35 percent were Muslim. The rest of the population was divided among several religious traditions: Orthodox Christian dissenters, Roman Catholics, German Lutherans, Jews, and Buddhist nomads. All of the Caucasus districts were mixed, both linguistically and religiously, but clear regional differences had emerged. The Kuban, Stavropol, Kutaisi, Tiflis, and Black Sea regions were predominantly Orthodox, while Dagestan, Baku, Elisavetpol, and Kars were mainly Muslim.

The vast majority of the region's population (87 percent) still lived in rural areas. However, that basic fact masked a trend that would become more important with the approach of the twentieth century, namely, the growth and transformation of urban environments. By the time of the Russian Revolution of 1905—which would usher in a short-lived parliament and set the stage for the growing disorder of the First World War—social cleavages and pent-up grievances were emerging. In the Caucasus the crucible of empire was no longer the old Cossack-patrolled lines, which had faded as the empire leached farther and farther into the mountains. It was now the burgeoning cities, where old elites jealous of their waning power, industrial workers attracted by the promise of socialism, and confessional groups suspicious of their neighbors' intentions created a volatile mix.

Bazaar and Boomtown

One of the legacies of the political fragmentation of the Caucasus over the centuries was the fact that, until rather late in the Russian Empire, few great cities emerged as obvious regional centers. Social life unfolded in upland hamlets, lowland villages, and feudal estates. Towns were by and large places that people passed through to get somewhere else—for example, to reach the trade fairs at Tabriz or to cross the Black Sea to Constantinople or Odessa. "Will we reach the town soon?" a Russian traveler asked his guide during a trip along the Caspian coast in the 1840s. "What do you mean? We've been in the town for a while now," the guide responded, pointing toward the small huts that dotted the landscape.[7]

When sizable cities emerged, they did so almost exclusively in response to the exigencies of imperial administration. The names of many of the region's modern cities hark back to their origins as imperial outposts, such as Vladikavkaz at the northern end of the Georgian Military Highway or Grozny in lowland Chechnya. Some of the old centers of local culture became minor regional towns renowned for a distinctive style of carpet or the presence of a lovely church, but few regained the prominence they might have had in times past.

The two great exceptions were Tiflis and Baku, ancient settlements that grew and changed as they became vital parts of the administrative and economic system of the late Russian Empire. Tiflis—known as Tbilisi since the 1930s—was a city tucked into the steep slopes along the banks of the muddy Kura River. Founded in the fourth century A.D., it began to flourish when the king of Kartli transferred his residence there in the sixth century. The city was repeatedly attacked and nearly destroyed, most spectacularly during the Persian campaign of 1795; parts of the city remained in ruins for decades following the Persian onslaught.[8] Tiflis had much to recommend it. Stark hills framed clusters of typical Georgian houses, their elegant, multilevel porches opening onto narrow streets. The hot springs along the river attracted both the healthy and the infirm. "I must not omit to mention that the baths of the city cannot be surpassed even by those of Constantinople," wrote a visitor in 1840. "They have also the additional recommendation of being remarkably clean and well kept."[9]

A walk through imperial Tiflis wound through several different worlds. The city was, in many ways, a miniature version of the entire Caucasus. Beginning on the southwest bank of the Kura River, known to Georgians as the Mtkvari, one could stroll down wide, straight streets, past public offices, the opera house, the palace of the viceroy, and the homes of wealthy merchants. The newer parts of the city boasted rows of trees planted along Golovinskii Prospekt, where well-dressed patrons took their evening constitutionals. The boulevard was lined with shops fitted with decorative vitrines that would not have looked out of place in St. Petersburg or Moscow, except that the signage might be in Russian, French, German, Armenian, or Persian.

To the southeast of this district lay the old town, more Asian than European to most visitors, its narrow streets twisting up toward the medieval citadel and slinking down toward the river. Houses were wedged one against the other, fronting unpaved streets where artisans—leather workers, jewelers, carpet salesmen, tinkers, shoemakers—plied their trades. Goods of local manufacture were offered beside furs from the high Caucasus, carpets from Tabriz, and silks from Bukhara. In the streets wagons and oxcarts competed with donkeys and the occasional string of camels. Above the rooftops one could see the drums and conical cupolas of Georgian and Armenian churches and the minarets of mosques, both Sunni and Shi'a. Descending to the river and crossing one of the principal bridges, one came upon the statue of Prince Vorontsov—the redoubtable old viceroy and the real maker of the modern city—standing guard near the district known simply as "the colony." There a community of German Protestants—invited by the tsarist government to settle throughout much of southern Russia—had created a very different environment. Rows of trees lined the main streets. Schools and churches, conducting their business in German, offered education and spiritual edification. Beer gardens provided the main entertainment.[10]

Tiflis became so well known as a desirable destination that visitors felt no need to describe it in any great detail."For me to add my small quota of information would be most unnecessary," said one writer in 1888.[11] But no one missed the central feature of Tiflis's urban landscape—that the city was in Georgia but not of Georgia. The countryside, from the vineyards of Kakheti in the east to the hazelnut groves of Mingrelia in the west, was inhabited by Georgian peasants, nominally freed from serfdom in the 1860s but still dependent on the feudal nobility. Faced with the meager resources of the countryside and attracted by the growth of small-scale manufacturing in the towns, some of these peasants had begun to leave the estates. Along with the influx of imperial administrators and newcomers from other parts of the empire, the city's population expanded rapidly. In 1811 Tiflis had a little over 8,000 inhabitants. By 1864 that figure had climbed to 60,000, and by 1902 it had reached around 190,000.[12] At the time of the outbreak of the First World War, Tiflis was the sixth largest urban center in the empire, with more than half the population consisting of migrants from other cities, towns, and villages.[13]

A newly arrived Georgian peasant would have found Tiflis almost wholly foreign. Business was conducted in many languages, with ethnic groups specializing in specific professions, such as Greek stonecutters, Persian plasterers, Ossetian cooks, Russian carpenters, and Jewish tailors.[14] The group that truly stood out in the economic and administrative life of the city was the Armenians. At the beginning of the nineteenth century Armenians accounted for perhaps three-quarters of the city's population. By the end of the century they were a little more than a third but remained the single largest cultural group.[15] They were responsible for financing the building boom of the latter half of the century and dominated the municipal administration. Oliver Wardrop, later to become the first British high commissioner in the Caucasus, provided the following assessment of the position of Armenians in the city's life in the 1880s: "Only those who have lived the life of the people in Trans-Caucasia know what a terrible curse the money-lending community are. A local proverb says, 'A Greek will cheat three Jews, but an Armenian will cheat three Greeks,' and the Georgian, straightforward, honest fellow, is but too often cruelly swindled by [them]. When the fraud is very apparent the Armenian often pays for his greed with all the blood that can be extracted from his jugular vein."[16] The same racist opinion would be echoed by many visitors, reflecting a view of urban relations they had picked up from Georgian intellectuals and Russian administrators who were jealous of the influence of Armenians in the city's economy and politics.

The Armenian issue would be central to the city's affairs during the First World War and the two Russian revolutions of 1917. However, the main outlines of Georgian nationalism—yet another product of urban life in Tiflis—developed in directions largely divorced from the Armenian dimension of the social landscape. The Georgian relationship with Russian power had always been complicated. On the one hand, the Georgian aristocracy was absorbed into the Russian system of noble ranks, and people of Georgian birth emerged as major partners in the Russian expansion into the Caucasus. On the other hand, there were regular uprisings by dissident members of the nobility, sometimes in league with discontented peasants. In 1832 a conspiracy of nobles nearly brought Russia's expansion to a halt. It was only in the last decades of the century that two distinct sources of dissatisfaction came together: a concern among Georgian intellectuals for the status of Georgian language and culture in the face of the Russification policies of the tsarist state, and the movement for reform that would eventually find expression in populism and socialism.

The growth of modern Georgian nationalism is usually charted in terms of "groups," or different generations and factions of intellectuals, each of which developed distinct points of view with respect to Georgian identity, Georgia's political and historical destiny, and the nation's relationship with Russia. The so-called first group of national elites (the *pirveli dasi*, in Georgian) is associated with the life and career of Ilia Chavchavadze, the great writer and activist, now considered

Georgia's national poet. The second group (*meore dasi*), roughly contemporary with the first, was active from the 1860s onward and was associated with the work of such bourgeois liberals as the journalist Giorgi Tsereteli. Both groups were part of a broader movement of nationalists, progressives, and populists inspired by reformist currents in other parts of the Russian Empire and western Europe. They challenged the old order of Russian autocracy and drew encouragement from liberal nationalists outside Georgia, hence the collective label sometimes applied to them—the *tergdaleulni*, or "those who have tasted the waters of the Terek," that is, men who traveled to Russia and abroad and brought back to Georgia ideas of national rebirth and political reform. However, it was the third group (*mesame dasi*) that, rising to prominence in the opening years of the twentieth century, would eventually form the basis for Georgia's first experiment in independence. Composed of more radical young men, many of them products of the Tiflis theological seminary, the third group questioned the political orientations of their predecessors, finding their inspiration not in the various forms of liberal nationalism then current in western Europe but rather in Marxism.

More than other parts of the Russian Empire, Georgia was uniquely suited to the growth of a strong socialist movement.[17] There was a tradition of radical peasant activism, especially in western Georgia, which also happened to be the birthplace of many Georgian Marxists. There was a small but well-educated urban class eager for political modernization. A growing proletariat—primarily railway workers and those in the mining industries—proved receptive to progressive ideals. A nobility ambivalent toward Russia—at times cooperative, at other times resentful of linguistic and cultural Russification—provided an articulate and wealthy class of patrons. Socialism and populist nationalism were thus not irreconcilable enemies in Georgia, as they were in other parts of Europe, but natural allies.

At the turn of the century underground political organizations fomented public unrest. Industrial workers held strikes. May Day celebrations—first held in Tiflis in 1899—sometimes ended in rioting, with soldiers firing at crowds. Bad harvests brought new waves of peasant migrants into the towns, creating a mass of discontented and displaced laborers susceptible to radical politics. In 1901 the Georgian branch of the Russian Social Democratic Workers' Party, the empire's major Marxist organization, held its first conference, bringing together many of the members of the third group and cementing ties between Georgian activists and the socialist movement in the wider empire.

The stage was set for the massive street demonstrations and public protests that characterized the period from the 1905 revolution through the First World War.

Unlike Tiflis, which grew steadily through trade and imperial administration, Baku was a classic boomtown. A settlement had existed there since antiquity. It was built around the natural fires, fueled by escaping gas, that were sacred to Zoroastrians. Perched on a narrow peninsula jutting out into the Caspian Sea, the town and its fortress became strategically important during Peter the Great's forays into the Caspian region in the 1720s, when the town was captured and held for several years by the tsar's forces. The city was fully integrated into the Russian Empire following the signing of the Treaty of Gulistan in 1813.

By the late nineteenth century Baku was alive with activity, spurred on by the realization that the sticky petroleum deposits on its outskirts could be used for something other than making torches and keeping flies off cattle. Although the Russian state was the earliest commercial exploiter of these resources, the decision to end the tsarist monopoly in the early 1870s opened the Baku fields to international companies. The Swedish businessmen Robert and Ludvig Nobel invested in a small refinery and laid the groundwork for the rise of the Nobel brothers' petroleum empire. The industry would soon attract financiers such as the Rothschilds and international firms such as Shell. Old hand-dug pits gave way to drilled wells and modern refining techniques. Transportation in barrel-laden carts and camel caravans was supplanted by rail cars, pipelines, and steamships. In 1893 there were 458 operational wells scattered around Baku; in 1914 there were 2,541.[18] By the time of the Bolshevik Revolution, over 150 different oil companies were active in the city.

As in Tiflis, the old town and the newer sections were marked by contrasts. The old palace of the khan was perched on a hill overlooking the sea, its steep, narrow streets winding inside massive stone walls, some of Persian origin, others of older Arab design. A warren of alleys encircled mosques and houses, all grouped around the landmark Qız Qalası, or "maiden's tower," a former watchtower that had been transformed into a lighthouse. Farther to the east lay the new town, a product of the city's recent wealth, with its boulevards and public buildings inspired by French architectural fashions. Despite the violent northwesterly winds, Baku's excellent harbor made it a natural entrepôt for goods arriving from the Caspian Sea and beyond, including cotton from Transcaspia, dried fruit from Persia, and fish from the sea itself. Rail lines connected the city to the other side of the Caucasus—to Poti and Batumi on the Black Sea, as well as to the north Caucasus railway network via Derbend and Petrovsk on the Caspian. The outskirts of the city contained a forest of derricks, the most visible sign of the industrial economy upon which the modern city was being built.

Bakuvians quickly learned how to cater to the tastes of their new foreign neighbors. Hotels, clubs, and casinos sprang up almost as fast as oil rigs. At the Metropole, described by some visitors as the finest restaurant in the Caucasus, deals were brokered and promises broken over salmon fillets, large sturgeon steaks, and generous dollops of caviar, that other oily product of the Caspian Sea. According to Harry Luke, a foreign diplomat, the city combined "the opulence of a Riviera Casino, the vulgarity of some upstart town in the New World, the unrestrained lavishness of pre-War Russia and the colours and savours of the mediaeval East."[19] By the time of the 1897 census, the city and its hinterland contained nearly 183,000 inhabitants, of which about 35 percent were Azerbaijani Muslims, 25 percent Russians, and 12 percent Armenians. Early in the next century the population of the city and its suburbs topped 200,000, rivaling Tiflis as the largest urban space in the south Caucasus. Like the viceregal center, it was a city of immigrants. By the beginning of the twentieth century, less than half the population had been born there.[20]

The wealth produced by the petroleum industry created a new class of Muslim entrepreneurs and industrialists whose influence and investments are still evident today even beneath the grime of the city's post-Soviet boom. Grand houses dating from the late nineteenth and early twentieth centuries, such as that of the industrialist Zeynalabdin Taghiyev (now the state history museum), reflected a unique combination of European and Middle Eastern tastes, some featuring reception rooms with both European-style chairs and carpet-covered divans. Public buildings in beaux arts and other contemporary styles, from banks and theaters to shopping arcades and public schools, dotted the new city close to the seashore. Local Muslim entrepreneurs—landowners who became rich following the discovery of oil—fostered public foundations and charitable organizations and established newspapers and libraries, all of which helped to transform the city in relatively short order.

This Baku—where East and West mixed both furtively and fortuitously—also became one of the centers of a great renaissance of Muslim cultural life in the empire, the seat of a modernizing movement among Caucasus Muslims that produced a raucous, creative, and Islamic fin-de-siècle. An Azerbaijani-language press flourished during periods when publication in the language was not banned by tsarist authorities. New schools and educational practices—which stressed literacy in Azerbaijani and Russian and taught mathematics as well as other practical subjects—competed with traditional Qur'anic educational foundations. Reformist discussion groups eventually evolved into political parties that called for greater civil liberties and a cultural identity that simultaneously embraced reformist Islam, a Turkic heritage, and citizenship in the Russian state.

As in any boomtown, social relations in Baku were sometimes fraught with tension. New arrivals threatened established elites. Villagers drawn to the town competed with older urbanites for jobs in the new economy. Baku was a city of young men on the make, seeking employment and a way to relieve their boredom. There was no urban space in the Russian Empire more ripe for social conflict than Baku, with its sizable industrial proletariat, ostentatious bourgeoisie, and history of communal discord between Christians and Muslims. Things came to a head in the opening years of the twentieth century, when this opulent city, precariously balanced at the edge of the sea, would embark on more than a decade of self-destruction.

In the countryside peasant insurrections and brigandage—a perennial feature of the Caucasus in the imperial period—were on the rise. In the city general strikes were staged in 1903 and 1904, prompted by poor working conditions and the agitation of socialist parties. Social unrest reached its climax in August 1905, when rioters torched entire stretches of Baku. Oil facilities were decimated, textile mills destroyed, and printing facilities broken up. International firms were closed down as their managers fled the city. Despite the imposition of martial law, the streets belonged to gangs of violent toughs.

Labor unrest became tangled up with communal issues as Muslim rioters attacked Armenian neighborhoods and burned the property of Armenian shopkeepers. Mutual fear—that the Armenians were planning an uprising to eliminate the Muslims, and that the Muslims were now repeating the anti-Armenian pogroms regularly perpetrated across the border in the Ottoman lands—created opportunities for settling old scores, as well as for simple thievery. Both were facilitated by local police and other state authorities. Once violence began, it quickly took on a life of its own irrespective of motive. "They themselves do not know why they are killing each other," the mayor of Baku is reported to have said at the time.[21]

Although the city had long been culturally diverse, confessional communities traditionally lived in their own neighborhoods, or *mahalles*, where they led separate but parallel lives. Those lines were breached during the bloody August days when entire Armenian *mahalles* were leveled and their inhabitants put to flight. The most extreme forms of violence had subsided by the spring of 1906, when martial law was lifted, but it would soon return. Further strikes were initiated in 1913. Labor uprisings continued throughout the First World War, devastating the city's industrial works and further contributing to hatred between Christians and Muslims. "When one speaks of the streets of a town running with blood one is generally employing a figure of speech," wrote Harry Luke about his experience in the city. "If one is referring to Baku . . . one is being starkly literal."[22]

The Uses of War

Far beyond the street violence of Baku, the overall political situation across Eurasia and the Near East was changing. Although Russia had lost the Crimean War to the Ottomans and their Western allies in 1856, the outcome of that contest provided necessary breathing space for the empire to restore full control over the Caucasus. Troops were freed up, which allowed them to be deployed against the Circassians in the final years of the wars of conquest. When the Russians and Ottomans came to blows again in the war of 1877–78, the outcome was even more advantageous for the tsar. The port of Batumi was brought under Russian control and converted into a naval station within easy striking distance of Ottoman possessions along the coast. Kars, the fortress in eastern Anatolia, was likewise turned into a Russian outpost, effectively blocking any potential Ottoman invasion of the south Caucasus. Roads and railway links ensured rapid troop movement in the event of conflict.

Russia, however, faced clear challenges. On the eve of the First World War, German interests in southeastern Europe—from the Balkans to Anatolia—were manifest. German-born princes had been elevated to the kingships of Romania and Bulgaria, which seemed to guarantee that these countries would join Germany in any pan-European conflict. Berlin exerted influence in the Ottoman military, where German officers had been training and reorganizing the army and navy for more than a decade. Railway projects in Anatolia, bank-rolled by German financiers, improved the ability of the Ottomans to move troops and equipment closer to the Russian border. Most important, the virtual elimination of Ottoman power in continental Europe—in the wake of the Balkan wars of 1912 and 1913—shifted that empire's real sphere of interest from Europe to its Asian expanse. Ottoman military officers and intellectuals increasingly stressed the natural affinities between Ottoman Turks and the Muslims of the Caucasus and Central Asia. A position in the Caucasus that only a few decades earlier had seemed unassailable—pacified highlands, good communication systems, a weak neighbor, an oil-rich economy—now appeared to the Russians to be increasingly threatened.

When war broke out in the summer of 1914, Germany and the Ottoman Empire were bound by a secret alliance that provided for mutual assistance in the event of international hostilities. During the early months of the war German war planners did little to press their special relationship with Constantinople. However, after suffering losses on both the western and eastern fronts, the Central Powers came to see the Turks as critical players in the game of separating Russia from its allies in the West. By autumn 1914 the insistence of the Germans and the strategic designs of the Ottoman Military had combined to produce a military situation that Sultans had assiduously avoided for centuries, namely, war with Russia, France, and Britain—all at the same time.[23]

At the beginning of the war many of the Russian forces in the Caucasus were transferred to Russia's western front, where German and Austro-Hungarian troops hoped to immobilize the tsar and prevent him from opening a route to the Balkans. Among these forces was the famous Dikaia diviziia, the so-called Wild Division of highland Muslims, commanded by Grand Duke Michael, the tsar's younger brother. The remaining Caucasus army consisted of perhaps 100,000 regular infantry, 15,000 cavalry, and 256 guns, along with another 150,000 or more Muslim, Georgian, and Armenian volunteers.[24] Forays along the Russian-Ottoman border resulted in few decisive victories for either side. Yet an Ottoman miscalculation in the winter of 1914–15 determined the future of military operations in eastern Anatolia and the Caucasus.

The military engineer of the Ottoman winter offensive was Enver Pasha, one of the leaders of the Committee of Union and Progress, or Young Turks, the group that had seized power in the empire after a revolution in 1908. Emboldened by the weak showing of Russian forces in early encounters, Enver planned to rush toward Kars and break through the Russian defenses into the south Caucasus. He believed that the arrival of Ottoman troops would encourage a general uprising by Caucasus Muslims and create a solid wall to block Russian movement southward. The plan was daring but poorly executed. Ottoman soldiers were inadequately provisioned and lacked everything from accurate topographical maps to winter shoes and clothing. By the middle of January, after weeks of heavy fighting in appalling conditions, the Ottoman offensive ground to a halt near Sarıkamış, well to the southwest of Kars. Enver's army, which began the campaign with some ninety-five thousand men, was now reduced to only eighteen thousand.[25]

The failure of the Sarıkamış expedition had significant repercussions. The Ottoman setback in the east may have inclined Allied planners to launch their own offensive in the west—the disastrous 1915 campaign to take the Dardanelles. From the Ottoman perspective this failure was attributable in part to the small but lethal bands of local guerrillas, especially Armenians, whom the Russians had employed against the regular Ottoman army. For the Russians the Caucasus forces had achieved a signal victory, but commanders realized that it was owing more to the topography of eastern Anatolia and the Caucasus borderlands than to the superior skills of the Russian army. A reorganization was launched to beef up the number of Russian soldiers by drawing them from Cossack regiments north of the mountains, redeploying them from the European front, and mobilizing Caucasus locals.

In addition to these high-level military changes, social tensions were on the increase. People took advantage of the breakdown in social order to settle old scores. Disputes between religious groups took on a political edge. Older differences—from family feuds to struggles over agricultural land—were cloaked in the language of national survival and, eventually, revolution. The confluence of greed, personal grievance, and communal fear and loathing was readily apparent in the Ottoman domains of eastern Anatolia. Wartime violence in that region would have a profound influence on the future of the Caucasus as a whole—but especially on the old province of Yerevan, that is, modern Armenia.

Irrespective of the period, Caucasus violence was usually a matter of what would now be called irregular warfare. Mountains, high plateaus, and deep gorges made traditional military operations difficult for imperial forces. Battles involved the fight for a strategic choke point in the form of a valley, river crossing, or mountain pass rather than a prearranged meeting of regular armies on an open field. Tribal and clan-based social organization, a tradition of intertribal raiding, the long experience of successive anti-imperial wars, and the martial ethic of highland societies all fueled guerrilla organizations and armed insurgency.

In all of these operations local knowledge was critical. Unfamiliar landscapes forced imperial soldiers to rely on cooperative villagers for information about topography and for the provisioning of troops. Modern empires and native societies were thus partners as well as opponents. The state was highly dependent on local techniques of violence already employed in the mountains. Russians treated some groups as loyal and cooperative and others as potentially inimical and suspect. Indigenous groups, in turn, could become violent subcontractors, settling scores with old enemies by offering their superior knowledge and warrior skills to imperial powerbrokers. As in any borderland, the obverse of resistance was not acquiescence but rather the active pursuit of personal and communal interests within frameworks provided by the empire itself.

Over the course of the nineteenth century, religious identity became a useful rule of thumb for deciding which groups to trust. Russia assumed the mantle of protector of Eastern Christians—which had been one of the key catalysts of the Crimean War—while the Ottomans often attempted to utilize Islam as a link to Caucasus Muslims in Circassia and Dagestan. The place where both these strategies came together was in eastern Anatolia, along the Russo-Turkish border. There Muslim and Christian populations mingled freely. Armenians, Greeks, and Assyrians lived in close proximity to Turkish- or Georgian-speaking Muslims and Kurdish nomads. Adding to this mix was a long tradition of intergroup conflict associated with feuds, nomadic targeting of settled groups, and religious retribution against nonbelievers. The relocation of Circassians to eastern Anatolia in the 1860s heightened to these tensions.

The Ottoman government frequently took advantage of these social divisions, using them as a lever against perceived Christian disloyalty to the empire. In the mid-1890s, during the reign of Sultan Abdülhamid II, a series of pogroms against Armenians and other Anatolian Christians was perpetrated by specially outfitted irregular troops composed of local Kurds and, less frequently, Circassians or other Caucasus highlanders. During the First World War army columns moved back and forth through the region, requisitioning livestock, commandeering accommodations, and further disrupting social order. Moreover, Russia's support for Armenian village militias and guerrillas (*fedayin*) deepened the sultan's distrust of the Armenian population.

Eastern Anatolia during the First World War was ripe for genocidal violence. Armenian political groups were attempting to foment a national rebellion, with political goals that involved the territorial dismemberment of the Ottoman state. The Ottoman authorities were a relatively new and insecure cohort associated with the Young Turks. Their senior leadership had been exposed to irregular warfare in the Balkans—the 1908 conspiracy that brought the Young Turks to power had originated among Ottoman military units stationed there—and were well aware of the power of an armed insurgency fueled by nationalism. They came to see Armenian villagers as either tacit or overt supporters of the *fedayin* and therefore dangerous instruments in the hands of their Russian enemy. Armenians outside eastern Anatolia, including well-established urban intellectuals and business leaders who had been unfailingly loyal to the Ottoman state, were viewed as potentially suspect as well. In such a context, the Ottomans adopted a policy of resettling allegedly untrustworthy populations, a policy that soon escalated into a full-scale war by the Ottoman state against its own subjects. In the chaotic period from 1914 to the establishment of the Turkish Republic in 1923, Armenians, Greeks, and Assyrian Christians emerged as the primary targets of a state-led policy of relocation and extermination.

It is a standard trope of genocide deniers to demand that claims about genocide be substantiated by a document explicitly ordering mass murder. It is an equally widespread trope among survivors and their descendants that genocide was inevitable, the result of an almost genetic loathing for the victims by the perpetrators. The first view seeks to explain how genocide could not possibly have happened. The second seeks to explain how it could not have been otherwise. However, both simplify the reality of mass killing. In nearly all instances of large-scale violence, state manipulation and local circumstances come together in a contingent, complicated, and ultimately deadly mix. The Armenian genocide was neither explicitly ordered as a single act of violence nor was it the unavoidable consequence of some ancient quarrel between Muslims and Christians. Rather, it was the result of communal fear, ethnic reprisals, government paranoia, and fitful experimentation with targeted killing as a tool of modern statecraft.

In the popular imagination the Armenian genocide has come to be thought of as a single event—the imprisonment and killing of intellectuals and other leaders of the Armenian community in Constantinople on April 24, 1915. However, the violence of the First World War was a rolling phenomenon, swelling in some periods and declining in others, sweeping across parts of eastern Anatolia and pushing refugees across the border into the Russian province of Yerevan or southward into modern Syria and Iraq. The focus of the violence was readily apparent to scores of on-the-ground observers. Some were no doubt influenced by the pervasive anti-Ottoman prejudices of many Europeans and Americans, while others simply recorded what their own eyes could not fail to remark: the systematic ethnic cleansing of Christian villages and neighborhoods; the persecution of communal leaders by the Ottoman army and gendarmerie; and the forced deportation, on foot and under deplorable conditions, of entire communities. Eyewitness testimonies are legion, and they are unequivocal in their assessment of the organized nature of the expulsions and massacres.

Throughout the empire and its borderlands Muslims, too, suffered at the hands of both the Ottoman state and its wartime enemies. Kurds, formerly employed by Ottoman authorities as irregular troops, were also deported from sensitive borderlands or simply slaughtered. Muslims were attacked, moved about, and killed by Christian states and empires in both the Balkans and the north and south Caucasus. In round figures, these regions were emptied of more than a million Muslims during the First World War alone, not to mention the previous century of removals and atrocities by Balkan states and the Russian Empire.[26]

However, engaging in comparative victimology obscures the central fact about the Armenian genocide, namely, that it set in motion the wholesale cultural and demographic transformation of eastern Anatolia. Between 800,000 and 1.5 million Armenians were killed or died during the deportations. Countless other Christians also perished during the war years, which continued well past the armistice of 1918. Under the terms of the Treaty of Lausanne between the Turkish government and the Allied powers, in 1923 an additional 1.5 million Orthodox Christians—usually labeled "Greeks" regardless of their language or identity—and 350,000 Muslims were exchanged between Greece and Turkey.

The Turkish Republic, established as the successor to the defunct Ottoman Empire later that same year, inherited a territory largely denuded of its ancient Christian civilization, a blank slate upon which a new vision of past and future could be inscribed. The motto found on innumerable statues of Mustafa Kemal Atatürk, the republic's founder, encapsulates the restricted range of identities possible in a transformed Anatolia: "Ne mutlu Türküm diyene" (Happy is he who can say "I am a Turk"). After the First World War, one was now a citizen of a national republic, not a multireligious empire. Citizenship and nationality were intertwined in a way that would have seemed strange to the former inhabitants of the Anatolian hinterlands. Before the genocide, it was possible to be an Armenian and an Ottoman. Afterward it was impossible to be both an Armenian and a Turk.

While the genocide itself was an Anatolian affair, its aftereffects became a fundamental part of the modern history of the Caucasus. Most immediately, it contributed to the changing demographic structure of the southern provinces. The Armenian population in Russian Armenia—essentially the old Nakhichevan and Yerevan khanates, later the Yerevan *guberniia*—had grown steadily in the early nineteenth century, partly because of the emigration of Armenians from eastern Anatolia and partly because of the immigration of Muslims to the Ottoman lands. It was not until the early 1830s, however, that Armenians formed a bare majority of the region's population. That figure remained largely the same despite waves of migration fueled by each new Russo-Turkish conflict, from the Crimean War to the war of 1877–78. By the time of the 1897 census, Armenians (both Gregorians and Catholics) constituted 53 percent of the population of the Yerevan *guberniia*, with Muslims accounting for 42 percent.[27] The city of Yerevan retained a Muslim majority until the First World War.[28] All this changed in the wake of the genocide. Armenians flooded across the border into Russia. Muslims moved out in the opposite direction. Armed refugees in both camps engaged in attacks and reprisals. While Russian Armenia became a place of relative safety for Armenians, its centuries-old Muslim population found the atmosphere increasingly unwelcoming.

As Ottoman forces were emptying eastern Anatolia of Armenians, Russian troops were preparing for further operations along the frontier. The year 1916 brought a new Russian offensive and significant gains. Key fortresses in eastern Anatolia fell during the early months of the year, and by the spring Russian forces had reached the Black Sea and were quickly descending on Trebizond. The Ottomans were able to launch only limited responses since troop strength in eastern Anatolia continued to decline. From November 1915 to March 1917 Ottoman forces were reduced by some four hundred thousand men, with perhaps three-quarters of that figure lost in the campaigns against the Russians.[29] Farther to the east, preparations were under way for a massive joint operation in which Russian forces would link up with British troops in Mesopotamia. The campaign was designed to deal a decisive blow to Ottoman power in the greater Middle East. Had it succeeded, it might well have shortened the war by several months—but then came the Russian revolution.

In February 1917 workers in Petrograd staged an uprising that ushered in the creation of a provisional government for the old empire. News of the abdication of the tsar quickly spread throughout the Russian army. Desertions increased. Propaganda activity, spurred on by party representatives of all stripes, politicized the ranks. The officer corps was in disarray. For much of 1917 the disintegration of the Russian lines had created a kind of equilibrium: The Russians were too weak to press their advantage, but Ottoman forces were engaged on other fronts and were too poorly provisioned to capitalize on their enemy's political crisis.

The new Russian Provisional Government formally ended the institution of the Caucasus viceroy, replacing it with a special commission. In practice, however, power was vested in an array of local soviets controlled by socialist parties or by self-serving elites who sought to take advantage of the disorder. Virtually overnight, across the Caucasus mayors became ministers, newspaper editors became diplomats, and underground activists stepped into the public arena as would-be presidents and prime ministers.

The Bolshevik seizure of power in Petrograd in October 1917 brought some degree of clarity to the confusing situation. The real threat was no longer political chaos but rather the political ambitions of the Bolsheviks. Leaders in the provinces and districts of the south Caucasus established a Transcaucasus Commissariat—which excluded Bolshevik representation—to serve as a government until the results of the Bolshevik Revolution could be assessed and its impact on the Caucasus fully understood.

The Bolsheviks returned the favor. No representatives of the new Transcaucasus government were included in the peace talks between Bolshevik Russia and the Central Powers at Brest Litovsk in March

1918. The Bolsheviks were now making peace above the heads of the politicians most immediately threatened by the collapse of the Caucasus and Anatolian fronts. The resulting Treaty of Brest Litovsk provided for the evacuation of Russian troops from precisely those border districts over which the tsarist forces had been fighting for the entire war—and which were regarded by Transcaucasus leaders as essential buffers against Constantinople. These provisions proved even more disheartening given the fact that representatives of the Transcaucasus government had already been engaging in talks with Ottoman negotiators over a future peace deal. However, once the Treaty of Brest Litovsk had been signed, the Ottomans demanded the immediate evacuation of the disputed districts along the old Russian-Ottoman boundary. A hastily convened meeting of Transcaucasus politicians in Tiflis responded by declaring war on the Ottomans, who were already moving toward the pre-1914 frontier.

The Transcaucasus government had little choice but to make a formal break with Russia, whose Bolshevik leadership seemed willing to sell out the Caucasus in exchange for peace. The Democratic Federative Republic of Transcaucasia was declared an independent country in late April 1918, but it was to be a fleeting entity. A little more than a month later, its constituents—a collection of former imperial provinces, soon to be renamed Armenia, Azerbaijan, and Georgia—went their separate ways, bracing themselves against the machinations of the Bolshevik government, an offensive by tsarist loyalists from the north, and the continued Ottoman threat from the south. The independence of these new states was likewise to prove ephemeral. Although they spent their brief existence (from 1918 to 1920 and 1921) fending off attacks from all sides, they were nevertheless of critical importance. Not only did they represent the first instance of modern statehood for the south Caucasus—and, in Azerbaijan's case, the world's first Muslim parliamentary republic—but they also created rivalries over territory and identity that would return to haunt the new, post-Soviet countries some seventy years later.

Phantom Republics

As historical losers go, few rival the Mensheviks. First there is the name. At the 1903 congress of the Russian Social Democratic Workers' Party (held in exile), delegates were divided over the wording of the party's statutes, particularly the section that defined party membership.

One faction, headed by Vladimir Lenin, favored a narrow definition, while another, led by the longtime socialist activist Iulii Martov, supported a more inclusive one. Lenin's vision was of a small, elite, conspiratorial party, Martov's of a broad workers' movement perhaps even open to compromise with bourgeois parties. The congress at first backed the latter position, but due to a walk-out by some of Martov's supporters, Lenin's view received the support of a slim majority of the delegates still left in the assembly hall. That accident of history produced the name with which the Martov group would eventually be stuck—*men'sheviki*, literally "the minoritarians"—while Lenin's less popular faction claimed the title "majoritarians," that is, *bol'sheviki*, or Bolsheviks.

The two groups remained at odds until the Mensheviks' "voluntary" liquidation by the Bolsheviks in 1924. The Mensheviks never managed to put forward a leader to rival Lenin's charisma or Stalin's ruthless resolve. Their ideology of inclusiveness on the Left was perhaps fated to fall victim to a faction founded on the idea of conspiracy. However, prior to October 1917 it was precisely this broader vision of the workers' movement that allowed the Mensheviks to attract a more diverse body of followers on the margins of the Russian Empire, particularly among the non-Russian nationalities. The one region where they succeeded politically—even after the Bolshevik Revolution—was on the periphery, in Georgia.

Georgian Mensheviks were active in the socialist underground well before 1905. When the revolution of that year prompted Tsar Nicholas II to agree to the establishment of a parliament, or Duma, they became critical voices in the new legislature. The experiment with representative government ultimately proved futile; the tsar soon reasserted his power by ensuring that social classes most loyal to autocratic ideals controlled the assembly. However, the Duma became the crucible where party politics, of a kind, could develop. Many of the Menshevik leaders in the Duma were Georgian, and when the Russian Revolution of February 1917 destroyed the old empire, they also became leading figures in the Provisional Government in Petrograd. With the coming to power of the Bolsheviks in October 1917, Georgian Mensheviks retreated to the Caucasus, where they declared an independent Georgia on May 26, 1918.

Although the Mensheviks formed the major party in Georgia, the political elite as a whole was divided along lines of both class and ethnicity. The Mensheviks were mainly ethnic Georgians, particularly from the western reaches of the country. Their constituencies were the urban working class, such as it was, and the Georgian peasantry, where their message of land reform and full constitutional rights attracted supporters. However, the remnants of former imperial army units, which had disbanded during the war, were still around. Composed largely of Russian peasants, these conscripts had been receptive to the work of socialist activists of various denominations and in time became a key constituency for the Bolsheviks. In Tiflis, by contrast, the urban bourgeoisie was largely Armenian, with political loyalties that lay further to the Right, among liberal parties, than those of Menshevik and Bolshevik supporters.

Despite the dominance of ethnic Georgians in the republic's social and political life, Georgian independence was not clothed in the language of historical destiny and national self-determination. The Mensheviks were congenitally ill-suited to become nation builders, focused as they were on questions of social justice and class relations rather than ethnic nationalism. Noe Jordania, the Georgian parliamentary chairman and *mesame dasi* leader, noted at the time that independence was both "a historical and a tragic act." It was occasioned not by a collective commitment to national sovereignty but by the necessity of Georgia's "self-preservation in the current historical tempest."[30] As the preamble to the republic's declaration of independence affirmed, the decision to join the Russian Empire more than a century earlier had come about because of the strategic need to ensure the country's survival against foreign enemies. Leaving the Russian embrace was prompted by a similar set of circumstances.[31]

The Georgian government first turned to Germany as its protector, a decision that rested on the desire for a strong ally to defend the country against both Turks and Russians. However, with the capitulation of Germany to the Allies in November 1918, that relationship came to an end. Britain was now the key foreign player in Georgian politics. British troops were already on the ground in the Caucasus, having originally been sent to prevent an Ottoman seizure of Baku's oilfields, and they extended their mandate to make sure that the terms of the armistice with both the Ottomans and the Germans were fulfilled.

Amid the swirl of international politics and changing strategic relationships, political institutions developed apace. The remnants of earlier revolutions were still visible. There were representatives of the Tiflis soviet, the local council that had been established along the lines of similar socialist-led bodies in other parts of the defunct empire. Representatives of the old Russian Provisional Government were around, too, still claiming to speak for a national government that had vanished beneath the tide of Bolshevism. With the end of the war, Menshevik leaders championed the establishment of a new constitutional order based on parliamentary democracy. The government enacted a wide-ranging land reform program in an effort to counter the peasant revolts that had engulfed some parts of the country. Elections for a new Georgian parliament in January 1919, the first with universal suffrage, gave the Mensheviks 109 out of 130 seats.

Although the Bolsheviks were defeated politically in Georgia, they remained active underground. In Tiflis they carried out raids and engaged in agitprop activities. In the countryside they attempted to foment armed rebellion. Problems of internal order were compounded by Georgia's relations with the Whites, the remnants of the old imperial army, which, having regrouped and reorganized, were engaged in an all-out civil war with the Bolsheviks in other parts of the former empire. North of the Caucasus mountains, the Whites were represented by the so-called Volunteer Army led by Gen. Anton Denikin. Convinced that the new Caucasus republics were aiding anti-Russian forces in the north Caucasus—the "fanatics and adventurers who were using cruel reprisals to mobilize the people," as Denikin claimed in his memoirs—in November 1919 the general initiated an economic blockade of Georgia and Azerbaijan.[32] Fighting flared up between Georgian troops and Denikin's forces, particularly along the Black Sea coast, while other detachments of the Volunteer Army pressed southward. Securing the state—both against Bolshevik agents within the country and against Denikin's troops at its borders—became the government's paramount concern. In 1919 Tiflis assigned half the national budget to the Ministry of Defense.[33]

In the past, the Russian Empire's approach to Georgia had been to insinuate itself into the old feudal network, supporting the power of local elites and depending on them to quell peasant insurrections. In the period of revolution and fitful state building, similar mixtures of old and new were evident. The combination of revolutionary zeal and traditional patterns of governance could be strikingly bizarre. In the summer of 1919 members of the American legation to Georgia traveled to Khevsureti to assess the situation there. This area of upland Georgia was remote—even during the imperial period it could never really be counted as being under Russian control—and there was some concern that it would soon rebel against the Georgian authorities. The Americans were surprised at what they found. The old system of village headmen was still in place, only now it had been transformed into a network of men calling themselves "commissars," all of whom owed allegiance to a particular chief commissar located in one of the larger villages. When the chief commissar formally received the American diplomats, he appeared in a *cherkeska* and Russian cavalry trousers, armed with two daggers, a sixteenth-century broadsword, a revolver, a Russsian army rifle, an iron-clad shield, and a seventeenth-century inlaid Persian helmet. He addressed the group in fluent Georgian and Russian and at one point explained the intricacies of Khevsur politics in Esperanto. He reported that he had attended Esperanto congresses in Krakow and Antwerp and was now putting into practice the internationalist and revolutionary message being preached by the Bolsheviks, much to the chagrin of the Menshevik authorities.[34]

In the midst of political and social upheaval life went on. The venerable old Marxist Karl Kautsky visited Georgia in the winter of 1920–21 and found the republic developing as "the antithesis to Bolshevism," with democratic institutions, a workable economy, and personal freedom generally respected.[35] The opera continued to function even without proper costumes and scenery, staging original Georgian pieces as well as such classics as *Tosca* and *Eugene Onegin*. Tea parties and grand dinners were arranged for the many foreign dignitaries who passed through or were posted to the capital. In October 1919 several of young Georgian ladies were invited to parade before the chief of the American mission. President Woodrow Wilson, it seems, had personally requested that the diplomat provide a report on the legendary beauty of Caucasus women.[36]

Events such as these created a fantastic, Ruritanian atmosphere in the republic, a sense that the new state was embarking on a grand experiment in self-governance, with little idea of how to rule itself, how to deal with its neighbors, or how to make the best case for recognition on the world stage. Relations with Armenia alternated between tension and open warfare. Denikin's Volunteer Army was a constant menace. Agitators of every political persuasion plotted terrorist attacks and assassinations. "If I were a symbolist, I should portray Georgia as a racehorse," commented the writer Odette Keun, who was living in Tiflis at the time, "palpitating, furious, rushing forward blindly it knows not where; rearing at the least check, not having yet learnt what is required of it, or what it can do; falling at the first slackening of the reins into a fantastic, prancing gait; a creature made for a parade, and for the pleasure of the eyes rather than for utility."[37]

━ ━

The Azerbaijan Democratic Republic was founded on May 28, 1918, just two days after Georgia's declaration of independence. Although independence had been thrust upon the Azerbaijanis by Georgia's withdrawal from the Transcaucasus federation, it grew out of the ideals of Islamic reformism that had been alive within the Russian Empire for decades. Since the late nineteenth century Muslim intellectuals had been engaged in a host of cultural activities designed to spur a sense of nationhood among the Turkic population of the southeast Caucasus, a group that had long been referred to by outsiders as "Tatars."

The democratic alternative to tsarism found expression in several local parties, the most important of which was Müsavat (Equality), which was founded just before the First World War. Like the Mensheviks in Georgia, Müsavat was socialist in form but nationalist in content—a party that changed, in the tumultuous period of the war, from a movement of leftist intellectuals into one that saw itself as the bearer of national identity and the agent of national revolution. The very name "Azerbaijan" reflected the party's aspirations as well as those of other inhabitants of the new republic. Some party leaders hoped that, under German or Turkish protection, the new state might be fused with the historic region of Azerbaijan, located across the border in northwestern Persia, an area with an even larger population of Turkic-speaking Shi'a Muslims. However, the only real enthusiasm displayed by Persian Azerbaijanis was the proclamation of their own phantom republic of Azadistan (lit."Freedomland"), which lasted only a few months during the summer of 1920. By that point the Azerbaijan republic had already disappeared from the map.

The territory of republican Azerbaijan roughly corresponded to the old imperial provinces of Baku and Elisavetpol. However, in the two years of its existence the government never managed to gain full control of the territory that it claimed as its own. At the time of the declaration of independence, the would-be capital, Baku, was outside the purview of republican forces. The city's tortuous history in 1917 and 1918 is one of the thorniest features of an already complex political and social landscape. Baku was by far the most variegated urban space in the region. It had an industrial proletariat that had grown up around the petroleum industry. It had a well-developed and wealthy urban bourgeoisie and a native intelligentsia. All these included Muslims,

Armenians, and Russians. Relations between these groups were tense, a legacy of the urban violence of 1904–6 now compounded by political uncertainty and the twin tempests of war and revolution.

Following the October Revolution, city government in Baku fell to the Bolsheviks. Although the party was in no sense the most numerous or popular, the Bolsheviks had two things that Müsavat initially lacked: a capable leader in the person of the resourceful Armenian activist Stepan Shaumian and a knack for exploiting ethnic divisions for their own gain. These issues came to a head in March 1918, when bloody clashes engulfed the city, nominally pitting Bolsheviks and Armenian socialists against the Müsavat party and its allies. However, the violence amounted to a replay of the communal conflict between Muslims and Armenians of a decade earlier. The outcome was a victory for the Bolshevik-dominated Baku soviet and the effective exile of Müsavat forces to the western city of Ganja.

That situation might well have lasted for some time had it not been for the assistance the Ottomans were now providing to the republicans. Ottoman officers and Caucasus volunteers, collectively known as the Army of Islam, gathered strength and by midsummer were preparing an offensive against Baku to oust the soviet and take control of the capital. It was this offensive—which to the Allied powers seemed an Ottoman operation in Azerbaijani guise—that led to the deployment of British troops. In August 1918 a small infantry force was dispatched northward from Persia, trailing an artillery detachment, two armored cars, and an undermanned machine-gun company. Led by Maj.Gen. Lionel Dunsterville, this group, known to history as "Dunsterforce," was tasked with preventing an Ottoman seizure of Baku and protecting oil facilities and railway lines. The men of Dunsterforce arrived aboard a requisitioned Russian warship and, lacking a British ensign, hoisted the Russian imperial tricolor upside down, which turned it into the Serbian national flag.[38] Despite its opéra bouffe beginnings, Dunsterforce succeeded in stalling the Ottoman advance, but in September the Army of Islam managed to march into the city. The taking of Baku also led to one of the signal events in the history of the Bolshevik Revolution and the Russian civil war: Twenty-six Bolshevik commissars, including Shaumian, fled the city and ended up on the eastern shore of the Caspian Sea, where they were executed by tsarist loyalists.[39]

The victory of the Army of Islam proved hollow. On October 9, 1918, the Ottomans signed the Mudros Armistice with the Allies, an agreement that paved the way for the full British occupation of Baku, the city's demilitarization, and the establishment of Allied control over the petroleum industry and rail transport. During the following year the capital was governed by administrators who neither recognized Azerbaijani sovereignty nor were sympathetic to the government's claims. Azerbaijan's real independence—in name if never completely de jure—thus lasted only from August 1919 until April 1920, from the departure of British troops until the final assault by the Bolsheviks.

The new republic's parliament met for the first time in December 1918 in the old Taghiyev School for Girls located in downtown Baku. Müsavat dominated, with about a quarter of the seats; the remainder was accounted for by Muslim parties of more nationalist or social democratic orientations. The largest minorities, the Armenians and Russians, were given set-aside seats.[40] Organizations of ethnic minorities were also set up to protect communal rights. In the months following the elections and the subsequent British withdrawal, the government managed to establish a program of Azerbaijani language instruction in schools (most state officials still preferred Russian), to found Baku University, and to get on with the work of state building, including repairing roads, training teachers, and founding libraries. Previously nationalized oil companies were returned to their owners. Stipends were created to send young people to Russia and western Europe to study engineering, shipbuilding, architecture, aviation, medicine, law, and other subjects.[41] Revealingly, however, half the republic's budget was set aside for defense and railway maintenance.[42]

As in Georgia, the establishment of the republic was seen by some political leaders not as the fulfillment of national ideals but as a matter of necessity. "Our separation from Russia is not a hostile act," declared parliamentary chairman Mammed Amin Rasulzade at the assembly's first session. "Our behavior can be explained . . . as a result of the anarchy now reigning in Russia." The country's new tricolor flag represented the multiple aspirations and traditions that now converged in the creation of a new government: the blue of Turkic civilization, the green of Islam, and the red of European socialism. Russia, Rasulzade said, should seek to overcome its own problems of anarchy and political extremism and join Azerbaijan in the social democratic project.[43]

Armenia shared the socialist ideals of Azerbaijan. The two republics were founded on the same day (May 28, 1918), and both were likewise based on preexisting imperial boundaries—in Armenia's case the old *guberniia* of Yerevan and the district of Kars. However, Armenian independence was really won on the battlefield. In a series of spectacular victories in late May 1918 Armenian units of the old tsarist army, along with irregular volunteers, defeated much larger Ottoman forces. Those victories made possible the establishment of a distinct Armenian republic, centered in the old garrison town of Yerevan. Armenian intellectuals and professionals from across the Russian Empire and beyond flooded to the city and organized a provisional parliament, which convened in August. The Armenian Revolutionary Federation, or Dashnaks, had the largest number of members, but the parliament also consisted of representatives of other parties, most with a reformist and progressive orientation. It also included significant Muslim representation—a nod to the fact that the new Armenian state contained a sizable Muslim population.

The provisional government instituted a national currency and reformed the legal system and tax code. But the social turmoil caused by years of warfare, the disgruntled Muslim minority, and the intrigues of Georgians, Azerbaijanis, and Bolsheviks—all with interests in the republic's fate—imperiled the fragile government. Armed bands roamed the countryside, establishing their own rule at gunpoint. Internal order was hampered by the activities of large numbers of demobilized soldiers and simple thugs who had learned to survive outside the bounds of legality.

Armenia's geographical position—on the shifting front of a brutal war—also meant that the refugee situation was extreme. According to one estimate, in 1919 there were 511,000 refugees in Armenia, some from across the Turkish border, others displaced from homes within Russian Armenia itself. Added to this number were perhaps 150,000 refugees from other parts of the Caucasus, including many Muslims, plus some 20,000 orphans being cared for by relief organizations.[44] Oliver Wardrop, the British commissioner for the Caucasus, described the scene near Echmiadzin, the holy see of the Armenian church, during a visit in October 1919: "I cannot give you any idea of the state of affairs here. There are 200,000 absolutely destitute, almost naked refugees in this small town and its district. Typhus, cholera, malaria and fevers of all kinds are raging among these poor people who are living out in the open air breathing the infected dust which the wind carries into their faces. The children pick up scraps of anything eatable they can find in the dirt.... [The people] will sell their children for bread."[45] "Starving Armenians" became a catchphrase of the American and

European press—and for a generation thereafter American mothers used it to shame persnickety children into eating their vegetables.

In Yerevan political divisions were rife. Political parties disagreed over how to build the new country and deal with the worsening international situation. Even within individual parties factions were deeply divided over how to respond to rampant lawlessness or how to deal with the opposition of Muslims, particularly peasants and landholders, who controlled parts of the countryside. Armenian delegates at the Paris peace talks clashed with the republican government, deepening longstanding rifts between Armenian communities from the old Russian Empire and those from the defunct Ottoman state. Adding to the uncertainty was the fact that all the republic's borders were in dispute, with territories claimed by Georgia in the north, Azerbaijan in the south and east, and the Turkish army in the south and west.

National elections in June 1919 resulted in a new parliament dominated by the Dashnaks, who held seventy-two of the eighty available seats. The government now effectively created a one-party state, with the Dashnaks controlling the levers of power, including key personnel appointments in state institutions. That outcome further alienated local Muslims and provided fodder for Turkish, Azerbaijani, and Bolshevik agents. A full-scale insurgency among Muslims in the Arax River valley erupted that summer, while clashes with Azerbaijan over disputed borderlands flared up later in the year.

In the summer and autumn of 1919 British troops departed from the Caucasus, beginning in Baku and moving west toward Batumi. The reasons for the evacuation was simple: The original goal of the British deployment was to secure oil and rail links during the war, and the war—at least as far as the British were concerned—had now come to an end. Denikin's Volunteer Army was pressing south and engaging in skirmishes with the nascent Georgian army. To many British strategists it would not have been a bad thing had Denikin simply swept through the region and restored Russian control. "We are in the Caucasus to help the small States not against Russia," declared the British war secretary, Winston Churchill, "but against anarchy."[46]

The Allies had little hope of crafting a clear policy as long as the final status of the three republics remained unsettled at the Paris peace talks. Armenian, Azerbaijani, and Georgian delegates crowded the antechambers of the peace conference, as did their opponents: representatives of pro-Russian imperial interests, proponents of land swaps that would have benefited Turkey, and assorted agitators and propagandists with single political issues or territorial claims they hoped to impress on the Allied negotiators. In January 1920 word reached Tiflis and Baku that the Allies had granted de facto recognition to Georgia and Azerbaijan, a last-ditch effort to firm up the states as buffers against the growing threat of the Bolsheviks. (Armenia was recognized de facto a short time later, and Georgia de jure the following year.) Cheering crowds poured into the streets. A grand ball was organized in Tiflis, with the Armenian prime minister and representatives from Azerbaijan in attendance.[47] The celebration proved premature, however. Even preliminary international recognition—especially one that was not yet sealed by international treaty—could not alter the Allies' disinclination to provide real assistance. "I am sitting on a powder-magazine," wrote Wardrop to his wife from Tiflis, "which thousands of people are trying to blow up."[48] In the end not a single territorial issue in the Caucasus was resolved by the Paris negotiations. They were all settled by force.

The crux of the matter was not the maneuverings of Bolshevik agents and sympathizers, although plenty were active in the region after the British departure. Rather, it was the unstable situation in Dagestan, to Azerbaijan's north. In May 1918 political leaders among the north Caucasus highlanders had established the North Caucasus Mountain Republic, which nominally included the peoples and territories from the Black to the Caspian seas.[49] From the beginning, both Bolsheviks and Whites worked to undermine its legitimacy, while local elites curried favor with whichever outside force seemed to be in the ascendant.[50] Even if the Allies had wanted to aid the Dagestanis and other highlanders, it was virtually impossible to get good intelligence indicating who was in charge. The ghosts of the past even made an appearance. A grandson of Shamil emerged from obscurity claiming to speak for the Dagestani mountaineers, but he was deliberately ignored by the Allies and treated as delusional.[51]

Fighting was raging in Dagestan between members of the parliament of the Mountain Republic and Denikin's forces; refugees were streaming across the border into Azerbaijani territory.[52] All this was merely the prelude to the Bolshevik seizure of the north Caucasus. Denikin's free hand in the region had caused many highlanders to turn to the Bolsheviks in a desperate attempt to prevent a return to tsarist rule. By the autumn of 1919 that alliance of convenience proved powerful enough to beat back both Denikin and the forces still loyal to the Mountain Republic. In early 1920, with Bolshevik control of the north Caucasus imminent, the Georgian and Azerbaijani governments launched a series of diplomatic offensives aimed at making peace with Moscow and securing their northern borders. The game was already over, however. In late April the Red Army took Baku and presented an ultimatum to the Azerbaijani parliament declaring an end to the Müsavat-led government. The parliament accepted the transfer of power to the Bolsheviks.

Next in line was Armenia. In May 1920 Bolshevik agents fomented an uprising that quickly spread across the entire republic. The rebels were joined by discontented units of the Armenian army as well as by leaders of some Muslim areas. In response, the Dashnaks declared martial law and moved to wipe out the rebellious military units and their leaders. The rebellion was quashed, and troops were dispatched to Muslim areas, where villages were emptied and citizens expelled across the border into Turkey. Armenian villagers were moved into the evacuated districts, at last securing control over the Arax plain, the heart of Armenia's agricultural economy. The army prepared to launch a further push to the south, into the disputed region of Nakhichevan, but that plan was soon derailed. Turkish troops were pressing into Armenian territory, using the disorder in the republic as a pretext for full occupation. Bolsheviks troops, having taken Azerbaijan, were moving into the republic as well. Faced with a choice between the two occupiers, in December Yerevan handed over power to the Bolsheviks.

After the fall of Armenia and Azerbaijan, things moved rapidly in Georgia. It was a time of confusion and dissembling. The Bolsheviks had earlier seemed to accept Georgian independence, even signing a treaty of friendship to that effect. "Well, construct socialism there in your own way, the democratic *petit-bourgeois* kind, and we will construct ours in a revolutionary way," Lenin reportedly told a Georgian diplomat in 1920.[53] However, in February 1921 Bolshevik troops moved from Armenia into Georgia. Soon Bolshevik infantry and cavalry detachments also entered Georgia from Azerbaijan. Moscow maintained that the military engagements were a local affair—just another instance of Caucasus factionalism—even though it was obvious that things were being directed from Moscow. Red Army troops next poured into Georgia from the north. At the same time, the Turkish government took advantage of the situation and demanded that Georgian forces retreat from two sensitive border areas.

For more than a year refugees had been making their way down the Georgian Military Highway, fleeing the violence in the north Caucasus and lumbering toward Tiflis in motorcars, carts, and on foot.[54] To these were now added a massive movement of people from Georgia toward the Black Sea coast in an attempt to escape the retribution that would come with a Bolshevik victory. In late February, Georgian troops evacuated Tiflis, leaving the city open to the Red Army, and headed toward Batumi with the idea of making a final stand there. By mid-March Bolshevik troops were at the outskirts of the port city, which soon fell to both Bolshevik and Turkish forces. The remnants of the Georgian government narrowly escaped on one of the last steamers to put to sea. People associated with the former government or army, peasants who resisted the requisitioning of food and animals, and people deemed unsympathetic to the Bolsheviks were rounded up or summarily executed.

On March 27 the exiled Georgian leadership—President Noe Jordania, Minister of Foreign Affairs Evgeni Gegechkori, Constituent Assembly president Karlo (Nikolai) Chkheidze, and Minister of Internal Affairs Noe Ramishvili—issued an appeal from their makeshift offices in Istanbul to "all socialist parties and workers' organizations" of the world, protesting against the invasion of Georgia and the end of the Menshevik government.[55] The appeal went unheeded. Apart from passionate editorials in some newspapers and calls for action from such old Georgia hands as Oliver Wardrop, the international reaction was silence. "Our file is little more than a record of the horrors of which you speak," wrote the British Foreign Office in response to one of Wardrop's many appeals, "but, alas, there seems no possible course for us to adopt beyond giving as much publicity as possible to this campaign of terror."[56] When the Georgians sought arms and ammunition to counter the Bolshevik invasion, the French provided an unusable cache of rusty carbines and machine guns that had been left in an Istanbul warehouse by the defeated Russian Whites.[57] When the Georgian republic's ambassador to the United Kingdom attempted to present his credentials, the response was a flurry of bureaucratic memos requesting that someone undertake the unpleasant task of informing the ambassador that he no longer had a country to represent. Similar rebuffs were made to other exiles.[58] By this point the independent republics of the Caucasus were gone.

Exiles

The former Georgian leadership set up shop first in Istanbul and then in France, finally landing in the village of Leuville-sur-Orge, south of Paris. Housed in a small villa, the government—now an unrecognized government-in-exile—continued to circulate petitions and send letters to Western leaders, begging them to make good on their earlier recognition.

Times had changed. No Allied country was willing to roll back the Bolshevik conquests or to support large-scale subversive movements inside Soviet territory. The territorial disputes that had divided the republics were settled—at least for the time being—since each was encased inside the Bolshevik state. The idea of a greater Armenia was dead, as was the vision of a greater Azerbaijan or an independent Georgia. The north Caucasus was lodged administratively inside Russia itself. The political uncertainty of the 1918–21 period was now resolved.

However, the founders of the original republics were still around—albeit with titles preceded by the word "former"—and they were rarely silent. Travelers in the nineteenth century often remarked that nearly every Georgian seemed to be a prince of some sort. Between the two world wars every Georgian in Europe seemed to be a former government minister. They could be found at virtually any public event related to international politics and the affairs of Eurasia.

These individuals and their sympathizers attempted to keep the flame of national independence alive and to lobby Western governments to face up to the Soviet threat. In Prague, Paris, and Warsaw small groups of exiles set up committees, organized conferences, and issued proclamations intended to buck up their fellow émigrés and pressure governments into doing something to liberate the captive nations of Eurasia.[59] Much of their work was centered around the Paris-based journal *Prométhée*, named for the figure from Greek mythology who was exiled to the Caucasus for bringing fire to mankind and thereby disobeying the gods. The journal's supporters included a variety of groups working to roll back Bolshevik gains, all united under the broad label of "Prometheanism."

Throughout the 1920s and early 1930s there appeared to be a reasonable chance of success. The rise of a strongly anti-Bolshevik leader in Poland—Józef Piłsudski, who assumed power in a coup in 1926—presented the émigrés with a ready patron, and during that period the Polish government provided direct assistance, both moral and financial, to Caucasus exiles. Scholarships were given to émigré students. Money for propaganda and counterintelligence activities flowed to willing recipients. Warsaw set aside funds for the publication of journals and newspapers, not just *Prométhée* but periodicals in regional languages as well. Müsavat published its *Kurtuluş* (Liberation) in Berlin. The Georgians published *Sakartvelo* (Georgia) in Paris. Exiled leaders of the Mountain Republic produced *Severnyi Kavkaz* (North Caucasus) in Warsaw. Even Cossacks published their own *Vol'noe Kazachestvo* (Free Cossackdom) in Prague.[60] The old phenomenon of the "captive Pole," fighting alongside highlanders against the Russian Empire, found new life as Warsaw became the chief source of sustenance for the Caucasus cause against the Bolsheviks.

The Caucasus exiles were a regular presence at seminars, scholarly conferences, and society balls, where they repeatedly made their case. Many had been active at the Paris peace conference, and the tactics of insistent lobbying and cocktail-party diplomacy continued even after 1921. Throughout the interwar years they continually affirmed that Soviet Russia's days in the Caucasus were numbered. "We see an enemy that is ill," wrote Noe Jordania a decade after the end of Georgian independence, "paralyzed by incurable plagues, decomposed and caught up in a web of internal contradictions, almost ready to give up the ghost."[61]

From the beginning there was dissension within and between the various national communities, offshoots of old quarrels that bloomed anew in the hothouse world of emigration. Cossacks, who had also established fleeting political formations in the north Caucasus during the revolution, operated awkwardly within a collection of peoples whom they had spent much of their history fighting. The collaboration of some Cossack communities with White armies against the Mountain Republic also made cooperation with other exiles difficult, even though they were now struggling against a common Bolshevik enemy. Some Muslim leaders supported pan-Turkism, but that orientation sat uneasily with the pan-Islamic ideology of other Muslim politicians and the programs of non-Turkic, Christian groups, such as Georgians and Armenians.

The old lines of political allegiance were also difficult to overcome. One of the few interstate agreements that the briefly independent republics managed to hammer out was a treaty between Georgia and Azerbaijan renouncing territorial pretensions. The Armenians had been sidelined in that process—Yerevan still had serious territorial conflicts with both Tiflis and Baku—and the isolation of the Armenian community continued throughout the interwar years. Georgian and Azerbaijani leaders were convinced that the Armenians were in the pocket of the Soviets—"the most loyal subjects of the Bolsheviks," as one author in *Prométhée* wrote.[62] These divisions blocked the creation of a genuinely united Caucasus front during the republican period and thereafter.

In the summer of 1934, at a conference in Brussels, former politicians from Georgia, Azerbaijan, and the north Caucasus announced the establishment of a "Caucasus Confederation" based on what they described in their communiqué as "the geographical and economic unity of the region."[63] The conceptual basis for the confederation was later described as "national centralism," a grand coalition of national governments-in-exile that represented the only attempt in history to unite the entire Caucasus—at least in theory—within a single independent state.[64] Delegates stressed that space was to be reserved for a future Armenian component of the new country should Armenian leaders eventually decide to join.

All this was moot, however. The 1934 confederation was a paper state, formally declared but incapable of being built. The Caucasus exiles must have known that time was not on their side. Relations between the Soviet regime and the West were warming. In 1929 the Soviet Union became a signatory to the Kellogg-Briand Pact, a diplomatic instrument designed to outlaw war. A special protocol, brokered by Maxim Litvinov, the Soviet commissar for foreign affairs, made the pact specifically applicable at the regional level, which meant there was now a clear sign of rapprochement between the Soviet Union and the frontline states of Poland, Romania, Turkey, Persia, and the Baltic republics—all countries that the Caucasus governments-in-exile had seen as their natural allies. Anti-Bolshevik groups operating in Istanbul were closed down and their activists arrested or handed over to Moscow. In 1932 France and Poland signed nonaggression pacts with Stalin. In 1933 the United States formally recognized the Soviet state, and the following year the Soviet Union joined the League of Nations.

Fearing the propaganda activities of the governments-in-exile, Soviet leaders had previously taken measures to interdict any publications that they might attempt to send to sympathizers inside the Soviet Union.[65] Now the exclamation point became a surrogate for real political influence. "Down with the Muscovite yoke!" the exiles proclaimed in one issue of *Prométhée*. "Long live the liberty of peoples! Long live the united Caucasus front! Long live the independent confederation of the Caucasus!"[66] Over time their activities came to look more and more quixotic, a crusade by vituperative old men from vanished countries, unable to reconcile themselves to the new realities of international politics.

The desperate activities of the former political leaders under-scored one critical issue following the Bolshevik conquest: Were the new Soviet administrative units in the Caucasus—the republics of the south and the autonomous republics and regions of the north—the legitimate successors of the national movements of 1918, or were they cheap perversions of the national ideal? Did the locus of legiti-macy lie on the ground in Tbilisi (the renamed Tiflis), Yerevan, and Baku or among the aging remnants of the old guard in Paris and London? Who, in other words, spoke for the nation? The stakes were high, for how one answered these questions cut to the heart of what it meant to be an Armenian, Azerbaijani, Georgian, and north Caucasus highlander. The global and at times deadly nature of these debates became readily apparent on a cold Christmas Eve in 1933.

The Armenian archbishop was a large man—over six feet tall—so when he used the crosier to steady himself, the staff doubled under his weight and sent him sprawling face down onto the church floor. Some two hundred parishioners had assembled for the Sunday service at Holy Cross Church, located on West 187th Street in New York City. Even those in the procession did not immediately sense that something was wrong. The deacon continued to wave the censer. The choristers kept up the invocational hymn. But when the archbishop's bodyguard came scrambling down the aisle, drawing his pistol and shoving peo-ple out of the way, it quickly became apparent what had happened. The primate of the Armenian Apostolic Church, the religious leader of Armenians throughout the western hemisphere, had been attacked and now lay dying, cross in hand, before the altar of a New York church.[67]

The crowd swarmed the assailants. Witnesses later reported seeing two men slash at the archbishop with a large butcher knife, its han-dle wrapped in newspaper to hide fingerprints. As evidence presented at the trial would show, the two murderers were part of a larger conspiracy. The archbishop had been threatened several times in the preceding weeks, having been shouted down at a speech in Chicago and set upon by thugs at a church picnic in Worcester, Massachusetts. Those events had caused him to hire an armed bodyguard. In all, nine men were eventually convicted. Two of them were sentenced to die in the electric chair, a punishment that was later commuted to life imprisonment.

The murder of Archbishop Levon Tourian was a front-page story in several American newspapers. The trial of his assassins dragged on through the spring and summer of 1934 and received coverage around the world. The requiem service, held at the Cathedral of St. John the Divine, drew more than five thousand people. Tourian did not join the pantheon of martyrs for the Armenian cause, nor is his death generally commemorated. It was, however, a signal event in the history of Armenia and Armenians. The murder cemented divisions within the Armenian diaspora that have remained in place until today, for unlike the many other perpetrators of violence against Armenians—from Ottoman pashas to Soviet commissars—the authors of the twentieth century's most spectacular public murder of an Armenian cultural leader, inside an Armenian church, were Armenians.

The Tourian case is illustrative of the major challenge that faced all émigré communities during the interwar period: how—or whether—to reconcile themselves to the new Soviet Union and achieve some sort of balance between patriotic sentiment and the realities of the new Communist order. In each of the various forms of nationalism in the Caucasus, the concepts of identity, community, and territory existed in a complicated interrelationship. North Caucasus nationalism—and, to a degree, Azerbaijani nationalism as well—might be described as classically postcolonial in form. The structure and content of the national idea owed a great deal to the experience of empire: the creation of distinct national categories in censuses; the demographic engineering of empire builders; and even the emergence of old imperial and clerical languages—Russian, Turkish, or Arabic—as the lingua franca in which nationalist elites felt most comfortable Moreover, there have always been alternative poles of allegiance in the north Caucasus that have competed with the nation. Islam and pan-Islamist movements were one; among Turkic-speaking populations, pan-Turkism was another.

Things were different in Georgia. Georgian nationalism entailed the reworking of an already established heritage by groups of dedicated cultural entrepreneurs, with a focus on gathering in the lands that once belonged to an older state. The idea of a Georgian nation stretching back into the mists of time is as ephemeral as all ideologies of the nation. However, an ecclesiastical tradition and literary language, a unique writing system, an ancient royal house, and the willingness of conquering empires to reinforce noble privileges rather than supplant them meant that basic questions of identity, community, and territory were settled much earlier than in other areas. Where Circassian and

Azerbaijani intellectuals looked to the national idea as a way of pulling their populations into modernity, Georgians saw the nation as a route back to an imagined past.

Armenian nationalism, both as an idea and as a movement, combined elements of both these forms—part modernizing, part revivalist. Its mixed character was a function of the environment in which it arose. The fact that one thinks of Armenia today as both Armenian and part of the Caucasus is largely an accident of history. For much of the modern period, the lands that would constitute the Armenian republic were Muslim, overseen by Muslim khans and inhabited mainly by Turkic-speaking Muslim nomads and some settled farmers. The real centers of Armenian life were in eastern Anatolia. The ancient city of Ani was a major site of Armenian learning and ecclesiastical governance before its destruction by an earthquake in the fourteenth century. Quite apart from the territorial question, the highly mobile nature of Armenian populations and their connections with international commerce dating back to the Middle Ages caused Armenian communities to thrive in what might seem like unlikely places: Venice, Krakow, Istanbul, Jerusalem, even Calcutta.

Within these dispersed Armenian communities there developed several competing—and in many ways incompatible—visions of what and where Armenia was. An ecclesiastical definition of the nation was nurtured in Armenian monasteries and religious centers across the Middle East, but even that was variegated. Unlike other Eastern churches, the Armenian Apostolic Church has two ecclesiastical heads: one based in Echmiadzin, outside Yerevan, and another in Antelias, Lebanon. The split is an artifact of the Crusades, when a separate Armenian kingdom was proclaimed in Cilicia along the northeastern Mediterranean and, in the mid fifteenth century, a separate *catholicos*, or patriarch, named for the Cilician church. Throughout the world today two separate networks of subordinate churches look to the holy sees either at Echmiadzin or at Antelias as their spiritual center. Linguistic differences also contributed to the growth of different notions of the nation. The western variant of the Armenian language, spoken in the Anatolian regions of historic Armenia and among the European and Levantine diasporas, is significantly different from the eastern variant spoken in the Armenian republic, Iran, and among the populations originating in these areas.

In the late nineteenth century political differences further complicated these social divisions. Two major political parties—the Hunchaks (from the Armenian for "tocsin") and the Dashnaks—were founded in Geneva in 1887 and in Tiflis in 1890, respectively. Both were part of the general progressive movement in the late Russian Empire and in western Europe, which sometimes combined the language of social justice and class consciousness with the power of national revival. However, the parties differed on cooperation with nonsocialist parties, the relationship between national and class struggles, and the tactics to be pursued in seeking their overall aim of resolving the political status of Armenian communities in the Ottoman Empire and Russia. They also existed alongside a host of other political orientations, from conservatives to bourgeois liberals, as well as the multiple influences of the Armenian church hierarchies. By the time of the Russian revolutions, the Dashnaks had become dominant among Armenian communities in the Caucasus. Their authority over guerrilla fighters in eastern Anatolia was augmented by victories on the battlefield. They thus assumed the mantle of defender of the Armenian national idea and became the leading voice in republican Yerevan.

The place of the Dashnaks in the republic also gave the party something that no previous Armenian political movement could claim, namely, the position of founder of a national state. When the republic collapsed in 1920, the end of independence was therefore a particularly severe blow to those Armenians whose personal histories had been tied to the rise, momentary triumph, and ultimate defeat of the Dashnak party. Other Armenian communities and political leaders continued with the work of supporting Armenians wherever they might reside, making their peace with new political realities, and focusing on the existence of an Armenian republic—even a Soviet one—as essential to the survival of Armenian identity. The Dashnaks, by contrast, saw the Bolshevik conquest as a tragedy for the party as well as the nation.

All of these things converged in New York City in December 1933. Archbishop Tourian's credentials as an Armenian patriot were unimpeachable. He was born in Istanbul, had survived the genocide, and, as bishop of Smyrna, had joined the wave of Greeks, Armenians, and other Christians who fled from that city before the Turkish army in 1922. The central issue, however, was the archbishop's relationship to the Armenian Soviet republic. In the eyes of some Dashnaks, he had revealed himself as a traitor to the national cause. By allowing the Soviet flag to fly at Armenian events rather than the old red-blue-orange tricolor of the republic, he had acquiesced to the Bolshevik takeover and Armenia's subjugation to Moscow. The murderers' conspiracy was aimed at liquidating a man who they believed had betrayed both his nation and the defunct republic.

Further violence followed the Tourian murder. Dashnaks took over a church in Philadelphia. Small-scale riots hit ethnic neighborhoods in Boston and Chicago. The real ramifications were deeper and longer-lasting. The old divisions within the diaspora were now unbridgeable. Pro-Dashnak congregations broke with the rest of the church, establishing their own ecclesiastical body. In the 1950s this new congregation of Armenian churches in the United States was placed under the aegis of the *catholicos* of Cilicia, thus separating these communities from the holy see at Echmiadzin. The diaspora was no longer a single group—if it had ever been—but rather two often antagonistic, separate wings. One, associated with the Dashnaks, called for muscular solutions to Armenian problems, including the targeted use of violence; the other, associated with more moderate parties and civic organizations, sought to influence the policies of Western governments while making peace with the new regime in Yerevan. Those divisions have remained in place down to the present. That is why there are now two archbishops in New York and other major cities, two separate lobbying organizations in Washington, D.C.—even two networks of summer camps for Armenian youth. The ghosts of the recent past— beyond the Caucasus and within a single ethnic community—have proven difficult to escape.

The prosecutor in the Tourian case provided a succinct summary of the nature of the archbishop's assassination. It was "a political murder," he said, in which otherwise reasonable men were simply "carrying out in America the grudges and antipathies of the old world."[68] He was right in at least one sense: Violence was always a part of the exile experience. What individual Armenians and the well-established network of the Dashnak party had failed to achieve in Anatolia they managed to do abroad. In 1921 Talaat Paşa, the former Ottoman interior minister and one of the architects of the genocide, was assassinated by an Armenian in Berlin. Similar attacks killed Cemal Paşa, the former Ottoman minister of war, as well as a former Ottoman grand vizier and a former Azerbaijani interior minister. A new wave of violence erupted in the 1970s and early 1980s when Armenian terrorists murdered over thirty Turkish diplomats and embassy employees in a string of attacks stretching from Los Angeles to Sydney. Georgians, too, were caught up in violence. Noe Khomeriki, a former Georgian minister of agriculture, returned to Georgia in 1924, where he was promptly shot by the Bolsheviks as a participant in a failed rebellion that year. In 1930 Noe Ramishvili, who served as Georgian prime minister and interior minister, was murdered in Paris, perhaps by a Soviet agent.

The men who founded the interwar republics were, in many ways, obvious losers. They were pushed aside by the Bolshevik invasion, forced to flee on crowded ships from harbors teeming with other refugees. They spent the rest of their lives in Paris, Istanbul, and elsewhere, working in vain for the liberation of their old homelands. When they approached Western diplomats, hoping to press their case for independence as Europe plunged into the Second World War, they were kept at arm's length. "The movement which he represents," reported a British Foreign Office representative upon meeting a Georgian Promethean in 1939, "seems somewhat academic."[69] Yet in a profound sense the émigrés would eventually become the real winners. When the Soviet Union suddenly collapsed in 1991, what emerged from the rubble was precisely the thing that the exiled leaders had been working for all along—the old republics of Armenia, Azerbaijan, and Georgia, now once again independent.

None of the émigrés was around to bask in the glow of belated victory, however. Karlo Chkheidze, former chairman of both the Petrograd soviet and the Georgian constituent assembly, committed suicide in France in 1926. Mammed Amin Rasulzade, head of the Azerbaijani Müsavat party, died in Turkey in 1954. Even Anton Denikin, the great enemy of the Caucasus republics, slipped away quietly in Ann Arbor, Michigan, in 1947. Noe Jordania, the former Georgian president, died not long after in Paris in January 1953. It must have been some small comfort to Jordania to know that, whatever else might have happened in his checkered political career, he still managed to outlive Denikin, his old nemesis, by six years. Had he lasted a few months longer, he would even have outlived his alter-ego, the younger, rougher, and rather more successful Georgian Marxist Ioseb Jughashvili—Joseph Stalin.

Cleansing

Jordania met Jughashvili for the first time in 1898 when Jordania was working as editor of the Tiflis weekly *Kvali* (The Furrow), the first legal Marxist newspaper in the Russian Empire. Jughashvili arrived at the editorial offices and introduced himself as an avid reader of the newspaper and a dedicated socialist—so dedicated, in fact, that he planned to leave his studies at the Tiflis theological seminary and join the workers' movement. Jordania questioned the eager young man about his knowledge of sociology, history, and political economy.

Jughashvili failed in every subject. His entire education seemed to have come from reading back issues of *Kvali* and a smattering of Marxist theory. Jordania sent him on his way with sage advice—stay in seminary—which Jughashvili studiously ignored.[70]

From that initial encounter between two Georgian social democrats, both of them former seminarians, the two men's lives went in radically different directions. One, an urbane man with a slight stutter who briefly served as president of an independent, vaguely democratic republic, would be forced into exile and slip into obscurity, forgotten by all but the most dedicated Georgian patriots. A few decades after meeting Jordania, the other would become the undisputed leader of the Soviet Union.

For many years after Stalin's ascendancy, the main approach to understanding his success was to psychoanalyze him, to attribute his particular brand of ruthlessness and destructive drive for power to some deep traits of character. That was certainly the view of those he defeated—most famously Leon Trotsky. More recently the trend has been to find some explanation in Stalin's origins in the Caucasus: his childhood beneath the wing of a doting Georgian mother; his adolescence inside the macho clannishness of Georgian society; or perhaps his coming of age amid the Oriental intrigues of the bazaar.

Such attempts fail, however, for the simple reason that there were plenty of other Georgians—and many other people from the wider Caucasus—who took different paths, supporting republican government over tyranny and working diligently for reform and openness. It would be too much to lionize the losers of the early 1920s, men such as Jordania and Rasulzade. There was plenty in the politics of 1918–21— from the treatment of Muslims in Armenia to the Mensheviks' use of the military against dissenters—that confirmed their own low tolerance for opposition. But the mere existence of alternatives to Bolshevism points to the fact that there is little in the Caucasus itself to explain Stalin's political pathologies or the callousness with which he dealt with his homeland once he had consolidated his power in Moscow. Even Stalin seems not to have thought of himself as, first and foremost, a man of the Caucasus. He mainly spoke Russian (with an accent), although he was known to converse with old associates in Georgian on occasion. He spent most of his life and career outside the region. In 1937 he committed a culturally unforgivable act that marked the final break with his Caucasus past: He failed to attend his mother's funeral. In fact, had Stalin been a better Georgian—loyal to friends and family; honorable to a fault; mindful of old debts; committed to the interests of his Caucasus homeland—the twentieth century might have turned out a little less bloody.[71]

To understand Stalin's particular relationship with Georgia—as well as with the entire phenomenon of national identity—one need only consult his treatise on the subject entitled "Marxism and the National Question," which was first published in 1913 in the St. Petersburg journal *Prosveshchenie* (Enlightenment).[72] Stalin's views may well have changed over the course of his life, from his early years as an aspiring Bolshevik activist, hoping to catch the attention of Lenin and other party leaders, to his last years as supreme leader of a one-party state. But there were certain themes that consistently defined his view of what constituted a nation and on how the multinational Soviet Union, as well as his own multinational Caucasus, was to be ruled.

Stalin began by distinguishing nations from races, tribes, linguistic groups, or people who simply inhabited the same territory. A nation was a community that was "historically evolved" and "stable." It could be defined in terms of a common culture consisting of "language, territory, economic life, and psychological make-up."[73] None of these criteria of nationhood, however, was timeless. Nations, like all historical phenomena, were subject to change; they arose and disappeared at definite times and in specific ways. Nor was any one of these things more important than any other. Nations were agglomerations of traits, and when one or more of them changed, so would the nation.

Being a good Marxist, Stalin saw the rise of national sentiment primarily as a response to oppression by some other national group. National consciousness, like consciousness of class identity, came about in circumstances in which a distinct national community found itself in a position subordinate to some other. Once constituted, however, the nation must be given the right of self-determination. This was, he said, the policy of all proper socialists: "The right of self-determination means that a nation can arrange its life according to its own will. It has the right to arrange its life on the basis of autonomy. It has the right to enter into federal relations with other nations. It has the right to complete secession. Nations are sovereign and all nations are equal."[74]

The difference between the socialists and the bourgeois parties was that the former used self-determination as a way of alleviating national discord, thereby allowing workers of different nationalities to recognize their common aims in the class struggle. The latter fanned nationalist animosities, calling on all classes to rally around the national banner in a single common cause. Only in a political system that allowed for nations to develop freely and to express their reasonable desire for self-determination could conflict be alleviated and its chief beneficiaries—the national bourgeoisie—removed from power. Stalin was quick to point out that self-determination had to be understood only in terms that would be in the best interests of the workers. Simply because a few bourgeois elites—the "beys and mullahs" of Azerbaijani Muslims, for example—called for seceding from the Russian Empire, this did not automatically mean that full secession would benefit the Muslim working class. The form of self-determination fundamentally depended on the historical and social condition of the nation concerned.

Much of Stalin's treatise was directed against the Bund, the social democratic movement among Jews of the western Russian Empire. Stalin believed that Bundist attempts to separate the interests of the Jewish working class from those of the working class as a whole could only play into the hands of class enemies, bourgeois parties that would always be superior in their ability to wield the language of nationalism. However, Stalin reserved an entire section of "Marxism and the National Question" for the application of his theories to the Caucasus. Here his target was the Mensheviks and others who argued for national autonomy, those who seemed to piggy-back the class struggle on top of Georgian, Azerbaijani, or other forms of nationalism. For Stalin, "national cultural autonomy is meaningless and nonsensical in relation to Caucasian conditions."[75]

The reason was simple, he argued: The Caucasus was nearly devoid of real nations. The region contained many "peoples," some with literary languages and others with only primitive dialects, some with a coherent economic system and others with only barter and the bazaar, but few genuine "nations." Stalin conceded that the Georgians might be a nation, albeit one that had only arisen during the past half century or so. However, smaller groups would eventually be faced with the choice of assimilating to larger nations or developing their own premature independence movements. Both courses, Stalin believed, served the bourgeoisie. The solution to this dilemma lay in territory, that is, to define self-determination in such a way that it embraced the largest possible territorial unit, allowing individual peoples to flourish within it but providing a check on social discord. The south Caucasus as a whole, not the individual peoples that constituted it, should be the unit of self-determination, carrying on the class struggle by pooling the legitimate interests of nations and nations-in-the-making.

The essence of Stalin's views was that socialism and national flourishing were not incompatible if properly understood. Not all aspects of national traditions needed to be celebrated. Any practices that were retrograde or inimical to the improvement of the workers' lot—such as the veiling of women in Muslim lands—would have to be eliminated in a socialist state. However, the nation could be a progressive force when tied to modernization and internationalism. In the Caucasus, as in other parts of the Soviet Union, these ideas contributed to the creation of a vast system of political institutions that ended up embracing rather than abjuring a certain brand of nationalism.

❥ ❥

The entire Soviet system—how demographic data were created and used; the way internal administrative borders were drawn; the style of everything from popular culture to museum displays—made a fetish of cultural identity, what in Russian was usually called *natsional' nost'* (ethnicity or nationality). Marx famously claimed that the workers have no country, that national distinctiveness, like the state, would wither away once the chief engine of nationalism—the self-interested bourgeoisie—passed from the historical stage. Yet the Soviet state, in its own self-conception and in its way of presenting itself to the outside world, privileged the ethnonational. The Soviet Union was portrayed not as a place where ethnic identity had ceased to matter but as a happy union of many discrete ethnonational groups collectively striving to create modern, classless nations that would eventually fuse into a single Soviet people. Over the seventy years of Soviet power, state policy on the nationalities question went through many different phases, at times highlighting the central importance of Russian language and culture, at other times stressing ethnic uniqueness. A constant theme, however, was the paradoxical—or, as Marxists would say, dialectical—union of ethnonational flourishing and cultural assimilation. The former had to do, first and foremost, with how basic questions of territory were decided.

The absorption of the Caucasus into the new Soviet order was presented as the will of the people, the "voluntary" union of the workers of the south Caucasus with their brothers north of the mountains. In fact, it was little more than the reacquisition of former Russian imperial lands, albeit by a new, Bolshevik-led state. By 1921 Moscow controlled almost all of the territory once encompassed by the imperial viceroyalty of the Caucasus, the only exceptions being the border areas seized by Turkish forces from Georgia and Armenia in the winter and spring of 1920–21—principally the district of Kars—which eventually fell to republican Turkey.

There was resistance, however. Northwest Caucasus highlanders fought on until the summer of 1921. Bolshevik operations against Chechen and Dagestani "bandits" continued until 1925. The defeated Dashnaks in Armenia continued to launch small-scale attacks through the spring of 1921. Svaneti, the upland district of northwestern Georgia, was barely under Bolshevik control for most of 1922 and 1923. In the largest revolt, underground Mensheviks, allied with émigré agitators, staged an abortive rebellion in Georgia in the spring of 1924. Although the Mensheviks were never able to march on Tbilisi, they did present a formidable threat to the Red Army. Hundreds of alleged Menshevik sympathizers were rounded up and executed by Georgian Bolsheviks and Red Army units.[76] By and large, however, the reconquest of the south Caucasus was relatively easy. With the three republics divided both internally and among themselves, most of the former republican leaders in exile, Turkey looking for Bolshevik support in its own war of liberation against the Allies, and no support forthcoming from Britain, France, or the United States, the fate of the south Caucasus was effectively sealed.

Figuring out how to govern this new territory was more complicated. The devastation of the war was still evident. Famine and disease were rampant, especially in Armenia. A plague of locusts descended on Azerbaijan in 1922.[77] In March of that year the central executive committees of the three south Caucasus republics—the new political authority under Soviet rule—approved the formation of a single Federal Union of Soviet Socialist Republics of the Transcaucasus. There might have been some argument for making the north and south Caucasus into a single administrative region; after all, that formula had been serviceable for more than a century under the tsars. However, since the Soviet Union did not yet exist—it would not be formed until the end of 1922—the Transcaucasus federation was technically an independent state and merely an ally of Soviet Russia. Separating north and south also fit into the overall Soviet strategy of creating buffer zones between the Russian heartland and foreign neighbors, especially Turkey and Iran. In December 1922 a newly created republic—now called the Transcaucasus Soviet Federative Socialist Republic, with its capital in Tiflis—entered the Soviet Union as a single entity. In 1936 the three south Caucasus republics were made separate union republics, the highest-level constituents of the Soviet state.

North of the mountains territories underwent several administrative changes through the late 1930s, when autonomous republics and regions broadly resembling the present-day configuration were finally put in place. In the northeast, Dagestan was separated into a single administrative unit, and the region from Chechnya westward was initially incorporated into another. Rather than separate out the lowland Circassian and highland Turkic populations in the northwest, the Soviet leadership combined them into conglomerate administrative units—with Cherkes and Karachai in one and Kabardians and Balkars in another—which eventually gave rise to today's hyphenated republics of Karachaevo-Cherkesia and Kabardino-Balkaria.

Things were equally complex south of the mountains. In the Georgian republic three regions were given special status. Abkhazia in the northwest, with its capital in the port city of Sukhumi, was made a separate Soviet socialist republic, united by treaty with Georgia. Achara in the southwest, with its capital in Batumi, was made an autonomous republic. In north-central Georgia, the region of South Ossetia, centered in the city of Tskhinvali, was made an autonomous province (*oblast'*). Similar arrangements were made in Azerbaijan. The region of Nagorno-Karabakh, near the Armenian border and with its capital at Khankendi (modern Stepanakert), was given autonomy. The same was done for the territory of Nakhichevan even though it was physically separated from Azerbaijan by the Zangezur region, which was made part of Armenia. This strange territorial sandwich—a piece of Azerbaijan (Nakhichevan) in the west, disconnected from the rest of the republic; a slice of Armenian territory (Zangezur) in the middle; and a piece of Armenian-majority territory inside Azerbaijan (Nagorno-Karabakh) in the east—would become the source of one of the region's bloodiest conflicts in the late 1980s. Only Armenia was made a single republic without administrative subdivisions, but that was small recompense. Most of the richest farmland and the historically significant sites—from the old royal city of Ani to Mount Ararat, the central symbol of Armenian identity—were now across the border in Turkey.

All the administrative units of the north and south Caucasus could claim some degree of legitimacy based on ethnic contours and longstanding economic and cultural ties among the peoples inhabiting these regions. For example, it would have made little sense to draw clear territorial boundaries around Circassian speakers and Turkic speakers in the northwest Caucasus, grouping each into a separate "national" homeland. Circassians living along the Kuban River had maintained far more intense economic relations with highland Karachai than their own linguistic kin, the Kabardians living near the Terek River. However, the origins of the modern map of the Caucasus differed in each case. In mountainous Karabakh and Nakhichevan the ethnic principle could be applied. The former had an Armenian majority, the latter a Muslim majority, and some argument could be made for granting each a special status. In Georgia, Abkhazia had been a major scene of fighting between Mensheviks and White forces during the civil war. Offering it special status thus created a buffer along what had recently been a hotly contested border. There was also an international component to these decisions. Largely to placate Turkish concern over the fate of Muslim minorities in the south Caucasus, the Bolshevik government agreed to special treatment for the Muslim areas of Achara and Nakhichevan even before Red Army units had marched into Georgia and Azerbaijan. Under the terms of the treaties of Moscow and Kars in 1921, Soviet Russia and Turkey settled their border in the south Caucasus and agreed on the administrative status of these areas even though they lay inside what would become the Soviet Union. They remain a rare instance in international law in which the internal administrative structure of one country has been secured by a treaty with another.

The decision of Soviet leaders to draw boundary lines in one place and not another thus had little to do with any putative grand strategy to make the Caucasus into a ticking time bomb of territorial disputes. Indeed, if Soviet officials had been able to foresee the violence that would erupt over precisely these borders in the 1980s and 1990s, they might well have opted for a different arrangement. In any case, local autonomy was of little immediate consequence. With a highly centralized party and a federal government in Tiflis—soon to be replaced by powerful republic-level governments in Yerevan, Baku, and Tiflis/Tbilisi—there was little reason to expect that how one drew the dotted lines of internal provinces would one day have international consequences.

Vladimir Lenin believed that the transition to socialism in the Caucasus should move "more slowly, more carefully" than in Russia, taking account of local conditions, especially the large peasantry and the natural resources that would be in great demand in Western markets.[78] That view was rejected by his successors. "You hens! You sons of donkeys! What is going on here?" Stalin screamed to a group of Bolsheviks shortly after the takeover of Georgia. "You have to draw a white hot iron over this Georgian land! . . . Impale them! Tear them apart!"[79] In the early years of the Soviet Caucasus, Bolshevik forces were energetically involved in the liquidation of alleged class enemies, the suppression of full-scale rebellion, and the creation of a new cadre of "highlander-revolutionaries" who could spread the message of class liberation to the laboring masses in the mountains.[80]

The same national groups that had been adjuncts in the Russian conquest of the Caucasus, principally Georgians and Armenians, continued to play pivotal roles in the Bolshevik consolidation of power. People of Muslim heritage, such as Azerbaijanis, Dagestanis, and others, were represented as well, although in lesser numbers. All were beneficiaries of the official policy of *korenizatsiia*, or indigenization, in the late 1920s. That policy sought to "root" the Communist Party and the apparatus of the Soviet state in the national republics by giving preferential treatment in hiring and promotion to members of underrepresented national groups—sovietization through affirmative action, as it were.[81] Today, nationalist histories portray the Soviet period as the extension of Russian rule into a new era, with Russian commissars simply taking the place of Russian viceroys. However, even more than in the imperial period, throughout the 1920s and 1930s both the achievements and tragedies of the new order in the Caucasus were produced by people from the region itself.

Indigenous Communist elites became some of the most enthusiastic campaigners against traditional forms of social organization and cultural practices that they viewed as retrograde. In the mountains, bride kidnapping, child marriage, and blood feuds were denounced as "crimes of custom" (*bytovye prestupleniia*) punishable by confiscation of property, fines, and imprisonment.[82] Peasant smallholders, briefly empowered by land reforms effected during the republican period, were forcibly enrolled in state farms and collectives. Mechanized agriculture began to change the countryside, although the disruptive speed of rural reform meant that many peasant families barely survived after delivering up their crops to the state. The cult of modernity—involving vast electrification schemes, building programs, and industrialization—became the hallmark of the new era.

The rise of a new political elite, uncertain of its success and congenitally suspicious of class enemies and foreign plots, ultimately produced the same show trials, disappearances, and summary executions in the Caucasus that were experienced in other parts of the Soviet state. The origins of the political purges of the 1930s lay in the vast expansion of the size of the Communist Party in the first two decades of Soviet power. Rivals to the Bolsheviks were progressively eliminated, and membership in the only dominant party became essential for advancement. Since its earliest days the party had periodically carried out investigations of party membership, verifying documents and going over membership lists, in part as an attempt to flush out police informers or inactive members, in part simply as a bureaucratic exercise in accurate record keeping. Once they assumed power, however, the Bolsheviks made the purge a mechanism of social control, a way of testing the loyalty of party members and eliminating rivals who threatened the growing power of Stalin, by now the supreme leader.

By the early 1930s party leaders had begun to worry that alien elements—opportunists, old class enemies, morally suspect cadres—had flooded onto the party rosters during the great intake of new members over the previous decade. A verification of party lists was soon carried out at all levels of the Soviet state. The outcome was the reduction of the size of the party by perhaps more than a million members, many—if not most—of them purged for reasons that had little to do with high politics. In relatively short order the small coterie of leaders around Stalin found the purge to be an effective tool for ridding party and state structures of real or potential rivals. A template had been found for dealing with those who deviated from the line set down by Stalin and his associates. The party was now returning to its origins: not as a mass political organization but as a relatively small, conspiratorial clique where secrecy and loyalty were the supreme virtues. Terror—against alleged class enemies, spies, and wreckers—had become an instrument of the state. In the Caucasus the person who wielded that instrument with brutal resolve was Lavrenti Beria.

There is a terrifying photograph of Beria taken at the Seventh Congress of Soviets, held in Moscow in 1935. Among the items on the agenda was preparatory work for a new Soviet constitution to be adopted the following year. Beria is seated in the center, his trademark pince-nez squeezing his eyes together in the middle of his round Georgian face. At this stage he was the leader of the Communist Party of Georgia. It would be another three years before he was appointed to the all-union People's Commissariat of Internal Affairs, the NKVD, a post from which he would oversee the later stages of the most horrific Stalin-era purges. In the photograph he is flanked by the other leaders of the south Caucasus: Nestor Lakoba, the party leader of Abkhazia, with his neatly trimmed mustache; Aghasi Khanjian, party first secretary in Armenia, with his bouffant hair and thick glasses; and Ghazanfar Musabekov, chairman of the Transcaucasus regional government and president of the Central Executive Committee of the Soviet Union, looking mischievously into the camera. All the men are seated in a row, hunched over a set of papers, working diligently on some resolution or other matter of state. What is shocking is the fact that within three years Beria would have the other three killed: Lakoba and Khanjian in 1936; Musabekov in 1938.

Beria was the central player in the chaotic era of denunciations, arrests, and cleansings of the party and state apparatus in the late 1930s, the period of the Great Purges. He was Stalin's chief henchman on the ground, first secretary of the Community Party of Georgia from 1931 to 1938, and the virtual ruler of the Caucasus at a time when Stalin was preoccupied with matters far beyond his native land. For much of this period he also held the position of chief of the Transcaucasus party committee, with responsibility for Armenia and Azerbaijan. Beria was twenty years Stalin's junior. He had joined the party at the time of the October Revolution and had no connection to the old Bolsheviks, who had been with Lenin in the underground years. He thus represented the new face of the party, an organization even more secretive and paranoid than when it had been a subversive force within the Russian Empire. He had made his career in the secret police, the Cheka, and had brought to his party work the same concern for—even obsession with—internal dissent and intrigue that had characterized his time as an agent. Like Stalin, he was a Georgian, but of a particular type: a Mingrelian, born in the riotously green valleys of Abkhazia. He was a man from the periphery of the periphery, armed with ruthless determination, who ascended to the highest levels of the Soviet state.

Beria's rise depended almost exclusively on his proximity to Stalin, and he repaid his patron's attentions by providing him with a usable past. Stalin's actual role in the emergence of Bolshevism in the Caucasus was of middling importance at best. He was not particularly distinguished in socialist circles, as Noe Jordania understood. He held few posts of consequence until after the October Revolution. However, in July 1935 Beria delivered a speech to a gathering of party activists in Tbilisi entitled "On the Matter of the History of Bolshevik Organizations in Transcaucasia."[83] The innocuous title masked its content. It was, in fact, nothing less than a complete rethinking—even fantastic retelling—of the history of the Communist Party. Stalin emerged from Beria's narrative as the young but farsighted Koba, one of his early *noms de révolution*, the obvious leader of Bolshevik subversives in the Caucasus. A visionary and persecuted champion of the interests of the working masses, Stalin was placed, Zelig-like, at the scene of major events. He was praised for masterminding workers' demonstrations in Batumi, leading the Tiflis Bolshevik organization and, later, heading the entire south Caucasus Bolshevik movement.

This reading of history was critical, for it allowed Stalin to elevate himself above the other old Bolsheviks who were still around. It also provided some justification for the ensuing moves against the well-established party elite, now considered latent rivals to Stalin and his favorites. Over the next several years Beria launched an all-out attack on local party leaders in the Caucasus. Earlier he had publicly claimed that remnants of the Dashnaks, Müsavatists, and Mensheviks were still scheming to fulfill their nefarious goals within the ranks of the Communist Party. By the late 1930s he had both the administrative apparatus and the patronage from the top to unmask the supposed bourgeois nationalists. Georgian Bolsheviks, some of whom had gone on to administrative positions across the Soviet Union, were removed from their posts and in many cases executed. Nestor Lakoba, a genuinely popular political leader in Abkhazia, was poisoned in 1936 on Beria's orders, and over the next few years nearly every member of Lakoba's immediate family was imprisoned or killed. Armenian commissars and party leaders who could be linked, however remotely, to the Dashnaks were exposed and placed on trial. Even onetime associates of Beria when he had worked in the secret police organs of Azerbaijan were progressively eliminated.

The same cascading motives that existed in other parts of the Soviet Union were at work in the Caucasus. Powerful figures in party and state institutions made rooting out internal enemies the central way of demonstrating loyalty and preserving one's career—and often one's life. The purges were launched from the top by Stalin, Beria, and their associates, but they evolved into an entire social system—terror as a way of life. From the highest-ranking officials to those at the bottom of the system, individuals had an incentive to denounce others before they themselves were targeted—to preserve their own positions, avenge old wrongs, and dispense with rivals while securing the gratitude and praise of superiors. Across the Soviet Union roughly twenty-nine million people—ordinary criminals, political prisoners, peasants, and those who happened to become the target of denunciation by a boss, subordinate, or neighbor—passed through state-run labor camps or were deported en masse during the Stalin era.[84] Among these was an entire generation of political leaders in the Caucasus, men and women who had been active since the earliest days of Soviet power but happened to fall afoul of Beria and his lieutenants.

When he departed the Caucasus to take up the post of NKVD chief in Moscow, Beria left his tentacles behind. His oversight of the purges resulted in a party structure denuded of old Bolsheviks and controlled by people loyal to Beria himself. It amounted to yet another revolution in a region that had already witnessed several: a massive turnover of elites at all levels of the party and state administration, from the top-level party politburos and councils of people's commissars to city and regional party committees, newspaper editorial boards, and schools.[85] A place that had produced Stalin was now decidedly Stalinist, controlled as never before from the Soviet center, purged of people with ties to the former Bolshevik underground and the pre-Soviet past, and deeply affected by the full-blown cults of personality that now enveloped both Stalin and Beria.

Just as his own success depended on his servility to Stalin, so the existence of a new generation of cadres in the Caucasus depended on Beria. In Georgia Kandid Charkviani, the new party leader, basked in Beria's favor while presiding over a new array of elites in a republic overturned by the purges. In Armenia Grigor Arutiunov took over the party leadership and launched what amounted to sweeping-up operations in a party and state structure shaken by years of summary executions and show trials. In Azerbaijan Mir Jafar Baghirov oversaw a continuing purge of officials who had been singled out as alleged instruments of pan-Turkism, pan-Islamism, or other great power interests. Some of these new leaders managed to survive politically for decades, while others fell victim to Stalin in a new round of purges just prior to the supreme leader's death. In the end, the influence of many of these local Berias lasted only as long as Beria himself, whose power was similarly dependent on the grace and favor of Stalin.

Before any of these officials left the scene, however, there was one massive purge still left to be accomplished. It took place on both sides of the mountains, in the north and south Caucasus, but its origins lay less in the need to expose political rivals and class enemies than in the desire to control and punish supposedly disloyal populations. In the frenzied atmosphere of the Second World War, the Soviets again applied the same tactic that had been used in the region with cruel effectiveness almost a century earlier—the wholesale deportation of targeted ethnic groups.

◆ ◆

When the Red Army fought its way into Berlin in the spring of 1945, a Georgian was on hand to help make history. Together with a Russian comrade, Sgt. Meliton Kantaria planted the hammer-and-sickle flag on the roof of the Reichstag, an iconic image that was captured by a quick-witted photographer. After the war Kantaria initially returned to his old job on a Georgian collective farm. However, he was soon swept up in the postwar glorification of wartime achievements and the leading role of Stalin, his fellow Georgian. He was made a "Hero of the Soviet Union" and given a comfortable billet in Abkhazia, where he remained until the Georgian-Abkhaz war of the early 1990s. Old and infirm, he was evacuated to Moscow and died in a Kremlin hospital. He is still invoked by Georgian politicians as a symbol of Georgia's commitment to resisting oppression.

Although Kantaria helped carry the war to the west, war had earlier come to the frontiers of his own home region. The southern reaches of the Soviet Union were in the forefront of German war aims in 1942. By then Hitler had begun to formulate plans for an invasion of the Middle East, which in turn depended on neutralizing Soviet forces in the Black Sea and Caspian regions. German plans called for a three-pronged attack, moving from northwest to southeast, to secure control of the Don River, the mountain passes of the Caucasus, and such major ports as Novorossiisk, Poti, Batumi, and eventually the oilfields of Baku.

The German push to the east and south in the summer of 1942, code name "Operation Blue," was rapid at first. Bridgeheads were made east of the Don. Soon the city of Rostov and oil facilities at Maikop were under German control. Along with Romanian troops, the Germans advanced down the Black Sea coast, taking several ports despite strong resistance. By August the advance had slowed due to an increase in the effectiveness of Soviet resistance. In another operation, code name "Edelweiss," German infantry and tank corps pushed into the mountains from July to November of the same year, hoping to take control of the major passes before the onset of winter. With the first snowfall the advance ground to a halt. German forces came within five miles of the regional center of Ordzhonikidze (the renamed Vladi-kavkaz), but that turned out to be a historic moment. It was the easternmost point the Wehrmacht ever reached.

The Soviet response had been to flee in the face of initial German advances and then attack when enemy supply lines were overextended and troops fatigued. In the end, Hitler's own obsession—the conquest of Stalingrad—diverted German attention away from the Caucasus and trumped military necessity. There was little reason to target the city on the lower Volga River. Taking it might have helped secure an east-west line of communication between the Don and the Volga, but its real value was symbolic. The chance to defeat the Red Army in a city named for Stalin himself was a powerful temptation. The determined resistance in the city itself; the daring Soviet counteroffensive; the lack of coordination among German and other Axis troops; the operational overstretch of all Axis forces; and, crucially, the weather of 1942–43 contributed to a German defeat. Soon German forces were retreating westward from the Volga, the lower Don, the north Caucasus, and the Black Sea coast. Soviet forces moved to reoccupy the evacuated ports, passes, and flatlands.

While many individuals and indigenous groups in the Caucasus experienced the initial German advance as a disaster, others saw it as an opportunity. Accompanying German armies in the push toward the mountains and Black Sea coast were former exiles, including old White officers, Cossacks, and Caucasus highlanders, who viewed the German invasion of the Soviet Union as a chance to fight again the battles they had lost in the early 1920s. The extent of local collaboration with the Nazis is difficult to gauge. German war planners actively encouraged Karachai, Chechens, and others to revolt against Soviet authorities. "Highlanders are by nature very naïve and frivolous," Hitler wrote to one of his commanders in the north Caucasus. "It is easier to work with them than with other nationalities."[86] No large-scale uprisings resulted, but the threat of local nationalities aiding the German war effort was significant enough for Beria to step up surveillance of mountain communities.[87]

Before the war ended, Soviet officials had become convinced that large-scale collaboration was, in fact, taking place. Such collaboration was viewed not as the fault of disloyal individuals but rather of entire, congenitally rebellious ethnic groups. Forced relocation became the official policy for dealing with it, a tactic that had been used repeatedly—often in the same territories—by tsarist generals and Bolshevik commissars alike. In 1943 the Soviets embarked on a wave of deportation and exile, much of it overseen by Beria himself, that once again altered the demographic profile of the Caucasus. Some 70,000 Karachai were removed to Kazakhstan in November 1943. More than 300,000 Chechens and 80,000 Ingush were sent to various parts of Central Asia in February 1944. Over 37,000 Balkars were deported in March.[88] The populations of entire villages and districts were wiped away, their places taken by new (usually Russian) migrants. Among those sent into exile were significant numbers of people who had actually served in Soviet forces during the war. According to official records, 4,428 deported Chechens, 946 Ingush, 2,543 Karachai, and

1,045 Balkars were Red Army veterans.[89] Focusing on the question of collaboration thus misses the essential point, namely, that the deportations of the Second World War were part and parcel of the persistent Soviet—and earlier Russian—insistence on demographic engineering as state policy. According to one calculation, from 1918 to 1952 the Soviet government organized fifty-two separate relocation campaigns, removing millions of people from their homes and sending them abroad or to unfamiliar, often inhospitable, parts of their own country.[90]

Specific ethnic populations were targeted, as was virtually any group thought to be potentially disloyal, from alleged class enemies to foreign citizens, or individuals simply classed as "enemy elements." In 1936 tens of thousands of Poles and Germans were relocated from Ukraine to Kazakhstan. They were followed by the forced migrations, both during and after the Second World War, of Koreans, Jews, Crimean Tatars, Kalmyks, Moldovans, and other peoples. Sometimes deportations were ordered out of fear of potential political treachery, while at other times their origins lay in the desire to shift the demographic weight of one or another ethnic group or fill a newly emptied territory with settlers. Ethnic Greeks were evacuated to Kazakhstan from the south Caucasus and the Black Sea coast. Boxcars of Armenians were sent to Siberia. Meskhetian Turks, Armenian-speaking Muslims, and Kurds were removed from the southern borderlands of Georgia. By 1949 some two million members of ethnic and religious minorities were living in deportation camps or resettlement colonies, some having been precipitously removed from their homelands and others having been born into what amounted to internal exile.[91]

Insofar as it was possible, these operations were carried out in secret. "The operation proceeded in an organized way," reported Beria matter-of-factly on the removal of thousands of Chechen families in cattle cars, "without serious resistance or other incidents."[92] Western diplomats knew about them at the time, but word sometimes came from unlikely sources. In one instance an ethnic Greek maid on the staff of the British Embassy in Moscow happened to receive a letter from her sister informing her that the family was now living in Kazakhstan.[93] North Caucasus peoples remained the most numerous of the exiled groups, accounting for nearly a fifth of all deportees by the late 1940s. Among these, the Chechens were by far the single largest ethnic population—a group that, as a result, nearly ceased to exist in its traditional homeland. The full magnitude of the suffering inflicted on more than a dozen distinct cultural groups during the Second World

War would come to light only after the death of Stalin and the beginning of de-Stalinization. In the Chechen case the history of exile would also come to play a powerful role as a source of grievance following the demise of Soviet power.

⚊ ⚊

During the war Beria continued to rise through the party and state hierarchy, assuming the title of marshal of the Soviet Union and taking charge of the atomic weapons program. As had happened before, however, Stalin began to question the allegiance of those closest to him. One of the final purges concerned the so-called Mingrelian affair, which came to light in the autumn of 1951. A conspiracy was uncovered among leading officials of Mingrelian origin within Georgia. The core of the plot was an attempt to shield corrupt cadres within the party and state elite. Several Georgian officials were dismissed, including some who were close to Beria. (The fact that Beria himself was of Mingrelian origin did not go unnoticed.) In the end, Beria managed to survive, if for no other reason than that Stalin's worsening physical condition made him less skillful at managing political intrigues than he might have been fifteen years earlier. However, Stalin's death in March 1953 opened the floodgates for those seeking to move against Beria and his henchmen.

The structure that Beria had built was crumbling. Charkviani, his associate in Georgia, had been dismissed as first secretary already in 1952. In Armenia Arutiunov was removed from the party secretaryship the next year, along with most of the Beria-era political elite. In Azerbaijan Baghirov was arrested and executed as a traitor. Beria himself was arrested in June 1953 in a conspiracy engineered by Nikita Khrushchev. His trial uncovered a host of alleged crimes, many of them fabrications and none connected with his true offenses, including mass murder and false imprisonment. He was later shot.

Soon the reputations of those who had fallen in the earlier purges or whose legacies were tainted by association with nationalism or bourgeois interests were rehabilitated and re-enshrined in the pantheon of local heroes. Khrushchev's denunciation of Stalin's crimes in 1956 met with praise in many parts of the Soviet Union, but the process of de-Stalinization did not always go smoothly. It sparked deadly rioting in Georgia, whose citizens cherished the memory of their two native sons, Stalin and Beria, regardless of the destruction that both had visited upon their native land. Deported populations were eventually officially rehabilitated as well, but not all of them were immediately allowed to return to their homelands; some had to wait until the fall of the Soviet Union to do so. For those who did return, rebuilding their lives in changed republics and competing with newcomers for jobs and housing created social tensions.

Still, the Caucasus was settling into a period of relative calm and isolation, when it would once again become the remote edge of an enigmatic empire. Western officials who happened to travel there returned with accounts that resembled those compiled by foreign visitors of the eighteenth century. "The people of Daghestan are the driftwood of numerous migrations," noted one diplomat following a visit in 1950. "The men are small, agile and dark, with hawk noses, and sharp faces.... The women have a more Mediterranean plumpness."[94] A land that had experienced decades of political turmoil, economic revolution, and war was once again a place of wonder and mystery.

The post-Stalin elite—those who came to power after the fall of Beria's lieutenants—would stay in power until the late 1960s and early 1970s, when they were replaced by a cadre of younger political figures whose long careers would come to characterize the late Soviet period in the Caucasus. Members of this newer generation, who came of age during the relatively liberal post-Stalin thaw, proved to be remarkable political survivors. They eventually oversaw the transformation of their homelands from Soviet republics into independent nation-states. However, they also presided over a time when social change, intellectual ferment, and long-simmering territorial questions were pushing the Caucasus toward a new era of unrest.

FIVE

Time of Troubles

It was, of all places, between Tiflis and Baku that I lost my political innocence.

Arthur Koestler (1954)

What is most important to the history of the world? Some stirred-up Muslims
or the liberation of Central Europe and the end of the cold war?

Zbigniew Brzezinski (1998)

THE CAUCASUS IN THE LAST QUARTER of the twentieth century
was defined by the long tenure of the Communist Party first
secretaries in the three union republics of the south: Karen
Demirchian in Armenia (1974–88), Heydar Aliyev in Azerbaijan
(1969–82), and Eduard Shevardnadze in Georgia (1972–85). Each held
the prime party post for more than a decade, a period in office rivaling
that of the generation that came to power in the wake of the Beria
purges of the late 1930s. All three were beneficiaries of the desire for
stability following the disruptions caused by de-Stalinization. Until
the Gorbachev reforms of the late 1980s, they managed to carve out
virtual fiefdoms in their own domains, governing the south Caucasus
under the aegis of Leonid Brezhnev, the party's general secretary, and
his immediate successors.

All three also turned out to be remarkable survivors. Returning to politics after the collapse of the Soviet Union, they occupied major positions in their old homelands, now independent countries: Demirchian as speaker of the Armenian parliament and Aliyev and Shevardnadze as presidents of Azerbaijan and Georgia, respectively. Demirchian and Aliyev left office in coffins, the former at the hands of an assassin in 1999, the latter from natural causes in 2003. Only Shevardnadze managed to have a life after politics. In 2003 he was swept from power in a peaceful revolution but was allowed to spend his retirement living quietly in the old presidential compound on the outskirts of Tbilisi.

During the late Soviet era these figures led the process of modernization, industrialization, and social change in their republics. Roads and other transport systems were upgraded. New factories were opened. Agricultural production was upgraded, providing much-vaunted models for the rest of the Soviet Union. Grand new building projects—such as the completion in 1979 of an Armenian nuclear power plant at Medzamor and the unveiling in 1984 of one of the world's tallest hydroelectric dams, located on the Inguri River in Georgia—highlighted the republics' progress. A generation that had no memory of Stalin began to enter the party and state machinery. As in the past, elites from the republics also found leadership positions at the top of the Soviet hierarchy. Aliyev left the office of party secretary to join the all-union Politburo (the first "cultural Muslim" holder of such a position), while Shevardnadze rose to the post of Soviet foreign minister. Throughout their careers the three first secretaries also spent much of their tenure combatting precisely the phenomenon that would occupy them in the post-Soviet period—corruption.

Brothers and Rivals

Postwar scarcity in the early 1920s—exacerbated by collectivization in the late 1920s and early 1930s and compounded by the purges and the Second World War—created a social system based on the need for access to limited goods. In such an environment, having privileged connections was indispensable. Moreover, in an economy dominated by the state, there was ample opportunity for overreporting the consumption of raw materials in industry and then skimming off the surplus for private gain, underreporting production and directing the difference to friends and patrons, and charging extra for services that were meant to be provided free or at an established price. From dealings at the top of the Soviet state to interactions between average citizens and the police, bus drivers, and physicians, survival depended on learning how to become creatively corrupt.

Anticorruption efforts were a feature of the Soviet order from its inception, but since the incentives for dishonest behavior were inherent, there was little to be done to counteract it other than to appeal to the moral sensibilities of citizens and "campaign" against the very practices that the system encouraged. One of Shevardnadze's earliest tasks after assuming the first secretary's position in Georgia was to institute a multiyear purge of state and party personnel accused of graft. Similar campaigns were launched in Armenia and Azerbaijan, targeting "swindlers, bribe-takers, and various adventurers," as Heydar Aliyev put it at the time.[1] Ministers and functionaries were sacked or publicly disgraced, with instances of venality given wide coverage in the republican press. None of the purges reached the bloody levels of the 1930s, and being accused of corruption did not amount to denunciation as a wrecker or an enemy of the people, as had been the case earlier. Nevertheless, campaigning as a style of governance remained essentially the same: applying the language and tactics of warfare—assaults, raids, and frontlines—against a set of social behaviors that were the products of systemic incentives, not just individual pathology. Predictably, the anticorruption campaigns were spectacular failures. Rather than reforming the system, they encouraged further duplicity, with officials professing the need for good socialist governance while at the same time continuing to rob the state. That, in turn, deepened the cynicism of ordinary citizens about the system as a whole and their ability to improve it.

One important effect of these features of Soviet life was the strengthening of familial and patron-client relationships, the networks of debt and responsibility that are often given the label "clans." Clan networks were traditionally an important element of Caucasus society, both north and south of the mountains. Circassian families were organized into groups composed of a number of households all stemming from a single, often mythical, progenitor. In Chechen and Ingush regions several extended families could be tied together into a single *teip*, a broad collection of people with links to a particular village or district. In Dagestan multiple villages were sometimes grouped together into distinct *jamaats*, headed by a council of elders. In Georgia clan relationships might run along regional or sub-ethnic lines, such as

Mingrelians from the Abkhaz borderlands or Gurians from western Georgia.

One would have expected the importance of such premodern social conventions to decline with time, but in many ways the Soviet system strengthened them. In an economy of scarcity, social networks were critical in providing access to goods and power, and the clan networks of the past served that purpose. Among Chechens, for example, the *teip* system seems to have been enhanced by the experience of exile in the unfamiliar environment of Central Asia.[2] Moreover, migration to the cities brought the old practices of the village into an urban setting. In the south Caucasus towns had historically been "foreign" spaces dominated by ethnic minorities. Over the course of seven decades of Soviet power, however, urban areas became more like the countryside that surrounded them, with social structures arranged according to traditional hierarchies and values that privileged personal loyalty over duty to society as a whole.[3] What anticorruption campaigners were fighting, then, was not simply the greed of unscrupulous officials. Armed with inadequate tools, they were taking on habits of behavior that had been grafted onto preexisting patterns of social interaction and obligation.

A revealing case in point is the State Automobile Inspectorate, an institution known to Caucasus citizens by its Russian initials, GAI. What distinguished the GAI from its nearest equivalent, the highway patrol in the United States, was that the GAI did not actually patrol. GAI officers, their large round caps perched jauntily on the backs of their heads, would set up mobile roadblocks and permanent guardhouses along major thoroughfares and routinely flag down cars with their trademark batons. At the entrances to towns and cities throughout the former Soviet Union, small GAI buildings can still be seen today, perched on an elevated concrete plinth and resembling the old Cossack watchtowers of the north Caucasus lines.

The purpose of the GAI roadblocks was nominally to make sure that citizens were complying with Soviet laws on car licensing, maintenance, and road safety. In practice, however, the GAI levied an informal tax on drivers. Once a car had been stopped, the GAI officer would almost certainly find something wrong with the car or with a driver's disposition. A fine would be imposed, with payment conveniently made to the officer himself. This system—an obvious form of police extortion—was extremely complex. A hierarchy developed within the GAI in the form of a pricing system for the "purchase" of jobs in the inspectorate based on which sites were likely to be the most profitable. For example, a roadblock on the way to a fashionable restaurant outside Tbilisi or to Lake Sevan in Armenia commanded the highest price because citizens were reckoned to be carrying a significant amount of cash on their way to these destinations. The officer would then recoup his initial financial outlay, plus a profit, through the collection of fines.

This entire system, a form of what economists would call tax farming, could have particularly perverse effects. The GAI would hardly ever give chase if someone ignored a baton-waving officer, but the fear of police power was such that most people complied with the officer's demands and stopped, knowing full well that they were in for a shakedown. Daring souls driving expensive cars—a large, late-model Volga, for example, rather than the diminutive Zhiguli—might attempt to speed through the checkpoint, waving smartly as they passed. Officers rarely objected in these cases since the assumption was that only someone of importance and connections would dare ignore the GAI's order to halt. Flouting a lawman's power was often a way of avoiding being fined for driving cautiously and respecting police authority.

In some areas the entire GAI system was rooted in preexisting social networks. One might allow a relative to purchase a plum roadblock spot at a reduced price. GAI members active in ethnic minority areas—such as Azerbaijanis in eastern Georgia or Lezgins in northern Azerbaijan—might be persuaded not to levy a fine if both driver and police officer belonged to the same minority group. It was not so much that the Caucasus had never moved beyond the clan and "tribal" forms of social organization of the nineteenth century. Rather, the structures of Soviet governance helped breathe new life into them. The GAI, although renamed, survived well into the post-Soviet period. In fact, it was not until 2004 that the Georgian government abolished the institution of the standing automobile checkpoint, replacing it with roving patrol cars. The result was a considerable increase in public confidence in the police and no noticeable decline in road safety.

Alongside the deepening of traditional networks and the waves of anticorruption campaigns, there were important social changes taking place during the tenures of Demirchian, Aliyev, and Shevardnadze. The republics were growing and, with them, their burgeoning capital cities. Tbilisi grew from 695,000 people in 1959 to over 1 million in 1979. During the same period, Yerevan and Baku both grew to a little over 1 million people. By the time of the 1979 census, all three republics had become more urbanized than ever before. On average, in the south Caucasus 56 percent of the population lived in towns and cities. Those trends would continue into the Gorbachev era. At the time of the last Soviet census in 1989, Baku had a population of 1.8 million, Tbilisi 1.3 million, and Yerevan 1.2 million. Regions that less than a century earlier had been largely rural, with towns floating in a sea of nomads and peasant farmers, now had urban spaces that proclaimed the cult of modernity and development that was a central message of Soviet power.[4]

In addition, as time went on all three south Caucasus republics were becoming more "national." By 1989 only Armenia was close to being ethnically homogeneous, at 93 percent Armenian, but even Azerbaijanis and Georgians were living in union republics that, more than at any time in their history, were dominated by the ethnonational group for which they were named. Ethnic Azerbaijanis accounted for 83 percent of Azerbaijan's population and Georgians for 70 percent of Georgia's population—figures that had increased, on average, by nearly 9 percentage points over the previous thirty years. The cities, too, were coming to look more and more like the republics in which they were situated. Migration from the countryside to urban environments had been a constant feature of the postwar period (and even earlier), but now the cities were attracting more new migrants than ever before. The cultural contours of the urban landscape changed as newly arrived Armenian, Azerbaijani, and Georgian villagers found themselves in competition with more established communities in towns and cities.

The ethnic homogenization of the south Caucasus in favor of the so-called titular nationalities was largely replicated north of the mountains. There the same ethno-territorial system was in place. Almost all the administrative units of the region were named for one or more ethnic groups—Adygeia (Circassians/Adyga), Karachaevo-Cherkesia (Karachai and Circassians), Kabardino-Balkaria (Circassians/Kabardians and Balkars), North Ossetia (Ossetians), and Checheno-Ingushetia (Chechens and Ingush)—even though the precise administrative status of these regions and their borders changed over time. Of all the territories included in the old imperial delineation of the Caucasus, only the Krasnodar and Stavropol regions (*krais*) and the Dagestan autonomous republic had nonethnic monikers. Almost all these units were becoming more indigenous with the passage of time. By 1989, with the exception Circassians/Adyga in Adygeia, titular nationalities formed an absolute majority in their homelands. Most dramatically, the Chechen and Ingush populations increased from around 41 percent of their region's total in 1959 to 80 percent in 1989. The proportion of ethnic Russians, by contrast, had fallen precipitously during the preceding decades. Emigration by Russians and other minorities, higher birth rates among some Muslim groups, and the return of formerly deported peoples from Central Asia all contributed to the relative homogenization of the north Caucasus. According to official rhetoric, the Soviet Union was meant to encourage the fusion of nationalities into a single Soviet people. In reality, the Soviet experience made the political units of the Caucasus considerably less ethnically diverse and more clearly national than they had been in the past.

❧ ❧

"It is a magical place, Georgia," wrote John Steinbeck during a visit in the late 1940s, "and it becomes dream-like the moment you have left it."[5] After the Second World War, plenty of writers and artists would have agreed. As it had been during the Russian imperial era, the Caucasus remained a peculiar kind of fantasy, a place of freedom and liberation of sorts, but one that could now be visited on workers' holidays. For people from other parts of the Soviet Union, the Caucasus was an attractive venue for tourism and relaxation. State-sponsored recreation areas were built alongside tsarist-era resorts, which had already begun to flourish in the nineteenth century. The spas of Mineral'nye Vody in the Stavropol region, the end point of pilgrimages by both Pushkin and Lermontov, were still a desirable destination. Building projects in the 1930s created a grid of new streets in towns such as Kislovodsk. Bathhouses, public gardens, and sanatoria were rebuilt after the war. Visitors to Lermontov's old haunts in Piatigorsk were promised relief from cardiovascular, digestive, and gynecological disorders, all within refurbished spa facilities dating from the tsarist period. Sochi, on the Black Sea coast, became the largest health facility in the entire Soviet Union. Formerly the site of a Russian imperial fort, it received its new name in 1896 and, during the waning days of the empire, became a fast-growing beach resort and holiday center. Gazebos, scenic overlooks, parks, and hotels were constructed during the early Stalin period. The city was transformed into a military convalescence station during the Second World War. After the war it flourished as the premier retreat for both party elites and average Soviet citizens, the jewel of the Red Riviera.

With a state-sponsored tourist industry spreading throughout the region, the Caucasus now shaped how Russians and other Soviet citizens conceived of their own country. North Caucasus dance troupes with their tight-fitting *cherkeska* tunics and fuzzy *papakha* hats; Georgian wine and the institution of the *supra*, or feast, and the *tamada*, or ebullient toastmaster; buttery Armenian brandy and souvenirs made from the republic's ubiquitous tuff, or volcanic rock; an entire genre of well-known jokes that featured the credulous announcers of a fictional "Radio Yerevan"; dinners of *shashlyk* and *lavash*, or shish kabob and flatbread; colorful carpets and kilims from Azerbaijan—all became not simply recognizable cultural artifacts of the Caucasus but also aspects of a broader Soviet way of being and feeling.

The appeal of the Caucasus lay not just in its perennial exoticism but also in the degree to which that exoticism could now be made one's own. It could be embraced and celebrated—even satirized—rather than feared. Popular films solidified the image of the Soviet south as the home of good-natured locals with a zest for life. In the comedy *Mimino* (1977), directed by Giorgi Danielia, a Georgian helicopter pilot realizes his dream of flying jetliners for Aeroflot, only to discover that travel abroad intensifies his longing to return to his bountiful homeland. The Caucasus even figured in the adventures of Shurik, the lead character of several Soviet slapstick comedies. In Leonid Gaidai's wildly popular *Prisoner Girl of the Caucasus* (1966), an old trope is given a comic treatment as Shurik rescues a beautiful and sporty Communist maiden from the clutches of hawk-nosed but harmless kidnappers.

While comedy and adventure were important trends in portrayals of the Soviet Caucasus, they were not the dominant ones in the region itself. If there is a unifying thread in the development of art, literature, and the imagination in the Caucasus after 1945, it is the escape into abstraction and high art on the one hand, and into the past on the other. There was a tradition of experimental literature and art in the south Caucasus that went back to prerevolutionary times. Georgian writers in particular were solidly in step with—and, in some cases, led—the cutting-edge movements of the immediate postrevolutionary era. This tradition survived the rise of socialist realism and sprang into full bloom following the Second World War. The work of the filmmaker Sergei Paradjanov, who was born into a Tiflis Armenian family in the 1920s, provided some of the most evocative representations of the Caucasus, as well as some of the signal contributions to world culture by a Soviet artist. His first major film, *Shadows of Forgotten Ancestors* (1964), was set in western Ukraine but developed themes of retribution and remembrance that would inform his later work. *The Color of Pomegranates* (1969) explored the life of Sayat Nova, the eighteenth-century Armenian troubadour and Persian court poet. Imprisoned as a dissident for part of the 1970s and 1980s, Paradjanov continued to create art that combined themes of the non-Russian, national past with experimental narrative forms. His *Legend of the Suram Fortress* (1984) retold a Georgian folktale in high-art style, while his *Ashik Kerib* (1988), based on a work by Lermontov, was a filmic homage to Andrei Tarkovsky, his peer and one of the legends of Soviet abstract filmmaking. In all his later work Paradjanov managed to combine elements of Georgian, Armenian, and Turkic Muslim culture while at the same time transcending national categories. Other intellectuals, such as the Abkhaz novelist Fazil Iskander, created indelible images of mountainous homelands and quizzical natives for adoring Soviet readers.

The past also had other uses, serving not simply as a source of inspiration but as an object of invention and glorification. Beneath the public avowals of Soviet brotherhood and friendship among peoples, intellectuals engaged in heated debates over contentious points of history and national origin. Historians argued over whether particular ancient peoples could properly be claimed as the legitimate antecedents of modern nations. Linguists debated the delineation of language families and which languages ought to be considered mere dialects of others. Alphabets were invented, reworked, and discarded. Major events and personalities from the past—from Shamil to early Bolsheviks—were reinterpreted and at times rehabilitated, transformed into the leaders of inchoate progressive movements or proponents of national distinctiveness within a multinational state. New public art celebrated national heroes and poets. Folk dancers and costumed choirs staged extravaganzas that explored the essence of being a member of one or another national group.

While the details differed, the way in which the peoples of the Caucasus spoke about their own past was structurally similar: from ethnogenesis in antiquity, through the rise of kingdoms, khanates, and principalities in the Middle Ages, to the birth of national movements in the nineteenth century under the beneficent tutelage of Russia, and finally toward incorporation into the enlightened and liberating Soviet Union. In virtually any major history text published in the Soviet Caucasus after the Second World War, the narrative is essentially the same except for the proper nouns. The Caucasus thus moved into the late 1980s with versions of history that privileged the nation, underscored its connection to a particular piece of real estate, and fundamentally excluded other ways of interpreting historical truth.

Moreover, all this was taking place in cities and republics that were more national, in demographic terms, than at any point in the recent past.

Both routes of escape—toward abstraction and toward the invention of a straight line from the ancient past to the present—could at times produce profound works of art, literature, and scholarship. Yet they also set the Caucasus on a perilous path. Almost without exception the region lacked the crucial set of voices for liberal values, tolerance, and public engagement that allowed other parts of the Communist world to weather the simultaneous collapse of an ideology, a political order, and an economic system. Even the peculiarly Caucasus variants of the early twentieth century—the social democratic orientations of the Dashnaks, Müsavat, and Mensheviks—were now discredited in the Soviet Union. Where they still held on—for example, among old Dashnaks and their children in the Armenian diaspora— they tended to inflame nationalism rather than temper it.

Of course, dissidents and occasionally dissident movements did emerge. Many individuals suffered indescribable cruelty in Soviet prisons and camps. However, their motivating ideologies were largely derived from the desire for national flourishing against what was perceived to be an antinational, Russian-dominated state. Three of the largest public demonstrations in the Soviet Union before the era of perestroika took place in the Caucasus. One, which occurred in Yerevan in 1965, commemorated the fiftieth anniversary of the Armenian genocide and called on the Soviet government to recognize it. Two years later the city unveiled a large memorial with an eternal flame, the focal point for future commemoration activities. The others, in Yerevan and Tbilisi in 1978, were sparked by plans to give the Russian language a status comparable to that of Armenian and Georgian in the republics' educational systems and administrative apparatus. The rallies successfully blocked the proposed change, and Armenia and Georgia remained the only Soviet republics with official languages— the local ones. All these events revealed the degree to which human rights issues were intertwined with, and sometimes wholly consumed by, questions of national identity and destiny. Well into the 1980s the response of the state to displays of national discontent was to issue stentorian statements about the degree to which cultural problems had been resolved in the multinational Soviet Caucasus—and to arrest dissidents who failed to agree with that claim. In 1983, for example, the two hundredth anniversary of the Treaty of Georgievsk was marked by official celebrations in Tbilisi, together with the imprisonment of several men who had publicly denounced the treaty as a milestone in Georgia's path toward national subjugation.[6]

The south Caucasus republics were rushing headlong into an era of political change, with few people who could argue convincingly for reappropriating the brand of democracy that had seemed promising, for a fleeting moment, at the end of the First World War. When Armenia, Azerbaijan, and Georgia became fully independent in 1991, they adopted the same flags that the Bolsheviks had pulled down seventy years earlier: the red-blue-orange tricolor in Yerevan, the blue-red-green tricolor in Baku, and the crimson, black, and white flag in Tbilisi. But rather than inheriting these earlier republics' aspirations for social justice and reform, the new ones seemed to inherit only their problems: economic chaos, social discord, territorial conflicts, and international isolation.

Land and Struggle

One of the preeminent cultural artifacts of the late Soviet period is the film *Repentance*, directed by the acclaimed Georgian filmmaker Tengiz Abuladze. The film centers on the death of Varlam, the despotic mayor of an unnamed town. The town's leaders gather to mourn the loss of the great man but soon discover that his corpse has a life of its own: Varlam's body keeps escaping from its grave. The agent of Varlam's wanderlust turns out to be a woman, Keti, who secretly digs up the body each time it is reburied. Keti is eventually caught with shovel in hand and brought to trial. On the witness stand she recounts her own story about Varlam's persecution of her parents and her promise to take revenge. Keti is ruled insane, but the truths she has exposed eventually destroy the cult of the dead mayor.

When it was released in 1986, the film was an overnight sensation. Eduard Shevardnadze, who had become Soviet foreign minister, proved to be a key patron, encouraging the film's public release and protecting Abuladze against official reprisals.[7] The messages of the film—that the Soviet Union had yet to come to terms with its past and that ghosts of old despots were still haunting the land—were unmistakable. In the first year of its commercial release, the film was viewed by at least thirty million individuals, an astonishing achievement for a film that mixed surrealist plot elements and avant-garde techniques.[8] *Repentance* became symbolic of Mikhail Gorbachev's new policy of glasnost and helped spur on public conversations about history, memory, and persecution.

Beginning in 1985, the nearly seven years of Gorbachev's tenure as general secretary of the Communist Party and later president of the Soviet Union produced the promise of systemic transformation. In time, however, what had seemed a hopeful beginning led to the dismantling of the entire state. Lithuania declared its independence in March 1990. Georgia followed in April 1991. The organizers of the Moscow coup of August 1991 hoped to reverse the disintegration of the union but instead hastened it. Armenia, Azerbaijan, and other republics soon followed the course set by Lithuania and Georgia. By the end of the year, Gorbachev was president of a country that no longer existed. Yet the remarkable fact about the end of the world's largest state is that it disappeared from the map in a mostly peaceful manner. Dozens of civil wars did not erupt across Eurasia. The new countries that rose from the Soviet rubble did not attack one another or seek territorial aggrandizement. If the Soviet Union and its satellite states could be called an empire, it is fair to say that no empire in the twentieth century—the Austro-Hungarian, Russian, Ottoman, or even the British—unmade itself in so civil a fashion.

The Caucasus was a major exception. Virtually all the armed conflicts associated with the end of Soviet power occurred there, including the territorial wars over Nagorno-Karabakh in Azerbaijan, over South Ossetia and Abkhazia in Georgia, and over Chechnya in Russia. The first of these was also Eurasia's only interstate war since it involved the attempt by Armenians in Nagorno-Karabakh to secede from Azerbaijan with the assistance of the Armenian republic. Even lesser conflicts—riots, pogroms, and ethnic cleansing—decimated ancient communities and left tens of thousands of refugees and displaced persons eking out an existence far from their homelands.

How could a region that had remained something of a backwater following the Second World War—the land of jolly mountaineers and holiday makers in the Soviet imagination—end up this way? The fate of the Caucasus in the late twentieth and early twenty-first centuries was not inevitable. Rather, the violent politics and territorial uncertainties were the result of, among other things, basic structural features of the Soviet state, the decisions of key political elites, and the fact that dysfunctional politics can sometimes serve the interests of politicians themselves even as they lead the people they claim to represent toward certain ruin. In the 1990s and early 2000s, it was not so much that

Varlam's dead body—history and the pent-up grievances of the Soviet era—had returned to haunt policy makers and the public. Rather, it was that the peculiar politics of state collapse had begun to push parts of the Caucasus over the brink into civil war and inter-ethnic violence. As with the citizens in Abuladze's *Repentance*, most people are content to weather political change by continuing to do precisely what they have done in the past, namely, to keep old myths in place and resign the bodies of despots to their graves. It is only when highly committed individuals begin digging up the past—and when those around them have an incentive to hear their cases and respond accordingly—that political change begins to occur. In the Caucasus the real story of the late twentieth century is not about deep-rooted sentiments of ethnicity or ancient grievances but about the ways in which personal ambition, structural incentives, and the simple presence of sufficient quantities of guns led to bloody conflict.

In the south Caucasus the late 1980s were characterized by the rise of opposition movements and the weakening of the Communist Party establishment. Experienced elites like Aliyev and Shevardnadze spearheaded the modernization of their republics in the 1970s and successfully suppressed public expression of discontent, but they were succeeded by less able bureaucrats. The pace of events on the ground, fueled by movements for reform and political change in other parts of the Soviet Union, outstripped the ability of local elites to manage them. In Baku the Popular Front of Azerbaijan was formed by intellectuals and activists in mid-1989 and quickly became the pole around which opposition groups could rally, taking its cue (and its name) from similar organizations in the Baltic republics. In Tbilisi the Round Table / Free Georgia bloc, headed by the prominent literary critic and dissident Zviad Gamsakhurdia, emerged as an umbrella organization that included a host of interests, from nationalists bent on independence to human rights activists from Georgia's emerging civil society. In 1990 the bloc garnered nearly two-thirds of the votes in the republic's first multiparty parliamentary elections. Gamsakhurdia was first elevated to the chairmanship of the republican parliament and to the post of president the following year. In Yerevan members of the intelligentsia were similarly motivated by the sense of reform and openness fostered by Moscow. The republic's inadequate response to the massive earthquake of December 1988—which killed some twenty-five thousand people and left half a million homeless—underscored the crisis of governance then facing the Soviet state.

Across the south Caucasus, however, the nature of political change was bound up with questions of borders. Although the dispute over the territory of Nagorno-Karabakh, located near the Armenian-Azerbaijani border, was not the first instance of open inter-ethnic rivalry within Gorbachev's Soviet Union, it was the first to involve the interests of two union republics. The territory was included in the Azerbaijani Soviet republic after the Bolshevik conquest of 1920. Part of its upland reaches—mountainous Karabakh (Russ. *Nagornyi Karabakh*)—was granted special status as an autonomous district shortly thereafter.[9] Nagorno-Karabakh was mainly populated by ethnic Armenians, comprising 76 percent in 1979, the last prewar census that can be trusted.[10] Clashes between ethnic Armenians and Azerbaijanis were not infrequent during the Soviet period, but they manifested themselves in different ways: heated debates among historians in learned journals; ethnic hooliganism during soccer matches between Baku and Yerevan teams; or underground publications about human rights abuses against ethnic Armenians in Azerbaijan. Within an atmosphere of increased openness under Gorbachev, questions about the past and future of the Nagorno-Karabakh territory became a natural focal point of discontent.

In 1988 Armenian leaders in the autonomous district called for its transfer to Armenian republican jurisdiction, repeating a demand that had been made by local Armenians many times before. Although only partially related to events in Nagorno-Karabakh, anti-Armenian pogroms in the Azerbaijani cities of Sumgait in 1988 and Baku in 1990 convinced ethnic Armenians that the territorial question was not only a matter of administrative boundaries but also one of national survival. Profound grievances were voiced by both sides. From the Armenian perspective, repeated attacks against ethnic Armenian communities were reminiscent of the Ottoman-era genocide, especially given the massive outflow of migrants (over 180,000 by mid-1989) from Azerbaijan.[11] From the Azerbaijani perspective, Armenians were attempting to squelch the nascent Azerbaijani national movement by destroying the republic's territorial unity, not to mention carrying out their own ethnic cleansing of ethnic Azerbaijanis from Yerevan and other parts of the Armenian republic.

Events in Nagorno-Karabakh and the rest of Azerbaijan were intimately linked to developments inside Armenia. Just as the growing national movement in Azerbaijan looked to the territorial issue as one of its central mobilizing themes, so the opposition movement in Armenia—centered around a group of intellectuals known as the Karabakh Committee—used the plight of Armenians in the neighboring republic to spur street protests and calls for reform. As in other parts of the Soviet Union, nationalism provided the basic vocabulary through which political opposition could be expressed. In 1989 the Armenian parliament and the Nagorno-Karabakh district council adopted a joint resolution declaring the unification of the two administrative units. Paramilitary groups began to form inside Nagorno-Karabakh, with substantial assistance from Armenia. The Azerbaijani government responded by forcibly evacuating villages near the Armenian border and imposing a road and rail blockade on the autonomous district and eventually on Armenia as well. An attempt by Soviet authorities to calm the situation by placing Nagorno-Karabakh directly under Moscow's control failed.

Hostilities escalated following the collapse of the Soviet center. Armenians in Nagorno-Karabakh's capital of Stepanakert announced the creation of a wholly separate Republic of Nagorno-Karabakh in September 1991, which was confirmed in a referendum on independence several months later. Full-scale war followed. By the middle of 1992 Nagorno-Karabakh forces had opened a land corridor linking the region to Armenia and had driven the Azerbaijani army from Shusha, the last remaining Azerbaijani stronghold and a strategic highland from which the military had been able to bombard Stepanakert. Armenian successes were accompanied by atrocities committed against local Azerbaijanis, such as the notorious massacre of civilians in the village of Khojaly in 1992, an event that came to occupy the same position for Azerbaijanis as the Sumgait and Baku massacres for Armenians. A major offensive in 1993 created an Armenian-controlled buffer zone around the old autonomous district, essentially bringing most of historic Karabakh, both highland and lowland, under Armenian control—and denuding it of Azerbaijani inhabitants in the process. After several unsuccessful mediation attempts, in May 1994 Russia managed to secure a lasting if imperfectly enforced ceasefire. Negotiations on a final settlement were launched under the auspices of a multinational coalition that included Russia and the United States, but those talks wound on for more than a decade with little real progress.

The pattern of events in Nagorno-Karabakh paralleled those in the autonomous republic of Abkhazia in northwestern Georgia. Abkhazia had a special administrative status going back to the Bolshevik seizure of power, even though the precise nature of that status changed over the course of the Soviet period. Repeated attempts were made by local intellectuals and activists to separate from Soviet Georgia and join the Soviet Russian federal republic. Unlike in the Nagorno-Karabakh case, however, the history of Georgian-Abkhaz relations was perhaps one of the more peaceful ones in the south Caucasus. There was a history of violence from the time of the First World War and the Russian civil war, but those conflicts were not generally drawn along ethnic lines. Georgians did not view the Abkhaz as illegitimate interlopers—as some Armenians were inclined to see Azerbaijanis inside Nagorno-Karabakh—nor did the Abkhaz typically stoke anti-Georgian sentiment. Religious distinctions were likewise not clearly drawn. Most Abkhaz, if they claimed a religious affiliation at all, were Orthodox Christians, as were Georgians. But when a revitalized Georgian national movement emerged in the waning days of Soviet power, eventually staging a referendum on Georgia's exit from the Soviet Union, the Abkhaz population demanded the opportunity to leave Georgia and take their territory with them.

The biggest difference between Abkhazia and Nagorno-Karabakh was demographic. Armenians comprised a majority of the population of Nagorno-Karabakh, but ethnic Abkhaz represented only a fraction of Abkhazia's (about 18 percent in 1989). The Abkhaz had been a minority group in the region for the better part of a century, following the expulsion of Abkhaz communities by the Russian Empire in the 1860s. The policy of the Soviet government, particularly under Beria, had been to encourage the immigration of ethnic Georgians into the autonomous republic, in part to help boost agricultural production there, in part to alter the ethnic balance further in favor of Georgians. To Abkhaz intellectuals and regional leaders, Georgia's exit from the Soviet Union promised to diminish further their influence in their own homeland. The coming to power of a new, more vocally nationalist leader in Tbilisi in the person of Gamsakhurdia also deepened Abkhaz fears.

Clashes soon erupted between Abkhaz and local Georgians. Gamsakhurdia, perhaps acting against type, made progress in dampening these disputes, but his ouster in a coup in Tbilisi scuttled any chance for a peaceful settlement. In early 1992 Eduard Shevardnadze returned from Moscow and assumed power as leader of the Georgian government. Shevardnadze proved incapable of controlling those politicians who called for a quick military solution to the Abkhaz problem. Georgian troops and paramilitary forces marched into Abkhazia—the proximate cause of the incursion is still debated on both sides—and succeeded in capturing and holding the capital of Sukhumi. By the end of 1993 Abkhaz militias, assisted by Russian government forces and irregular troops from the north Caucasus, had pushed back the ill-prepared Georgian troops to the Inguri River, the dividing line between Georgia proper and Abkhazia. A Russian-brokered agreement in May 1994 provided for the deployment of a peacekeeping mission of the Commonwealth of Independent States—although in practice wholly Russian—to monitor the security zone along the river. Negotiations on Abkhazia's final status, brokered by the United Nations, were soon set in motion. However, as in Nagorno-Karabakh, the ceasefire continued well into the 2000s with little sign of a final resolution.

Unlike the Abkhaz, the Ossetians were historically tied to a region outside Georgia, the autonomous republic of North Ossetia in the Russian Federation. The autonomous district of South Ossetia, in Georgia, maintained a relatively steady ethnic make-up throughout the Soviet period (two-thirds ethnic Ossetian), but Georgian popular opinion tended to see the Ossetians as newcomers who demanded more than their fair share of Georgian real estate. Georgian historians and writers pointed to the long-ago migration of Ossetians across the mountains to the south and their privileged status as reliable partners in Russian imperial expansion, both of which were marshaled to support claims that Ossetians should be no more than grateful guests inside Georgia. Despite a history of strong intercultural ties between Georgians and Ossetians, the political climate of the late 1980s encouraged escalating demands for local autonomy and independence. In 1988 and 1989 the Georgian government adopted measures to strengthen the use of the Georgian language in public life. Shortly thereafter it rejected calls by district leaders for an upgrade in South Ossetia's status from autonomous district to autonomous republic, the same as Abkhazia's.

The spark that touched off violence occurred in 1990, when the South Ossetian district administration declared a separate South Ossetian republic within the Soviet Union, moved to unite with the Russian republic of North Ossetia across the mountains, and shortly thereafter held elections for a separate parliament—a variation on the Nagorno-Karabakh theme. In response, the Georgian parliament voted to revoke South Ossetia's existing autonomous status. Gamsakhurdia ordered troops to the district, but their entry met with the fierce resistance of Ossetian irregulars and their supporters from North Ossetia and other parts of Russia. In July 1992 a ceasefire agreement provided for the cessation of hostilities and final-status negotiations. As in Abkhazia and Nagorno-Karabakh, those negotiations wound on throughout the 1990s and early 2000s with occasional flare-ups in violence among the contesting sides.

For more than a decade following the end of large-scale conflict, the political elites who had engineered these wars, both in the national capitals and in the secessionist regions, mostly remained the same. Eduard Shevardnadze was Georgian president until 2003, the same year that saw the death of Heydar Aliyev. Robert Kocharian, the former president of Nagorno-Karabakh, became president of Armenia in 1998. Many people in the Caucasus continued to refer to the events of the perestroika period as explanations for why a stable settlement remained elusive. Nagorno-Karabakh's leaders spoke of the revocation of their local autonomy and massacres of Armenians in Azerbaijan. Abkhaz and Ossetians listed Georgia's oppressive cultural policies and the dilution of local autonomy. Ethnic majorities talked of the treachery of minority populations intent on tearing apart their states.

None of these views was completely wrong. In all these conflicts, there were repertoires of violence that defined the basic issues, delineated the contending sides, and provided ready justifications for war. Nagorno-Karabakh and Abkhazia were sites of ethnic conflict in the truest sense of the term: wars that sometimes involved neighbors killing neighbors, even door to door. The minority populations believed that the weakening of the Soviet center would lead to a concomitant expansion of the power of ethnic majorities in the union republics. Republican governments, in turn, were convinced that the minorities were either tools of a revitalized Russia—fifth columns that would be used by Moscow to undermine their newfound independence—or simply ungrateful citizens intent on redrawing borders to realize their own national designs. Moreover, the presence of significant prewar populations of Georgians in Abkhazia, Georgians in South Ossetia, and Azerbaijanis in Nagorno-Karabakh gave these conflicts an additional complicating factor. In denying secession to the Abkhaz, Ossetians, and Karabakh Armenians, the governments of Georgia and Azerbaijan could also claim to be protecting the interests of ethnic Georgians and ethnic Azerbaijanis who once lived in the secessionist regions.

At various points in the late 1980s and early 1990s, violence might have been averted had visionary leaders proved more assertive and those most committed to fomenting conflict less able. In many ways, however, the Soviet system itself sanctioned violence as a viable instrument of politics. In two infamous instances Soviet troops attacked pro-independence demonstrators in Tbilisi in April 1989, leaving more than twenty people dead, and intervened in Baku in January 1990, killing more than a hundred. Those incidents were not directly related to the brewing territorial struggles, but they did signal Moscow's desperation in a part of the Soviet Union that seemed to be spiraling out of control. In such a context, the escalation of territorial disputes to all-out war was not fated, but those arguing for peace—and there were such voices on all sides—were increasingly drowned out by those intent on violence.

Tens of thousands of people were killed in fighting inside the three conflict areas. Refugees flooded out of them: some 1.2 million from Nagorno-Karabakh, Armenia, and the occupied territories; 270,000 from Abkhazia and surrounding areas; and 50,000 from South Ossetia.[12] Many spent the rest of the decade (and beyond) living in allegedly temporary housing in old Soviet hotels and dilapidated resorts in other parts of Georgia and Azerbaijan. The most visible of these refugee camps—the multi-storey Hotel Iveria in downtown Tbilisi—stood as a stark reminder of the unsettled nature of these disputes and the enormous human cost of the end of Soviet power. (It was subsequently renovated and reemerged as a luxury hotel in the early 2000s). The cruel irony of Soviet-era tourist complexes being used as refugee centers was not lost on the victims of war themselves.

After the early 1990s, most central governments and international organizations did virtually everything that the conventional wisdom on conflict resolution suggested in order to reach an equitable solution. Generally stable cease-fires, monitored by outside parties, were put in place. Regular negotiations were set up under the aegis of international organizations, with the support of the United States and the Russian Federation. To varying degrees governments amended their constitutions, citizenship laws, educational statutes, and local administrative structures to provide for civil rights guarantees and local autonomy.

The real block on a final settlement was the fact that, beneath the facade of unresolved grievances and international negotiations, political elites in the secessionist regions were going about the process of building states that, in some instances, functioned about as well as the recognized countries of which they were still formally constituents. Moreover, these unrecognized entities were shielded by independent military forces large enough to fend off an attack by the recognized states: fifteen to twenty thousand men in Nagorno-Karabakh; between fifteen hundred and five thousand in Abkhazia; and anywhere from a few hundred to two thousand in South Ossetia—all with supplies of armor and equipment either inherited from Soviet forces or purchased from Russia or on the international market.[13] At the same time, interest groups outside the conflict zones learned to live with the effective division of their countries by finding ways to profit from a state apparatus that was chronically weak—and, in the process, ensuring that it remained so. The history of the south Caucasus in the 1990s and early 2000s was thus not simply about state collapse and territorial secession but about how people learned to survive and even thrive in otherwise miserable circumstances—and how this adaptive mechanism ended up perpetuating the status quo.

The politics of state disintegration produced violence, not the other way around. There would have been no post-Soviet wars in the Caucasus if elites at the republican level had not tried to prevent their regional counterparts from claiming rights to secession and sovereignty—the very rights, of course, that the republican elites were claiming vis-à-vis Moscow. In no case did war break out because one ethnic group suddenly decided to slaughter another. Large-scale violence came about because of the weakening of the Soviet state and the commitment of its successor governments—both those that had achieved international recognition and those that had not—to use force to realize their goals. These wars were fundamentally about controlling turf, not more rarefied questions of history, identity, or national destiny.[14] Each of the disputed areas was blessed with having an autonomous administration at the time the Soviet Union began to falter, and local elites in each of these regions set about transforming their Soviet-era institutions into the accoutrements of independent statehood. Regional councils became parliaments. Factory managers and local intellectuals became ministers and presidents. Without those administrative structures and the personal ambition of those who held pivotal positions within them, the post-Soviet wars might never have gotten off the ground.

As the conflicts progressed, what had been quintessentially political disputes took on an ethnic tinge. Today the conflicts are memorialized as victorious wars of national liberation or tragic struggles for the integrity of the fatherland. An entire generation of schoolchildren has grown up imbibing one or another of these narratives. In the secessionist regions history curricula have been redesigned to highlight the citizens of the unrecognized states as the indigenous inhabitants of their territory and to strengthen the connection between previous and current forms of statehood. Children who were not even born when the conflicts began have been schooled to believe that the republics they inhabit represent ancient nations now reborn through war and sacrifice. As a South Ossetian textbook proclaimed in 2000: "The war killed and maimed thousands of our citizens; left tens of thousands of innocent people without shelter, work, and means of survival; razed our infrastructure; robbed the people of kindergartens and schools; and made peaceful citizens into refugees. Nevertheless, these years have a special historical significance for us, because we not only managed to defeat the aggressor but also to build our own statehood."[15] This way of seeing the past, though, is little different from the equally tendentious arguments used to justify the existence of many other new Eurasian states.

Overall, the post-Soviet order in the Caucasus was not the natural outcome of individual nations striving for independence but rather a reflection of the international community's capacity to tolerate one kind of secessionist but not another. In the end, the narratives of the successful secessionists—Armenia, Azerbaijan, and Georgia—were legitimated through international recognition and membership in multilateral organizations. Those of the unrecognized regimes—Nagorno-Karabakh, Abkhazia, and South Ossetia—were viewed by outsiders as desperate attempts to rationalize the whims of separatists. One obvious difference, however, was simply size. All of the secessionist regions were tiny: under two hundred thousand people each in Abkhazia and Nagorno-Karabakh; perhaps as few as seventy thousand in South Ossetia. Still, they represented significant parts of the recognized states, accounting for roughly 15 percent of the territory of Georgia and Azerbaijan. Yet well into the early 2000s it was difficult for a visitor to tell the difference between life in an unrecognized state and life in a recognized one—at least outside the national capitals. Electricity was often in short supply, roads went unrepaired, government was capricious, and politics was intertwined with corrupt businesses. State weakness, arbitrary governance, and economic uncertainty had little to do with territorial status. These ills were experienced equally by citizens across the Caucasus regardless of whether their countries were real or imagined.

Whose Nations? Whose States?

During the first decade following independence, the rise of nationalist extremists, hesitant democratization, multiple coups d'état, the consolidation of control by Soviet-era elites, and the passing of power to a new generation of politicians were the major signposts in the fractious affairs of the south Caucasus. In the 1990s and early 2000s, amid the twists and turns of post-Soviet change, the region had become less a collection of independent countries and unrecognized republics than a constellation of city-states—Yerevan, Baku, and Tbilisi. These cities were the principal recipients of external aid and foreign investment, the main destinations for migration from the countryside, and the central arenas in which fitful reform and reaction were played out. Somewhere between a third and half the republics' total populations resided in the capitals, making the south Caucasus appear demographically far closer to the developing world than to many other east European states. In the far corners of these countries entire towns and neighborhoods lay abandoned. If one asked what people did for a living, the answer was nearly universal in both the recognized countries and the secessionist zones. For men it was driving taxis, working abroad, or lugging merchandise to and from the capital cities. For women it was, in Russian, "Nu, torguem"—"Well, we sell stuff"—trying desperately to make ends meet by buying and selling cheap consumer goods in a local bazaar.

The three capitals experienced something of a renaissance, however. Aid programs helped transform urban landscapes. Foreign investment picked up. In Baku in particular the promise of profits from Azerbaijan's rich oil and gas sector turned the city into a boomtown on the model of a century earlier, with foreign restaurants, luxury hotels, and casinos. The city became the largest urban environment in the Caucasus—larger than Yerevan and Tbilisi and, according to some estimates, more populous even than Armenia and Georgia. Per capita income grew in all three countries, fueled by remittances from immigrants working in Russia, western Europe, and the United States. Dire poverty continued to define life in the countryside, but to many visitors it was masked by the growth of new businesses in the three capitals and the emergence of a younger, English-speaking, often Western-educated elite. At nearly every turn, though, hopes for genuine political change, democratization, and long-term stability were dashed by the eagerness of small factions to sacrifice the interests of their countries for personal gain.

— ◆ ◆ —

Armenia emerged as an independent country with the anti-Communist opposition in power in parliament and one of the leaders of the Karabakh Committee, the literary historian Levon Ter-Petrosian, as president. Ter-Petrosian was among the less radical members of the dissident movement, which had taken up the plight of Armenians in Nagorno-Karabakh as its central theme, but his moderation was rarely a virtue in the turbulent politics of the immediate post-Soviet period. Months after his election in the autumn of 1991, mass rallies demanding his resignation were held in Yerevan. The president soon came up against one of the major dividing lines in the new republic—the gulf between Soviet Armenians and diaspora returnees and their sympathizers, particularly those associated with the revived Dashnak party.

Nurtured in the centers of the Armenian diaspora, which stretched from Beirut to Los Angeles, the Dashnaks once again became a force in domestic Armenian affairs, seeking to regain the position they had lost as a result of the Bolshevik invasion in 1920. Although few members of that earlier generation were present, their successors looked to the ideology of national rebirth as a source of inspiration following the end of communism. The creation of an independent Armenia was the signal event in the life of the diaspora, and community leaders from the West flocked to Yerevan hoping to find long-lost brothers willing to open their homes, their economy, and their political system. Armed with funds from abroad, the Dashnaks and their associates were able to found newspapers and start businesses, field candidates for office, and wield significant power in the new state. Their successes worried many local Armenians, who saw them as newcomers with little experience of the hardships of the Soviet era and even less respect for its achievements. In late 1994 Ter-Petrosian formally moved against the party, banning it for the alleged role of its members in the assassination of a prominent former politician.

Faced with the residual effects of the 1988 earthquake, then a hot war and tense standoff with Azerbaijan, along with a road and rail embargo enforced by both Azerbaijan and Turkey, the Armenian state spent much of the 1990s lurching from one crisis to another. Ter-Petrosian won another term as president in 1996 in an election widely disputed by opposition parties. Looking to outflank his nationalist critics, he eventually named Robert Kocharian, the former president of Nagorno-Karabakh, to the post of Armenian prime minister. That appointment marked the beginning of what many regarded as the takeover of the state not by its Western diaspora but rather by its Eastern one, specifically politicians, businessmen, and war veterans from Nagorno-Karabakh. In early 1998 Ter-Petrosian was forced to resign as president largely as a result of his perceived willingness to compromise with Azerbaijan. New presidential elections marked the ascendancy of Kocharian, who moved from the prime ministership to the president's office, lifted the ban on the Dashnaks, and began to consolidate the position of pro-presidential forces within the legislature. Armenia was now moving in a direction being followed by several post-Soviet republics: toward the concentration of power in the hands of a president who had been placed in office through questionable elections and with his own presidential party in control of the national assembly.

In his resignation speech Ter-Petrosian pointed out what many Armenian intellectuals and analysts had come to believe—that the conflict with Azerbaijan was only one aspect of a much thornier debate within Armenian society itself, namely, whether the future lay in a civic definition of statehood based on principles of democracy and openness or in a more radically ethnic vision that rewarded those politicians best able to protect ethnic Armenians at home and abroad.[16] Kocharian's ascendancy assured the triumph of the latter vision and, concomitantly, the militarization of Armenian society. The number of men under arms in Armenia (along with those in Nagorno-Karabakh) remained broadly comparable to the number in Azerbaijan, even though the defense budgets and populations of the two countries were widely disparate. Increasingly, it was the needs and desires of the military establishment—veterans who were now in control of key political institutions—that appeared to set the agenda of the country as a whole. From the late 1980s through the early 2000s men from the old Karabakh Committee gave way to men from Nagorno-Karabakh itself.

Like its neighbors, post-Soviet Armenia had its share of assassinations, attempted assassinations, and armed plots to eliminate one or another rival for political or economic reasons—or an imponderable combination of both. The most shocking incident took place in October 1999. A small group of gunmen entered the parliament building and opened fire on the floor of the assembly, leaving eight prominent politicians dead, including Vazgen Sargsian, the prime minister, and Karen Demirchian, the parliamentary speaker and former Communist Party head. Although the gunmen were eventually tried and sentenced, the origins of the plot remained murky even years after the tragic events. Some insisted that it had been launched in an effort to forestall a deal on Nagorno-Karabakh, which seemed to be in the offing at the time of the shootings. Others claimed to see the hand of the most powerful political figure still standing in the aftermath of the assassinations—President Kocharian himself.

One afternoon in 1930 the poet Osip Mandelstam found himself in a boat on Lake Sevan, the stunning Armenian lake that is home to a famously succulent species of trout. In the boat with Mandelstam were two Armenians. One was a certain Professor Khachaturian. He had formerly been director of an Armenian secondary school in Kars, but after the Bolshevik Revolution he moved to Yerevan to take up a chair in archaeology. He still dressed in an Ottoman-style black frock coat. He had never been to Russia and spoke Russian only haltingly. The other was a Comrade Karinian. He had previously served as chairman of the Central Executive Committee of Soviet Armenia. He smoked cardboard-tipped Russian cigarettes and read proletarian experimental fiction. The three men conversed freely about literature and art, but the two Armenians held radically different views of things. One, an old-world intellectual, was convinced of the power of tradition in Armenian intellectual life. The other, a member of the new Communist elite, was enamored of the revolutionary changes that Soviet power had wrought.[17]

The two men symbolized the choices facing Armenians in the twentieth century: One represented the old Armenia, a Near Eastern civilization tied to the heritage of the Ottoman Empire and Persia; the other, a product of migration, genocide, and Soviet state-building, looked to Russia for salvation from the horrors of the early twentieth century. Today's Armenians are a pluralistic nation bound together by a distinct Christian culture and the memory of the genocide yet divided by the same ties to place and the past that defined the professor and the comrade in Mandelstam's boat. The distinctive sights and sounds of different Armenian communities—those with roots in Turkey, Persia, or the republic—are evident to any visitor to the major centers of Armenian life. Successive waves of migration have transformed these communities. Glendale, California, once the seat of émigrés who fled the genocide, is now filled with the pop music and fashions of more recent arrivals from the former Soviet Union. Old fissures within the diaspora, some of them dating back to the murder of Archbishop Tourian in 1933, keep churches separate and social networks distinct. Who is an Armenian, who speaks for the nation, and who owns the right to define *Hay Dat*—the "Armenian cause"—are questions that continue to be problematic both culturally and politically.

In Armenia itself the days of the most intense struggle between the spiritual descendants of Khachaturian and Karinian have now passed. Local enthusiasm for the political program of the Dashnaks has remained muted. If the ties of nation and brotherhood were motivating factors in the early 1990s—demanding that all true patriots sacrifice themselves for the common cause of Nagorno-Karabakh—by the early 2000s it was the dire state of the economy and rampant corruption that prompted street demonstrations. During the first decade and a half following independence, what became increasingly evident was how little Armenians knew about people whom they regularly called brothers, whether in the republic, in Nagorno-Karabakh, or in the diaspora.

For Armenians abroad, the central issue has remained securing Turkish recognition of the genocide. While admitting that many Armenians were killed in the Ottoman lands during the First World War, the Turkish government has insisted that these deaths were no different from the normal, albeit regrettable, civilian casualties of any armed conflict. Moreover, as Turkish officials and many Turkish historians affirm, plenty of Muslims were killed by local Armenians as well as by Balkan governments, Russia, and the occupying Allies. Nevertheless, the lack of recognition of the Armenian genocide has had terrible repercussions. For one, it has prevented the growth of an honest and sophisticated understanding of the Ottoman past and the creation of the Turkish Republic. It is possible to weave a narrative of modern Turkish history that acknowledges past crimes while valuing the republican ideal, but only a few Turkish historians—sometimes at great risk to themselves and their reputations—have slowly begun to explore these themes. In 2007 the murder in Istanbul of Hrant Dink, a well-known Armenian newspaper editor, demonstrated the deadly passion that these issues could incite.

Commemorated in popular memory and public memorials, the genocide has emerged as the defining tragedy in the history of the Armenian nation, the lens through which national history is interpreted, and the inescapable collective experience that shapes relations between Armenia and its neighbors. One cannot visit modern Yerevan—with the fabled Mount Ararat peering down on the city from the other side of the tense Armenian-Turkish border—and fail to appreciate the roles that landscape, memory, and death continue to play in Armenian national consciousness. But the centrality of the genocide has hardened a narrative of loss and denial that has worked against genuinely complex understandings of the past. It has encouraged an avoidance of themes both painful and promising, from the multifaceted nature of Armenian identity to questions of collaboration and survivorship in times of devastating violence. Most problematic, it has encouraged a patriotism built on victimhood, which in turn yields an inferior brand of *patria*, one worriedly building levees against the past instead of confidently looking to the future. More than a decade after independence from the Soviet Union, conflicts over different ways of being Armenian have remained at the heart of the Armenian republic and its relationship with the diaspora.

Politics in Azerbaijan has not been similarly influenced by diaspora concerns, although the status of Azerbaijani speakers in Iran has occasionally contributed to the already tense relationship between Baku and Tehran. Unlike its two south Caucasus neighbors, Azerbaijan participated in the March 1991 referendum on the future of the Soviet Union organized by the Gorbachev leadership. While Azerbaijanis voted overwhelmingly for preserving the union, that result hid deep divisions within Azerbaijani society. The major opposition movement, the Popular Front, was continually harassed by Azerbaijani authorities. Its most radical members were firmly in favor of exiting the Soviet Union and launching an all-out war against Armenia over the Nagorno-Karabakh controversy. When the Moscow coup thrust independence upon Azerbaijan, it was the old guard, not the Popular Front, that initially assumed control. Ayaz Mutalibov, the Communist Party first secretary, was elected president, but a string of military losses in the Nagorno-Karabakh campaign inflamed the opposition. After massive street protests in Baku in early 1992, the Popular Front succeeded in deposing Mutalibov. New elections elevated Abulfaz Elçibey, the Popular Front's leader, to the presidency.

Elçibey's tenure in office was no less fraught than that of his predecessor. The influx of refugees from Nagorno-Karabakh and the Armenian-occupied territories illustrated the poverty of the government's approach to the territorial issue. In the summer of 1993 a renegade army, partially composed of former Nagorno-Karabakh fighters and led by the military commander Surat Hüseynov, seized the western city of Ganja and pushed toward Baku—a replay of the Army of Islam's march to the sea in 1918. Fearing for his position and his life, Elçibey called on Heydar Aliyev, the old Communist Party first secretary—who by this time had become chairman of the regional assembly in his native Nakhichevan—for assistance.

Aliyev was made speaker of the national parliament in Baku, but rather than assisting the embattled Elçibey, Aliyev ended up supplanting him. Baku eventually fell bloodlessly to Hüseynov's rebel army, but that victory proved hollow, as it had in 1918. In the political turmoil that followed the army's arrival, Aliyev managed to secure the president's post for himself, relegating Hüseynov to the position of prime minister. Allegations that Hüseynov was behind yet another uprising the following year led to his dismissal and subsequent flight to Russia. Aliyev's position as supreme leader was now secure, although another armed uprising, which the president harshly suppressed, threatened social stability. Actual or alleged coups d'état became an almost annual occurrence—in 1994, 1995, 1996, and 1998—but in the aftermath of each one, Aliyev was able to augment his power over both rivals and old associates. Unlike his many opponents, Aliyev stood at the center of a vast network of friends and colleagues from his days as Communist Party leader and, even more crucially, from his earlier career as head of the Baku branch of the KGB.

As in Armenia, the president began building a base of support within the legislature through the creation of his own pro-presidential organization, the New Azerbaijan Party. During the years following Aliyev's rise, the party emerged as the preeminent faction in successive elections, none of which was believed by international observers to meet democratic standards. However, party politics turned out to be far less important than the clan politics that encouraged loyalty to Aliyev yet also motivated his staunchest opponents. Aliyev's base of support remained the cadre of old friends and personal connections from the autonomous republic of Nakhichevan in western Azerbaijan. This loose community worked to secure control over state institutions, and its members also emerged as critical players in the booming energy sector. Aliyev's son, Ilham, became vice-chairman of the state oil company, which negotiated with Western investors for access to Azerbaijan's oil fields. When clear rivals to Aliyev's power emerged, they did not necessarily come from the fractured democratic opposition, whose own commitment to liberal ideals was often shaky, but rather from clans that derived their base of support from parts of Azerbaijan other than Nakhichevan or from among the ranks of ethnic Azerbaijanis expelled from Armenia in the late 1980s and early 1990s. Backroom machinations, not the dialectic of reform and reaction, defined Azerbaijani politics well into the early 2000s.

Political and economic success was largely a function of personal loyalty to the president. During his tenure Aliyev created a personality cult that was generally absent from the other two south Caucasus states (although still modest compared to those of some other Eurasian rulers). His image adorned billboards across the capital and the countryside. His visionary leadership was credited with bringing Azerbaijan back from the brink of civil war and nurturing international interest in the country's hydrocarbon reserves. None of this was exactly untrue. The country had repeatedly been on the edge of serious civil disorder, and Aliyev's iron hand no doubt played a role in preventing chaos. However, in the process of preserving order he forged the most clearly authoritarian state in the south Caucasus.

When Aliyev announced that he would not run for another term in 2003, he chose a method of political succession familiar to authoritarian leaders around the world—he handed power to his son. Ilham Aliyev was duly elected president in a race that was again viewed by both local and international monitors as deeply flawed. The younger Aliyev spent his early years in office shoring up control within his father's old party, pushing forward piecemeal reform, and strengthening relations with foreign investors. The oil and gas wealth of the country became the central theme in foreign relations, with revenues transforming the lives of some Azerbaijanis. It has remained an open question, however, whether the grand strategic games over the riches of the Caspian Sea will bring about a well-governed, democratic state.

In Georgia the administration of Eduard Shevardnadze spent much of the early 1990s quelling the internal conflicts that had brought fighting to the streets of Tbilisi. His predecessor, Zviad Gamsakhurdia, was by training a linguist and literary historian, someone most comfortable in the arcana of medieval Georgia, who brought to the presidency a faith-based zeal for reviving the Georgian nation.[18] Shevardnadze was in many ways his opposite. As a trained Soviet bureaucrat, he cared less about renewal than stability and saw his essential task as to consolidate Georgia's statehood, not realize its millennial destiny. The new president managed to corral many of the paramilitary groups that had once roamed the country. By late 1993 he had defeated the major formations still loyal to the old president, who had been ousted by a military junta shortly before Shevardnadze's arrival. (Gamsakhurdia died under uncertain circumstances—either suicide or assassination—at the end of that year.) Following the declaration of cease-fires in Abkhazia and South Ossetia, the secessionist zones remained relatively quiet during the balance of Shevardnadze's tenure—if for no other reason than the fact that the Abkhaz and South Ossetians, having effectively won the wars of the Soviet succession, were preoccupied with building their own states. The absence of open warfare, however, did not lead to a genuinely stable, multiparty, and free state even in those areas still under central government control.

The military defeats in Abkhazia and South Ossetia sobered Shevardnadze and illustrated the need for a solid political base on which to consolidate his power. That took the form of the Citizens' Union of Georgia. Like similar pro-presidential parties in Armenia and Azerbaijan, the Citizens' Union was driven less by ties of ideology and class than by loyalty to Shevardnadze and a desire by local elites to secure their political and economic positions amid civil war and state collapse. Shevardnadze grounded the party on the network of district-level administrative personnel, factory managers, and party bosses who had proved themselves trusted friends in his role as Communist Party first secretary. The Citizens' Union also attracted a small group of younger, reform-minded leaders from among the civic organizations that had sprung up at the end of the Gorbachev era.

For most of the 1990s Shevardnadze remained the single most important player in Georgian politics. Under the country's strongly presidential system, he was the ultimate decision maker both within the state and within his party. Even the few political figures who openly broke with the Citizens' Union remained staunchly devoted to the president. His leadership style was characterized by an effort to balance competing interests and to ensure that no single faction was able to challenge his authority as head of state, head of government, and head of the ruling party. At times he seemed supportive of younger reformists, even appointing them to senior positions within the government and handing them a mandate for change. At other times he repeatedly cut deals with Aslan Abashidze, one of the least progressive figures on the political scene as the local potentate of the autonomous republic of Achara along Georgia's southwestern coast. The peculiar nature of electoral politics sometimes deepened this relationship. For example, in exchange for Shevardnadze's recognition of his iron rule in Achara, Abashidze guaranteed a high voter turnout in his autonomous republic and aided Shevardnadze in winning Georgia's 2000 presidential race.

Shevardnadze's political party in effect became a mechanism for capturing the state rather than transforming it. The administrative cadres, factory bosses, and security officials who ran Georgia during the Soviet period remade themselves into a new class of entrepreneurs in the largely dysfunctional economy, benefiting from the opportunities to acquire old state enterprises under the country's murky privatization program. Shevardnadze helped create a state in which the ruling party and the administrative system were fused, a style of politics borrowed from the Soviet era. As was the case during his tenure as first secretary, Shevardnadze spent much of the 1990s dealing with the problem of corruption—or at least attempting to convince Western aid agencies that he was doing so. On most lists Georgia ranked as one of the world's most corrupt states; even within the former Soviet Union, it stood near the top.[19] Despite Shevardnadze's support for well-funded public campaigns to unmask corrupt practices—from extortion by traffic police to misappropriation of international loans—the results were less than stellar. That fact was not lost on Georgians themselves. In 1996 42 percent of Georgians expressed high or moderate confidence in local government institutions; by 1998 the figure had fallen to 25 percent. In 2000 roughly 67 percent reported having no faith in parliament or the president, with some 80 percent saying the same for tax and customs officials.[20]

In the 1990s Georgia became one of the world's largest per capita recipients of American democracy assistance and economic development aid, totaling nearly a billion dollars during the eleven years of Shevardnadze's tenure.[21] Much of this aid was dispensed to political parties that demonstrated little ability to attract voters, local government institutions that only superficially reformed themselves, and anticorruption efforts that had little impact on both the petty and gargantuan thievery that had become commonplace. However, persistent Western engagement did help solidify a new class of political entrepreneurs increasingly dissatisfied with the sclerotic leadership of a former Communist boss and his unwieldy party.

Opposition groups—many headed by onetime Shevardnadze loyalists—made the 2003 parliamentary elections into a test case of the president's commitment to genuine reform. When it became clear that Shevardnadze intended to manipulate the results, street protestors stormed the parliament building and called on the president to resign, a confrontation dubbed the Rose Revolution in honor of protestors who dispensed roses to troops guarding government offices. After first declaring a state of emergency, Shevardnadze thought better of his legacy and agreed to resign. The presidency passed to the speaker of parliament, who organized new elections early in 2004. Legitimated by international observers, the vote overwhelmingly awarded the presidential post to Mikheil Saakashvili—thirty-something, Columbia

University–educated, multilingual, and one of the major figures cultivated during the previous decade by U.S. democracy-assistance programs.

The Rose Revolution was a peaceful protest modeled on the demonstrations that had brought down Yugoslav president Slobodan Milošević in 2000. It would, in turn, provide inspiration for the Orange Revolution in Ukraine in 2004 and the Tulip Revolution in Kyrgyzstan in 2005. Like these later political transformations, the Rose Revolution was hailed in the West as a breakthrough for democracy in the post-Soviet world. Although it did produce some immediate changes, such as a much-needed reform of the police sector, the toppling of Shevardnadze was remarkably similar to what had happened in Georgia in 1992, Azerbaijan in 1993, and Armenia in 1998, namely, a change in administration effected through street rallies and political maneuvering. More than a decade and a half following independence, most of the Caucasus had yet to install a new chief executive through free, fair, and boringly uneventful elections. The political norm remained one of being ushered out of office by a crowd—whether a cortege or a tide of protestors.

The Tragic North

Despite the turbulent politics of the 1990s, the south Caucasus entered the new millennium with some degree of justified hopefulness. Local economies—at least in the capitals—were expanding after years of persistent contraction. New, younger leaderships were taking charge as men of the Shevardnadze and Aliyev *père* generations passed from the scene. Territorial conflicts remained unresolved, but the threat of armed conflict seemed less severe than it had been during the previous decade. Individuals were traveling and working abroad, bringing back to their independent countries not only much-needed cash but also innovative ideas for reform, greater openness, and a more functional government. This simple desire to live in a "normal" country promised to reshape political and social life in the years ahead.

The north Caucasus was another matter. The political instability that attended the emergence of the three south Caucasus states in the early 1990s remained a fundamental feature of the north well into the early 2000s. Russia fought two full-scale wars in Chechnya, one lasting from 1994 until 1996, during the presidency of Boris Yeltsin, and another that commenced in 1999 under his successor, Vladimir Putin.

Political killings and inter-ethnic discord afflicted virtually every Russian republic in the north—especially those closest to Chechnya itself, such as Dagestan and Ingushetia. For much of the immediate post-Soviet period, instability was confined to the northeast, the same areas that had demonstrated concerted resistance to Russian rule in the nineteenth century. By the early 2000s violence had spread to the center and northwest as well. In September 2004 forces loyal to Shamil Basaev, the most ruthless of Chechen field commanders, laid siege to a school in Beslan, North Ossetia, on the opening day of classes. Children and their teachers were herded into the gymnasium, where an elaborate system of explosives had been rigged to keep the hostages in check. The subsequent storming of the school building by Russian rescuers ended with the deaths of some 330 civilians, of which more than half were children. In October 2005 an armed attack against police and government buildings in Nalchik, the capital of the republic of Kabardino-Balkaria, heralded the possibility of violence spreading even farther westward, into historical Circassia.

The reasons for the violent politics of the north Caucasus were varied. In some areas national revival followed lines similar to those in the south, where ethnic grievances first articulated by local intellectuals were subsequently hijacked by older political elites looking to find a way of preserving their own relevance. In other areas disputes over land and property provided the impetus for ethnic cleansing and pogroms. In still others the Russian state, seeking to forestall the same secessionist domino effect that had brought an end to the Soviet Union, responded with overwhelming force or devolved power to local authoritarian leaders, who were encouraged to stamp out opposition and ensure loyalty to Moscow. As the 1990s and early 2000s progressed, yet another source of mobilization in the form of revivalist Islam was added to the mix. As in the past, the peoples of the north Caucasus were divided over their relationship with Russia and the place of religion in the social life of the region, especially the puritanical forms preached by small groups of committed proselytizers. The inescapable source of many of these problems, however, was Chechnya.

During the late Soviet period, social mobilization in Chechnya was not wildly different from the national movements that arose in other union republics and autonomous territories. Chechens, Ingush, and other north Caucasus nationalities had ample reason to oppose continued Russian control once the Soviet Union began to weaken. Few groups had a longer list of grievances or a richer history of armed opposition—from the legacy of Shamil's activities in Chechnya in the 1840s and 1850s, to anti-tsarist and anti-Bolshevik uprisings from the 1870s to the 1920s, to the Stalinist deportations of the 1940s. Still, the form of early Chechen mobilization had little in common with these historical antecedents. Instead, it proceeded largely along the lines found in other republics and regions. Indeed, in opposing first the Soviet and later the Russian center, the Chechens were following a pattern set in other parts of the Soviet Union and, more important, one also followed in almost every major administrative unit on the other side of the mountains, including Armenia, Azerbaijan, and Georgia, as well as in most of these republics' sub-units, such as Abkhazia, South Ossetia, and Nagorno-Karabakh. To ask why the Chechens chose to defy Moscow is to miss a basic point: Defying central authority and questioning old forms of sovereignty were what nearly everyone was doing in the late 1980s and early 1990s.

In 1988 Chechen and Ingush intellectuals, calling for greater attention to environmental issues, cultural freedom, and openness, established their own Popular Front to support Gorbachev's perestroika initiative. Local party and state elites united in a common cause with the Popular Front and managed to use the growing social movement in order to push for control of government institutions by ethnic Chechens. Again following a model found in other Soviet regions, the Popular Front quickly produced its own rivals in the person of other intellectuals who demanded more far-reaching reforms and genuine national renewal. The poet Zelimkhan Yandarbiev created a rival organization, the All-National Congress of the Chechen People, which in turn assembled an armed guard headed by Jokhar Dudaev, a Soviet air force general of Chechen origin. Yandarbiev's organization was more radical than the Popular Front in the sense that it sought free elections and the transformation of the Chechen-Ingush Autonomous Republic into a sovereign administrative unit outside Russia but still within the Soviet Union. At this stage, however, neither of the major opposition organizations sought full independence.

During the August 1991 coup in Moscow, Communist Party authorities in Chechnya followed the example of many other elites on the periphery, initially supporting the putschists and then denouncing them when it became clear that Gorbachev was still in control. This wavering provided an opening for Dudaev, the most vocal leader on the scene. His irregular soldiers stormed the local parliament, ousted the authorities, and made plans for new presidential and parliamentary elections, which he and his supporters won handily. In November the new parliament proclaimed a fully independent Chechen Republic of Ichkeria—the name derived from the highland region of Chechnya—with Dudaev as its founding president.

By this stage the Russian Federation had also declared its independence from the Soviet Union, and its president, Yeltsin, was loath to accept Chechen self-determination. He declared a state of emergency in the republic and dispatched troops to the capital of Grozny. However, Yeltsin quickly backed away when it became clear that violence would be opposed from above and below—by Gorbachev, still in his lame-duck role as Soviet president, and Dudaev, in his post as the elected Chechen leader. The key issue at this point was not the relationship between Yeltsin and Dudaev but rather the internal politics of Chechnya itself. Dudaev's efforts to consolidate power in Chechnya bore remarkable resemblance to those being pursued by Yeltsin in Moscow: a shaky president, faced with serious internal opposition, who was not shy about using military force to disperse his rivals—even elected parliamentarians.[22] To many local observers Yeltsin's decision to shell the Russian parliament in 1993 simply replayed, on a much grander scale, Dudaev's attack on Chechnya's legislature two years earlier.

Scholars and journalists have offered a variety of explanations for the origins of the first Chechen war, from the capriciousness of the mustachioed, trilby-sporting Dudaev, to the history of Chechen rebelliousness, to the martial culture of highland peoples in general. All of these no doubt played some role. Dudaev was far from a committed democrat and actively sought confrontation with Moscow in order to buttress his own power. Chechen leaders self-consciously resurrected the memory of Sheikh Mansur and Shamil. The social networks of *teips*, which had grown stronger during the period of Chechen exile, served as lines along which political forces could mobilize—even though people from the same clan might equally see themselves as mortal enemies.[23]

These explanations, however, miss the mark. They might account in part for why Chechens proved to be vocal opponents of Moscow precisely when other Russian republics and regions were cutting advantageous deals with the federal center. But the origin of the Chechen wars was much simpler, namely, the decision by a small coterie of military men and policy makers within the Yeltsin administration to respond to Dudaev with force. Personalities, social habits, and historical antecedents allowed Chechens to seek independence, but it was the political decision of Kremlin planners to attack Grozny that turned popular mobilization into large-scale violence. One need not take a position on the legitimacy of Chechen self-determination to accept a basic counterfactual proposition. Had Mikhail Gorbachev chosen to respond to the secession of union republics the way that Boris Yeltsin handled Chechnya, the creation of an independent Armenia, Azerbaijan, and Georgia would have been far bloodier affairs than they actually became. Gorbachev was content to let the union republics go. Yeltsin was not prepared to follow the same course in Chechnya. Over time, what had begun as a military intervention by federal authorities was transformed into an intractable guerrilla conflict, fueled by the same mix of sunk costs and war profiteering that makes any war harder to end the longer it goes on.

More than three years elapsed between the initial Chechen declaration of independence and the Russian invasion of December 1994. Up to that point Yeltsin had mainly been concerned with consolidating his power in Moscow and patching together compromises with regional leaders in other parts of the federation in order to prevent Russia's complete disintegration. By 1994 Yeltsin had established the supremacy of the president over the Russian parliament. He had also come to see Dudaev as an intransigent local politician and Chechen defiance as a virus that might spread to other parts of the federal state. He worried that if Chechnya could effectively secede, the copycat effect in other restive areas would be irresistible. Moreover, the rise of clear, armed opposition to Dudaev within the republic—organized by former Communist Party elites, old members of the Popular Front, and disaffected Dudaev loyalists—eventually convinced a small cadre within the Kremlin that a military response was both necessary and sure to succeed.

The decision to invade the republic seems to have been made in haste, with little thought to the operational requirements of the task at hand. Revealingly, the attack on Grozny—launched on New Year's Eve—was not even assigned an official code name.[24] Russian tanks and troops rolled into the city and quickly seized control of the major road and rail links. Soon, however, the inexperienced conscripts who formed the bulk of the Russian force found themselves pinned down by snipers, their tanks and other armor ripped apart by rocket-propelled grenades. The mutilated cadavers of Russian soldiers littered the city. Yeltsin's response to this humiliation was to intensify indiscriminate attacks against the Chechen capital, the first instance of heavy aerial bombing of a European city since the Second World War. Dudaev had slipped away at the beginning of the invasion, but the civilians who remained, many of whom were ethnic Russians, spent the winter huddled in cellars, creeping out to find food and water in a city devastated by an army that was, after all, their own. Grozny—built by Ermolov to showcase imperial Russia's ferocity to the mountain tribes—now demonstrated post-Soviet Russia's astonishing disregard for human life.

The outrage in other parts of Russia was palpable, both at the government's bungling of the military operation and its later attempt to recoup its losses by using even more devastating force. Sergei Kovalev, a longtime human rights campaigner and chairman of the Russian government's human rights commission, was unequivocal in his criticism. Kovalev denounced the crimes being committed by the Yeltsin administration. He and his colleagues estimated that twenty-five thousand civilians had been killed by bombs and artillery fire in the attack on Grozny, with an additional thirty-five thousand civilians and soldiers killed thereafter.[25] The Chechen conflict galvanized Russian public opinion. In often remarkable displays of the country's emerging civil society, intellectuals, human rights advocates, politicians, and the mothers of soldiers united to protest a war that was quickly taking its toll on Russian youth and Chechen civilians and was adversely affecting Russia's international reputation.

As the war wound on, things only got worse for Russian troops on the ground. Chechen forces managed to regroup after the initial Russian counteroffensive, and by August 1996 Russian units were forced to retreat from Grozny. Dudaev was not around to witness the victory. He had been killed in the spring, and was succeeded first by Yandarbiev, his old colleague, and then by Aslan Maskhadov, a former Soviet artillery officer and leader of the anti-Russian Grozny campaign. It was this single military act—the triumphant entry of Chechen guerrillas into the republican capital—that demonstrated the bankruptcy of the Russian war effort and eventually helped convince Yeltsin to seek a political settlement. Brokered by retired Russian general Alexander Lebed'—who had garnered a reputation as an iron-fisted peacemaker in another post-Soviet war in Moldova—the so-called Khasaviurt Agreement marked the end of the first Chechen conflict. It was signed in the Dagestani city of the same name in August 1996. The agreement, a combination cease-fire and formal peace treaty, committed all sides to rejecting the use of force and affirmed the right of self-determination. It also established a framework for arriving at a settlement regarding Chechnya's final status. A joint commission composed of Russian and Chechen representatives was to be set up to help govern the republic and work out the terms of a permanent peace settlement, which was to be concluded by the end of 2001. Russian troops were evacuated from the republic.

What followed the end of Russian-Chechen hostilities was not so much peace as an absence of war. Nearly two years of conflict had radicalized an entire generation of younger Chechens, intensified the rifts within the Chechen leadership, and proven that violence could provide a reasonable source of livelihood in a context in which the state had effectively collapsed. The experiment in Chechen self-governance after Khasaviurt turned out to be a miserable failure. Violence and kidnappings continued, although now they involved clans and criminal gangs rather than Russian soldiers and Chechen guerrillas. The Islamic dimensions of the struggle also became more pronounced. Chechens, Arabs, and others who had fought with the mujahideen in Afghanistan and who now saw Chechnya as the next battleground in the global jihad moved into positions of power. The foreign Islamist presence was never as large in Chechnya as is often claimed, nor did Arabs and other imported fighters form a unified group. Moreover, traditional religious elites were wary of these newcomers, whose teachings were at odds with religious practices in Chechnya. But their arrival did change the social and political calculus of Chechen elites. It made adherence to a particular brand of Islamic orthodoxy a mark of political viability, and it provided a claim to legitimacy that Maskhadov's many opponents used to undermine the president's power. One of the most ambitious figures within the Maskhadov regime, the field commander Shamil Basaev, wrapped himself in the mantle of revivalist Islam and used it to justify his own increasingly outrageous activities, such as setting up private military formations and political institutions and staging spectacular mass hostage takings.

In 1994 Yeltsin seems to have believed that a short, victorious war in Chechnya would seal his position of strength in Moscow and prevent other republican elites from following the Chechen model of secession. Vladimir Putin appears to have believed something similar five years later. However, in Putin's case there were added incentives for doing something about the Chechen problem, namely, the growing radicalization of Chechen politicians, the perceived influence of outside Islamists, and the real threat that freelancers like Basaev posed for other north Caucasus republics. A raid by Basaev's forces into Dagestan in the summer of 1999 plus a series of terrorist attacks in Russian cities—some of which have never been conclusively linked to Chechen fighters—provided the proximate causes for the resumption of war.

Following more than a week of aerial bombardment, in October 1999 Putin launched a new ground offensive in Chechnya aimed at deposing the Maskhadov government and putting an end to disorder.

Grozny was fairly easily retaken. The Russian soldiers sent to do the job included seasoned security personnel, border guards, and interior-ministry troops. In the first Chechen war the Russian side numbered around forty-five thousand men at the height of the conflict, about 93 percent of whom were conscripts. By contrast, the ninety-three thousand men deployed by Putin was roughly the size of the Soviet expeditionary force sent to Afghanistan.[26] The nature of the conflict came to resemble a long-term counterinsurgency operation, not the full-scale but poorly planned maneuvers of the first Chechen campaign. However, many of the techniques that had previously been used—including the wholesale roundup of men and boys of fighting age, the "cleansing" (*zachistka*) of territories thought to contain rebel sympathizers, and the "disappearance" of men and women with alleged terrorist connections—were pursued with renewed zeal. Over time the Russian state increasingly subcontracted its duties to local authorities, who, while professing loyalty to Moscow, were building up their own paramilitary units and profiting from the chaos of conflict. Putin's long-term plan was not so much to use federal forces to subdue guerrillas and "terrorists" but rather to hand off the job of securing Chechnya to local Chechens, who could be trusted to neutralize the anti-Russian fighters still roaming the hills and valleys.

The human and material costs of the two Chechen wars are impossible to gauge with any precision. In the second war the Russian government restricted press access, a technique that would have been familiar to Ermolov and Vorontsov. The profitable industry of kidnapping—a favored practice on all sides—ensured that even the most intrepid observers generally stayed away. However, the broad outlines of the wars' devastating effects are clear. Estimates for the total dead range from forty thousand to one hundred thousand (out of a prewar population of about 1.3 million), most of them civilians.[27] The level of Russian military casualties approached that sustained by the Soviet Union during its ten-year quagmire in Afghanistan. Russian leaders seemed to believe that this level was politically sustainable so long as soldiers were being killed in half dozens rather than in tens and twenties. (Russian military planners reportedly calculated that a casualty figure of 12 to 15 percent in any major operation would not produce a significant public response.)[28] Cities were leveled by Russian bombs, and hundreds of thousands of Russian citizens were made refugees in neighboring republics and countries. In contrast to the first Chechen war, these losses did not generate widespread opposition among the Russian public outside the conflict zone. The Putin administration had found a method of making war that seemed to work: minimizing the use of conscripts in the most difficult engagements, controlling press coverage, and casting the enemy not as nationalist secessionists but as self-serving bandits and cold-blooded terrorists linked to a global Islamist holy war.

Tit-for-tat assassinations became routine. Dudaev had already been killed in 1996 by a Russian missile programmed to track the signal of his satellite telephone. The prominent field commander Salman Raduev died while in Russian custody in 2002. Dudaev's immediate successor as acting president, Yandarbiev, was assassinated in Qatar in 2004, probably by Russian agents. Akhmad Kadyrov, who headed the pro-Russian government in Grozny, died in a bomb attack by secessionists in 2004. Dudaev's successor as elected president, Aslan Maskhadov, was killed by Russian special forces in 2005. Maskhadov's successor, Abdul-Khalim Sadulaev, was likewise killed the following year. This spiral of violence also extended to the heart of Russia itself. In October 2002 Chechen fighters seized a Moscow auditorium full of theatergoers, setting off a crisis that ended in the deaths of more than a hundred hostages during a gas attack by Russian security services. Two years later the attack on the Beslan schoolhouse in North Ossetia became the single largest incident involving civilian deaths outside the war zone. Events such as these—along with the appearance of Chechen suicide bombers who were responsible for, among other things, bringing down Russian commercial aircraft—increased public support for the war and eased discontent over the concentration of power in the hands of the Russian president. Building an effective and powerful state, Putin affirmed, should be the primary goal, especially in the face of organized violence bubbling up from the south.

As the war wound on and its effects spread to other areas, Western governments became even less interested in the region's fate. What had initially been a mildly critical attitude gave way to a propensity to treat the north Caucasus as a legitimate battleground against the international network of radical Islam. The detention and torture of young men and the wanton theft and destruction of property—all of which were documented in innumerable reports by Russian and Western human rights groups—became some of the defining features of Russia's war effort in Chechnya. While the government admitted that some atrocities had taken place, federal soldiers were only rarely held accountable. By 2003 fifty-one Russian servicemen had been court-martialed for crimes against civilians. Of these, only nineteen served prison sentences.[29] If Yeltsin's war was purportedly about preserving the federation, Putin's was cast as a war to defend the federation against bandits, terrorists, and religious zealots. Both rhetorical devices played well abroad. President Bill Clinton and other American officials publicly compared the conflict in Chechnya to the American Civil War. Following the terrorist attacks against the United States on September 11, 2001, Putin repeatedly stressed that Chechnya was simply another theater in the new global war on terror.

Putin's claim was less easy to dismiss than the portrayal of Yeltsin as a latter-day Lincoln, especially after the United States began to engage in some of the very wartime techniques in Iraq and Afghanistan for which American presidents had earlier criticized the Yeltsin leadership. There were, no doubt, some Chechens who continued to fight for national liberation, but their numbers were diminishing as the second Chechen war dragged on. Rebels lacking an overall strategic plan for victory—known in Russian simply as *boeviki*—came to dominate what had been a multifaceted Chechen political elite. They and their spokesmen became skilled at resurrecting allegedly traditional social norms—particularly the glorification of the highland bandit (*abrek*), the martial way of life, and holy war—and transforming them into a code of violence for its own sake.[30] The wars thus had a doubly deleterious consequence for the Russian state: at first keeping it at arm's length from Western institutions and then making it the West's partner to the rhetoricians of radical Islam.

Historical analogies are easy to propose—and they are often wrong. But one could not observe Russian and Chechen behavior without being reminded of the nineteenth century. The Russian state worked to "Chechenize" the conflict by devolving authority to locals who could fight guerrillas on their own turf and with equal brutality. It set aside concerns for governance and focused mainly on security. It carried out punitive expeditions for each act of violence and, in the process, provided new recruits for the rebels. The line between Russian and Chechen blurred as fighters on both sides used the same unscrupulous tactics, carried out impromptu raids against alleged collaborators, and worked assiduously to derive some personal profit from the wartime economy. As the second Chechen war continued, the people who were doing the killing and dying on both sides were most often ethnic Chechens, some wearing the uniform of the Russian

Federation and others the camouflage fatigues and green headbands of a putative worldwide jihad.

The guerrillas also learned to speak about the war by using the vocabulary of Islamist fighters in other conflicts and the terminology of earlier eras. Web sites such as kavkazcenter.com—a major channel of communication with the rest of the world—consistently appropriated the Islamic lexicon found in Shamil's letters written 150 years earlier. Rather than "Russians," the Web masters spoke of "unbelievers" (*kafirs*). Rather than pro-Russian Chechens, they spoke of "hypocrites" (*munafiqs*). Casualties on the Chechen side were always "martyrs" (*shahids*). There is a world of difference between the Russian Empire's wars in the Caucasus and those of the Russian Federation, but in the Chechnya of the early twenty-first century the past still provided a dark template for action. Just as Imam Shamil frequently wrote letters to the Ottoman sultan and Russian commanders explaining the nature of his struggle, Chechen leaders also understood the power of public relations. In early 2006 Shamil Basaev published his own e-memoir, *Book of a Mujahideen* [*sic*], which he made available for purchase online with a major credit card. (Within only a few months Basaev was killed in an explosion in Ingushetia, an event that seemed to mark a turning point in the conflict and was heralded by Moscow as the beginning of the end for the guerrillas.)

The tragedy of the long-running war was not that there was no one to speak for the people of Chechnya, its real victims. It was that those who claimed that mantle—in Moscow, Grozny, and the highlands—preferred a pyrrhic victory to a lasting peace. That same logic seemed to be spreading to other parts of the north as well. One of the pressing analytical questions of the 1990s was why Chechnya erupted into large-scale violence while other parts of the north Caucasus remained quiet. By the early 2000s that question appeared naively time-bound. The relative peace that had prevailed in Dagestan, based on a complex distribution of power among the republic's many clans and ethnic groups, proved uniquely sensitive to external and internal shocks, such as targeted assassinations and raids launched from Chechnya. North Ossetia continued to face the prospect of violence between ethnic Ossetians and Ingush over property ownership and social power, following a pattern previously set in clashes in the early 1990s. Karachaevo-Cherkesia and Kabardino-Balkaria were moving into the 2000s burdened by local authoritarianism, the politicization of Islamic practice, and tensions between Circassian and Turkic populations.

In general, the region's persistent ethnic and religious disputes were usually proxies for other, often deeper contours of discord. People displaced by the Soviet regime found themselves at odds with those who now lived in their homes and worked their fields. Individuals to whom the Kremlin had devolved control clashed with those left out of Russia's new imperial bargain. People who had learned to profit from the post-Soviet disorder succeeded at the expense of those who struggled merely to survive in it. The Caucasus still had plenty of ghosts, but they were not those of ancient hatreds among peoples and religions. They were much younger ones, born of the Soviet system and now revealing a cold and unexpected paradox—that it is possible to gain one's freedom and lose it at the same time.

Conclusion: Continental Shift

*The suppression of the Polish insurrection and the annexation of the Caucasus, I regard
as the two most important events to have taken place in Europe since 1815.*

Karl Marx, writing to Friedrich Engels (1864)

We have always been on the threshold of Europe, and now we want to be Europeans.

Evgeni Gegechkori, Georgian foreign minister (1919)

W HEN THE BRITISH TRAVELER Henry Barkley loped out of
the hills and plains of eastern Anatolia in 1878, dusty after
riding along the limits of the south Caucasus, he inquired
about the amenities to be found in Trebizond, the port on the southeastern coast of the Black Sea. It was, he hoped, a far cry from the hinterland, a city where steamers arrived weekly from Marseille, Odessa,
and other points to the west, and where a hodgepodge of traders and
travelers from across Europe met local Muslims, Greeks, and Armenians on the quays. Are there good streets, good houses, good shops,
and, above all, a good hotel, Barkley asked. Yes, of course, a local man
assured him: "Trabzon Avrupa!"—Trebizond is Europe.[1]

Good streets, good houses, good shops, and good hotels. More than
a century later, that is still the view from the periphery—Europe as the
civilized terminus of a long, aspirational journey. For Czechs and Poles

in 1989, rejoining Europe involved rediscovering a cultural heritage that had been buried beneath the gray moraine of communism and foreign occupation. For Romanians and Bulgarians today, Europe represents the promise of economic success and consolidated if still imperfect democracy. For Ukrainians it may eventually become the winch that helps pull their unlikely country out of Eurasia. For Turks it has encouraged an unprecedented program of government reform that may one day stretch the European continent across the Bosphorus. Trabzon Avrupa, indeed.

In the Caucasus the magnetic utility of Europe is less clear. On the one hand, all the independent states of the region repeatedly affirm their European credentials: in Armenia's case as the first Christian nation; in Azerbaijan's as the first Muslim republic; in Georgia's as the inheritor of an ancient culture that produced Byzantine-era emperors as well as George Balanchine. All three countries are members of the Council of Europe, an organization that has become something of a large antechamber for prospective applicants to the European Union. The flags of both bodies are conveniently the same, consisting of a circle of twelve gold stars on a blue field. That simple fact allowed Georgian authorities to begin flying the flag outside government buildings in 2004—a symbol of where the country already was and an affirmation of where it wanted to go.

On the other hand, when one is standing on the pebbly beaches of the Black Sea or the salty dunes of the Caspian, Europe seems very far away. The nature of politics in the Caucasus—guerrilla war, secessionist disputes, consolidated authoritarianism, rickety democracy—is at odds with the growth of responsive and responsible governance closer to Europe's center, even in the once disorderly Balkans. Indeed, in the early 2000s it was still the United States, not Europe, that was the preeminent player across the wider Black Sea zone. On one side of the sea, in Romania, the United States announced the opening of two new military bases in 2005. On the other side, in Georgia, a military training program provided facilities and know-how to the Georgian army. Both Georgia and Armenia were slated to benefit from the Millennium Challenge Account program sponsored by the United States, an aid effort that promised to deliver over five hundred million dollars to the two countries for designated infrastructure projects. All three south Caucasus states remained among the largest per capita recipients of U.S. development aid in the world. In Armenia's case that flow of resources was enhanced by investment and assistance from U.S.-based members of the global Armenian diaspora. Azerbaijan had earlier been under an arms ban by the United States—limiting direct military assistance as long as Azerbaijan maintained an embargo against Armenia—but the lifting of those restrictions under President Bill Clinton permitted a deepening of the bilateral relationship. Hydrocarbons also played a significant, even dominant, role. In 2006 a new pipeline running from Baku, via Tbilisi, to the Turkish Mediterranean port of Ceyhan began carrying oil to Western markets—a route that significantly bypassed older pipelines running through Russia. For years before and after, one could not enter a bar or restaurant in Baku without finding a contingent of Texas oilmen and their nouveau riche Azerbaijani counterparts.

Politically, if not geographically, all of the south Caucasus capitals have remained far closer to Washington than to Brussels. Within the European Union there is little sign that either politicians or the public are eager to change that state of affairs. However, rather than being peripheral to European interests, there is much about the nature of political life and historical memory in the Caucasus that makes it a quintessentially European space. In order to grasp this point, one has to understand something about the transformation of Europe during the last half century and the peculiar relationship between Europeans and their past.

After 1945 the concept of Europe as an idea and an ideal, rather than a place, became a way of addressing a set of perplexing questions about the nature of political and social life on this small appendage of western Eurasia. How might a set of diminutive, irascible states provide for their own security and prosperity? How might they bind themselves, Ulysses-like, against the siren calls of nationalism, chauvinism, and militarism? How might they pool their political and economic resources and reclaim their destiny from two global powers, the United States and the Soviet Union?

Answering these questions—a process that came to be known as the European project—was less a matter of farsighted leadership, although that certainly played a role, than a result of the utter failure of the alternatives. European states had never abided hegemony on their own continent even as they rushed to impose it on others. Any vision of European unity that rested on the dominance of a single state or empire soon prompted a reaction. This traditional system of adversarial balancing could produce unity of a sort, but it was usually short-lived. In the middle of the twentieth century the devastation of mechanized war cleared the ground to such a degree that the old system of would-be hegemonic states and counteralliances became unworkable. But envisaging a different future—one that entailed acting, as it were, contrary to type—required thinking about what came before in radically new ways, that is, viewing the horrors of the first half of the twentieth century not as the logical outcome of Europe's past but as a long and deadly detour away from the natural norms and behaviors that might yet transform the continent into an arena of peace and cooperation.

In other words, Europe could be something other than what Europe had done. This Europe—the "organized and living Europe" invoked by French foreign minister Robert Schuman in his May 1950 proposal to create what would eventually become the European Coal and Steel Community (the kernel of the current European Union)—was conspicuous for one thing: It had never previously existed. As Schuman realized, this Europe would be made, not begotten, crafted "through concrete achievements which first create a de facto solidarity." As time went on, the emphasis shifted from making a continent to rediscovering one. Building on the momentum of Franco-German reconciliation, a nucleus of committed states and leaders was soon engaged in a movement of radical return, embracing such "European values" as respect for individual rights, skepticism about the unrestrained market, preference for diplomacy over force, and an identity that might be called rooted cosmopolitanism—national yet "multi-" and "trans-" as well. Through the remarkable alchemy of memory, it was only after 1945, the story now went, that Europe at last became genuinely European.

Part of modern Europe's history involves the withering of the grand old ideological narratives of the Right and the Left and, in the space left behind, the development of a uniquely "European" model of politics, economics, and social relations. As the historian Tony Judt has remarked, this Europe was not the product of vision and optimism but rather "the insecure child of anxiety," a continent congenitally nervous about the forces and failings that had enabled the massive destruction of the Second World War.[2] In laying the foundation for what, in 1992, would become the European Union, Europeans were not charging boldly into the future so much as raising barricades against the past.

The birth of this new Europe cannot be understood without reference to the miserable state of affairs at the end of the Second World War. The scale of the damage is still shocking to contemplate: over thirty-six million dead, more than half noncombatants; tens of millions displaced and deported; entire cultures (and countries) wiped away;

utter economic and political collapse. The war upended everything, in senses both horrible and ultimately providential. The continent was divided, but that very division helped spur the consolidation of its western half. Institutional and economic devastation permitted original thinking about how to organize the state. The substitution of new international rivalries for old ones meant that there was now room—and powerful incentives—for reconciliation. What followed was a complete continental transformation, but one that oscillated between optimism and pessimism over the continent's future: the postwar reckoning and recovery, the emergence of cold war politics, the dialectic of affluence and rebellion, the waning of power and expectations, the revolutionary dreams of 1989, and the emergence of a united yet complicated continent. Europeans have both literally and figuratively spent the last half century crawling out from under the rubble, dusting themselves off, and trying to make sense of the ruins around them.

The war, however, did more than destroy an old system. It also set up one of the enduring themes in Europe's long march away from 1945, namely, the conscious struggle to misremember the past. Trauma can produce three kinds of reactions. One is rugged determination, a courageous commitment to remake and rebuild. Another is nostalgia, a way of recalling the past that is selective and sepia-tinged. The third is creative amnesia, an effort to refashion the past so that it provides a coherent link to the imagined present. This third reaction is a basic marker of modernity, and as such, it is the defining attribute of Blanche DuBois, nationalists, and, to a great degree, modern Europeans.

Amnesia has its uses. It has facilitated the creation of a European quasi state that was barely conceivable a few decades ago, a multifaceted and multilevel form of political and economic union that has knitted together the continent, improved the quality of life for its citizens, and inspired political change on its periphery. The next era in world affairs—if one believes in eras—might well be Europe's, or at least this Europe's. The old ghosts—ethnic exclusivism, fractious politics, governments that promise too much and deliver too little—are still there, but the barricades, by and large, have held. What has been built up behind them is, as Marxists used to say, of world-historical importance.

The irony is that this Europe emerged out of a particular kind of victim narrative ("never again can we do this to ourselves") that has imparted to the European project a uniquely anxious relationship to history. That, as it turns out, is precisely the structure of the narratives that spawned the twentieth century's problems in the first place. A

Europe that sees its own recent history as tragedy and invents an older, more civilized past to which it is now returning: can this Europe become something other than the insular, fearful, self-absorbed countries it was meant to replace? The answer lies in the future of continental shift: whether Europe can now reimagine itself in such a way that real engagement with lands farther east—Turkey, Ukraine, and even the Caucasus—becomes part of the natural future of the European continent. Much of this will depend on what happens in the Caucasus itself, a region now facing a struggle with its own ghosts that bears more than a passing resemblance to the one the rest of Europe has been waging for the past fifty years.

With the accession of Romania and Bulgaria in 2007, the European Union became a Black Sea power; if Turkey ever gains admission, it will almost become a Caucasus one as well. But the Caucasus remains a feared and poorly understood specter at the edge of Europe's thinking about its own future. Brussels has barely begun to chart what its "Caucasus policy" might look like in the next few decades, although debates among analysts and pundits about the future of the Black Sea and Caspian zones are now more vigorous than ever. As new issues come to the fore—the future of Iraq and the greater Middle East; the prospects for political change in Iran; and the evolution of Russia's consolidated authoritarianism—the Caucasus will fall squarely within the interests of European states. Still, for the time being, the core concerns of the United States and Russia—oil, security, and the building of political systems that pass for democracies—are likely to remain the prime movers in the political and economic life of the Caucasus.

What, then, of Russia? Under both Boris Yeltsin and Vladimir Putin, post-Soviet Russia has remained something resembling an empire—an electoral and increasingly wealthy one perhaps, but a political system whose essential attributes look rather different from those of a modern state. Central power is exercised through subalterns, who function as effective tax and ballot farmers. In exchange for being permitted to manage their own fiefdoms, they surrender up a portion of local revenue and deliver the votes for the center's designated candidates in national elections. Viceroys sent from the capital keep watch over local potentates but generally leave them to their own devices. State monopolies or privileged private companies secure strategic resources and keep open the conduits that provide money to the metropolis. The military, weak and in crisis, is given the task of policing the restless frontier, from supervising a low-level war in Chechnya to superintending the cease-fire lines of unresolved conflicts in the borderland emirates of Moldova, Georgia, and Tajikistan. Such arrangements do make for federalism of a sort, but in an older sense of the word. The concept, after all, is derived from ancient Rome's practice of accommodating threatening peoples by settling them inside the empire and paying them to be *foederati*, or self-governing border guards. It is federalism as an imperial survival strategy, not as a way of bringing government closer to the governed. The problem with this system is not its fragility. As a form of political and economic organization covering vast stretches of territory, it has a track record far longer than that of the nation-state. It is, however, incompatible with the basic norms of liberal democracy and the free market.

Russia is in many ways the last of the Soviet successor states to develop a clearly national—or more accurately ethnonational—sense of self.[3] The other successor states exited the Soviet Union in a vast crusade to reclaim their heritage as nation-states—by, of, and for a distinct ethnonational group—in contrast to the soporific multiethnicism preached by official Soviet ideology. Russia, a power comfortable with the legacies of empire, has long resisted the allure of the ethnonational. However, one of Vladimir Putin's major achievements has been to transform Russia into a confident international actor that is equally sure of its own historical destiny. One need only look at school curricula or visit newly refurbished museums in Moscow to sense the shift in attitude toward a national, culturally Russian perception of the past and of the state itself.

All this has been happening within a context in which Russia is, in fact, becoming less "national" as a society. From 1989 to 2002 the ethnic Russian proportion of the country's population slid by almost two percentage points—from 81.5 to 79.8 percent. During the same period Russia's minority groups grew considerably. The ethnic Armenian population more than doubled, the number of Azerbaijanis grew by 85 percent, and the number of Lezgins by 60 percent. Despite the war in Chechnya, there were over 50 percent more Chechens reported in Russia's first census in 2002 than in the last Soviet census in 1989.[4] If current trends continue, Russia faces a future in which its population will be smaller, more multi-ethnic, and considerably more Muslim than it is today.

Throughout the Caucasus, the post-Soviet era has seen an intensive "de-Russification" of local societies, a process of emigration by ethnic Russians that has begun to reverse nearly two centuries of Russian and Soviet demographic engineering.[5] Still, part of what it means to be Russian continues to include elements that are fundamentally linked to the cultures, histories, and traditions of the mountains, from the dress of Cossack dancers to habits of feasting and toasting. Russia is not quite Russia without the Caucasus. Yet the peoples of the region—especially Muslims—are routinely denigrated as thievish and inherently rebellious, blanketed with collective responsibility for everything from organized crime to terrorism, and portrayed as the chief threat to Russia's internal security and stability. In the Russian imagination to be a "person of Caucasian nationality" (*litso kavkazskoi natsional'nosti*) is to be dark rather than light—of complexion, yes, but also of spirit and purpose. "Cossack! Do not sleep. In the gloomy dark, the Chechen roams beyond the river," wrote Pushkin in "Captive of the Caucasus." Those fearful lines about the southern menace continue to evoke and inspire images of Chechens, Dagestanis, Circassians, and others in Russian popular culture and to inform the behavior of state officials, from traffic cops to senior politicians. They are right in only one respect. With unfinished territorial disputes still smoldering in the south Caucasus, the expansion of violence in the north could trigger a nightmare scenario in the early twenty-first century: the eruption of multiple armed conflicts involving not only the region's many political entities and ethnic groups but also its four sovereign states of Russia, Armenia, Azerbaijan, and Georgia.

Given all these problems, can one ever really think of the Caucasus as Europe? To conceive of Europe as a place that does not stop at the Oder River or even the Bosphorus became possible once Europe refashioned itself as a set of values rather than a self-evident set of boundaries. Seeing things in that way has required a gargantuan effort to forget, to shove into the dark corners of the past those values that have most often defined Europeanness: nationalism, chauvinism, and a penchant for the authoritarian state. In other words, it requires that today's Europeans and those who wish to join them continue to do what they have done since 1945—to engage in a collective rethinking of the past that enables a creative, liberating, and humane imagining of the future.

The time of troubles in the Caucasus is by no means over. There may yet be even more devastating things to come for the people who inhabit the hills and plains on either side of the great mountain range. But if a European continent that spent the first half of the twentieth century devising ever more creative ways of destroying itself can misremember its past as an inexorable march toward liberal values, human rights, and democratic governance, there may yet be hope that the Caucasus can do the same.

Notes

Abbreviations Used in Notes

ACA	Alpine Club Archives, London
AKAK	*Akty sobrannye Kavkazskoiu arkheograficheskoiu kommissieiu*
BL	British Library, London
GRR	Georgia (Republic) Records, Houghton Library, Harvard University
GSCACH	Georgian State Central Archive of Contemporary History, Tbilisi
HIA	Hoover Institution Archives, Palo Alto
KS	*Kavkazskii sbornik*
NAUK	National Archives of the United Kingdom (formerly Public Record Office), Kew
OWP	Oliver Wardrop Papers, Bodleian Library, Oxford
RGB-OKI	Russian State Library, Department of Cartographic Publications, Moscow
SMOMPK	*Sbornik materialov dlia opisaniia mestnostei i plemen Kavkaza*
SRA	Soviet Red Archives, Records of Radio Free Europe/Radio Liberty, Open Society Archives, Budapest
SSKG	*Sbornik svedenii o kavkazskikh gortsakh*
UP	David Urquhart Papers, Balliol College, Oxford
WC	Wardrop Collection, Bodleian Library, Oxford

Introduction: Nature's Bulwark

1. Herodotus, *The Histories*, new ed., trans. Aubrey de Sélincourt (London: Penguin, 1972), 80.

2. Robert Ker Porter, *Travels in Georgia, Persia, Armenia, Ancient Babylonia, &c. &c., During the Years 1817, 1818, 1819, and 1820*, 2 vols. (London: Longman, Hurst, Rees, Orme, and Brown, 1821–22), 1:44–45, 64–65.

3. Jacques-François Gamba, *Voyage dans la Russie méridionale, et particulièrement dans les provinces situées au-delà du Caucase, fait depuis 1820 jusqu'en 1824*, 2 vols. (Paris: C. J. Trouvé, 1826), 2:37–38.

4. W. E. D. Allen, *Béled-es-Siba: Sketches and Essays of Travel and History* (London: Macmillan, 1925), 204.

5. George Kennan, "The Mountains and Mountaineers of the Eastern Caucasus," *Journal of the American Geographical Society of New York* 5 (1874): 177. The author was the great-uncle of George F. Kennan, the famous American diplomat and expert on Russia.

6. James Bryce, *Transcaucasia and Ararat, Being Notes of a Vacation Tour in the Autumn of 1876*, 4th rev. ed. (London: Macmillan, 1896), 62.

7. W. E. D. Allen, "The Caucasian Borderland," *Geographical Journal* 99 (May-June 1942): 230.

8. Julius von Klaproth, *Travels in the Caucasus and Georgia, Performed in the Years 1807 and 1808*, trans. Frederic Shoberl (London: Henry Colburn, 1814), viii.

Chapter 1: Empires and Boundaries

1. Jacques-François Gamba, *Voyage dans la Russie méridionale, et particulièrement dans les provinces situées au-delà du Caucase, fait depuis 1820 jusqu'en 1824*, 2 vols. (Paris: C. J. Trouvé, 1826), 1:66.

2. Frederika von Freygang, *Letters from the Caucasus and Georgia* (London: John Murray, 1823), 32.

3. Michael Khodarkovsky, *Where Two Worlds Met: The Russian State and the Kalmyk Nomads, 1600–1771* (Ithaca, N.Y.: Cornell University Press, 1992).

4. Quoted in David Marshall Lang, *The Last Years of the Georgian Monarchy, 1658–1832* (New York: Columbia University Press, 1957), 143.

5. See W. E. D. Allen, ed., *Russian Embassies to the Georgian Kings, 1589–1605*, 2 vols. (Cambridge: Cambridge University Press, 1970).

6. "Vsepoddanneishii raport gen.-l. Knorringa, ot 28-go iulia 1801 goda, za No. 1," *AKAK*, 1:426.

7. Lang, *Last Years*, 231–32.

8. "Vysochaishii Manifest 12-go sentiabria 1802 g. [*sic*]," *AKAK*, 6:433.

9. Bernard Eugène Antoine Rottiers, *Itinéraire de Tiflis à Constantinople* (Brussels: Chez Frechet, 1829), 77–82.

10. Marie-Félicité Brosset, "Nouvelles recherches sur l'historien Wakhoucht, sur le roi Artchil et sa famille, et sur divers personnages géorgiens enterrés à Moscou," *Mélanges asiatiques* 3 (1859): 533–75.

11. Wakhoucht [Vakhushti Bagrationi], *Description géographique de la Géorgie*, trans. M. Brosset (St. Petersburg: L'Académie Impériale des Sciences, 1842), 63–64, 79, 287, 413.

12. John Chardin [Jean Chardin], *Travels in Persia* (London: Argonaut Press, 1927), 184.

13. Lang, *Last Years*, 91–102. For further investigations of the eastern experiences of Georgian families, see Hirotake Maeda, "On the Ethno-Social Background of Four *Gholam* Families from Georgia," *Studia Iranica* 32 (2003): 243–78.

14. Gamba, *Voyage dans la Russie*, 2:350–51.

15. A. L. Narochnitskii, ed., *Istoriia narodov Severnogo Kavkaza (konets XVIII v.–1917 g.)* (Moscow: Nauka, 1988), 19.

16. Quoted in Michael Kemper, "Communal Agreements (*ittifāqāt*) and *'ādāt*-Books from Daghestani Villages and Confederacies (18th–19th Centuries)," *Der Islam* 81 (2004): 121.

17. For an early exploration of this idea, see "Pis'mo gr. Nessel'rode k gen. Ermolovu, ot 13-go iulia 1820 goda," *AKAK*, 6:1:646–52.

18. "Raspolozhenie krepostei i ukreplenii na Kavkaze, 1818–1855 gg." (n.d.), RGB-OKI, KO 105/V-83.

19. See the strategy outlined as early as 1816 in "Mémoire sur les frontières de la Russie avec la Perse et la Turquie d'Asie," *AKAK*, 5:983–92.

20. Thomas M. Barrett, "Lines of Uncertainty: The Frontiers of the North Caucasus," *Slavic Review* 54, no. 3 (autumn 1995): 578–601.

21. Moritz Wagner, *Travels in Persia, Georgia and Koordistan; with Sketches of the Cossacks and the Caucasus*, 3 vols. (London: Hurst and Blackett, 1856), 1:127.

22. Barrett, "Lines of Uncertainty," 587.

23. On the strategic uses of precisely this state of affairs, see Alexei Vel'iaminov, "Korpusnomu komandiru (1833)," *KS* 7 (1883): 145–55.

24. Robert Lyall, *Travels in Russia, the Krimea, the Caucasus, and Georgia* (London: T. Cadell, 1825), 1:395.

25. Thomas Alcock, *Travels in Russia, Persia, Turkey, and Greece, in 1828–9* (London: E. Clarke and Son, 1831), 19. See also Wagner, *Travels in Persia*, 1:315.

26. "Otnoshenie barona Rozena k gr. Chernyshevu, ot 21-go marta 1832 goda," *AKAK*, 8:342–46.

27. Wagner, *Travels in Persia*, 1:314–17.

28. Ibid., 1:275, 283; 2:241.

29. Ibid., 1:295–96.

30. Edmund Spencer, *Travels in Circassia, Krim-Tartary, &c., Including a Steam Voyage Down the Danube, from Vienna to Constantinople, and Round the Black Sea*, 3rd ed., 2 vols. (London: Henry Colburn, 1839), 2:252.

31. Don Juan van Halen, *Mémoires de D. Juan van Halen*, 2 vols. (Paris: Jules Renouard, 1847), 2:117.

32. Alexander Pushkin, *A Journey to Arzrum*, trans. Birgitta Ingemanson (Ann Arbor, Mich.: Ardis, 1974), 15.

33. Quoted in John F. Baddeley, *The Russian Conquest of the Caucasus* (1908; reprint, London: Routledge Curzon, 2003), 97.

34. Baddeley, *Russian Conquest*, 107–8.

35. Wagner, *Travels in Persia*, 1:37.

36. Alexei Vel'iaminov, "Sposob uskorit' pokorenie gortsev (1828)," *KS* 7 (1883): 67–77.

37. A. P. Ermolov, *Zapiski A. P. Ermolova, 1798–1826* (Moscow: Vysshaia shkola, 1991), 302.

38. Quoted in Baddeley, *Russian Conquest*, 112.

39. Ibid., 156.

40. Ibid., 167.

41. David Marshall Lang, "Griboedov's Last Years in Persia," *American Slavic and East European Review* 7, no. 4 (1948): 319.

42. Platon Zubov, *Kartina kavkazskogo kraia* (St. Petersburg: Konrad Vingeber, 1834), 159.

43. Michael Khodarkovsky, *Russia's Steppe Frontier: The Making of a Colonial Empire, 1500–1800* (Bloomington: Indiana University Press, 2002), 22.

44. On the Shvetsov incident, see Thomas M. Barrett, "Southern Living (in Captivity): The Caucasus in Russian Popular Culture," *Journal of Popular Culture* 31, no. 4 (1998). See also Liubov Derluguian, "The Unlikely Abolitionists: The Russian Struggle Against the Slave Trade in the Caucasus, 1800–1864" (Ph.D. diss., State University of New York, Binghamton, 1997), 141–48.

45. According to one estimate, there were already three thousand Russian deserters and prisoners in Abkhazia in 1820, many of whom were prevented from leaving by their new Abkhaz in-laws. See "Notions sur Soukhoum-Kalé et sur les Abazes, données par R. de Scassi," *AKAK*, 6:1:650.

46. Spencer, *Travels in Circassia*, 2:227.

47. Wagner, *Travels in Persia*, 2:296–318.

48. "Raport gen. Raevskago ot 8-go aprelia [1838], No. 1," *AKAK*, 9:454.

49. See the letter from Hasan Efendi, the Circassian representative in Constantinople, to David Urquhart, received October 31, 1863, UP, Box 15, File IJ9: Circassia.

50. Edouard Taitbout de Marigny, *Three Voyages in the Black Sea to the Coast of Circassia: Including Descriptions of the Ports, and the Importance of Their Trade* (London: John Murray, 1837), 235–38.

51. Edmund Spencer mentions his encounter with a multilingual Silesian Jewish silversmith who was taken captive by a Shapsug prince in the 1830s. See Spencer, *Travels in Circassia*, 230–31.

52. See E. A. Verderevskii, *Plen u Shamilia* (St. Petersburg: Tipografiia Koroleva, 1856). See also Anna Drancey, *Souvenirs d'une française captive de Chamyl*, ed. Edouard Merlieux (Paris: Ferdinand Sartorius, 1857).

53. On the particular role of Scottish missionaries, see the following: Donald Mackenzie Wallace, *Russia* (1877; reprint New York: AMS Press, 1970), 377–78; William Glen, *Journal of a Tour from Astrachan to Karass* (Edinburgh: David Brown, 1822), 3; Ebenezer Henderson, *Biblical Researches and Travels in Russia* (London: James Nisbet, 1826), 446–50; and Richard Wilbraham, *Travels in the Trans-Caucasian Provinces of Russia* (London: John Murray, 1839), 154, 165.

54. A. L. Gizetti, *Sbornik svedenii o poteriakh Kavkazskikh voisk vo vremia voin kavkazsko-gorskikh, persidskikh, turetskikh i v Zakaspiiskom krae;* quoted in *Shamil': Illiustrirovannaia entsiklopediia*, ed. Sh. M. Kaziev (Moscow: Ekho Kavkaza, 1997), 162.

55. Ehud R. Toledano, *The Ottoman Slave Trade and Its Suppression, 1840–1890* (Princeton, N.J.: Princeton University Press, 1982), 89.

56. Charles White, *Three Years in Constantinople; or, Domestic Manners of the Turks in 1844*, 3 vols. (London: Henry Colburn, 1845), 2:290–91, 304.

57. J. A. Longworth, *A Year Among the Circassians*, 2 vols. (London: Henry Colburn, 1840), 2:279, 281. See also Taitbout de Marigny, *Three Voyages*, 49–50, 238–39.

58. August von Haxthausen, *Transcaucasia: Sketches of the Nations and Races Between the Black Sea and the Caspian* (London: Chapman and Hall, 1854), 8.

59. Wagner, *Travels in Persia*, 1:47.

60. Ibid., 1:42–43.

Chapter 2: Rule and Resistance

1. Marie Bennigsen Broxup, ed., *North Caucasus Barrier: The Russian Advance towards the Muslim World* (New York: St. Martin's, 1992).

2. Muhammad Tahir al-Qarakhi, "The Shining of Dagestani Swords in Certain Campaigns of Shamil," in *Russian-Muslim Confrontation in the Caucasus: Alternative Visions of the Conflict Between Imam Shamil and the Russians, 1830–1859*, ed. and trans. Thomas Sanders, Ernest Tucker, and Gary Hamburg (London: Routledge Curzon, 2004), 14.

3. Moshe Gammer, *Muslim Resistance to the Tsar: Shamil and the Conquest of Chechnia and Daghestan* (London: Frank Cass, 1994), 58.

4. Gammer, *Muslim Resistance*, 60.

5. John F. Baddeley, *The Russian Conquest of the Caucasus* (1908; reprint, London: Routledge Curzon, 2003), 286.

6. Baddeley, *Russian Conquest*, 287–88.

7. Edmund Spencer, *Travels in Circassia, Krim-Tartary, &c., Including a Steam Voyage Down the Danube, from Vienna to Constantinople, and Round the Black Sea*, 3rd ed., 2 vols. (London: Henry Colburn, 1839), 2:222.

8. "The Wood-Felling," in *Collected Shorter Fiction*, by Leo Tolstoy, trans. Louise and Aylmer Maude and Nigel J. Cooper, 2 vols. (New York: Knopf, 2001), 1:60.

9. N. A. Volkonskii, "Pogrom Chechni v 1852 godu," reprinted in *Rossiia i Kavkaz skvoz' dva stoletiia*, ed. G. G. Lisitsyna and Ia. A. Gordin (St. Petersburg: Zvezda, 2001), 403, 405.

10. Baddeley, *Russian Conquest*, 398.

11. "Dnevnik poruchika N. V. Simanovskogo, 2 aprelia–3 oktiabria 1837 g.," reprinted in Iakov Gordin, *Kavkaz: Zemlia i krov'* (St. Petersburg: Zhurnal "Zvezda," 2000), 404.

12. Leo Tolstoy, *The Cossacks*, trans. Peter Constantine (New York: Modern Library, 2004), 160.

13. A. L. Gizetti, *Sbornik svedenii o poteriakh Kavkazskikh voisk vo vremia voin kavkazsko-gorskikh, persidskikh, turetskikh i v Zakaspiiskom krae* (Tiflis, 1901), quoted in *Shamil': Illiustrirovannaia entsiklopediia*, ed. Sh. M. Kaziev (Moscow: Ekho Kavkaza, 1997), 162.

14. Richard Wilbraham, *Travels in the Trans-Caucasian Provinces of Russia* (London: John Murray, 1839), 230–31.

15. Gammer, *Muslim Resistance*, 98.

16. Baddeley, *Russian Conquest*, 361–63.

17. J. A. Longworth to the Earl of Clarendon, July 20, 1855, in "Correspondence Respecting Circassia: 1855–1857," NAUK, FO881/1443, f. 13.

18. Al-Qarakhi, "The Shining of Dagestani Swords," 11–74.

19. "Pis'mo kadi, alimam, starshinam, vsem zhiteliam Khaidaka i Tabasarana," June 2, 1850, in *100 pisem Shamilia*, ed. Kh. A. Omarov (Makhachkala: Izdatel'stvo DNTs RAN, 1997), 56.

20. Dibir M. Mahomedov, "Shamil's Testament," *Central Asian Survey* 21, no. 3 (2002): 241–42.

21. Quoted in Gammer, *Muslim Resistance*, 140.

22. L. Hamilton Rhinelander, "Russia's Imperial Policy: The Administration of the Caucasus in the First Half of the Nineteenth Century," *Canadian Slavonic Papers* 17, nos. 2–3 (1975): 218–35.

23. Iakov Gordin, ed., *Osada Kavkaza: Vospominaniia uchastnikov Kavkazskoi voiny XIX veka* (St. Petersburg: Zvezda, 2000), 406, n. 1. For firsthand accounts, see *Darginskaia tragediia: Vospominaniia uchastnikov Kavkazskoi voiny XIX veka* (St. Petersburg: Zvezda, 2001).

24. Gammer, *Muslim Resistance*, 155.

25. W. E. D. Allen, *Béled-es-Siba: Sketches and Essays of Travel and History* (London: Macmillan, 1925), 143–63.

26. See the mission reports and correspondence in NAUK, FO195/443.

27. Gammer, *Muslim Resistance*, 277.

28. "Pis'mo Shamilia Mukhammadaminu," November 24, 1859, in Omarov, ed., *100 pisem Shamilia*, 231.

29. Quoted in Gammer, *Muslim Resistance*, 293.

30. Hadji Hayder Hassan and Kustan Ogli Ismael, "To the Queen from the Circassian Deputies," August 26, 1862, in Stewart E. Rolland, *Circassia: Speech of Stewart E. Rolland, at a Public Meeting Held at the Corn Exchange, Preston, October 1, 1862, to Receive the Deputies from Circassia* (London: Hardwicke, 1862), 3.

31. The Russian government never denied that it intended to remove the Circassians from the coastal areas and the uplands, but officials maintained that the point was to allow colonization of the tribal lands by Cossacks and Russian settlers, groups deemed more politically reliable than the highlander natives. The distinction between being voluntarily relocated and forcibly exiled must have been lost on the natives themselves. See L. V. Burykina, *Pereselencheskoe dvizhenie na severo-zapagnyi Kavakaz v 90-e gody XVIII-90-e gody XIX veka* (Maikop: Adygeiskii gosurdarstvennyi universitet, 2002). See also Lord Napier (St. Petersburg) to Earl Russell, May 17, 1864, NAUK, FO881/1259, f. 7.

32. For various accounts, see I. Drozdov, "Posledniaia bor'ba s gortsami na zapadnom Kavkaze," *KS* 2 (1877): 387–457. See also V. Soltan, "Voennyia deistviia v Kubanskoi oblasti s 1861-go po 1864-i god," *KS* 5 (1880): 345–470.

33. Lord Napier to Earl Russell, May 23, 1864, NAUK, FO 881/1259, ff. 11–12.

34. "Bulletin du Caucase," *Journal de St. Pétersbourg*, May 19, 1864, quoted in NAUK, FO881/1259, f. 11.

35. "Doklad Komissii po delu o pereselenii gortsev v Turtsiiu, 18 fevralia 1865 goda, g. Tiflis," reprinted in T. Kh. Kumykov, *Vyselenie adygov v Turtsiiu: Posledstvie Kavkazskoi voiny* (Nalchik: El'brus, 1994), 21–46.

36. Lord Napier to Earl Russell, May 23, 1864, NAUK, FO881/1259, f. 13.

37. The lower figures are given in a British Foreign Office report dated May 1864 and cited in "Memorandum Respecting Circassian Emigrants in Turkey," NAUK, FO 881/3065, f. 6. Mark Pinson estimated the figure at 500,000; see his "Demographic Warfare: An Aspect of Ottoman and Russian Policy, 1854–1866" (Ph.D. diss., Harvard University, 1970), 99. That figure is generally accepted by contemporary Russian and Caucasus historians. Ottoman sources seem to put the figure at closer to 300,000 for the 1863–64 period alone; see Bedri Habiçoğlu, *Kafkasya'dan Anadolu'ya göçler ve iskanları* (Istanbul: Nart, 1993). Total Muslim emigration from Russia, including Crimean Tatars and Caucasus Muslims, has been estimated at between

700,000 and 900,000 from 1856 to 1864. See Alan W. Fisher, "Emigration of Muslims from the Russian Empire in the Years After the Crimean War," *Jahrbücher für Geschichte Osteuropas*, 35, no. 3 (1987): 356–71. For a careful discussion of available sources, including those that give the two million figure, see A. V. Kushkhabiev, *Cherkesskaia diaspora v arabskikh stranakh (XIX–XX vv.)* (Nalchik: K.B.N.Ts., Russian Academy of Sciences, 1997), 42–44.

38. Consul Stevens (Trebizond), December 21, 1863, quoted in "Memorandum Respecting Circassian Emigrants in Turkey," NAUK, FO881/3065, f. 3; Consul Stevens (Trebizond) to Earl Russell, February 17, 1864, NAUK, FO881/1259, f. 1; Stevens to Russell, May 19, 1864, NAUK, FO881/1259, f. 14; Consul Cumberbatch (Smyrna) to Earl Russell, September 23, 1864, NAUK, FO97/424, f. 1; Consul Dickson (Constantinople) to Stuart, November 4, 1864, NAUK, FO97/424, f. 2; Dickson to Stuart, October 9, 1864, NAUK, FO97/424, f. 2.

39. Consul Clipperton (Kerch) to Earl Russell, May 10, 1864, NAUK, FO97/424, f. 6.

40. Sir H. Bulwer (Constantinople) to Earl Russell, May 3, 1864, NAUK, FO881/1259, f. 5.

41. Consul Dickson (Soukoum-Kalé) to Earl Russell, February 22, 1864, NAUK, FO881/1259, f. 2.

42. A. P. Berzhe, *Kratkii obzor gorskikh plemen na Kavkaze* (1858; reprint Nalchik: n.p., 1992), 5–6.

43. My calculations are based on *Obshchii svod po imperii rezul'tatov razrabotki dannykh Pervoi vseobshchei perepisi naseleniia, proizvedennoi 28 ianvaria 1897 goda*, ed. N. A. Troinitskii, 2 vols. (St. Petersburg: n. p., 1905). See also "Statisticheskiia svedeniia o kavkazskikh gortsakh, sostoiashchikh v voenno-narodnom upravlenii," *SSKG* 1 (1868): 14 (separate pagination).

44. Drozdov, "Posledniaia bor'ba," 457.

45. Sir H. Bulwer (Constantinople) to Earl Russell, May 3, 1864, NAUK, FO881/1259, f. 6.

46. Mark Pinson, "Ottoman Colonization of the Circassians in Rumili After the Crimean War," *Études balkaniques* 8, no. 3 (1972): 79.

Chapter 3: The Imaginary Caucasus

1. V. A. Potto, *Kavkazskaia voina*, 5 vols. (1885–87; reprint, Stavropol: Kavkazskii krai, 1994), 1:7.

2. Johann Anton Güldenstädt, *Reisen durch Russland und im Caucasischen Gebürge*, 2 vols. (St. Petersburg: Kayserlichen Akademie der Wissenschaften, 1787, 1791). For a Russian translation, see *Puteshestvie po Kavkazu v 1770–1773 gg.*, trans. T. K. Shafranovskii and ed. Iu. Iu. Karpov (St. Petersburg: Peterburgskoe vostokovedenie, 2002).

3. T. K. Shafranovskii and Iu. Iu. Karpov, "Ot perevodchika i redaktora," in Güldenstädt, *Puteshestvie po Kavkazu*, 13–20.

4. Julius von Klaproth, *Travels in the Caucasus and Georgia, Performed in the Years 1807 and 1808*, trans. Frederic Shoberl (London: Henry Colburn, 1814), 4.

5. Ibid., 5.

6. Julius von Klaproth, *Reise in den Kaukasus und nach Georgien*, 2 vols. (Halle: Hallisches Weisenhaus, 1812–14). All text references are to the English edition.

7. Klaproth, *Travels in the Caucasus and Georgia*, 344.

8. Selections from Güldenstädt's work had been published. See, e.g., Johann Anton Güldenstädt, *Geograficheskoe i statisticheskoe opisanie Gruzii i Kavkaza* (St. Petersburg: Imperatorskaia Akademiia Nauk, 1809).

9. Semyon Bronevskii, *Noveishiia geograficheskiia i istoricheskiia izvestiia o Kavkaze*, 2 vols. (Moscow: Tipografiia S. Selivanovskago, 1823).

10. Ibid., 1:xxvii.

11. Quoted in Semyon Mikhailovich Bronevskii, *Istoricheskiia vypiski o snosheniiakh Rossii s Persieiu, Gruzieiu i voobshche s gorskimi narodami, v Kavkaze obitaiushchimi, so vremen Ivana Vasil'evicha donyne*, ed. I. K. Pavlova (St. Petersburg: Russian Academy of Sciences, St. Petersburg Branch of the Institute of Oriental Studies, 1996), 179 n. 1. On Pushkin, see 181 n. 10.

12. Quoted in T. J. Binyon, *Pushkin: A Biography* (New York: Knopf, 2003), 113.

13. I. K. Pavlova, "O sochinenii Bronevskogo," in Bronevskii, *Istoricheskiia vypiski*, 11.

14. Susan Layton, *Russian Literature and Empire: Conquest of the Caucasus from Pushkin to Tolstoy* (Cambridge: Cambridge University Press, 1994), 24.

15. Ibid., 24–34, 103.

16. See, e.g., the account of one Lieutenant Simanovskii, "Dnevnik poruchika N. V. Simanovskogo, 2 aprelia–3 oktiabria 1837 g., Kavkaz," in Iakov Gordin, *Kavkaz: Zemlia i krov'* (St. Petersburg: Zhurnal "Zvezda," 2000), 377–429.

17. "The Poet's Death," in *Major Poetical Works*, by Mikhail Lermontov, trans. Anatoly Liberman (Minneapolis: University of Minnesota Press, 1983), 107–11.

18. "My Native Land," in *Major Poetical Works*, 239.

19. "The Debate," in *Major Poetical Works*, 255–59.

20. See Susan Layton, "Ironies of Ethnic Identity," in *Lermontov's "A Hero of Our Time": A Critical Companion*, ed. Lewis Bagby (Evanston, Ill.: Northwestern University Press, 2002), 64–84.

21. "Mtsyri," in *Major Poetical Works*, 311–29.

22. Mikhail Lermontov, *A Hero of Our Time*, trans. Paul Foote (London: Penguin, 1996), 54.

23. Leo Tolstoy, "The Wood-Felling," in *Collected Shorter Fiction*, by Leo Tolstoy, trans. Louise and Aylmer Maude and Nigel J. Cooper, 2 vols. (New York: Knopf, 2001), 1:49–50.

24. Ibid., 1:53–54.

25. Leo Tolstoy, *The Cossacks*, trans. Peter Constantine (New York: Modern Library, 2004), 13.

26. Ibid., 88.

27. Leo Tolstoy, *Hadji Murad*, in *Collected Shorter Fiction*, 2:607–8.

28. J. Buchan Telfer, *The Crimea and Transcaucasia*, 2 vols. (London: Henry S. King, 1876), 1:291.

29. Max von Thielmann, *Journey in the Caucasus, Persia, and Turkey in Asia*, trans. Charles Heneage, 2 vols. (London: John Murray, 1875), 1:256–57.

30. Jacques-François Gamba, *Voyage dans la Russie méridionale, et particulièrement dans les provinces situées au-delà du Caucase, fait depuis 1820 jusqu'en 1824*, 2 vols. (Paris: C. J. Trouvé, 1826), 2:12. See also Ebenezer Henderson, *Biblical Researches and Travels in Russia* (London: James Nisbet, 1826), 475–76.

31. Alexander Pushkin, *A Journey to Arzrum*, trans. Birgitta Ingemanson (Ann Arbor, Mich.: Ardis, 1974), 20–21. See also Robert Lyall, *Travels in Russia, the Krimea, the Caucasus, and Georgia*, 2 vols. (London: T. Cadell, 1825), 1:457–59.

32. Frederika von Freygang, *Letters from the Caucasus and Georgia* (London: John Murray, 1823), 35.

33. Docteur Kimmel, *Lettres écrites dans un voyage de Moscou au Caucase* (Moscow: N. S. Vsevolojsky, 1812), 44. See also Lyall, *Travels in Russia*, 1:500.

34. Thomas Alcock, *Travels in Russia, Persia, Turkey, and Greece, in 1828–9* (London: E. Clarke and Son, 1831), 26–27.

35. John Abercromby, *A Trip Through the Eastern Caucasus* (London: Edward Stanford, 1889), 294–95.

36. Kimmel, *Lettres*, 58.

37. Pushkin, *A Journey to Arzrum*, 19.

38. Il'ia Radozhitskii, "Doroga ot reki Dona do Georgievska na prostranstve 500 verst," *Otechestvennyia zapiski* 15 (1823): 344.

39. These numbers are based on my count of sources listed in the following: Gordin, *Kavkaz*; M. Miansarof, *Bibliographia caucasica et transcaucasica* (1874–75; reprint, Amsterdam: Meridian, 1967; and V. K. Zelenin, *Bibliograficheskii ukazatel' russkoi etnograficheskoi literatury o vneshnem byte narodov Rossii, 1700–1910 gg.* (St. Petersburg: Tipografiia A. V. Orlova, 1913).

40. G. P. Dolzhenko, *Istoriia turizma v dorevoliutsionnoi Rossii i SSSR* (Rostov: Izdatel'stvo Rostovskogo universiteta, 1988), 21–22. For early detailed mapping of the region, see "Podrobnaia karta Kavkazskogo kraia" (1842), RGB-OKI, KO 4/V-S; "Marshrutnaia karta Kavkazskogo kraia" (1847), RGB-OKI, KO 13/V-20; and "Karta Kavkazskogo kraia" (1847), RGB-OKI, KO 14/IV-3.

41. V. A. Merkulov, *Putevoditel' po goram Kavkaza* (St. Petersburg: Izd. Krymsko-kavkazskago gornago kluba, 1904).

42. Clinton Dent, "The Ascent of Tetnuld Tau," *Alpine Journal* 13 (1886–88): 242.

43. Douglas W. Freshfield, "Search and Travel in the Caucasus," *Proceedings of the Royal Geographical Society and Monthly Record of Geography*, n.s., 12, no. 5 (1890): 258. See also Telfer, *The Crimea and Transcaucasia*, 1:vii.

44. Douglas W. Freshfield, *The Exploration of the Caucasus*, 2 vols. (London: Edward Arnold, 1896), 1:4.

45. Ibid., 1:6.

46. Ibid., 2:171.

47. Ibid., 2:171–72.

48. Freshfield, "Search and Travel," 277–78.

49. For an analysis of the controversy surrounding the Circassian's achievement—long denied by Freshfield and other British climbers—see Audrey Salkeld and José Luis Bermúdez, *On the Edge of Empire: Mountaineering in the Caucasus* (Seattle.: The Mountaineers, 1993), 241–44.

50. The names of Caucasus peaks can be confusing since modern names do not always correspond to their nineteenth-century equivalents. The modern Koshtan was known as Dykh-Tau, while the peak now known as Dykh-Tau was variously called Koshtan, Guluku, or other names. To further confuse matters, the modern Shkhara was also sometimes called Koshtan. One of Freshfield's contributions was to help fix the names of these peaks.

51. My account of the Koshtan expedition is based on the following sources: Clinton Dent, "The History of the Search Expedition to the Caucasus," *Alpine Journal* 15 (1890–91): 26–39; Freshfield, "Search and Travel," 257–86; Freshfield, *Exploration of the Caucasus*, 2:59–92; and reports and letters published in the *Times* (London) on October 6, 15, 24, December 8, 31, 1888, and August 17, 1889.

52. Clinton Dent to Andreas Fischer, October 11, 1888, Andreas Fischer Papers, ACA, C126/8.

53. See Donkin's account in the *Alpine Journal* for May 13, 1887, which is reprinted in Salkeld and Bermúdez, *On the Edge of Empire*, 50–66.

54. See Douglas W. Freshfield, *Travels in the Central Caucasus and Bashan* (London: Longmans, Green, 1869). In subsequent climbs, however, Freshfield found the locals to be rather more accommodating. See Freshfield, *Exploration of the Caucasus*, 2:46.

55. Diary of H. Fox, Tuesday, August 28, 1888, ACA, D93 (typescript); and Freshfield, "Search and Travel in the Caucasus," 265–66.

56. Clinton Dent, letter, *Times* (London), August 17, 1889.

57. Freshfield, "Search and Travel," 280.

58. Ibid., 282.

59. John Hunt and Christopher Brasher, *The Red Snows* (London: Travel Book Club, 1960), 74–75; Salkeld and Bermúdez. *On the Edge of Empire*, 103.

60. Edmund Spencer, *Travels in Circassia, Krim-Tartary, &c., Including a Steam Voyage Down the Danube, from Vienna to Constantinople, and Round the Black Sea*, 3rd ed., 2 vols. (London: Henry Colburn, 1839), 2:267.

61. *Dundee Advertiser*, October 24, 1862, quoted in David Urquhart, *The Secret of Russia in the Caspian and Euxine: The Circassian War as Affecting the Insurrection in Poland* (London: Robert Hardwicke, 1863), 10–11. See also G. Poulett Cameron, *Personal Adventures and Excursions in Georgia, Circassia, and Russia*, 2 vols. (London: Henry Colburn, 1845), 1:189.

62. Spencer, *Travels in Circassia*, 2:206. See also Cameron, *Personal Adventures*, 1:334–36.

63. Bronevskii, *Noveishiia*, 2:101–2.

64. E. Demidoff, Prince of San Donato, *Hunting Trips in the Caucasus* (London: Rowland Ward, 1898), 133–34.

65. Tolstoy, *The Cossacks*, 12.

66. Freshfield, *Travels in the Central Caucasus*, 84.

67. Irakli Makharadze and Akaki Chkhaidze, *Wild West Georgians* (Tbilisi: New Media Tbilisi, n.d.).

68. Phineas T. Barnum, *Struggles and Triumphs: or, Forty Years' Recollections* (1869; reprint, New York: Arno Press, 1970), 580.

69. Ibid., 581.

70. Barnum to Greenwood, May 14, 1864, in *Selected Letters of P. T. Barnum*, ed. A. H. Saxon (New York: Columbia University Press, 1983), 125, 127.

71. *Biographical Sketch of the Circassian Girl, Zalumma Agra; or, Star of the East* (New York: Barnum and Van Amburgh Museum and Menagerie Co., 1868).

72. On the cultural meanings of the Circassian beauties, see Linda Frost, *Never One Nation: Freaks, Savages, and Whiteness in U.S. Popular Culture, 1850–1877* (Minneapolis: University of Minnesota Press, 2005), 62–85.

73. Pushkin, *A Journey to Arzrum*, 15–16.

74. See Thomas M. Barrett, "Southern Living (in Captivity): The Caucasus in Russian Popular Culture," *Journal of Popular Culture* 31, no. 4 (1998). See also Jeffrey Brooks, *When Russia Learned to Read: Literacy and Popular Literature, 1861–1917*, 2nd ed. (Evanston, Ill.: Northwestern University Press, 2003).

Chapter 4: Nations and Revolutions

1. Semen Bronevskii, *Noveishiia geograficheskiia i istoricheskiia izvestiia o Kavkaze*, 2 vols. (Moscow: Tipografiia S. Selivanovskago, 1823), 2:38–39. A graphic representation is provided in "Karta Kavkazskikh zemel' s chastiiu Velikoi Armenii izdannaia Semenom Bronevskim" (1823), RGB-OKI, KO 12/I-34.

2. Austin Jersild, *Orientalism and Empire: North Caucasus Mountain Peoples and the Georgian Frontier, 1845–1917* (Montreal: McGill-Queen's University Press, 2002), 75.

3. Collections of these materials can be found in *SMOMPK* and *SSKG*, a genuine treasure trove of information on social practices, folklore, and local history that would have been lost if not for the dedication of amateurs and academics.

4. Gustav Radde, *Kratkii ocherk istorii razvitiia Kavkazskago muzeia* (Tiflis: Tipografiia A. A. Mikhel'sona, 1892), 61–64.

5. Oliver Wardrop, *The Kingdom of Georgia: Travel in a Land of Women, Wine, and Song* (1888; reprint, London: Luzac and Co., 1977), 15–16. For photographs of the mural and the exhibits, see *Kollektsii Kavkazskago muzeiia*, 6 vols. (Tiflis: Tipografiia Kantseliarii Namestnika Ego Imperatorskago Velichestva na Kavkaze, 1912), vol. 6.

6. Census data are taken from N. A. Troinitskii, *Obshchii svod po imperii rezul'tatov razrabotki dannykh Pervoi vseobshchei perepisi naseleniia, proizvedennoi 28 ianvaria 1897 goda*, 2 vols. (St. Petersburg: n.p., 1905).

7. I. N. Berezin, *Puteshestvie po Dagestanu i Zakavkaz'iu*, 2nd ed. (Kazan: Universitetskaia tipografiia, 1850), pt. 3, 112–13.

8. Frederika von Freygang, *Letters from the Caucasus and Georgia* (London: John Murray, 1823), 128.

9. G. Poulett Cameron, *Personal Adventures and Excursions in Georgia, Circassia, and Russia*, 2 vols. (London: Henry Colburn, 1845), 1:83.

10. Augustus H. Mounsey, *A Journey through the Caucasus and the Interior of Persia* (London: Smith, Elder, 1872), 37–50; James Bryce, *Transcaucasia and Ararat, Being Notes of a Vacation Tour in the Autumn of 1876*, 4th rev. ed. (London: Macmillan, 1896), 145–51, 158.

11. John Abercromby, *A Trip Through the Eastern Caucasus* (London: Edward Stanford, 1889), 1.

12. Iu. D. Anchabadze and N. G. Volkova, *Staryi Tbilisi: Gorod i gorozhane v XIX veke* (Moscow: Nauka, 1990), 24. These figures apply to the city itself, not its outskirts.

13. Judith Pallot and Denis J. B. Shaw, *Landscape and Settlement in Romanov Russia, 1613–1917* (Oxford: Clarendon Press, 1990), 257; Ronald Grigor Suny, *The Making of the Georgian Nation* (Bloomington: Indiana University Press, 1988), 153.

14. Anchabadze and Volkova, *Staryi Tbilisi*, 73.

15. Ibid., 29.

16. Wardrop, *Kingdom of Georgia*, 13–15.

17. See Stephen F. Jones, *Socialism in Georgian Colors: The European Road to Social Democracy, 1883–1917* (Cambridge, Mass.: Harvard University Press, 2005).

18. D. Gambashidze, *The Caucasian Petroleum Industry and Its Importance for Eastern Europe and Asia* (London: Anglo-Georgian Society, 1918), 8–9.

19. Harry Luke, *Cities and Men: An Autobiography*, 3 vols. (London: Geoffrey Bles, 1953), 2:108.

20. Audrey L. Altstadt, *The Azerbaijani Turks: Power and Identity Under Russian Rule* (Stanford, Calif.: Hoover Institution Press, 1992), 29–30. See also J. D. Henry, *Baku: An Eventful History* (London: Archibald Constable, 1907), 11.

21. Quoted in Henry, *Baku*, 156.

22. Luke, *Cities and Men*, 2:108. For another firsthand account, see Luigi Villari, *Fire and Sword in the Caucasus* (London: T. Fisher Unwin, 1906).

23. W. E. D. Allen and Paul Muratoff, *Caucasian Battlefields: A History of the Wars on the Turco-Caucasian Border, 1828–1921* (Cambridge: Cambridge University Press, 1953), 239.

24. Ibid., 241.

25. Ibid., 283–84.

26. See Justin McCarthy, *Death and Exile: The Ethnic Cleansing of Ottoman Muslims, 1821–1922* (Princeton, N.J.: Darwin Press, 1995).

27. Troinitskii, *Obshchii svod po imperii rezul'tatov*, 1:256, 259.

28. George A. Bournoutian, "The Ethnic Composition and the Socio-Economic Condition of Eastern Armenia in the First Half of the Nineteenth Century," in *Transcaucasia, Nationalism, and Social Change: Essays in the History of Armenia, Azerbaijan, and Georgia*, ed. Ronald Grigor Suny, rev. ed. (Ann Arbor: University of Michigan Press, 1996), 78–80.

29. Allen and Muratoff, *Caucasian Battlefields*, 439.

30. "Iz protokola pervago zasedaniia Natsional'nago Soveta Gruzii," in *Dokumenty i materialy po vneshnei politike Zakavkaz'ia i Gruzii* (Tiflis: Tipografiia Pravitel'stva Gruzinskoi respubliki, 1919; reprint, Tbilisi, 1990), 332–33.

31. "Akt nezavisimosti Gruzii," in *Dokumenty i materialy po vneshnei politike Zakavkaz'ia i Gruzii*, 336–38.

32. Anton Denikin, *Put' russkogo ofitsera* (Moscow: Bagrius, 2002), 459.

33. "Raspisanie gosudarstvennykh dokhodov Gruzinskoi Respubliki," GRR, reel 8.

34. "Autobiography," Robert Pierpont Blake Collection, HIA, Box 1, f. 30. On the particular problems of Khevsureti, see also Odette Keun, *In the Land of the Golden Fleece: Through Independent Menshevist Georgia*, trans. Helen Jessiman (London: Bodley Head, 1924), 45.

35. Karl Kautsky, *Georgia: A Social-Democratic Peasant Republic* (London: International Bookshops Ltd., 1921), 8.

36. Oliver Wardrop to Margrethe Wardrop, October 5 and November 3, 1919, OWP, no ff. See also C. E. Bechhofer, *In Denikin's Russia and the Caucasus, 1919–1920* (1921; reprint, New York: Arno Press, 1971), chap. 2.

37. Keun, *In the Land of the Golden Fleece*, 179–80.

38. L. C. Dunsterville, *The Adventures of Dunsterforce* (London: Edward Arnold, 1920), 219.

39. The definitive history of the Baku events is by Ronald Grigor Suny, *The Baku Commune, 1917–1918: Class and Nationality in the Russian Revolution* (Princeton, N.J.: Princeton University Press, 1972). Ronald Sinclair, a British agent in Transcaspia, was

among those accused of having masterminded the plot. See his papers in BL, MSS Eur C313/12.

40. "Spisok chlenov Azerbaidzhanskogo parlamenta," in *Azerbaidzhanskaia Respublika: Dokumenty i materialy, 1918–1920 gg.*, ed. Dzh. B. Guliev (Baku: ELM, 1998), 214–16.

41. "Spisok studentov, napravlennykh na uchebu za rubezh," in Guliev, ed., *Azerbaidzhanskaia Respublika*, 413–17.

42. "Kopiia diagrammy raskhodnogo biudzheta Azerbaidzhanskoi respubliki po proektu rospisi na 1919 god," in Guliev, ed., *Azerbaidzhanskaia Respublika*, 132.

43. "Rech' predsedatelia Natsional'nogo soveta M.-E. Rasulzade, 7 dekabria 1918 g.," in Guliev, ed., *Azerbaidzhanskaia Respublika*, 92.

44. "Report on Trans-Caucasia and Daghestan," Tiflis Party, Russian Field Mission, American Commission to Negotiate the Peace, Tiflis (April 13, 1919), Joseph C. Green Collection, HIA, Box 4, File "Caucasus and Daghestan," f. 46.

45. Oliver Wardrop to Margrethe Wardrop, October 16, 1919, OWP, no ff.

46. Minutes, Inter-Departmental Conference on Middle Eastern Affairs, March 6, 1919, NAUK, FO 371/3661, f. 385.

47. Oliver Wardrop to Margrethe Wardrop, January 11 and 18, 1920, OWP, no ff.

48. Oliver Wardrop to Margrethe Wardrop, February 11, 1920, OWP, no ff.

49. The name of the republic is variously rendered in historical sources as the "mountain republic" or the "highlander republic."

50. At one point there was even talk of offering the presidency of the republic to the Oxford don Francis "Sligger" Urquhart, a descendant of David Urquhart, one of the British spies active in Circassia in the 1830s. See Luke, *Cities and Men*, 2:198.

51. Mehmet Kiamil to the British government, December 18, 1918, NAUK, FO 371/3667, f. 161.

52. See the telegrams from Mehmet Jafarov, the Azerbajani foreign minister, to Oliver Wardrop, Sept. 20, 1919–Oct. 2, 1919, BL, IOR/L/PS/11/158/P6846.

53. David A. Sagirashvili, "Kak proizoshlo priznanie nezavisimosti Gruzii sovetskim pravitel'stvom," unpublished MS (Munich, 1953), quoted in Roy Stanley de Lon, "Stalin and Social Democracy, 1905–1922: The Political Diaries of David A. Sagirashvili" (Ph.D. diss., Georgetown University, 1974), 46–47.

54. Oliver Wardrop to Margrethe Wardrop, March 28, 1920, OWP, no ff.

55. Noe Jordania, Evgeni Gegechkori, Nikolai Chkheidze, and Noe Ramishvili, "Vsem sotsialisticheskim partiiam i rabochim organizatsiiam," Constantinople, March 27, 1921.

56. Secretary of Lord Curzon to Wardrop, June 23, 1923, WC, no ff.

57. Chenkeli to the French Minister of War, June 10, 1921, GRR, reel 98.

58. NAUK, FO 372/1581, f. 14 verso; FO 372/1581, f. 19; FO 371/7726, f. 172; FO 371/7728, ff. 116–28, 236–41; FO 371/9275, ff. 88–119.

59. On the work of these groups, see the following: Charles Warren Hostler, *Turkism and the Soviets* (London: George Allen and Unwin, 1957); Etienne Copeaux, "Le Mouvement 'Prométhéen,'" *Cahiers d'études sur la Méditerranée orientale et le monde turco-iranien* 16 (1993): 1–36; Mitat Çelikpala, "The North Caucasian Emigrés Between the Two World Wars," in *Ottoman Borderlands: Issues, Personalities, and Political Change*, ed. Kemal H. Karpat and Robert W. Zens (Madison: University of Wisconsin Press, 2004), 287–314.

60. Hostler, *Turkism and the Soviets*, 158. On the Polish role in Prometheanism, see Timothy Snyder, *Sketches from a Secret War* (New Haven, Conn.: Yale University Press, 2005).

61. Noe Jordania, "À la nation géorgienne," *Prométhée* (March 1931): 3–4.

62. Gotthard Jäschke, "La Transcaucasie—l'une des parties de l'impérialisme rouge russe," *Prométhée* (January 1936): 9.

63. "Pacte de la Confédération du Caucase," *Prométhée* (July 1934): 3–6; O. N. M. Kritchinski, "Historique de l'idée de la Confédération Caucasienne," *Prométhée* (March 1935): 6–8.

64. B. Bilatti, "Le Centralisme national comme garantie du succès," *Prométhée* (August 1937): 24–30.

65. "V TsIK SSRG" (September 6, 1930), GSCACH, f. 284, op. 3, d. 434, l. 5.

66. "Appel aux peuples du Caucase," *Prométhée* (May 1937): 1–2.

67. My account of the murder of Archbishop Tourian is based on reports published in the *New York Times* on the following dates: December 25–29, 1933; January 1–3, 11, 15, 19, 24–25; April 8–9, 30; June 12–13, 15, 20, 27–28; July 14, 25, 1934; March 18; April 10, 1935.

68. "2 Tourian Slayers Condemned to Die," *New York Times*, July 25, 1934.

69. Report by Laurence Collier of Northern Department, March 9, 1939, NAUK, FO 371/29635, f. 225. For the émigrés' activities following the war, see the periodical *Ob"edinennyi Kavkaz*, which was published in Munich beginning in 1950.

70. Noe Jordania, "Staline," *L'Écho de la lutte*, no. 65 (October 1936), Boris I. Nicolaevsky Collection, HIA, Box 144, File 3.

71. Robert Service, *Stalin: A Biography* (Cambridge, Mass.: Harvard University Press, 2005), 27.

72. Joseph Stalin, "Marxism and the National Question," in *Marxism and the National Question: Selected Writings and Speeches* (New York: International Publishers, 1942).

73. Ibid., 12.

74. Ibid. 23.

75. Ibid., 54.

76. "Liste des fusillés," Irakli Tsereteli Papers, Boris I. Nicolaevsky Collection, HIA, Box 32, File 8.

77. Armenian Refugees (Lord Mayor's) Fund, "Transcaucasia," February 1922, NAUK, FO 371/7728, ff. 190–207.

78. V. I. Lenin, "Tovarishcham kommunistam Azerbaidzhana, Gruzii, Armenii, Dagestana, Gorskoi Respubliki," in *Polnoe sobranie sochinenii*, 5th ed., 55 vols. (Moscow: Izdatel'stvo politicheskoi literatury, 1958–65), 43:199.

79. David A. Sagirashvili, *Memorias*, translated in Stanley de Lon, "Stalin and Social Democracy," 126.

80. Al. Todorskii, *Krasnaia armiia v gorakh* (Moscow: Voennyi vestnik, 1924), 159.

81. Terry Martin, *The Affirmative Action Empire: Nations and Nationalism in the Soviet Union, 1923–1939* (Ithaca, N.Y.: Cornell University Press, 2001).

82. V. K. Gardanov, *Kul'tura i byt narodov severnogo Kavkaza, 1917–1967* (Moscow: Nauka, 1968), 200–206.

83. Lavrenti Beria, *K voprosu ob istorii bol'shevistskikh organizatsii v Zakavkaz'e* (Moscow: Partizdat Ts.K. V.K.P.(b)., 1935).

84. Anne Applebaum, *Gulag: A History* (New York: Doubleday, 2003), 578–86. See also Oleg V. Khlevniuk, *The History of the Gulag* (New Haven, Conn.: Yale University Press, 2004).

85. Suny, *Making of the Georgian Nation*, 278–79.

86. Quoted in N. F. Bugai, *L. Beriia-I. Stalinu: "Soglasno Vashemu ukazaniiu..."* (Moscow: AIRO-XX, 1995), 59.

87. Earl F. Ziemke and Magna E. Bauer, *Moscow to Stalingrad: Decision in the East* (Washington, D.C.: U.S. Army Center of Military History, 1987), 372–73.

88. Bugai, *L. Beriia-I. Stalinu*, 62, 106, 132. Others place the figures rather higher: 393,000 Chechens, 91,000 Ingush, and 38,000 Balkars. See Pavel Polian, *Against Their Will: The History and Geography of Forced Migrations in the USSR* (Budapest: Central European University Press, 2004), 331. Contemporary documents give various numbers, some as high as 496,000 Chechens and Ingush, 68,000 Karachai, and 38,000 Balkars. See "Spravka ob otdele spetsposelenii NKVD SSSR," September 5, 1944, reprinted in N. L. Pobol' and P. M. Polian, eds., *Stalinskie deportatsii, 1928–1953* (Moscow: Materik, 2005), 552.

89. "Chislennost' spetspereselentsev, ranee sluzhivshikh v Krasnoi Armii," reprinted in Pobol' and Polian, eds., *Stalinskie deportatsii*, 765–66.

90. "Deportatsionnye kampanii i deportatsionnye operatsii v SSSR (1918–1952)," in Ibid., 789–98.

91. "Spravka o kolichestve vyselentsev i spetsposelentsev po sosstoianiiu na 15 iulia 1949 g.," reprinted in Pobol' and Polian, eds., *Stalinskie deportatsii*, 762.

92. Lavrenti Beria to State Defense Committee, March 1, 1944, reprinted in N. F. Bugai, ed., *Iosif Stalin—Lavrentiiu Berii: "Ikh nado deportirovat'"* (Moscow: Druzhba narodov, 1992), 105.

93. Joint memorandum by British and U.S. embassies, Moscow, NAUK, FO 181/1061, no ff.

94. "A Visit to Daghestan," NAUK, FO 371/94908 [1950], f. 6.

Chapter 5: Time of Troubles

1. *Bakinskii rabochii*, June 27, 1978.

2. Iu. A. Aidaev, ed., *Chechentsy: Istoriia i sovremennost'* (Moscow: Mir domu tvoemu, 1996), 185–90.

3. I wish to thank Ghia Nodia for conversations that inspired these ideas.

4. Statistical information has been derived from the following: *Itogi vsesoiuznoi perepisi naseleniia 1959 goda: SSSR* (Moscow: Gosstatizdat, 1962); *Itogi vsesoiuznoi perepisi naseleniia 1979 goda* (Moscow: Goskomitet po statistike, 1989), 4:1, bks 1, 3; *Itogi vsesoiuznoi perepisi naseleniia 1989 goda* (Minneapolis, Minn.: East View, 1998); and *Demograficheskii ezhegodnik SSSR: 1990* (Moscow: Finansy i statistiki, 1990). For a detailed treatment, see Paul B. Henze, "The Demography of the Caucasus According to 1989 Soviet Census Data," *Central Asian Survey* 10, nos. 1–2 (1991): 147–70.

5. John Steinbeck, *A Russian Journal* (New York: Viking, 1948), 195.

6. *Pravda*, October 29, 1983; Liz Fuller, "Ten Georgians Sentenced for Protesting Against Celebrating Bicentennial of Russian-Georgian Treaty" (March 26, 1984), SRA 300/80/1/227.

7. Eduard Shevardnadze, *The Future Belongs to Freedom* (New York: Free Press, 1991), 172–73.

8. Josephine Woll and Denise J. Youngblood, *Repentance* (London: I. B. Tauris, 2001), 91.

9. The region is known today by a variety of names, including Artsakh (Armenian) and Nagorno-Karabakhskaia Respublika (Russian). Nagorno-Karabakh is most frequently encountered in English.

10. *Itogi vsesoiuznoi perepisi naseleniia 1979 goda*, 4:1, bk 3, 50.

11. V. A. Zolotarev, ed., *Rossiia (SSSR) v lokal'nykh voinakh i voennykh konfliktakh vtoroi poloviny XX veka* (Moscow: Institute of Military History, Russian Ministry of Defense, 2000), 45.

12. All these figures are disputed. For discussions of the various arguments, see the following: special issue of the journal *Accord* (September 1999), published by Conciliation Resources, www.c-r.org; "Nagorno-Karabakh: Viewing the Conflict from the Ground," International Crisis Group Report No. 166 (September 14, 2005), www.crisisgroup.org; and Dennis Sammut, "Population Displacement in the Caucasus: An Overview," *Central Asian Survey* 20, no. 1 (2001): 55–62.

13. *The Military Balance, 2000–2001* (London: International Institute for Strategic Studies, 2000), 100; and *The Military Balance, 2005–2006* (London: International Institute for Strategic Studies, 2006), 423.

14. I owe this felicitous phrasing to Georgi Derluguian, *Bourdieu's Secret Admirer in the Caucasus* (Chicago: University of Chicago Press, 2005).

15. K. G. Dzugaev, ed., *Iuzhnaia Osetiia: 10 let respublike* (Vladikavkaz: Iryston, 2000), 4.

16. I wish to thank Aram Grigorian for this reference.

17. Osip Mandelstam, *Journey to Armenia*, trans. Sidney Monas (San Francisco: George F. Ritchie, 1979), 39.

18. See Zviad Gamsakhurdia, *The Spiritual Mission of Georgia* (Tbilisi: Ganatleba, 1991); idem, *Za nezavisimuiu Gruziiu: Avtobiografiia* (Moscow: n.p., 1996).

19. Georgia was not included in Transparency International's 2000 Corruption Perceptions Index, but in 1999 it received a score of 2.3, ranking it 84 out of the 99 countries surveyed. In the former Soviet Union only Azerbaijan, Uzbekistan, Kyrgyzstan, and Kazakhstan were viewed as more corrupt.

20. *Human Development Report: Georgia, 1999* (Tbilisi: United Nations Development Program, 2000), 57; GORBI, *Georgian Lifestyle Survey*, 2000, cited in *Human Development Report: Georgia, 2000* (Tbilisi: United Nations Development Program, 2001), 74.

21. See Charles King, "Potemkin Democracy: Four Myths about Post-Soviet Georgia," *National Interest* (summer 2001): 93–104.

22. Moshe Gammer, *The Lone Wolf and the Bear: Three Centuries of Chechen Defiance of Russian Rule* (Pittsburgh, Pa.: University of Pittsburgh Press, 2006), 205.

23. Marc Brody, "Entretien avec Akhmed Zakaev, envoyé spécial du Président Maskhadov pour les négociations de paix," *Central Asian Survey* 22, nos. 2–3 (2003): 221–30.

24. Gennadii Troshev, *Moia voina: Chechenskii dnevnik okopnogo generala* (Moscow: Bagrius, 2001), 28.

25. Sergei Kovalev, "Death in Chechnya," *New York Review of Books*, June 8, 1995. Later estimates put the figures even higher at seventy-five hundred Russian soldiers, four thousand Chechen fighters, and thirty-five thousand civilians. See John B.

Dunlop, "How Many Soldiers and Civilians Died During the Russo-Chechen War of 1994–1996?" *Central Asian Survey* 19, nos. 3–4 (2000): 329–39.

26. Pavel Felgengauer, "The Russian Army in Chechnya," *Central Asian Survey* 21, no. 2 (2002): 157–66.

27. Gammer, *Lone Wolf*, 210. The best analysis of the military elements of the war is Mark Kramer, "Guerrilla Warfare, Counterinsurgency, and Terrorism in the North Caucasus: The Military Dimension of the Russian-Chechen Conflict," *Europe-Asia Studies* 57, no. 2 (2005): 209–90. On the military lessons of the first Chechen war, see Troshev, *Moia voina*, 257–65.

28. Dmitri V. Trenin and Aleksei V. Malashenko with Anatol Lieven, *Russia's Restless Frontier: The Chechnya Factor in Post-Soviet Russia* (Washington, D.C.: Carnegie Endowment, 2004), 156.

29. O. P. Orlov, *Deceptive Justice: Situation on the Investigation on* [sic] *Crimes Against Civilians Committed by Members of the Federal Forces in the Chechen Republic During Military Operations, 1999–2003* (Moscow: "Memorial" Human Rights Center, 2003), 7.

30. For an insightful study of the uses of tradition, see V. O. Bobrovnikov, *Musul'mane Severnogo Kavkaza: Obychai, pravo, nasilie* (Moscow: Vostochnaia literatura, 2002).

Conclusion: Continental Shift

1. Henry C. Barkley, *A Ride Through Asia Minor and Armenia: Giving a Sketch of the Characters, Manners, and Customs of Both the Mussulman and Christian Inhabitants* (London: John Murray, 1891), 346.

2. Tony Judt, *Postwar: A History of Europe Since 1945* (London: William Heinemann, 2005), 6.

3. I wish to thank Dmitri Trenin for this point.

4. A. G. Vishnevskii, *Naselenie Rossii, 2003–2004* (Moscow: Nauka, 2006), 72. The Chechen figure is controversial. Some people have alleged that it is the result of counting "dead souls" in order to falsify voter-registration lists.

5. Vitalii Belozerov, *Etnicheskaia karta Severnogo Kavkaza* (Moscow: OGI, 2005); O. Glezer and P. Polian, eds., *Rossiia i ee regiony v XX veke: Territoriia, rasselenie, migratsii* (Moscow: OGI, 2005).

On Sources

In the pages that follow I discuss some of the primary and secondary sources that I found to be most useful in writing this book. Citations to further specialized items are given in the notes to each chapter.

Chapter 1: Empires and Boundaries

Russian engagement with the Georgian lands before the Treaty of Georgievsk can be traced in the documents collected in W. E. D. Allen, ed., *Russian Embassies to the Georgian Kings, 1589–1605*, 2 vols. (Cambridge, Eng., 1970). The basic primary source for nineteenth-century Caucasus history is *Akty sobrannye Kavkazskoiu arkheografi-cheskoiu kommissieiu [AKAK]*, 13 vols. (Tiflis, 1866–1904), a collection of documents mainly from the archive of the imperial viceroy. Ermolov's career can be traced in *AKAK* as well as in his own notes and memoirs, published as *Zapiski A. P. Ermolova, 1798–1826* (Moscow, 1991), which offer insights into his thinking on military strategy. For translations of the Nart legends, see John Colarusso, *Nart Sagas from the Caucasus* (Princeton, N.J., 2002).

In covering the basic facts of Caucasus history in the late eighteenth and early nineteenth centuries, I found the following especially useful: John F. Baddeley, *The Russian Conquest of the Caucasus* (reprint, London, 2003); Muriel Atkins, *Russia and Iran, 1780–1828* (Minneapolis, Minn.,1980); Mark Bliev, *Rossiia i gortsy Bol'shogo Kavkaza* (Moscow, 2004); and Mark Bliev and V. V. Degoev, *Kavkazskaia voina* (Moscow, 1994). Robert H. Hewson's *Armenia: A Historical Atlas* (Chicago, 2001) and Artur Tsutsiev's *Atlas etnopoliticheskoi istorii Kavkaza, 1774–2004* (Moscow, 2006) are outstanding achievements not only as geographical references but also as guides to the demographic and political history of the entire Caucasus. On the very early history of the

Caucasus, see Cyril Toumanoff, *Studies in Christian Caucasian History* (Washington, D.C., 1963). Thomas M. Barrett's groundbreaking article "Lines of Uncertainty: The Frontiers of the North Caucasus," *Slavic Review* 54 (1995), influenced my thinking on the importance of the Caucasus military lines. For sophisticated studies of the changing ecology and demographics of the steppe and the south Russian borderlands, see Michael Khodarkovsky, *Russia's Steppe Frontier* (Bloomington, Ind., 2002); idem, "Of Christianity, Enlightenment, and Colonialism: Russia in the North Caucasus, 1550–1800," *Journal of Modern History* 71 (1999); and Willard Sunderland, *Taming the Wild Field* (Ithaca, N.Y., 2004). My ideas about captivity were sparked by Linda Colley's insightful *Captives: Britain, Empire, and the World, 1600–1850* (New York, 2002). On the Caucasus slave trade, see the revealing study by Liubov Derluguian, "The Unlikely Abolitionists: The Russian Struggle Against the Slave Trade in the Caucasus, 1800–1864" (Ph.D. diss., State University of New York at Binghamton, 1997). Michael Kemper, one of the leading scholars in the study of local religious and social institutions in Dagestan, has coedited, with Anke von Kügelgen and Dmitriy Yermakov, the multivolume series *Muslim Culture in Russia and Central Asia from the 18th to the Early 20th Centuries* (Berlin, 1996–).

Indispensable overviews of the region and its divisions, from the earliest times to the twentieth century, include: W. E. D. Allen, *A History of the Georgian People* (London, 1932); David Marshall Lang, *A Modern History of Georgia* (London, 1962); Ronald Grigor Suny, *The Making of the Georgian Nation* (Bloomington, Ind., 1988); idem, *Looking Toward Ararat: Armenia in Modern History* (Bloomington, Ind., 1993); and Audrey L. Altstadt, *The Azerbaijani Turks* (Stanford, Calif., 1992).

Chapter 2: Rule and Resistance

Important primary sources for this chapter include *AKAK*, British Foreign Office records in the National Archives of the United Kingdom (formerly the Public Record Office), and the David Urquhart Papers at Balliol College, Oxford, supplemented by four major secondary works: John F. Baddeley, *The Russian Conquest of the Caucasus* 1908; reprint, London, 2003); Moshe Gammer, *Muslim Resistance to the Tsar* (London, 1994); N. I. Pokrovskii, *Kavkazskie voiny i imamat Shamilia* (Moscow, 2000); and Mark Bliev, *Rossiia i gortsy Bol'shogo Kavkaza* (Moscow, 2004). Some of Shamil's letters are collected in Kh. A. Omarov, ed., *100 pisem Shamilia* (Makhachkala, 1997). Two important contemporary chronicles of Shamil's movement are: Muhammad Tahir al-Qarakhi, "The Shining of Dagestani Swords in Certain Campaigns of Shamil," in *Russian-Muslim Confrontation in the Caucasus: Alternative Visions of the Conflict Between Imam Shamil and the Russians, 1830–1859*, ed. and trans. by Thomas Sanders, Ernest Tucker, and Gary Hamburg (London, 2004); and Abd al-Rahman al-Ghazi-Qumuqi, *Kratkoe izlozhenie podrobnogo opisaniia del imama Shamilia*, trans. N. A. Tagirova (Moscow, 2002). There are many contemporary accounts of the nature of highland warfare, but for important texts see: Iakov Gordin, *Kavkaz: Zemlia i krov'* (St. Petersburg, 2000); idem, ed., *Osada Kavkaza: Vospominaniia uchastnikov Kavkazskoi voiny XIX veka* (St. Petersburg, 2000); and F. F. Tornau, *Vospominaniia kavkazskogo ofitsera* (Moscow, 2000).

Four indispensable memoirs on Circassia and the wider Caucasus in the first half of the nineteenth century are: E. Taitbout de Marigny, *Three Voyages in the Black Sea to the Coast of Circassia* (London, 1837); Frédéric Dubois de Montpéreux, *Voyage autour du Caucase*, 6 vols. (Paris, 1839–43); J. A. Longworth, *A Year Among the Circassians*, 2 vols. (London, 1840); and James Stanislaus Bell, *Journal of a Residence in Circassia*, 2 vols. (London, 1840). For indigenous perspectives see the following by two of the century's major Circassian intellectuals: Shora Nogma, *Istoriia adykheiskogo naroda* (Nalchik, 1994), and Khan-Girei, *Zapiski o Cherkesii* (Nalchik, 1978). For modern studies of these thinkers, see Sufian Zhemukhov, *Filosofiia istorii Shory Nogma* (Nalchik, 2007); and idem, *Mirovozzrenie Khan-Gireia* (Nalchik, 1997). The expulsions can be followed in the documents published by T. Kh. Kumykov, *Vyselenie adygov v Turtsiiu* (Nalchik, 1994).

The best study of north Caucasus social mores and their transformation since the imperial period is V. O. Bobrovnikov, *Musul'mane Severnogo Kavkaza: Obychai, pravo, nasilie* (Moscow, 2002). The debate over the religious dimensions of Muridism is intense. For various perspectives see: Anna Zelkina, *In Quest of God and Freedom* (New York, 2000); and Alexander Knysh, "Sufism as an Explanatory Paradigm: The Issue of the Motivations of Sufi Resistance Movements in Western and Russian Scholarship," *Die Welt des Islams* 42, no. 2 (2002). My thinking on Shamil's reception in Russia was influenced by Thomas M. Barrett, "The Remaking of the Lion of Dagestan: Shamil in Captivity," *Russian Review* 53 (July 1994). The basic work on Mikhail Vorontsov in English is Anthony L. H. Rhinelander, *Prince Michael Vorontsov: Viceroy to the Tsar* (Montreal, 1990). The best recent treatment of the Circassian expulsions, based on Ottoman archives, is David Cameron Cuthell, Jr., "The Muhacirin Komisiyonu: An Agent in the Transformation of Ottoman Anatolia, 1860–1866" (Ph.D. diss., Columbia University, 2005). My ideas on imperial conquest were shaped in part by Austin Jersild's brilliant *Orientalism and Empire: North Caucasus Mountain Peoples and the Georgian Frontier, 1845–1917* (Montreal, 2002). I learned a great deal about the nature of Russian colonization on the ground from Nicholas B. Breyfogle's *Heretics and Colonizers: Forging Russia's Empire in the South Caucasus* (Ithaca, N.Y., 2005).

Chapter 3: The Imaginary Caucasus

Primary sources for this chapter include the writings of Güldenstädt, Klaproth, and Bronevskii, all of which are cited in the notes, along with the literary works (referenced in their easily available English translations) of Pushkin, Lermontov, and Tolstoy. There is a wealth of nineteenth-century travel writing on the Caucasus in English, French, and German, as well as a large Russian body of literature that grew steadily over the course of the century, specific examples of which are mentioned in the notes. The section on mountaineering relies on the firsthand accounts of Douglas Freshfield, including *The Exploration of the Caucasus*, 2 vols. (London, 1896), and *Travels in the Central Caucasus and Bashan* (London, 1869), as well as accounts by his contemporaries. In addition, I consulted reports published in the indispensable *Alpine Journal* and *Proceedings of the Royal Geographical Society*, as well as the archives of the Alpine Club,

London. For an excellent overview of Caucasus climbing, see Audrey Salkeld and José Luis Bermúdez, *On the Edge of Empire: Mountaineering in the Caucasus* (Seattle, Wash., 1993).

On the life and work of Güldenstädt and Klaproth, see Iu. Kh. Kopelevich, *Iogann Anton Gil'denshtedt, 1745–1781* (Moscow, 1997) and C. Landresse, "Notice historique et littéraire sur M. Klaproth," *Nouveau Journal Asiatique* 16 (Sept. 1835). My thinking on the Caucasus in Russian and Western popular culture has been influenced by Susan Layton's fascinating study *Russian Literature and Empire* (Cambridge, Eng., 1994), as well as by two articles by Thomas M. Barrett: "Cowboys or Indians? Cossacks and the Internationalization of the American Frontier," *Journal of the West* 42, no. 1 (2003); and "Southern Living (in Captivity): The Caucasus in Russian Popular Culture," *Journal of Popular Culture* 31, no. 4 (1998). The trope of the Caucasus captive is traced from Pushkin through Soviet popular representations by Bruce Grant in "The Good Russian Prisoner: Naturalizing Violence in the Caucasus Mountains," *Cultural Anthropology* 20, no. 1 (2005). I gained perspective on the image of the rebellious Caucasus mountaineer by reading Anthony Harkins's engaging *Hillbilly: A Cultural History of an American Icon* (Oxford, Eng., 2004). Although many sources mention the Circassian beauties, the best analyses of their cultural meanings are: Robert Bogdan, *Freak Show: Presenting Human Oddities for Amusement and Profit* (Chicago, 1988); and Linda Frost, *Never One Nation: Freaks, Savages, and Whiteness in U.S. Popular Culture, 1850–1877* (Minneapolis, Minn., 2005). My feel for the experience of Victorian-era popular entertainment was enhanced by a visit to the American Dime Museum in Baltimore, Maryland, which, sadly, is now defunct.

Chapter 4: Nations and Revolutions

This chapter is based on British Foreign Office records; the Oliver Wardrop Papers and Wardrop Collection, Bodleian Library, Oxford; the Georgia (Republic) Records at the Houghton Library, Harvard University; and the following named collections at the Hoover Institution Archives: Ralph G. Albrecht, Nikolai N. Baratov, Alexander Munro Barton, Robert Pierpont Blake, "Bureau de Presse et d'Information Armenien", Emin Vahan, Georgian Subject, Joseph Coy Green, Stanley K. Hornbeck, Pavel Alekseevich Kusonski, Nestor Apollonovich Lakoba, Charles Manuel, Boris I. Nicolaevsky (Iurii Semenov Papers, Irakli Tsereteli Papers, Noe Zhordania Papers), Wilbur E. Post, John Amar Shishmanian, Aleksei Vladimirovich fon Shvarts, T. G. Stepanov-Mamaladze, Alexandre Tarsaidze, Mariia Petrovna Vatatsi, Vrangel', Carl E. Wallen, and Samuel Graham Wilson.

Documents from the interwar republics are collected in: *Dokumenty i materialy po vneshnei politike Zakavkaz'ia i Gruzii* (1919, reprint Tbilisi, 1990); and Dzh. B. Guliev, ed. *Azerbaidzhanskaia Respublika: Dokumenty i materialy, 1918–1920 gg.* (Baku, 1998). The memoirs of Anton Denikin (*Put' russkogo ofitsera* [Moscow, 2002]) and Noe Jordania (*Moia zhizn'* [Stanford, Calif., 1968]), along with Jordania's collection of speeches (*Za dva goda: Doklady i rechi* [Tiflis, 1919]), provide contrasting views of a chaotic time. The basic source on the Promethean movement is the journal *Prométhée*, which was published in Paris in the 1920s and 1930s. Works by Essad Bey (Lev

Nussimbaum), such as his *Twelve Secrets of the Caucasus* (New York, 1931), are sometimes cited by historians, but for the most part I have found them to be unreliable fantasies. Three far more interesting primary sources on the post–First World War period are: the memoir by the feisty Odette Keun, *In the Land of the Golden Fleece: Through Independent Menshevist Georgia* (London, 1924); Karl Kautsky's trip report entitled *Georgia: A Social-Democratic Peasant Republic* (London, 1921); and Zourab Avalishvili's diplomatic memoir *The Independence of Georgia in International Politics, 1918–1921* (1940, reprint Westport, Conn.,1981). On Armenian nationalism, I learned a great deal from Louise Nalbandian, *The Armenian Revolutionary Movement* (Berkeley, Calif., 1963) and Razmik Panossian, *The Armenians: From Kings and Priests to Merchants and Commissars* (New York, 2006).

Soviet-era deportations can be traced through the important collections assembled by N. F. Bugai and his colleagues, including *"Po resheniiu pravitel'stva Soiuza SSR..."* (Nalchik, 2003); *L. Beriia–I. Stalinu: "Soglasno Vashemu ukazaniiu..."* (Moscow, 1995); and *Kavkaz: Narody v eshelonakh (20–60-e gody)* (Moscow, 1998). The most comprehensive collection of documents on the deportations—a truly monumental scholarly achievement—is *Stalinskie deportatsii, 1928–1953*, ed. N. L. Pobol' and P. M. Polian.

The basic source on the military history of the Caucasus through the early twentieth century is W. E. D. Allen and Paul Muratoff, *Caucasian Battlefields: A History of the Wars on the Turco-Caucasian Border, 1828–1921* (Cambridge, Eng., 1953). An excellent guide to the complex politics surrounding the First World War is Firuz Kazemzadeh, *The Struggle for Transcaucasia, 1917–1921* (New York, 1951). The best study of the development of Georgian socialism is Stephen Jones, *Socialism in Georgian Colors: The European Road to Social Democracy, 1883–1917* (Cambridge, Mass., 2005). The unrivaled history of the first Armenian republic is Richard G. Hovannisian, *The Republic of Armenia*, 4 vols. (Berkeley, Calif., 1971–96). The growth of Azerbaijani identity is traced in Tadeusz Swietochowski, *Russian Azerbaijan, 1905–1920* (Cambridge, Eng., 1985), as well as in Eva-Maria Auch's deeply researched study *Muslim— Untertan—Bürger* (Wiesbaden, Ger., 2004). The literature on the Armenian genocide is vast, and much of it is written with one or another agenda in mind. For recent insightful treatments, see: Taner Akçam, *A Shameful Act: The Armenian Genocide and the Question of Turkish Responsibility* (New York, 2006); Donald Bloxham, *The Great Game of Genocide* (Oxford, Eng., 2005); and Jay Winter, ed., *America and the Armenian Genocide of 1915* (Cambridge, Eng., 2003).

My ideas on Soviet nationality policy, like those of most scholars, have been shaped by Ronald Grigor Suny's study *The Revenge of the Past* (Stanford, Calif., 1993) and Terry Martin's book *The Affirmative Action Empire* (Ithaca, N.Y., 2001). Francine Hirsch's *Empire of Nations* (Ithaca, N.Y., 2005) is a detailed investigation of the making of ethnonational categories in the early Soviet state. Among a truckload of biographies of Stalin and Beria, four stand out: Sarah Davies and James Harris, eds., *Stalin: A New History* (Cambridge, Eng., 2005); Robert Service, *Stalin: A Biography* (Cambridge, Mass., 2005); Simon Sebag Montefiore, *Stalin: The Court of the Red Tsar* (New York, 2003); and Amy Knight, *Beria: Stalin's First Lieutenant* (Princeton, N.J., 1993). The best study of Stalinism in the region—especially in Azerbaijan—is Jörg Baberowski, *Der Feind Ist Überall* (Munich, 2003).

Chapter 5: Time of Troubles

This chapter is based on my own interviews and conversations in Armenia, Azerbaijan (including Nagorno-Karabakh), Georgia (including Abkhazia and South Ossetia), and Russia (including the Stavropol region, Kabardino-Balkaria, and North Ossetia) in 2000, 2004, 2005, and 2006. I also made use of the clippings files of the Soviet Red Archives at the Open Society Archives, Budapest. For up-to-date analysis, I have found the following particularly useful: Eurasianet (www.eurasianet.org); the International Crisis Group (www.crisisgroup.org); the Institute for War and Peace Reporting (www.iwpr.net); Conciliation Resources (www.c-r.org); the American Committee for Peace in the Caucasus (www.peaceinthecaucasus.org); the Jamestown Foundation's *Chechnya Weekly* (www.jamestown.org); and Human Rights Watch (www.hrw.org). Every scholar of Eurasia is indebted to Johnson's List (www.cdi.org/russia/johnson), the Web's foremost compendium of news related to Russia. The major outlet for north Caucasus guerrilla groups is www.kavkazcenter.com.

The Chechen conflict has produced some outstanding war reporting. On the first war, the best accounts are: Carlotta Gall and Thomas de Waal, *Chechnya: Calamity in the Caucasus* (New York, 1998); Anatol Lieven, *Chechnya: Tombstone of Russian Power* (New Haven, Conn., 1998); and Sebastian Smith, *Allah's Mountains*, rev. ed. (London, 2006). The interregnum (1996–99) is covered in Anne Nivat's haunting *Chienne de Guerre* (New York, 2001). On the second Chechen war, the most widely read work is by Anna Politkovskaya, who was murdered in 2006. See *A Dirty War* (London, 2001) and *A Small Corner of Hell* (Chicago, 2003). The voices of Chechens themselves can be heard in Valery Tishkov's *Chechnya: Life in a War-Torn Society* (Berkeley, Calif., 2004). On the horror of Chechnya as it was experienced by foreigners and journalists, there is no better guide than Scott Anderson's coverage of the disappearance of Fred Cuny, the well-known American aid worker, in *The Man Who Tried to Save the World* (New York, 1999).

The best reporting on the Caucasus as a whole, including Chechnya, is Yo'av Karny's *Highlanders: A Journey to the Caucasus in Quest of Memory* (New York, 2000). See also Thomas Goltz's fast-paced trilogy *Azerbaijan Diary* (Armonk, N.Y., 1998), *Chechnya Diary* (Armonk, N.Y., 2003), and *Georgia Diary* (Armonk, N.Y., 2006). There is still relatively little published on the three conflict zones in the south Caucasus. See Thomas de Waal's excellent volume on Nagorno-Karabakh entitled *Black Garden* (New York, 2003). On the role of the Armenian diaspora, see Markar Melkonian's memoir *My Brother's Road* (London, 2005), which tells the story of Monte Melkonian, the most famous Armenian-American to die in the conflict. Mathijs Pelkmans focuses on Achara—a region of Georgia that was separate but not separatist in the 1990s—in his *Defending the Border: Identity, Religion, and Modernity in the Republic of Georgia* (Ithaca, N.Y., 2006).

For a detailed scholarly overview of Caucasus politics in the 1990s, see Svante Cornell's *Small Nations and Great Powers* (Richmond, Eng., 2001). On Georgia in particular, the best study is Jürgen Gerber, *Georgien: Nationale Opposition und kommunistische Herrschaft seit 1956* (Baden-Baden, 1997). The north Caucasus beyond Chechnya has not received the attention it deserves. There are only a handful of specialists in the West who have written on Circassia and Dagestan, and the growing literature in Russian is infrequently based on real research. An exception is Georgi Derluguian's

Bourdieu's Secret Admirer in the Caucasus (Chicago, 2005), which is about an intriguing Circassian sociologist and an entire generation's transition from one kind of modernity to another. On debates over whether my Caucasus ancestors are older than yours, the best books are Victor Shnirelman's *Voiny pamiati: Mify, identichnost' i politika v Zakavkaz'e* (Moscow, 2003) and his *Byt' Alanami: Intellektualy i politika na Severnom Kavkaze v XX veke* (Moscow, 2006).

Index

Communist Party of the Soviet Union, 190, 192

Constantinople, 36, 53, 61–62, 89, 137–38, 145–46, 154, 158, 161
slave markets in, 59
See also Istanbul

Cooper, James Fenimore, 109

corporal punishment, 43

corruption, 201–6, 220, 229–30

Cossacks, 11, 22, 24–26, 31, 39–40, 42–3, 47, 52, 55, 61–62, 70, 73, 75–77, 83, 106, 115, 117–18, 120, 122–23, 132, 145, 155, 175, 196, 250
relations with highlanders, 41–44

The Cossacks (Tolstoy), 117, 135

Council of Europe, 244

Crimea, 26, 95, 103, 107

Crimean Tatars, 9, 23, 26, 40, 65, 93, 95, 101
deportation of, 197

Crimean War, 56, 88–90, 94–95, 116, 124, 153, 156, 159

Cyprus, 96, 137

Czechs, 243

Dagestan, 4, 10, 15–16, 23–24, 27, 36–37, 47–49, 53, 65–66, 68–70, 72, 88–89, 91–92, 94, 102–3, 112, 120–21, 124, 144–45, 171, 188, 199, 202, 232, 237, 241

Dagestani languages, xiv

Dagestanis, 28, 73, 82–3, 90, 112, 250

Danielia, Giorgi, 207

Dardanelles, 155

Dargin language, xiv

Dargins, 10

Dargo, 87

Darial Gorge, 8

Dashnaks, 169–70, 172, 179, 181, 193, 222–23

David (biblical king), 33

"The Death of a Poet" (Lermontov), 113

"The Debate" (Lermontov), 114

Decembrist uprising, 49–50, 113

Demirchian, Karen, 200–201, 223

Denikin, Anton, 164–65, 170, 182

Denmark, 61

Dent, Clinton, 125, 128–29, 130–33

deportations, 11, 17, 46, 92–98, 118, 158
of Circassians, 92–98, 118
during Second World War, 196–98

Derbend, 7, 16, 25, 30–31, 46, 49, 65, 151

desertion (from army), 54

dhikr, xv, 69

Dikaia Diviziia, 154

Dink, Hrant, 225

disease, 22, 43, 48, 84, 97

disguise tours, 60, 137

djabal al-alsun, 9

Dnepr River, 40, 110

Dnepropetrovsk, 109

Dolgorukov family, 108

Don River, 13, 25, 105, 119, 195–96

Donkin, W. F., 128–32

DuBois, Blanche (literary character), 247

Dudaev, Jokhar, 233–42

Duma, 162

Dumas, Alexandre, 17, 99 (epigraph)

Dundee Advertiser, 134

Dunsterville, Lionel, 167

Dykh-Tau, 7, 128

Echmiadzin, 11, 50, 169, 179

Eisenmann, Charles, 138

Ekaterinoda, 41

Ekaterinoslav, 109

Elbrus, 7, 114, 124–26, 128

Elçibey, Abulfaz, 226

Elisavetpol, 29
province, 144–45, 166

Enlightenment, 32

Enver Pasha, 154–55

Erekle II (king), 23, 27, 44, 102

Ermolov, Alexei, 20 (epigraph), 73, 85, 108, 113, 116, 139, 236, 238
life and career, 45–53

Esenç, Tevfik, 98

Jughashvili, Ioseb, 182–83. *See also* Stalin, Joseph
Julian calendar, xiv

Kabarda, 23–24, 26, 36–37, 49, 67, 88, 103, 105, 120, 142. *See also* Kabardino-Balkaria
Kabardians, 65, 68, 93, 120, 123, 188, 205. *See also* Adyga; Circassians
Kabardino-Balkaria, 6, 9, 15, 128, 188, 205, 232, 241
Kabyles, 73
Kadyrov, Akhmad, 239
kafir, 82, 241
Kaitag, 53
Kakheti and Kakhetians, 10, 21, 23–24, 32–33, 35, 85, 89, 147
Kalmyks, 22
    deportation of, 197
Kaluga, 91–92
Kandahar, 34
Kantaria, Meliton, 194
Karabakh, 31, 35–36, 49, 189. *See also* Nagorno-Karabakh
Karabakh Committee, 214, 221, 223
Karabulaks, 142
Karachaevo-Cherkesia, 9, 15, 188, 205, 241
Karachai, 17, 68, 188, 195, 205
    deportation of 196–98
Karachai language, xiv
Karaul, 128–29, 131
Kars, 51–2, 89, 144–45, 169, 153, 155
Kartli and Kartlians, 11, 23–24, 32–35, 85
Kartli-Kakheti, 26–7, 30–31, 102
Kartvelian languages, xiv, 10
Kautsky, Karl, 165
kavkazets, 100
Kazakhstan, 196–97
Kazbek, 7, 114, 124–25, 128
Kazi Mullah. *See* Ghazi Muhammad al-Daghestani
Kazi-Kumuk, 77
Kellogg-Briand Pact, 176
Kennan, Georg, 9

Kerch, 62
Keun, Odette, 165
KGB, 227
khanates and khans, 10, 24, 29, 31, 84–85
Khanjian, Aghasi, 191–92
Khankendi. *See* Stepanakert
Khasaviurt Agreement, 236–37
Khevsureti and Khevsurs, 10, 29, 68, 143, 164
Khojaly, 214
Khomeriki, Noe, 181
Khrushchev, Nikita, 198
kidnapping, 48. *See also* bride kidnapping; captivity
Kiev, 108
Kievan Rus', 109
kinjal, xv, 41
Kislovodsk, 122, 206
Kists, 142
Kizliar, 39, 53, 102
Klaproth, Julius von, 19, 104–8, 111–12, 126, 140
Klüge-von-Klugenau, Franz, 71, 78
Klukhor Pass, 124
Koba 192. *See also* Stalin, Joseph
Kocharian, Robert, 217, 222–24
Koestler, Arthur, 200 (epigraph)
Koreans. deportation of, 197
korenizatsiia, xv, 190
Koshtan, 124, 127–30, 132
Kovalev, Sergei, 236
Krasnodar, 9, 205
Kuban district, 97, 144–45
Kuban River, 9, 13, 27, 31, 40, 42–43, 48, 57, 67, 68, 93–95, 110, 142, 144, 188
Kuma River, 110
Kumyk khanate, 48
Kumyk language, xiv
Kumyks, 10, 143
Kura River, 11, 13, 23, 68, 122, 146
Kurds, 31, 97, 156–58
    deportation of, 197
Kurtuluş (publication), 175
Kustan Ogli Ismael, 64 (epigraph), 134
Kutaisi, 85, 144–45

Orel, 139–40
Orthodox Christianity, 11, 15, 32, 66, 118, 215
  dissenters, 145
  See also Georgian Orthodox Church
Ossetian language, xiv
Ossetians, 68, 115, 144, 147, 205
Ottoman Empire and Ottomans, 9, 12–16, 21–35, 40–42, 51–52, 57, 65–66, 73, 77, 79, 81, 88–89, 93, 96, 119, 141, 144, 211
  captivity in, 59–63, 137
Oxford University, 125

Pakhu Bikhe, 72
Pallas, Peter Simon, 101–3
pan-Islamism, 175, 178, 194
pan-Turkism, 175, 178, 194
papakha, xv, 41, 139, 207
Paradjanov, Sergei, 207–8
Paris, 46, 173–74, 177, 181–82
Paris peace conference, 170, 175
Pashtuns, 73
Paskevich, Ivan, 50–2, 71, 73
Paul (tsar), 28
Peace of Amasya, 22, 24
Pechorin (literary character), 115
perestroika, 233
Persia and Persians, 3, 10, 13, 16, 22–24, 28–35, 49, 51–52, 56, 66, 69, 73, 115, 150–51, 166–67, 176. *See also* Iran; Qajar dynasty; Safavid dynasty
Persian Gulf, 36, 64, 66
Persian language, 13, 146
Peter the Great, 5, 16, 25, 34, 40, 109
petroleum. *See* oil
Petrovsk, 151
Philadelphia, 181
Piatigorsk, 109–10, 113, 115, 117, 122–23
Pikes Peak, 124
Piłsudski, Józef, 174
pirveli dasi, 148–49
plague. *See* disease
podorozhnaia, 119

Poland and Poles, 55–56, 176, 179, 243
  deportation of 197
Polish uprising (1830), 55
Politburo, 201
Popular Front of Azerbaijan, 212, 226
populism, 148–49
Porter, Robert Ker, 5
posting, 119–20
Poti, 30, 51–52, 151, 195
Potto, Vasilii, 100
Powell, Charles Herbert, 130–33
Prague, 174–75
Prisoner Girl of the Caucasus (film), 207
Prometheanism, 173–77, 181–82
Prométhée (publication), 174, 176
Prometheus, 22, 125
Protestantism, 147. *See also* Lutheranism
Provisional Government (Russia), 160, 162, 164
Pshavs, 68
Pushkin, Alexander, 3 (epigraph), 6, 18, 45, 48, 64 (epigraph), 108–15, 117, 119–23, 127, 133, 139, 206, 250
Pushkin, Lev, 110
Putin, Vladimir, 231, 237–41, 248–49

Qadiri *tariqa* xv, 65. *See also* Sufism
Qajar dynasty, 10, 27, 31, 50–51, 81. *See also* Iran; Persia and Persians
Qing dynasty, 22
Qız Qalası, 150
Quba khanate, 31, 35
Qur'an, 22

race. *See* Caucasian race
Radde, Gustav, 143
Radio Yerevan, 207
Raduev, Salman, 239
Raevskii, Nikolai Nikolaevich, 110
raiding and banditry, 23–24, 29, 43, 52–53, 73–74, 92, 97, 120–21, 187, 240
Ramishvili, Noe, 173, 181

Tetnuli, 128
Texas, 9, 245
Thielmann, Max von, 120
Tiflis
    Armenians in. 147–48
    early history of, 146
    Persian attack on, 27, 146
    population, 147
    province, 144–45
    urban life in, 85–6, 121–22
    See also Tbilisi
Tiflis theological seminary, 149,
    182–83
Todtleben, Heinrich von, 26
Tolstoy, Leo, 6, 75, 116–19, 135
Tosca (Puccini), 165
Tourian, Levon, 177–81, 224
tourism, 206–7. *See also* Caucasus: travel
    and exploration
Transcaspia, 151
Transcaucasia, Democratic Federative
    Republic of, 161
Transcaucasus Commissariat, 160
Transcaucasus railroad, 13, 123
Transcaucasus Soviet Federative
    Socialist Republic, 187
*Travels in Russia and the Caucasus
    Mountains* (Güldenstädt),
    102–3
Travels in the Caucasus and Georgia
    (Klaproth), 105–6
Treaty of Adrianople, 52, 93
Treaty of Brest Litovsk, 160–61
Treaty of Bucharest, 30
Treaty of Georgievsk, 26, 28, 209
Treaty of Gulistan, 30, 26, 49–50,
    70, 150
Treaty of Kars, 189
Treaty of Küçük Kaynarca, 26
Treaty of Lausanne, 158
Treaty of Moscow, 189
Treaty of Turkmanchai, 51
Trebizond, 55, 59, 61–62, 96, 160,
    243
Trotsky, Leon, 183
Tsitsianov, Pavel, 28, 30, 85

Tskhinvali, 188
Tulip Revolution, 231
Turkey, 7–8, 11, 14, 23, 98, 137,
    157–59, 171, 176, 187–88, 225
    relations with Europe, 247
    See also Ottoman Empire and
    Ottomans
Turkic languages, 188
Turkish language, xiv, 12–13, 15, 32,
    36, 178
Turkomans and Turkmen, 27, 31,
    143
Tush, 68, 143
Tyrol, 8

Ubykh, 97
Ubykh language, xiv
Ukraine and Ukrainians, 40, 109, 197,
    207, 231, 244, 247
Ummayad dynasty, 65
United Nations, 216
United States, 19, 73, 109, 164,
    176, 187, 203, 218, 230,
    244–45
University College, Oxford, 125
Urquhart, David, 93
Ushba, 124
Ushurma. *See* Sheikh Mansur

Vakhtang V (king), 34
Vakhusht (Vakhushti Bagrationi),
    32–34
Van Halen, Juan, 45
Varna, 96
Vel'iaminov, Alexei, 47–48
Venice, 179
Victoria (queen), 64, 94
Vladikavkaz, 8, 31, 47, 105, 120, 130,
    132, 146, 195
Vnezapnaia (fort), 47
Vol'noe Kazachestvo (publication),
    175
Volga River, 13, 22, 24–25, 102, 119,
    196

Volga Tatars, 24
Volkonskii family, 108
Volunteer Army, 164–55, 170
Voronezh, 29
Vorontsov, Mikhail, 147, 238
  life and exploits, 84–90
vyshki, 42

Wagner, Moritz, 41–43, 56
Wardrop, Oliver, 148, 169, 171,
  173
warfare
  casualties in, 76, 87
  nature of, 44, 46–49, 67–69, 73–77,
    80, 87–88, 91, 113–14
Warsaw, 55, 174–75
Washington, DC, 181
Wehrmacht, 195
wheat, 62
White, Charles, 59–60
Whites (Russian civil war), 164, 171,
  173, 175, 189, 196
Wilson, Woodrow, 165
wine, 100

"The Wood-Felling" (Tolstoy), 75–76,
  116–17
Woolley, Hermann, 130–33

Yandarbiev, Zelimkhan, 233, 239
Yeltsin, Boris, 213, 234–42, 248
Yerevan
  khanate, 30–31, 35, 49–51, 159
  population, 204–5
  province, 144, 155, 159, 169
  See also individual subject entries
Young Turks, 154, 157
Yugoslavia, 231

zachistka, 238
Zalumma Agra, 138–39
Zangezur, 188
Zaporozhian Cossacks, 40. *See also*
  Black Sea Cossacks; Cossacks
Zhiguli (automobile), 4, 204
Zoberdie Luti, 138
Zoe Meleke, 138
Zoroastrianism, 66, 150